Violence and War in Culture and the Media explores the roots of violence and war through the lenses of five very different disciplines (history, culture, sociology, politics and gender) with a focus on very different subjects, ranging from an original interpretation of Manet's artwork '*The Execution of Emperor Maximilian*' to studies on early systems of communication in the Thirty Years War, culture and memories of violence and war, cyberwar, and rape narratives in South Africa, as well as war between Israel and Hezbollah in 2006, among other deeply researched chapters, all with a common denominator of media and communications. The result is totally unexpected and serendipitous, allowing disciplines that rarely speak to one another to inter-communicate – and learn from one another – for the very first time.

Hall Gardner, *Professor and Chair, Department of International and Comparative Politics, American University of Paris,* author of *Averting Global War* and *American Global Strategy and the 'War on Terrorism'*

From the postal system in the Thirty Years War to bondage imagery in fashion shoots, from hacker activists in Eastern Europe to rape narratives in South Africa, these essays offer new connections between violence and culture, between mediation and domination, between the politics of conflict and the conflicts of politics.

Graham Meikle, *Senior Lecturer in Communications, Media and Culture, University of Sterling,* author of *Future Active: Media Activism and the Internet*

Violence and War in Culture and the Media

This edited volume examines theoretical and empirical issues relating to violence and war and its implications for media, culture and society.

Over the last two decades there has been a proliferation of books, films and art on the subject of violence and war. However, this is the first volume that offers a varied analysis which has wider implications for several disciplines, thus providing the reader with a text that is both multi-faceted and accessible. This book introduces the current debates surrounding this topic through five particular lenses:

- the historical involves an examination of historical patterns of the communication of violence and war through a variety of sources
- the cultural utilises the cultural studies perspective to engage with issues of violence, visibility and spectatorship
- the sociological focuses on how terrorism, violence and war are remembered and negotiated in the public sphere
- the political offers an exploration into the politics of assigning blame for war, the influence of psychology on media actors, and new media political communication issues in relation to the state and the media
- the gender studies perspective provides an analysis of violence and war from a gender studies viewpoint.

Violence and War in Culture and the Media will be of much interest to students of war and conflict studies, media and communications studies, sociology, security studies and political science.

Athina Karatzogianni is Lecturer in Media, Culture and Society at the University of Hull, UK. She is author of *The Politics of Cyberconflict* (2006), *Power, Conflict and Resistance: Social Movements, Networks and Hierarchies* with Andrew Robinson (2010), and editor of *Cyber Conflict and Global Politics* (2009).

Media, War and Security
Series Editors
Andrew Hoskins
University of Glasgow
Oliver Boyd-Barrett
Bowling Green State University

This series interrogates and illuminates the mutually shaping relationship between war and media as transformative of contemporary society, politics and culture.

Global Terrorism and New Media
The Post Al-Qaeda Generation
Philip Seib and Dana M. Janabek

Radicalisation and the Media
Legitimising Violence in the New Media
Akil N. Awan, Andrew Hoskins and Ben O'Loughlin

Hollywood and the CIA
Cinema, Defense and Subversion
Oliver Boyd-Barrett, David Herrera and Jim Baumann

Violence and War in Culture and the Media
Five Disciplinary Lenses
Edited by Athina Karatzogianni

Military Media Management
Negotiating the 'Front' Line in Mediatized War
Sarah Maltby

Icons of War and Terror
Media Images in an Age of International Risk
Edited by John Tulloch and R. Warwick Blood

Violence and War in Culture and the Media

Five disciplinary lenses

Edited by Athina Karatzogianni

Routledge
Taylor & Francis Group

LONDON AND NEW YORK

This edition published 2012
by Routledge
2 Park Square, Milton Park, Abingdon, Oxon OX14 4RN

Simultaneously published in the USA and Canada
by Routledge
711 Third Avenue, New York, NY 10017

Routledge is an imprint of the Taylor & Francis Group, an informa business

British Library Cataloguing in Publication Data
A catalogue record for this book is available from the British Library

Library of Congress Cataloging-in-Publication Data
A catalog record has been requested for this book

ISBN: 978-0-415-66523-0 (hbk)
ISBN: 978-0-203-14330-8 (ebk)

Typeset in Baskerville
by Wearset Ltd, Boldon, Tyne and Wear

Contents

Notes on contributors   ix

Preface   xv

1 Violence and war in culture and the media through five
  disciplinary lenses   1
  ATHINA KARATZOGIANNI

PART I
Through the historical lens   11

2 Perceptions of violence in the early modern communications
  revolution: the case of the Thirty Years War 1618–1648   13
  PETER H. WILSON

3 Patrick Pécherot, eugenics and the Occupation of France   30
  ANGELA KIMYONGÜR

4 United States Army chaplains and magazines: censorship in
  World War II   46
  JENEL VIRDEN

PART II
Through the cultural lens   63

5 Hidden conflict, visible world   65
  KEITH TESTER

6 The ethics of remembering: Little Big Man and the
  exoneration of American guilt   78
  JAMES ASTON

7 Loving violence? The ambiguities of SM imagery in
  contemporary popular culture   92
  SARAH HARPER AND MAJID YAR

PART III
Through the sociological lens   111

 8 Defining the victims of terrorism: competing frames
    around victim compensation and commemoration
    post-9/11 New York City and 3/11 Madrid   113
    CRISTINA FLESHER FOMINAYA AND ROSEMARY BARBERET

 9 The returns of war: bodies, images and invented ritual in
    the war on terror   131
    MICHAEL S. DRAKE

10 Frames, forums and Facebook: interpreting British Muslim
    understandings of post-7/7 militarist media narratives   148
    LUCY MICHAEL

PART IV
Through the political lens   169

11 The Israel–Hezbollah War and the Winograd Committee   171
    RAPHAEL COHEN-ALMAGOR AND SHARON HALEVA-AMIR

12 Media actors in war and conflict: insights from political
    psychology and the Bosnian war   188
    MARIA TOURI

13 Virilio and the gaze of the state: vision machines, new
    media and resistance   204
    ANDY ROBINSON

14 Blame it on the Russians: tracking the portrayal of Russian
    hackers during cyber conflict incidents   221
    ATHINA KARATZOGIANNI

PART V
Through the gender studies lens   247

15 Making the pain count: embodied politics in the new age of
    terror   249
    GILLIAN YOUNGS

16 Corrective rapes: rape narratives in South Africa   260
    BEV ORTON

    Index   275

Contributors

Athina Karatzogianni is a Lecturer in Media, Culture and Society at the University of Hull. She is the author of *The Politics of Cyberconflict* (2006), *Power, Conflict and Resistance: Social Movements, Networks and Hierarchies* with Andrew Robinson (2010), and editor of *Cyber Conflict and Global Politics* (2009). Athina is currently preparing a research monograph *The Real, the Virtual and the Imaginary State*, and editing with Adi Kuntman *Affective Fabrics of Digital Cultures*. Other recent research articles published are focused on diverse themes: contemporary cyberconflicts, such as WikiLeaks, Google-China and the Climategate hack, conflict in collaborative networks, peer production, coverage of global hotspots and when in high mind, the spectrum and mechanisms of the inbetween space of the physical and virtual.

Peter H. Wilson is GF Grant Professor of History at the University of Hull, UK, and works on German political, cultural and social history and the history of warfare in Europe 1500–1900 and in the nineteenth-century world. His books include *Europe's Tragedy: A History of the Thirty Years War* (Penguin/Harvard, 2009), *From Reich to Revolution: German History 1558–1806* (Palgrave, 2004), *Absolutism in Central Europe* (Routledge, 2000), *The Holy Roman Empire 1495–1806* (2nd edn Palgrave, 2011; Japanese edition Iwanami Shoten, 2006; Chinese edition Peking University Press, forthcoming 2011), *German Armies: War and German Politics 1648–1806* (UCL Press, 1998), *War, State and Society in Württemberg, 1677–1793* (Cambridge University Press, 1995), and as editor, *The Blackwell Companion to Eighteenth-Century Europe* (2008), and (with Alan Forrest), *The Bee and the Eagle: Napoleonic France and the End of the Holy Roman Empire, 1806* (Palgrave, 2009).

Angela Kimyongür is a Senior Lecturer in French in the Department of Modern Languages at the University of Hull where she teaches French language and various aspects of twentieth-century French culture. Her research has focused for a number of years on the fiction of communist writer Louis Aragon and is the author of numerous articles on his work. She has published two monographs on Aragon: *Socialist Realism* *in Louis Aragon's Le Monde reel* (Hull University Press, 1995 and *Politics and Memory: Representations of War in the Work of Louis Aragon* (University of Wales Press, 2007). She is also joint editor, with Dr Angela Kershaw of the University of Birmingham, of *Women in Europe between the Wars* (Ashgate, 2007). Her current project is a monograph on French detective fiction, which will focus on representations of war within the genre and, more broadly, the way in which the genre is used as an articulation of political commitment or as a vehicle for the exploration of socio-political issues.

Jenel Virden is a Senior Lecturer in American History and Secretary General of the European Association of American Studies. She has published *America in the Wars of the Twentieth Century* (Palgrave, 2008), *Good-Bye, Piccadilly: British War Brides in America* (University of Illinois, 1996) and was an editor *America in the Course of Human Events: Presentations and Interpretations* (VU University Press, 2007). Her research interests are in United States social history in general and the US response to World War II specifically. Jenel is currently working on a monograph on United States Army chaplains in World War II that explores their work with servicemen at home and abroad. The underlying theme of the work looks at issues of morality and warfare. Past research has covered areas of immigration history, transatlantic relations and modern wars.

Keith Tester is a Professor of Sociology at the University of Hull and Kyung Hee University in Seoul. Some of his more recent publications include *Humanitarianism and Modern Culture* (Penn State University Press, 2009), *Eric Rohmer: Film as Theology* (Palgrave Macmillan, 2008), *Bauman Beyond Postmodernity: Conversations, Critiques and Annotated Bibliography 1989–2005* with Michael Hviid Jacobsen and Sophia Marshman (Aalborg University Press, 2007), *The Social Thought of Zygmunt Bauman* (Palgrave Macmillan, 2004), *Conversations with Zygmunt Bauman*, (Polity, 2001) and *Compassion, Morality and the Media* (Open University Press, 2001). His main research interest is in exploring the entwinement of culture and morality through the heritage of critical theory and, especially, the social thought of Zygmunt Bauman. Running alongside this area is an interest in questions of film and theology.

James Aston is Lecturer in Film Studies at the University of Hull and his principal research interests lie in the field of cinematic representations of the past especially in Hollywood during the 1960s and 1970s and post 9/11. He is also active in other research areas that focus on pre- and post millennium apocalyptic cinema and the films of Michael Haneke. Also, at present, he is collaborating on a book about sex and television for which he is writing a chapter on the viewing habits of adult television. Recent publications include 'Terrorist Attack!: The Spectacle of

Evil in the Blended Horror of Cloverfield' (*Scope*, February 2010) and 'The (Un)Spectacle of the Real: Forwarding an Active Spectator in Michael Haneke's Le Temps du Loup/Time of the Wolf (2003)' (*Studies in European Cinema*, Volume 7, no. 2, November 2010).

Sarah Harper studied sociology at the University of Hull. Her research interests include sexual culture and social theory. She is currently developing research around women's participation in BDSM practices.

Majid Yar is a Professor of Sociology at the University of Hull. He has written *Community & Recognition: Ethics, Inter-Subjectivity and the Foundations of Political Life* (VDM Verlag, 2009) *Cybercrime and Society* (Sage, 2006), has co-authored with Martin O'Brien *Criminology: The Key Concepts* (Routledge, 2008) and co-edited with Yvonne Jewkes *The Handbook on Internet Crime* (Willan, 2009). His research interests and activities span disciplines, with published work in the areas of social and political theory, crime and deviance, popular culture and new media. Majid's work explores the internet, including issues of crime, deviance, and regulation; intellectual property and the cultural commons; popular culture, especially Hollywood films; and social and cultural theory.

Cristina Flesher Fominaya holds a PhD in Sociology from the University of California, Berkeley and is Lecturer in Sociology at the University of Aberdeen. In addition to her research on the political and cultural aftermath of the 9/11 and 3/11 bombings, Flesher Fominaya's long term interest in alternative social movements has led to ethnographic research on the Spanish Green Parties, the British Anti-Roads Movement, and anti-globalization networks in Western Europe. Publications include 'The Madrid bombings and popular protest: Misinformation, counter information, mobilization and elections after 11-M' (*Contemporary Social Science* Volume 6, 3, 2011); 'Creating Cohesion from Diversity: The Challenge of Collective Identity Formation in the Global Justice Movement' (*Sociological Inquiry*, Volume 80, 3, 2010); 'Autonomous Movement and the Institutional Left: Two Approaches in Tension in Madrid's Anti-globalization Network' (*South European Society and Politics*, Volume 12, 3, 2007). Flesher Fominaya is a founding editor of *Interface: a journal for and about social movements* (www.interfacejournal.net), and founding co-chair of The Council for European Studies European Social Movements Research Network.

Rosemary Barberet is an Associate Professor in the Sociology Department at John Jay College of Criminal Justice in New York, where she currently directs the Masters of Arts degree program in International Crime and Justice. Rosemary's publications have dealt with self-reported youth crime, violence against women, business crime, crime indicators and comparative methodology. Her research interests include the use of criminal justice data and research in policy making, crime indicators, victimisation, gender and crime and cross-cultural methodology. Rosemary was awarded the Herbert Bloch Award of the American Society of Criminology for service to the society and to the professional interests of criminology, as well as the Rafael Salillas Award of the Sociedad Española de Investigación Criminológica.

Michael S. Drake is Lecturer in Sociology at the University of Hull. His work applies classical and recent social theory to organisations of violence, the body and society, culture and identity, and historical and political sociology, in order to develop new insights into the world in which we live. He has published journal articles and book chapters on social movement activism, sociology and war, disability politics, cultural identity, revolution, and a historical sociology of military power, *Problematics of Military Power: Government, Discipline, and the Subject of Violence* (Routledge/Cass, 2002). His most recent book is *Political Sociology for a Globalizing World* (Polity Press, 2010).

Lucy Michael is a Lecturer in Criminology at the University of Hull. Research interests relate to moral ordering and social control processes, in particular the problems of contemporary leadership in communities facing problems of crime, conflict and cohesion, and its relationship to both patterns of inter-generational conflict and cohesion, and the capacity of the community to access public institutions and mobilise effectively for a 'fair' share of social resources. Her publications include: 'Securing Civic Relations in the Multicultural City' (*Citizenship, Security and Democracy: Muslim Engagement with the West*, W. Krause, ed. International Institute of Islamic Thought, 2009); 'Youth and Leadership in British Muslim Communities', (2004), and 'Islam as Rebellion and Conformity: How Young Muslims in the UK Negotiate Space for and against Radical Ideologies' (*Journal of Religion, State and Society*, forthcoming, 2011).

Raphael Cohen-Almagor (D. Phil., Oxon), educator, researcher, human rights activist; Professor and Chair in Politics, University of Hull. He has published extensively in the fields of political science, philosophy, law, media ethics, medical ethics, sociology, history and education. He was Visiting Professor at UCLA and Johns Hopkins, Fellow at the Woodrow Wilson International Center for Scholars, Founder and Director of the Center for Democratic Studies, University of Haifa, and Member of The Israel Press Council. Raphael won many grants and scholarships, including Fulbright, the British Council, Volkswagen, Rich, Rothschild, Rockefeller and Yigal Alon. Among his recent books are *Speech, Media and Ethics* (2005), *The Scope of Tolerance* (2006), *The Democratic Catch* (2007), and his second poetry book *Voyages* (2007). His sixteenth book is scheduled to be published in 2011, dealing with public responsibility in Israel.

Sharon Haleva-Amir is a PhD Candidate and a research fellow at the Haifa
Center of Law and Technology (HCLT), Faculty of Law, University of
Haifa. Sharon has a Bachelor Degree in Law (LLB) from Tel-Aviv University and a Master degree (MA) in Information Science (specialising in internet and knowledge management) from Bar-Ilan University.
Before assuming her doctorate, she had practiced legal counseling,
editing and web mastering. Her fields of research include e-Democracy,
e-Politics, MPs web practices, websites content analysis and internet
ethics. Sharon has won a doctoral scholarship for excellent students
from the University of Haifa and a SHVIL (Transparency International–
TI) Israel scholarship for establishing a doctoral research plan which
will advance governmental transparency.

Maria Touri is a Lecturer in the Department of Media and Communications at the University of Leicester. She is involved in the analysis of
news framing and journalistic practices in situations of conflict and
crisis, and is currently completing a study on the coverage of the 2010
Greek financial crisis by the UK press. She is also working on a theoretical model of media-government interactions during conflict, using
game theory. Current research interests also include the media's role in
migration policy making.

Andy Robinson is a scholar and researcher working on critical theory, everyday life and the politics of oppression and resistance. He is co-author
with Athina Karatzogianni of *Power, Conflict and Resistance in the Contemporary World* (Routledge, 2010), which analyses the intersection of networks and hierarchies in the world-system. Other recent work includes
pieces on precarity, Deleuze and the social symptom, anarchism and
war, a post-colonial critique of global justice theory, and post-left anarchist utopianism.

Gillian Youngs has a background in academia, business and journalism.
Her broad research areas are globalisation, international relations and
international communications, and she has recently been working
on a range of issues related to the 'war on terror'. She led the ESRC
Research Seminar Series 'Ethics and the War on Terror: Politics, Mul-
ticulturalism and Media' (RES-451–25–4188, 2006–09) with Professor
Simon Caney (University of Oxford) and Professor Heather Widdows
(University of Birmingham). Her publications include *International
Relations in a Global Age: A Conceptual Challenge* (Polity, 1999), *Global
Political Economy in the Information Age: Power And Inequality* (Routledge,
2007), the edited volume *Political Economy, Power and the Body: Global
Perspectives* (Palgrave Macmillan, 2000), and the co-edited volume *Glo-
balizaton: Theory and Practice,* 3rd edn (Continuum, 2008). Her research
has appeared in numerous journals, edited collections and policy documents. She is currently University of Wales Alliance Research Chair and

Professor of Digital Economy at University of Wales, Newport. As well as practice and policy related work in UNESCO and NGO projects, her academic activities have included being a founding co-editor of *International Feminist Journal of Politics* from 1999 to 2005, and serving on the boards of several international journals.

Bev Orton is a PhD student and a teaching fellow in Criminology at the University of Hull. Bev had a wide-spanning career in theatre, film and TV, working in various dissident media in South Africa producing documentaries and films, before assuming a doctorate in Hull to enquire into female victimhood and emancipation in South Africa, under the supervision of Dr Susan Clisby and Dr Liz Walker. Beverley has taught diverse courses in criminology, sociology and cultural studies in a variety of higher education settings, as well as created emancipatory workshops, seminars and theatrical performances for marginalised and victimised women, as well as women who have been in prison.

Preface

Violence and War in Culture and the Media is bringing 18 experts for the first time together in one cross-disciplinary volume, focusing on theoretical and empirical issues relating to violence and war and the implications it has on media, culture and society.

The majority of the scholars participated in the 'Violence and War in Culture and the Media Lectures', I had the pleasure of organising for the Humanities Department and the Centre for Popular Cultures at the University of Hull, during the 2009–10 academic year. I am indebted to Professor George Talbot, former Dean of Arts and Social Sciences, for his encouragement and support in this endeavour.

Initially, the Violence and War lectures served as a space, to not only present research across units within departments, but also to understand interdisciplinarity issues in relation to violence and war across Departments within the Faculty of Arts and Social Sciences. Colleagues contributed from the areas Film (James Aston), Media (myself) and American Studies (Jenel Virden) within Humanities; from Sociology (Keith Tester, Majid Yar, Mick Drake, Sarah Harper), and Criminology (Lucy Michael, Bev Orton) within Social Sciences; and from the departments of Politics (Raphael Cohen-Almagor), Modern Languages (Angela Kimyongür) and History (Peter Wilson). I would like to thank my immediate colleagues for believing in this project, generously giving up their time for the lectures, and their exciting contributions to the volume.

Nevertheless, this book would not have the present diversity and intellectual reach, if colleagues from other universities in the UK and internationally did not offer their perspectives and contributions in the field. Therefore, I would like to reiterate my gratitude to the contributors Cristina Flesher Fominaya (Sociology, Aberdeen), Rosemary Barberet (Sociology, John Jay New York), Sharon Haleva-Amir (Law, Haifa), Gillian Youngs (Digital Economy, Wales), Maria Touri (Media, Leicester) and my close collaborator Andy Robinson (former Leverhulme Fellow, Nottingham), for believing in this project enough, to honor us with their valuable work. All contributors were involved in an internal peer review process, engaging with each other's work, which has added a further collaborative aspect to the project. The series editor Andrew Humphrys, and Isabel Jones, their team at Routledge, as well as the reviewers, also deserve our thanks for ensuring the book reached its readers in its best possible form.

I have saved for last, the reason for organising the lectures in the first place. I felt at home at no other research seminar series, as this subject area is too interdisciplinary to be addressed by any single unit or department. As a result, I had too much fun creating my own home in that regard, and you are welcome to it. I hope you engage with these works and stretch intellectually beyond your own ontology, discipline, methodology, and research interests. While pregnant with my son Sebastian, I definitely had to, in order to keep up with these scholars!

Lastly, I would like with the permission of all the contributors to dedicate this volume to our families and all our past, present and future students, and readers. Also, to newly born lives entering our world. I believe *they* are the inspirational motivations for more work on the study of violence and war in culture and the media.

Athina Karatzogianni
University of Hull, UK
17 April 2011

1 Violence and war in culture and the media through five disciplinary lenses

Athina Karatzogianni

Rationale

This volume is integrated around theoretical and empirical issues relating to violence and war, while attempting to transcend the boundaries of different fields and provide a variety of approaches of the implications of these phenomena on media, culture and society. In doing so, it is introducing current debates in relation to such representations through five particular lenses reflecting the specialisation of the contributors: the historical, the cultural, the political, the sociological and the gender studies perspectives. Although the contributions launch their inquiry from a specific disciplinary platform, it is evident that all authors, not only recognise the contributions made elsewhere, but they cross-fertilise their approaches with these other disciplinary lenses in the process. This introduction to the volume aims to demonstrate the need for diverse disciplinary perspectives and time frames, to introduce the authors and the themes explored in the volume, and how this interdisciplinary perspective is reflected in the general lay out of the book.

The logic of the volume becomes far more transparent, if the book is situated within the relevant scholarship. In the last 15 years or so, there has been a proliferation of books on the subjects of media violence, war coverage, or specific media and its relationship with violence and war, such as television or the internet, as well as the effect and expression of war and violence in traditional popular culture, as found for instance in books, film and art. Examples across the Arts and Social Sciences include: Barker and Petley's (1997) *Ill Effects*, a volume on media violence with audience studies and concentrating more on children, teenagers and women; Potter's (1999) *On Media Violence*, focusing on the effects of media violence and research/methodological limitations in this field in the 1990s; Sharrett's (1999) edited volume, *Mythologies of Violence in Postmodern Media*, which concentrates on film and television narratives exploring causes of violence and effects in the American context; Thussu and Freeman's (2003) volume *War and the Media*, specialised on 24/7 broadcasting with more of a television and early internet information warfare, new ways of managing and reporting conflict, with specific case studies such as 9/11, Iraq, and Afghanistan; Allan and Zelizer's (2004) volume *Reporting War: Journalism in Wartime*, specialised on reporting war, responses to war on terrorism, small wars and insurgencies, the role of journalists in covering the war and representations with Iraq War in focus; Hoskins and O'Loughlin's (2009) *Television and Terror*, which explains in great detail the link between the war on terror and news discourse produced for consumption in the contemporary global public sphere; and Malesevic's (2010) *The Sociology of War and Violence*, which tracks through the ages the effects of war and violence from a sociological perspective, with nationalism, propaganda, organised violence, gender violence and new wars as topics. The list also includes my edited volume *Cyber Conflict and Global Politics* (2009), which focused on new ICTs and political communication in relation to global politics.

In these efforts, there is the inevitable specialisation, which is defined first of all by the editor and the series the works are published, and the exact field the contributors are emerging from. From the examples I mention, it is evident, that usually, academics and writers in this field come from academics or practitioners based exclusively at specific disciplines, such as history, or military or history departments, sociology/cultural studies, or political communication and global politics. For instance, it has been widely accepted that history, political science and sociology, and within the latter the sub-areas of war studies, international conflict analysis, political communication, and cultural studies are the main disciplines assigned to deal with the subject of war and violence in politics, culture and the media.

Nevertheless, in order to do justice to the rich research strands across arts, humanities and social sciences, this volume serves as an attempt to aggregate a series of disciplinary approaches across time and space, to move beyond closed boundaries of specific disciplines, and to upset their standing as the privileged focal points. As a result, the volume focuses on violence and war through multiple perspectives, which has wider implications in seeking to develop links between this field and a body of theory that organically evolves out of other contexts, and in a way that would satisfy the demands of several disciplines, including communication studies, international relations, sociology and conflict theory, film, and literary theory. Such a broader interdisciplinary wealth of approaches and subjects enables future students of violence and war to understand and to analyse these phenomena, in a multi-perspectival way, which is not held ransom by the demands of a single discipline or school of thought. Complimentary to that, the volume attempts to update and enrich the current research output in the field, add to the current debates the individual contributors are engaged in, as well as presenting an original understanding of the multi-faceted effects of violence and war in society in general, by covering a wide range of subjects and not concentrating on just one subject through one disciplinary lens, which is usually the case.

The five lenses (historical, cultural, sociological, political and gender perspectives) proved useful in terms of theorising and analysing examples from different historical contexts (wars from different centuries to present conflicts), diverse communication media (art, film, literature, digital media and television), methods of analysis (others theoretical, others more empirical), with their own research techniques, (such as theoretical sampling, narrative and discourse analysis, archive, and interviews) and with scholars adhering to specific systems of thought while cross-fertilising with other perspectives. Theorising violence and war in culture and the media across disciplines and across case studies, and with a broader toolbox of research techniques, means that students from a variety of disciplines can engage not only with their own area, using their own methodologies, but can also be exposed to the research and understanding of other disciplines. This way, historians learn from sociologists and cultural theorists, political scientists learn from sociolologists and historians, while cultural theorists and media analysts borrow tool kits from politics, sociology and history. It is the ability to situate the specific case and example within a society, with a specific culture, in a specific historical moment, under different political systems in a global world, using the insight of different disciplines, which makes studying violence and war a truly fascinating subject. In more advanced studies on the professional academic level, specialisation and delving in the more intricate nature of the structurational elements of the subject matter is necessary (for example see Arquilla and Ronfledt, 2001; Van de Donk *et al.*, 2004; Hammond, 2009; Der Derian, 2009; Stahl, 2010; Karatzogianni and Robinson, 2010). Nevertheless, in the cases where scholarship is taught and transmitted to university students, or informs scholars from different areas of study, interdisciplinarity is key to broadening our understanding of what the analyses and theories have the potential to involve, and not just what we have been trained and told within our specific schools of thought and disciplines that it *should* involve.

The intention of the volume is to materialise this realisation, in a way that can be grasped by both the undergraduate and postgraduate student, but also by academics in different fields to engage with works on similar subjects emerging from an 'alien' theory, methodology and research technique to their own. In that sense, it is a challenge, which hopes to forge an openness to dialogue within the disciplines in Arts and Social Sciences, in a way that overly specialised volumes often fall sort of. In what follows, I introduce the five parts of the book and how the authors argue and link to each other and inform the overall rationale of the volume as such.

Through the historical lens

The first part 'Through the historical lens' serves as an example of the volume's rationale. The three contributors are based in different departments utilising specific disciplinary perspectives, coming from History (Peter H. Wilson), Modern Languages (Angela Kimyongür), and American Studies (Jenel Virden). Nevertheless, history is a critical factor in their analysis of the periods they examine. In some respects, there is a similarity in the way they write about their respective timeframes, although it is clear that methodologically, great differences remain, as for example, Virden examines the cultural and moral stance of chaplains through historical documents, Wilson examines historical patterns of the communication of violence and war through a variety of sources, such as diaries and newspapers, while Kimyongür relies on the literary novel by Patrick Pécherot to explore post-war France.

Peter H. Wilson, in his chapter 'Perceptions of violence in the early modern communications revolution: the case of the Thirty Years War 1618–1648', engages with aspects of the history of communication, but also looks into autobiographical and newspaper accounts of the period, in order to identify how perceptions of violence were influenced by the early modern communication revolution. His central thesis is that the experience of the war contributed to the general shift in European attitudes to violence. While medieval society saw violence as a moral problem to be solved by modifying behaviour, the experience of sectarian and civil war in the sixteenth and early seventeenth century, coupled with the early modern communication revolution, encouraged calls for a political solution to tame violence by entrusting greater power to the state to supervise daily life and to discipline society. This critical shift in popular perceptions of war enabled secular and religious authorities post-1618 to emphasise moral improvement, projecting sinful behaviour as the cause of war, and more importantly, emphasise subordination to recognised authorities, as the best guarantee to prevent a reoccurrence of such horror.

Angela Kimyongür, in her 'Patrick Pécherot, eugenics and the occupation of France', argues that novelist Patrick Pécherot continues this appropriation of the detective genre, in order to cast new light on forgotten victims of war-time violence in his 2005 novel *Boulevard des Branques*. Two levels, the historical and the cultural, are addressed in her analysis. The historical, where Pécherot offers a reconstruction of day-to-day life in Paris during the Occupation, offering a particular focus on the treatment of vulnerable minorities such as Jews, foreign nationals, and the mentally ill in wartime France; on a cultural level, Pécherot calls on a cultural memory of the Occupation through his adoption of Léo Malet's fictional hero, Nestor Burma, and through narrative parallels with his *120 rue de la Gare*. Pécherot, Kimyongür argues, uses the crime fiction genre to explore difficult truths about the Occupation period, and to offer a more complex historical memory of wartime France.

It is this interplay of history with culture, which is also the subject Jenel Virden explores in her 'United States Army chaplains and pulp magazines: censorship in World War II'. In her empirically rich account, we meet

United States Army chaplains of World War II who are grappled with problems associated with their work as religious counsellors to American GIs, trying to control influences on the GIs that could potentially lead to moral confusion or degeneracy. The chaplains are faced with the moral dilemma of what constituted immoral behaviour or immoral influences during wartime. Some chaplains took a very active role in issues of morality, safeguarding the men in their care from corrupting influences. Equally, some chaplains felt more at ease in dealing with the spiritual and pastoral needs of their men than with bigger and broader behavioural or moral issues. Virden argues in her analysis of the official communication between chaplains and the military, that the extent of a common policy towards the material was vague and highly personal. Moreover, World War II chaplains faced the problem of a changing and increasingly culturally exposed world where talk, discussion, imagery and awareness of issues, especially sexual issues, were more widespread and certainly more commonly imbibed than in any previous era. It is the cultural arena we must turn to next.

Through the cultural lens

The second part of the volume utilises the cultural studies perspective to engage with issues of violence, visibility and spectatorship; the ethics of remembering war; and ambiguities in cultural depictions of sadomasochistic imagery and alternative sexual practice communities. Again, the contributors come from different disciplinary, methodological and ontological backgrounds, from sociology (Keith Tester, Sarah Harper and Majid Yar), but also film studies (James Aston). Although at first instance the themes seem irreconcilable, it is the cultural studies perspective, coupled with sociological and political aspects, which all contributions utilise as an integrated platform, from where they launch their analysis.

Keith Tester, in his 'Hidden conflict, visible world' engages with Manet's painting of a historical moment in time, *The Execution of Emperor Maximilian*, to raise the point that conflict and the suffering it causes cannot be *assumed* to be visible. According to Tester, visibility is dependent, contingent to two conditions: *mediation*, whereby conflict and the hurts and humiliations it causes is only visible, if it appears in the media; and the second condition, whereby *the interpretation of the imagery*, as it appears in the media as relevant and, indeed, as offensive. His work explores the two aspects of visibility, mediation and imaginary, and asks whether conflict can also be hidden when visibility is not obtained though mediation and imaginary.

It is the cultural and political representational strategies, which James Aston's 'The ethics of remembering: Little Big Man and the exoneration of American guilt' examines in the film *Little Big Man*, which portrays the genocide of the Native American as a lamentation on their disappearance from the American West. The film exculpates white America's guilt and burden of that history, while conterminously forging direct associations with the war in Vietnam, and the huge loss of life experienced by the indigenous populations of South-east Asia. For Aston, *Little Big Man* has important repercussions in judging how effective revisionist or alternative historical narratives were in challenging dominant cultural forms. In his analysis he demonstrates, that the film smoothes over and renders less traumatic and controversial the war in Vietnam and the domestic unrest in America at the time.

Sarah Harper and Majid Yar in 'Loving violence? The ambiguities of SM imagery in contemporary popular culture', examine diverse fields of popular culture including film, fashion photography, advertising and music, to argue that mainstream imagery of Bondage Domination Sadism and Masochism (BDSM) culture, consistently glosses over the centrality of consent, reinforcing negative stereotypes about the practices and their practitioners. These media representations intersect with medico-moral and legal discourses, and work in concert to reproduce the supposed 'deviance' (and, indeed, 'criminality') of BDSM practitioners. Furthermore, Harper and Yar explore the ways certain practitioners actively embrace the status and symbolism associated with deviance, as an integral element in the production of a desired social and sexual identity.

Through the sociological lens

The enquiry to how violence and war impact on the victims and how terrorism, violence and war are remembered and negotiated in the public sphere is discussed in this third part of the volume, utilising the sociological lens. Contributors have a background in Sociology (Micheal S. Drake, Cristina Flesher Fominaya) and Criminology (Lucy Michael, Rosemary Barberet). Nevertheless, it is the interplay of the socio-political with the cultural, and by extension the ethico-legal, often in a global media environment in transformation due to ICTs, which informs the discussions here.

Flesher Fominaya and Barberet, in their 'Defining the victims of terrorism: competing frames around victim compensation and commemoration post 9/11 New York City and 3/11, Madrid', use a comparative analysis of the narrative patterns of *commemoration* and *compensation* in the cases of 9/11 and 3/11, arguing that the politics of victimhood have very real consequences for victims, not only in cases of internecine conflict, but also in cases of foreign-perpetrated terrorism. They have shown that national cultural narratives, legal frameworks and political arenas shape these in very different ways, as multiple competing hierarchies of victim stratification emerged in both 9/11 and 3/11, linked to claims about what victims were entitled to, be it commemoration, compensation, charitable donations, representation or medical psychological treatment.

The politics of commemoration are also the subject of Mick Drake's 'The returns of war: bodies, images and invented ritual in the war on terror'. Drake undertakes a comparative study of the public receptions of the war dead in the UK and the US, to produce insights into current conditions of the politics of mourning, in relation to the ineffectiveness of the antiwar movements and to remilitarisation processes in these national civic cultural contexts. Theoretically, he counterpoises the *politics* of mourning outlined by Gillian Rose to Judith Butler's work on the 'powers of mourning' after 9/11, which was intended to inform critical opposition to the Bush regime's response. Drake argues, that the strategy of the antiwar movement, reflected in Butler's argument, produces an impasse of what Rose calls 'aberrated mourning', leaving a vacuum, which has been filled by new forms of militarisation. For Drake, any counter-politics of war demands engagement in a struggle for the public meaning of the war dead.

Lucy Michael in 'Frames, forums and Facebook: interpreting British Muslim understandings of post-7/7 militarist media narratives', examines the frames through which British Muslims have interpreted the media reporting post 7/7. Muslims in the present study perceived media coverage through three dominant frames; the war at home; the unique (and unassailable) position of the state as arbiter of information and rights; and the identification of an enemy within. These three dominant frames, unlike those employed by British and international mass media, are borne of the local context from which participants viewed the war on terror. For Michael, what is observable from these personal responses to the dominant media discourses is that personal contributions to virtual discussion spaces illustrate the ways, in which the process of 'framing' is both an act of rejection of alternative understandings, and an emotional attachment to distant concepts and experiences.

Through the political lens

This part of the volume turns to the political to engage with the politics of assigning blame for war, the influence of psychology on media actors, and new media political communication issues, in relation to the state and the media. Here, the contributors institutionally are based in Politics (Raphael Cohen-Almagor, Andy Robinson), Media and Communications (Maria Touri and Athina Karatzogianni), and Law and Technology (Sharon Haleva-Amir), although there are evident quite a few interdisciplinary overlaps with the each other's areas in their actual academic research.

Raphael Cohen-Almagor and Sharon Haleva-Amir in 'The Israel–Hezbollah War and the Winograd Committee' examine the internal politics and international implications of assigning blame for the Olmert government's handling of the war with Hezbollah, and criticise the establishment of the committee and the results it reached, as a mockery of justice and a travesty of social responsibility. In a rich empirical analysis, Cohen-Almagor and Haleva-Amir, argue that the Israeli government responded hastily and without much thinking to the Hezbollah attack. Its massive attack on Lebanon brought about large-scale retaliation, which subjected more than one million Israeli citizens to continuous rocket attacks, and resulted in hundred of thousands of refugees, with hundreds of people killed or maimed. They argue that the war strengthened the Hezbollah in Lebanon, and weakened Israeli deterrence.

The need for a more systematic theoretical approach to the media's role in war and conflict is the focus of Maria Touri's chapter 'Media actors in war and conflict: insights from political psychology and the Bosnian war'. With the aid of prospect theory, Touri draws attention to the significance of the news media as a source of domestic cost for leaders in the context of an international conflict, with potential implications for their international behaviour. She offers an alternative interpretation of existing knowledge of the interaction between political leaders, the national media and the public in war and conflict. Touri applies this framework to the Bosnian conflict and argues that although media scholars have already recognised the media's potential pressure on Clinton's policy shift, prospect theory can help illuminate a potential mechanism through which this pressure was activated.

In 'Virilio and the gaze of the state: vision machines, new media and resistance', Andy Robinson uses Virilio's work to theorise the role of the state in an environment of global media transformation and its effect on war. Robinson argues that Virilio provides an account of the contemporary world, and the place of mass culture within it, which involves a novel, thought provoking theory of alienation. For Virilio, people are not simply alienated at the site of production, but in the channelling of sensory perception. A condition of 'telepresence' has corroded experiences of the local and created a generalised, mutual surveillance. The power of the state and the force of global markets are largely effects of this regime of telepresence. Robinson believes Vrilio's account is too pessimistic: new technologies which are part of the order of telepresence can often be converted into tools of resistance, reclaiming, in the lived immediacy of local lifeworlds, a site of affective counter-power which at its limits, becomes undeterrable.

My own contribution, 'Blame it on the Russians: tracking the portrayal of Russian hackers during cyber conflict incidents' employs cyber conflict theory, in order to engage with various aspects of cyber conflicts implicating Russian hackers, such as those involving Estonia and Georgia. The discussion reveals tensions and pressures in the transfer of physical conflict to cyberspace, such as the overall presence in culture and the media, of a residual, politicised, and ideological discourse, indiscriminately portraying individuals, often coming from a specific ethnic background, which nevertheless engages in fundamentally diverse ways, in order to effect change, to protest electronically, to support ethno-national causes or to engage in criminal activities in cyberspace. The chapter also examines the effect of such discourses on diplomacy, global politics and the question of defining and regulating cyber conflict, cyber protest and cyber crime on a global level.

Through the gender studies lens

In this final part, Gillian Youngs and Bev Orton, offer their analyses of violence and war from a gender studies viewpoint. Youngs focuses her discussion on a masculine public sphere, where pain is othered and excluded from mainstream political process and motivations, and which denies political meaning to the embodied experience of pain thanks to these binary constraints. This compliments Orton's analysis of rape narratives and rape myths in relation to lesbian corrective rapes in South Africa, and how these constrain the state's legal acknowledgement that 'corrective rape' is a violation of human rights.

To elaborate further, Gillian Youngs in 'Making the pain count: embodied politics in the new age of terror', argues that the realities of pain are distorted by the realities of the mainstream political lens. This is one explanation for the limited political effect of increasing exposure to the collective experiences of pain. She argues that working towards a holistic political public sphere is fundamental with the new media environment and its horizontal and interactive forms, helping to stretch and disrupt the familiar constraints of the public sphere. Youngs calls for a transformation, whereby the memory of pain, instead of being continually effaced in political senses, would gain potency, not only in relation to the present and future, but also the past. The links across time and space are central here, as are the connections between public and private. While the transformation and its effects relate to war and terror, they also relate to domestic violence.

This chapter and its theoretical polemic is especially relevant to Orton's 'Corrective rapes: rape narratives in South Africa', where she is discussing rape narratives and rape myths, using various studies and research on gender violence in South Africa. Orton analyses *Broken Dreams*, a play by Juliet Vuviseka Rozani, to highlight some of the issues, perceptions and threats confronting lesbians in townships in South Africa. In her analysis of the cultural and legal issues involved, she promotes support for the movement in South Africa by activists to petition the government to classify lesbian rape as a hate crime. She argues, that it is through changing the law, that perpetrators of lesbian rape would be subjected to harsher sentencing, and that there would be an acknowledgement that 'corrective rape' is a violation of human rights.

Conclusion

Lastly, the volume takes the reader through a journey of diverse perspectives and subjects of analysis, which often overlap and talk to each other, in order to discuss the role of the media and culture in framing acts of war and violence, in exonerating guilt and making conflict visible or hidden. In turn, the volume explores the structural constraints in the commemoration, perception and understanding of war and violence in a gendered public sphere, currently under new media transformation, which can offer the potentially for radical change in our understanding of victims, perpetrators, blame, pain and memory of war, and violence, in the frequently blurred public and private spheres, situated within the past, and the contemporary transformative cultural space-time.

References

Allan, S. and Zelizer, B. (eds) (2004) *Reporting War: Journalism in Wartime*, London and New York: Routledge.

Arquilla, J. and Ronfeldt, D. (eds) (2001) *Networks and Netwars: The Future of Terror, Crime and Militancy*, California: Rand.

Barker, M. and Petley, J. (eds) (1997) *Ill Effects: The Media Violence Debate*, London and New York: Routledge.

Der Derian, J. (2009) *Virtuous War*, London and New York: Routledge.

Hammond, P. (2009) *Media, War and Postmodernity*, London and New York: Routledge.

Hoskins, A. and O'Loughlin, B. (2009) *Television and Terror: Conflicting Times and the Crisis of News Discourse*, Palgrave Macmillan.

Karatzogianni, A. (ed.) (2009) *Cyber Conflict and Global Politics*, London and New York: Routledge.

Karatzogianni, A. and Robinson, A. (2010) *Power, Resistance and Conflict in the Contemporary World*, Routledge Advanced Series in International Relations and Global Politics, London and New York: Routledge.

Malesevic, S. (2010) *The Sociology of War and Violence*, Cambridge: Cambridge University Press.

Potter, W. J. (1999) *On Media Violence*, London: Sage.

Sharrett, C. (ed.) (1999) *Mythologies of Violence in Postmodern Media*, Detroit, MI: Wayne State University Press.

Stahl, R. (2010) *Militainment Inc.: War, Media and Popular Culture*, London and New York: Routledge.

Thussu, D. and Freeman, D. (eds) (2003) *War and the Media*, London: Sage.

Van de Donk, W., Loader, B., D., Nixon, P. G. and Rucht, D. (eds) (2004) *Cyberprotest: New Media, Citizens and Social Movements*, London and New York: Routledge.

Part I

Through the historical lens

2 Perceptions of violence in the early modern communications revolution

The case of the Thirty Years War, 1618–1648

Peter H. Wilson

Introduction

The Thirty Years War was the most destructive conflict in European history prior to the two twentieth-century world wars (Wilson 2009; Kampmann 2008). It was a struggle over the political and religious order in the Holy Roman Empire which encompassed what are now Germany, Austria, Czech Republic, parts of Denmark, France and Poland, as well as holding jurisdiction over northern Italy. This conflict was not inevitable, but resulted from the coincidence of adverse factors around 1600. War broke out when the Habsburg dynasty (holding the imperial title) was unable to contain the Bohemian Revolt, which began symbolically with the Defenestration of Prague in May 1618, when three of the emperor's officials were thrown from a window in Prague castle. The war continued, partly through the intractability of its underlying causes, notably disputed interpretations of the imperial constitution, but also through the successive intervention of foreign powers, each acting from their own motives. To some observers, it was a general European war, but in fact most saw it as distinct from other conflicts in western and northern Europe, which followed their own trajectories and were concluded separately. The termination of the Thirty Years War in the Peace of Westphalia is seen generally as the birth of the modern international system based on sovereign states.

Around 1.8 million soldiers and at least 3.2 million civilians died, reducing the Empire's population by at least one-fifth, and representing, proportionally, far higher losses than either of the two world wars – the Soviet Union, which suffered the most in the second of these two conflicts, lost about 12 per cent of its population. It is scarcely surprising that the Thirty Years War has become a benchmark to measure both earlier and later violence. One recent discussion of massacre considers the sack by the imperial army of the city of Magdeburg (1631), the worst single atrocity between the Mongol invasion of Europe in the thirteenth century and the Japanese 'Rape of Nanking' in 1937 (Bailey 1994: 36–7, 118). Many soldiers fighting in the trenches of World War I, or on the Eastern front during World War II, believed their situation was *almost as bad* as that of the Thirty Years War. The official announcement to the German people after Hitler's death explained the surrender to the Allies as necessary to prevent the level of destruction reaching that experienced in the early seventeenth century. In public opinion surveys, late twentieth-century Germans regularly placed the Thirty Years War ahead of the Black Death and the Nazi era as their country's greatest disaster. The prevalence of mass media images of more recent carnage has eroded this, but such views are often voiced in popular and local histories published in the twenty-first century. This sense of a conflict exceeding all known bounds draws our attention to the importance of contemporary perceptions of violence and how those perceptions were formed and communicated.

This chapter will briefly examine the early modern communications revolution and assess how it was accelerated by the war. It will then investigate the nature and level of violence during the war, before concentrating on how this was perceived by those experiencing it. The approach will be historical, locating perceptions of violence during the Thirty Years War within the context of longer term trends. The findings rest on a wide range of eyewitness testimony and other contemporary sources, of which only a selection can be presented here. Such sources are increasingly used systematically by historians to reconstruct past perceptions of events, rather than simply to supply information or as anecdotes. Opinions differ as to how reliable this material is, and the extent to which the thoughts of long dead central Europeans can be recovered in any meaningful way (Mortimer 2002; Woodford 2002). This chapter supports the growing consensus that we can distinguish between momentary experience (what Germans call *Erlebnis*) and accumulated experience (*Erfahrung*). The former can hardly be recovered, but the latter can at least be studied through diaries, letters and other reflective forms of testimony (Buschmann and Carl 2001; Münch 2001).

The main argument will be that the experience of the war contributed to the general shift in European attitudes to violence. Medieval society generally saw violence as a moral problem to be solved by modifying behaviour. This shifted in the sixteenth and early seventeenth century with the experience of sectarian and civil war, encouraging calls for a political solution to tame violence by entrusting greater power to the state to supervise daily life and to discipline society (Lademacher and Groenveld 1998; Oestreich 1982). Popular perceptions of the war escaping rational control contributed to this by conditioning subjects to accept a stronger state, despite the abject failure of existing authorities to provide protection during the conflict. Secular and religious authorities directed their efforts inwards towards their own subjects after 1618, fostering a sense that they were to blame for the war, having incurred God's wrath through their sinful behaviour. Alongside the traditional stress on moral improvement came a new emphasis on subordination to recognised authorities as the best guarantee to prevent a reoccurrence of such horror.

The early modern communications revolution

The war occurred during what has been labelled the 'early modern communications revolution', which began much earlier, but was greatly accelerated and expanded by the conflict (Behringer 2003). The revolution rested on the development of the first effective postal system in Europe, initiated when the emperor authorised the Thurn und Taxis family to run a service throughout the Empire in 1490. This private business enjoying a public monopoly proved hugely successful, not least for its operators who eventually rose to the ranks of imperial princes. The Empire was Europe's largest state, measuring 900 km North–South, East–West and took 30 days to cross by conventional means. The Thurn und Taxis post used relays of horses working day and night to reduce this to just five – speed not exceeded until the development of railways and telegraph in the 1830s. The service operated according to modern performance criteria, in an age otherwise still characterised by patronage and casualness. For example, detailed records were kept to identify the location and time of delays to improve performance.

'The early modern communications revolution was the mother of all communications revolutions' since subsequent developments in transportation and communication have followed principles established by the postal network: rail, road, air travel, telephone, cable, internet (Behringer 2003: 42). The German rail and road network essentially follows the post routes established in the sixteenth century, while Frankfurt am Main, the hub of the Thurn und Taxis operations, is the country's financial centre and location of its main airport. More fundamentally, all subsequent communications systems use the same structural principle of integration, regardless of the number of individual operators and users. The German princes tried to develop their own postal services, both for profit and for political reasons, but were compelled to accept that exclusive systems would not work – communication needs integration. Thus, while the political authorities encouraged the development of communications, they were unable to control it entirely.

The structure of the Empire greatly influenced this development. The Empire was a mixed monarchy, meaning that the emperor shared the exercise of key prerogatives with around 300 princes, counts and free cities collectively constituting the imperial Estates (*Reichsstände*). Political centralisation occurred at the level of the Empire's component territories (the imperial Estates), not the Empire as a whole (Wilson 2011b). Individual territories expanded their information gathering and supervision of their inhabitants, initiating a 'surveillance society', but nonetheless remained part of the wider imperial framework, not least, because most were too small to be viable as independent states, and continued to depend on higher imperial institutions until the Empire's collapse in 1806. The emperor asserted control over book licensing and copyright law around 1500, but it proved impossible to establish tight censorship, especially after the Empire officially adopted religious pluralism by granting equal legal rights to Lutherans, as well as Catholics, in 1555. The political structure remained porous, allowing the circulation of news and ideas, despite the continued efforts of imperial institutions and individual imperial Estates to control this.

The early modern communications revolution transformed the European perception of time, eroding the traditional pattern based on location and the seasons, which the mechanisation of time keeping had not changed, since clocks were set locally according to the sun. Communications integration propelled a common system of time keeping, exemplified by the time charts kept by the imperial post to help improve efficiency. This process continued despite important counter trends, notably the 'confessionalisation' of time following the Protestants' rejection of the Gregorian calendar as a papal invention in 1582, which resulted in the two groups observing different days of the week, until the general acceptance of the new system around 1700. The common framework was symbolised by the spread of the use of Mercury, the messenger of Zeus, in newspaper titles across the Empire, as well as a similar format for layout and news reporting.

The development of mail coach services using the postal routes revolutionised personal travel and, to an extent, still persists in some rural areas with the phenomenon of the post bus. Above all, the post system made newspapers commercially viable as a means to deliver current or at least recent news in print, since they could be distributed to a wider audience. Papers began in Strasbourg and Antwerp in 1605 and were followed by at least five others by 1618. The Empire led the way. There was no French equivalent until 1631, while most other countries only followed during the later seventeenth century (Weber 2006; Koopmans 2005). Improved distribution also encouraged a greater volume of other news forms, which had appeared by 1490 as part of the first 'print revolution'. These consisted of retrospective newsletters, which compiled information in longer chronologies, and were often produced during the early seventeenth century in Frankfurt. Broadsheets represented a cheaper alternative, which combined a striking image with a rhymed text that could be sung out by the news seller for a fee, if the audience could not afford or did not want to purchase the sheet. A third form were pamphlets commenting on current events that were often subsidised by, or written on behalf of governments as propaganda.

The development of a varied media landscape was directly related to the Empire's vast physical and decentralised political geography, which hindered centralised supervision. Commercial factors encouraged a degree of self-censorship, since newspaper publishers usually wished to sell across territorial and confessional boundaries. However, the uneven pattern of political authority created opportunities for subtle differences.

Publications in cities like Hamburg or Wolfenbüttel generally refrained from extremist views, because these venues wished to remain on good terms with everyone. Those in cities more firmly associated with one of the belligerents were more partisan, such as the main Viennese paper, which was usually favourable to the emperor, but occasionally printed more negative reports (Oggold 2001; Reisner 2001).

The Defenestration of Prague heralding the outbreak of war on 23 May was already reported in the Frankfurt paper in June 1618. The subsequent spread of the conflict beyond Bohemia fuelled rapid expansion with six new titles appearing in 1619 alone, followed by another 17 over the 1620s and 12 more after Swedish intervention in 1630. Several folded, or only appeared irregularly, but around 30 weekly papers were running in 1648 with a total distribution of 15,000 copies, compared to only 100 a week before 1618. Total readership was up to 20 times the distribution figure, because papers were circulated amongst friends or read aloud to illiterate neighbours. In addition, there was a dramatic expansion in other forms of communication and in the recording of information by the authorities, by their subjects and by those outside the immediate theatre of war who were impatient for news.

To understand how the war added impetus to the early modern communications revolution, we need to set the violence after 1618 into its longer-term context. The Thirty Years War represented a massive, sudden intrusion into what had been a relatively settled existence. There had been a number of localised conflicts in parts of the Empire which saw relatively little fighting, as well as peasant rebellions in parts of the Habsburgs' hereditary lands and rioting in some imperial cities. However, the Empire had not seen major military operations for 66 years before 1618, in stark contrast to France and the Netherlands which were ripped apart by civil wars since the 1560s. No one was prepared for a major conflict. Most German princes only maintained bodyguards and militias, while the Habsburgs had less than 2,000 professional soldiers at the time of the Defenestration and were in the process of disbanding these as too expensive. Within three years the war had spread from Bohemia to cover much of western Germany with around 80,000 to 100,000 men under arms. Danish intervention in 1625 prompted the formation of a new, larger imperial army, pushing total combatants to 160,000 and spreading the war northwards. Though Denmark was knocked out in 1629, Sweden invaded the following year and the conflict became general across the Empire. The number of soldiers peaked at a 250,000; a figure which can be doubled given that every soldier was usually accompanied by at least one non-combatant 'camp follower', or civilian providing logistical support and welfare. Growing devastation and economic dislocation contributed to a reduction in overall numbers, but there were still 160,000 men under arms when peace was signed in October 1648 (Wilson 2009: 770, 782–3). While the ratio of soldiers to civilians was lower than in twentieth-century conflicts, the proportional burden was in many ways greater, given that this was a pre-industrial age with virtually no ability to replace the missing labour power and very limited flexibility in production and exchange.

These numbers were far in excess of the capacity of pre-war institutions to sustain, forcing all belligerents to live off the land, often seizing hostages to compel communities to redirect their taxes from their lord to maintain the troops instead. The scale and immediacy of military demands presented civil authorities and society with major challenges. A well-stocked farm might have the equivalent of 500 daily rations, enough for it to survive for an entire year, but a single regiment required 3,000 or more individual rations each day (Pohl 1991: 63–9). Communities urgently required information on troop movements to prepare for their arrival, or to take precautionary measures such as moving inhabitants and livestock to a place of safety.

These military and material conditions help explain why the war represented a dramatic personal experience. It was recorded in a wide variety of eyewitness and personal testimony, ranging in terms of immediacy from letters through diaries, chronicles, autobiographies, to funeral sermons (Krusenstjern 1997). People wrote from a wide variety of motives, which have already been analysed elsewhere (Mortimer 2002; Schulze 1996; Woodford 2002). Their writing was greatly influenced by the communications revolution, notably the distribution of almanacs and printed calendars around 1600, which encouraged a more chronological sense of time, while the availability of newspapers and other sources contributed to the repetition of phrases and metaphors. In some cases, passages were copied verbatim or simply cut out and pasted into a hand-written account (Theibault 1993).

The nature and level of violence

Written testimony records varying levels and forms of violence, which require some discussion before we can analyse what such accounts tell us about contemporary perceptions. Not all violence was directly related to the war. Violence was a feature of other aspects of life at the time (Ulbrich *et al.* 2005), though much of it was verbal, rather than physical (Sabean 1990: 130–46, 163–4). Most people carried a weapon if they went out after dark or beyond sight of their home. It is debatable whether the war really increased the incidence of this 'background' violence, but this certainly was the contemporary perception. There was widespread belief across all sections of society in the general breakdown, not only of the settled order, but also individual morals (Fuchs 2002). Certainly, the incidence of banditry, highway robbery and housebreaking all increased with the dislocation of settled society, and the general problems of military supply.

Violence more directly related to the war fell broadly into two categories already identified in contemporary military discourse. What was termed 'major warfare' (*Hauptkrieg*) involved movement and contact between large bodies of troops and was intended to secure major strategic goals, such as key towns, as well as confront and where necessary defeat the enemy army. The significant increase in the overall size of armies was sustained for a generation, so that a sizeable proportion of the population by 1648 had known only war. The first half of the conflict was characterised by major operations in only one to three regions simultaneously. Swedish intervention and the rapid expansion in army size meant the war was fought in virtually every region in the Empire after 1631. The number of battles increased as forces contested control of particular regions. This intensified the demographic and material impact, since decisions on the battlefield often meant sudden reversals of fortune, forcing the defeated side to evacuate large areas, often precipitously. The extensive and rapid movement of forces spread plague and disease, both of which were the primary killers during the war (Eckert 1996).

However, major operations affected only a small proportion of the total population directly. Battles were fought within restricted areas within a single day between professional soldiers and, less frequently, mobilised militia. The civilian camp followers generally stayed to the rear, though they often returned to plunder the dead and could be caught if their side broke at the end of the engagement. Sieges affected more civilians, especially if the defending garrison refused to surrender and the town was taken by assault, as occurred notoriously at Magdeburg in 1631.

Direct exposure to violence more commonly occurred during what was termed 'little war' (*Kleinkrieg*), which involved what later generations have labelled variously irregular or guerrilla warfare, or special operations. These involved smaller parties of troops engaged in raiding, ambushes, or skirmishes intended to secure supplies or information, or to disrupt the enemy and deny him resources. Little war often accompanied major operations, as for example during scouting prior to a battle, or the pursuit of a defeated foe, but it was also an important feature in areas where the main armies were not operating. It was conducted by 'special forces', such as dragoons (mounted infantry), light cavalry, and selected parties of infantry. Foreign soldiers were often recruited for these tasks, notably Balkan peoples who were invariably called 'Croats', or Eastern Europeans who were usually termed 'Cossacks' regardless of their actual origin. The Swedish army also employed Finns and Scots, often as assault troops.

Special forces generally operated detached from the main army, further from supervision and with less access to regular forms of supply. They were sometimes assisted by members of the non-combatant 'camp community', especially when foraging (Lynn 2008), or by local civilians who joined for a great variety of reasons (Kaiser 2002b: 219–21). Partisans were a feature from the first campaign when Bohemian peasants attacked stragglers from the imperial army trying to suppress the Revolt. Though sometimes sanctioned by the authorities, they were usually ill-coordinated and generally directed at all the formal belligerents. The war provoked considerable unrest, and though this remains poorly studied, it is clear there were substantial risings in Westphalia 1622–23, Upper Austria 1626, and large parts of southern Germany 1633–34.

Civilians most commonly experienced the war as a succession of intrusions into their community (Asch 2000; Kaiser 1996). Teacher Ascher Levy recorded that it was too dangerous to go to the synagogue (Levy 1913: 62), while nun Maria Anna Junius noted how the bells in her hometown no longer tolled at the usual times for mass, during occupation by the Protestant Swedes (Junius 1890–91: 36). Most diaries are little more than lists of troops passing through the writer's community, seeking food and shelter, or (less often) coming to raid and destroy. Physical violence was frequently discussed, but usually as something that was feared or had allegedly occurred elsewhere. Eyewitness testimony of actual violence usually involved cases where foreign soldiers had been unable to make themselves understood, or where civilians had got in the way or offered resistance (Ulbricht 2004). Sometimes poorer inhabitants were injured or killed to frighten their richer neighbours into revealing hidden food stores or treasure. However, it is also clear that some soldiers used violence to reinforce their own group identity or to take revenge on those who despised them. Soldiers often deliberately destroyed things their victims held dear, or made them perform degrading acts. Authority figures were often targeted, either to coerce their communities into complying, or to mock them, such as making them wear fools' hats. It has been suggested that rape can also be explained this way (Burschel 1994: 27–53; Kaiser 2004; Theibault 1998).

Many of these elements can be found in contemporary accounts of the sack of Magdeburg in May 1631, which constituted the worst atrocity in the war. Around four-fifths of the city's 25,000 inhabitants perished when the city caught fire during the final imperial assault. The event received wide coverage in personal testimony, as well as all forms of print media, not least because the Swedes tried to exploit it to rally German support for their invasion (Kaiser 1997; Lohmann 1913; Medik 2001; Neubauer 1931).

Early modern definitions of violence

One final aspect requires our attention before we review contemporary perceptions. Early modern Germans identified four concepts of violence, though the distinctions between them were fluid, and most eyewitness accounts are unreflective and do not use these categories which were only fully explicit in learned discourse (Pröve 1997, 1999). Violence in the sense of the power to enforce one's will was labelled *Gewalt*, distinct from *potestas*, or power (as authority), *vis* or *virtus*, meaning power (as strength, virtue), and finally *violentia*, denoting violence (as physical act).

The contemporary discussion of war combined all of these elements through the concept of a 'just war' developed since the fourth century (Kaiser 2002a; Piirimäe 2002; Repgen 1985). This literature responded to war as a moral rather than a political problem and tried to reconcile the use of violence with Christian prohibitions, especially the commandment not to kill. For a war to be just it had to be waged by a properly constituted authority (*potestas*), be conducted by appropriate means (avoiding unnecessary *violentia*), and be directed towards upholding justice (*virtus*). In short, war was the continuation of legal arguments by other means; an exercise of *Gewalt* to force the other party to accept a reasonable settlement. Destruction was never – at least officially – an end in itself; something which is often forgotten given the popular image of the Thirty Years War, as both an all-destructive fury, and as the last and greatest of Europe's religious wars. Few, even among religious militants, advocated exterminating their foes (Brendle and Schindling 2006; Wilson 2008). The normative guidelines were codified in printed 'articles of war', which all recruits were obliged to swear to obey. These failed to prevent numerous infractions, but the key point is that contemporaries still distinguished between legitimate and illegitimate violence, according to broadly accepted norms, meaning that all belligerents were within the same normative system (Wilson 2011a).

Until recently, historians concentrated on assessing the level of violence by quantifying the demographic and material loss (Theibault 1997). The general trend has been to revise earlier estimates downwards, though the current conclusion is that both human and material losses were still very high. However, this raises the question why contemporaries thought the level of violence was even higher and to answer this, we need to examine contemporary perceptions.

Perceptions

Contemporary perceptions can be grouped into seven broad categories. A sense of excitement or adventure is expressed by a few writers. Several soldiers' accounts read like travelogues with the author commenting, at least as much, on the areas he passed through as the events he participated in (Peters 1993). Augustus von Bismarck (1611–70) noted with pleasure that the war had given him the opportunity to travel to Italy (Bismarck 1890: 97). Other perspectives falling into this category include those who benefited materially or socially from the war, either by acquiring pay or plunder, or social elevation, such as ennoblement. Excitement is also expressed occasionally by adults recalling childhood experiences, such as Friedrich Friese (born 1619) who recounts his fascination at first seeing soldiers at a military checkpoint in 1628 (Lohmann 1913: 186–7), or by soldiers surviving danger (Raymond 1917: 38–9). Sometimes, these authors were influenced by Humanist models of heroism, but their views were essentially subversive since they contradicted the general moral condemnation of violence.

Professionalism represented a second category, and was usually expressed as a sense of duty to a cause and/or to comrades, or as corporate loyalty to the military as a distinct group in society, or an interest in military practice from the perspective of efficiency. It was most common among serving or former soldiers, especially officers, since there are very few accounts by men who did not either start service as an officer, or work their way up from the ranks. Several British officers wrote accounts of their experiences in the Thirty Years War when they returned home, notably Robert Monro (1590–1680) and Sir James Turner (1615–86), intending these either to advance their careers or to disseminate military practice they had learned on the continent (Monro 1999; Lawrence 2009). A few civilian writers showed interest in technical military matters, like Sister Junius who records some detail of the tactics employed by the forces fighting near her convent outside Bamberg. Most soldiers' accounts were a non-committal, laconic recounting of events, often restricted to the names of settlements they passed through and how much distance they covered with each march. Criticism remained limited to matters of efficiency, such as Christian Vitzthum von Eckstädt's scathing remarks on the lacklustre conduct of the Saxon generals during the 1630s (Vitzthum von Eckstädt 1881). However, soldiers' accounts could be subversive through their inherent tendency to explain events in secular rather than spiritual terms, or as the outcome of arbitrary fortune (Knauer 1997).

Far more fall into a third category of writing dominated by a sense of apprehension, anxiety and fear. These emotions are most common in civilian accounts, though a few soldiers, like Raymond, confess having felt frightened in action. Civilian accounts indicate that many initially experienced the war at a distance through the news, commenting with mounting disquiet as operations approached their community. Some, usually clergy, were partisan at this stage, using terms like 'the enemy' to describe forces hostile to their own territory's government, and noting victories with approval (Junius 1890–91: 55–7, 69–70). Many remained confused, either unable or unwilling to discuss the conflict in political terms, and instead regarding it only as a danger which loomed larger as news came that soldiers were approaching. Landlords and nuns sometimes record the dilemma of whether to stay in their own homes, or to flee. The sense of war as something alien to settled existence is heightened by the prominence given to Croats and other foreigners in accounts of violence (Rullmann 1877: 242–3). Anxiety made most writers susceptible to rumour and stereotypes. The Hamburg papers reported in November 1631 that the Swedes had landed accompanied by ferocious Laplanders mounted on reindeer, while others thought the Finnish infantry possessed magical powers enabling them to cross rivers (Pleiss 1992). Junius readily believed the cliché that blood literally ran down the walls as the Swedes massacred the garrison of nearby Würzburg in October 1631 (Junius 1890–91: 18).

Fears could give way to relief and even guilt if actual encounters were less fearful than expected. Junius and the Catholic nuns in the Heiliggrab convent were obviously uncomfortable in escaping the worst of the Swedish occupation of Bamberg in 1631–32. Whereas the other citizens suffered billeting and heavy requisitioning, a senior Swedish officer posted guards to stop his troops troubling the nuns, whose main concern was a constant stream of other officers and their wives who wanted to visit the convent out of curiosity. Other writers were simply grateful to have been spared death.

Relief often proved only temporary giving way to disillusionment, an altogether more common experience, which usually developed following successive encounters with troops. Any prior distinctions between 'friends' and 'foes' were eroded as all behaved equally badly. Junius records the alarm caused by a sortie from the imperial garrison from Forchheim, despite this intended to disrupt Swedish occupation of her home city Bamberg. Imperial soldiers often proved more menacing towards the nuns than the Lutheran Swedes who were usually perfect gentlemen (Junius 1890–91: 37–8, 59, 169–70). Such ambiguities eroded the differences between legitimate and illegitimate violence, especially as chronic logistical problems encouraged soldiers to steal and extort supplies. Diaries or memoirs become accounts of mounting hardship, growing insecurity and, above all, decline which was often recorded as the death or departure of neighbours, and the physical deterioration of familiar surroundings. The latter contributed to one of the lasting stock metaphors of the war as leaving a once flourishing Germany devastated. Writers regularly recount grass growing in the streets, or fields left untilled for want of draught animals or human labour. The deaths of friends, relations or children are given prominence, even if they are usually recorded without much comment. The war also features in the destruction of homes, prized possessions and the loss of opportunity or social status (Kürschner 1913).

These comments were sometimes expanded into a general sense of moral decline, especially in writing by clergy and by poets and playwrights, who recounted children swearing in the streets, drunkenness and, above all, horror stories. Some stories undoubtedly had a basis in real events, but many used stock elements common to accounts of violence circulating before 1618, including news from the French and Dutch civil wars, campaigns against the Ottoman Turks, and accounts of Russian operations in the Baltic during the mid-sixteenth century. Some stories were migratory myths, which updated generic tales to suit current circumstances and provide information about dealings with soldiers. Others appear to have featured more to express horror or simply despair at a conflict seemingly out of control. Common elements include breaches of the articles of war, like the brutal murder of the defenceless (women, children, the elderly), whom soldiers were expressly instructed to spare or protect. The sense of atrocity was heightened by these events supposedly having taken place in sacred spaces; indeed, most hearsay or propaganda accounts of massacres have these occurring whilst the victims were attending church services. Many tales included accounts of rape or cannibalism – the latter usually alleged to have involved starving mothers eating their own children – all of which heightened the impression that violence knew no bounds and that civilisation was breaking down (Wilson 2011a). Hard evidence for such events is rarely forthcoming, but they were clearly believed. Many writers retreat into silence, as diaries break off, or autobiographies are left unfinished, suggesting that the experience was too overwhelming (Woodford 2002; 174).

Condemnation in the form of direct criticism of violence is relatively rare. Disillusionment could be expressed as criticism, though often indirectly as, for instance, when writers recorded how their neighbours hurled abuse at authority figures who fled in advance of the enemy's arrival, rather than staying to help protect them (Junius 1890–91: 27; Ulbricht 2004: 126). There was a millenarian aspect to some of the popular protests during the worst phase of the conflict during the 1630s. Several writers expressed the common early modern metaphor of the world turned upside down, which could be critical of the established order, but also a sign of anxiety as familiar rules no longer seemed to apply. Some were hostile to those who appeared to benefit from the war, while others resented their loss of social status as their wealth disappeared and they were forced to walk barefoot, or eat food normally consumed by the poor. Communal solidarity was strained, or even broke down when people saved themselves by telling soldiers to plunder richer neighbours instead.

However, few attacked violence or criticised the war in general. Where criticism was voiced, it usually took the form of official propaganda, or commentary by clerical observers. Such criticism was always partisan, attacking the enemy for perceived abuses in an attempt to rally sympathy from potential supporters. The concept of just war left no room for neutrality, because only one side could have God on its side. Some propaganda deliberately magnified accounts of violence to warn neutrals of the risks of standing idly by while the devil did his work. Those transgressing commonly accepted norms were routinely referred to as 'behaving worse than the Turks' to place them outside Christian civilisation (Kaiser 2008: 160–6). Significantly, such propaganda was rarely directed internally by the authorities, in an effort to mobilise their own subjects. Several belligerents did call out militia to supplement their regular forces, but none called for a peoples' war. Even the hard pressed Bohemian rebels preferred to negotiate with the Ottoman sultan in 1620, rather than consider arming their peasants or calling for a holy war against the invading imperial, Bavarian and Saxon troops. While enemies were criticised for breaching the laws of war, they were not demonised or presented as objects of popular hatred (Droysen 1903; Rystad 1960). Popular mobilisation would have contradicted the official attitude to war as the controlled application of force by a properly constituted authority.

The final category of writing presented the war as divine punishment (Asche and Schindling 2002). This was the official line promoted by secular and religious authorities and drew on the traditional view of war as a moral problem, but unwittingly developed it in a new direction. The common perception of violence as transgressive was embraced by official statements, indicating a broad coincidence of elite and popular views. The authorities claimed that the war was an intrusion from outside into ordered society, and thus a source of fear and anxiety. They also suggested that it was exceeding all rational limits and was posing a grave danger to society, but argued this was a result of society's own moral failure, not the enemy's depravity. Germans had brought the war upon themselves through their own sinfulness. The solution lay in internal reflection and moral improvement, which were officially encouraged by the declaration of regular days of fasting, prayer and repentance. However, the authorities went beyond previous practice and advocated a more complete subjection of the general population, thus presenting a political solution alongside the more traditional purely moral one. By transforming themselves into pious, thrifty and obedient subjects, people would earn divine benevolence and improve the authorities' capacity to defeat external threats and ensure public order. The emphasis on war as divine punishment relieved rulers from personal responsibility for the disaster and enabled them to distance themselves from it whilst still using it to justify demands on their subjects. This was woven into the official commemorations of the war, which began as peace celebrations around 1650, as troops were withdrawn, and continued as annual events into the mid-nineteenth century (and in some cases still persist today, for example in Augsburg) (Roeck 1998).

The scale and duration of the war accelerated the communications revolution and enabled more people to learn of developments beyond their immediate vicinity, but access to news also contributed to the widespread fear of violence. Likewise, information from across the Empire allowed people to relate personal or local experience to wider events, yet it also heightened the sense that the war had escaped all control and had become, as one contemporary broadsheet depicted, a monster devouring all before it.

After the war, it suited both sides in the debates on good government to emphasise the general perception of the conflict as an all-destructive fury. Opponents of stronger princely rule argued the war proved the futility of becoming involved in great power politics and claimed (with considerable justification) that it had left subjects too poor to pay high taxes. Princes and their advisors also stressed wartime devastation, but argued this could only be avoided in future, if subjects worked harder and paid the taxes needed for a new-style, well-ordered permanent army (in contrast to the marauding bands of the war years).

This trend to seeking a more political solution to violence was common throughout Europe. The civil wars in France and the Netherlands from the mid-sixteenth century encouraged calls to entrust greater power to the state to supervise daily life and discipline society, including Jean Bodin's idea of the state as constituting an indivisible sovereign. Thomas Hobbes advanced broadly similar views in his *Leviathan*, written in response to the chaos of the British civil wars in the mid-seventeenth century. What made the situation different in the Empire, where the Thirty Years War was effectively also a civil war, was that these calls were directed at strengthening the authorities in the individual territories, not the Empire as a whole. In particular, they were employed to distract attention from official failings during the conflict, such as the inability to preserve peace and order, and instead to legitimate post-war princely absolutism (i.e. *potestas*), an ideology of rule which projected a strong state as best guarantee against such horror (*violentia*) in the future. The outcome was paradoxical: violence was to be curbed by strengthening the state, the main institution capable of inflicting it.

References

Asch, R. G. (2000) 'Wo der soldat hinkömbt, da ist alles sein': Military violence and atrocities in the Thirty Years War', *German History* 13, 291–309.

Asche, M. and Schindling, A. (2002) (eds) *Das Strafgericht Gottes. Kriegserfahrungen und Religion im Heiligen Römischen Reich deutscher Nation im Zeitalter des Dreißigjährigen Krieges*, 2nd edn, Münster: Aschendorff.

Bailey, B. (1994) *Massacres and Account of the Crimes against Humanity*, London: Orion.

Behringer, W. (2003) *Im Zeichen des Merkur. Reichspost und Kommunikationsrevolution in der frühen Neuzeit*, Göttingen: Vandenhoeck und Ruprecht.

Bismarck, A. von (1890) Die Memoiren des Junkers Augustus von Bismarck, *Jahresberichte des Altmarkischen Vereins für Vaterländische Geschichte* 23, 90–105.

Brendle, F. and Schindling, A. (2006) (eds) *Religionskriege im Alten Reich und in Alteuropa*, Münster: Aschendorff.

Burschel, P. (1994) *Söldner im Nordwestdeutschland des 16. und 17. Jahrhunderts*, Göttingen: Vandenhoeck und Ruprecht.

Buschmann, N. and Carl, H. (2001) (eds) *Erfahrungsgeschichtlichen Perspektiven von der Französischen Revolution bis zum Zweiten Weltkrieg*, Paderborn: Ferdinand Schöningh.

Droysen, G. (1903) (ed.) *Gedruckte Relationen über die Schlacht bei Lützen 1632*, Halle: Max Niemeyer.

Eckert, E. A. (1996) *The Structure of Plagues and Pestilences in Early Modern Europe: Central Europe 1560–1640*, Basel: Karger.

Fuchs, R. P. (2002) Zeit und Ereignis im Krieg. Überlegungen zu den Aussagen Steinfurter Zeugen in einer Befragung zum Normaljahr 1624, in Sodmann, T. (ed.), *1568–1648: Zu den Auswirkungen des Achtzigjährigen Krieges auf die östlichen Niederlände und das Westmünsterland*, Vreden: Landeskundliches Institut Westmünsterland, 65–76.

Junius, M. A. (1890–91) Bamberg im Schwedenkriege, *Bericht des Historischen Vereins zu Bamberg*, 52–3, 1–250.

Kaiser, M. (1996) Inmitten des Kriegstheaters: Die Bevölkerung als militärischer Faktor und Kriegsteilnehmer im Dreißigjährigen Krieg, in Kroener, B.R. and Pröve, R. (eds) *Krieg und Frieden. Militär und Gesellschaft in der frühen Neuzeit*, Paderborn: Ferdinand Schöningh.

Kaiser, M. (1997) 'Excidium Magdeburgense.' Beobachtungen zur Wahrnehmung und Darstellung von Gewalt im Dreißigjährigen Krieg', in Meumann, M. and Niefanger, D. (eds) *Ein Schauplatz herber Angst*, Göttingen: Vandenhoeck und Ruprecht, 43–64.

Kaiser, M. (2002a) Maximilian I. von Bayern und der Krieg, *Zeitschrift für Bayerische Landesgeschichte* 65, 69–99.

Kaiser, M. (2002b) Überleben im Krieg – Leben mit dem Krieg, in Ehrenpreis, S. (ed.), *Der Dreißigjährigen Krieg im Herzogtum Berg und seinen Nachbarregionen*, Neustadt an der Aisch: Schmidt, 181–253.

Kaiser, M. (2004) die 'Magdeburgsiche' Hochzeit (1631), in Labouvie, E. (ed.) *Leben in der Stadt. Eine Kultur-und Geschlechtergeschichte Magdeburgs*, Cologne: Böhlau, 196–213.

Kaiser, M. (2008) Ärger als der Türck. Kriegsgreuel und ihre Funktionalisierung in der Zeit des Dreißigjährigen Kriegs', in Neitzel, S. and Hohrath, D. (eds) *Die Entgrenzung der Gewalt in kriegerischen Konflikten vom Mittelalter bis ins 20. Jahrhundert*, Paderborn: Ferdinand Schöningh, 155–83.

Kampmann, C. (2008) *Europa und das Reich im Dreißigjährigen Krieg*, Stuttgart: Kohlhammer.

Knauer (1997) Krieg, Gewalt und Erbauung, in Meumann, M. and Niefanger, D. (eds) *Ein Schauplatz herber Angst*, Göttingen: Vandenhoeck und Ruprecht, 83–104.

Koopmans, J. W. (ed.) (2005) *News and Politics in Early Modern Europe*, Leuven: Peeters.

Krusenstjern, B. von (1997) *Selbstzeugnisse der Zeit des Dreißigjährigen Krieges*, Berlin: Akademie.

Kürschner, W. (ed.) (1913) Aus dem Kirchenbuch von Reichensachsen (und Langenhain) von 1639–1653), *Archiv für hessische Geschichte und Altertumskunde*, new series 9, 48–55.

Lademacher, H. and Groenveld, S. (eds) (1998) *Krieg und Kultur. Die Rezeption von Krieg und Frieden in der Niederländischen Republik und im Deutschen Reich 1568–1648*, Münster: Waxmann.

Lawrence, D. R. (2009) *The Complete Soldier. Military Books and Military Culture in Early Stuart England, 1603–1645*, Leiden: Brill.

Levy, A. (1913) *Die Memoiren des Ascher Levy aus Reichshofen im Elsaß (1598–1635)*, Berlin: Lamm.

Lohmann, K. (ed.) (1913) *Die Zerstörung Magdeburgs von Otto von Guericke und andere Denkwürdigkeiten aus dem Dreißigjährigen Krieg*, Berlin: Gutenberg.

Lynn, J. A. (2008) *Women, Armies and Warfare in Early Modern Europe*, Cambridge: Cambridge University Press.

Medik, H. (2001) Historical Event and Contemporary Experience. The Capture and Destruction of Magdeburg, *History Workshop Journal* 52, 23–48.

Monro, R. (1999) *Monro, his Expedition with the Worthy Scots Regiment called Mac-Keys*, new edition, Westport CT: Praeger.

Münch, P. (ed.) (2001) *Erfahrung als Kategorie der Frühneuzeitgeschichte*, Munich: Oldenbourg.

Mortimer, G. (2002) *Eyewitness Accounts of the Thirty Years War 1618–48*, Basingstoke: Palgrave.

Neubauer, E. (ed.) (1931) *Magdeburgs Zestörung 1631*, Magdeburg: Stadt Magdeburg.

Oestreich, G. (1982) *Neostoicism and the Early Modern State,* Cambridge: Cambridge University Press.

Oggold, C. (2001) Druck des Krieges, in Weigl, A. (ed.), *Wien im Dreißigjährigen Krieg,* Cologne: Böhlau, 409–45.

Peters, J. (1993) *Ein Söldnerleben im Dreißigjährigen Krieg,* Berlin: Akademie.

Piirimäe, P. (2002) Just War in Theory and Practice. The legitimation of Sweden's Intervention in the Thirty Years War, *Historical Journal* 45, 499–523.

Pleiss, D. H. (1992) Finnische Musketiere in fränkischen Garnisonen, *Mainfränkisches Jahrbuch* 44, 1–52.

Pohl, J. (1991) *Die Profiantirung der Kayerslichen Armaden ahnbelangendt. Studien zur Versorgung der kaiserlichen Armee 1634/5,* Kiel: Horn.

Pröve, R. (1997) Violentia und Potestas. Perzeptionsprobleme von Gewalt in Söldnertagebüchern des 17. Jahrhunderts, in Meumann, M. and Niefanger, D. (eds), *Ein Schauplatz herber Angst,* Göttingen: Vandenhoeck und Ruprecht, 24–42.

Pröve, R. (1999) Gewalt und Herrschaft in der Frühen Neuzeit, *Zeitschrift für Geschichtswissenschaft* 47, 792–806.

Raymond, T. (1917) *Autobiography of Thomas Raymond and the Memoir of the Family of Guise of Elmore, Gloucestershire,* London: Camden Society.

Reisner, S. (2001) Die Kämpfe vor Wien im Oktober 1619 im Spiegel zeitgenössicher Quellen, in Weigl, A. (ed.), *Wien im Dreißigjährigen Krieg,* Cologne: Böhlau, 446–81.

Repgen, K. (1985) Kriegslegitimationen in Alteuropa, *Historische Zeitschrift* 241, 27–49.

Roeck, B. (1998) Die Feier des Friedens, in Duchhardt, H. (ed.), *Der Westfälische Friede,* Munich: Oldenbourg, 633–59.

Rullmann, J. (1877) Einwirkungen des Dreißigjährigen Krieges auf die Stadt Schlüchtern und ihre Umgebung, *Zeitschrift des Vereins für hessische Geschichte und Landeskunde* new series 6, 201–50.

Rystad, G. (1960) *Kriegsnachrichten und Propaganda während des Dreißigjährigen Krieges,* Lund: Skånska Centraltryckeriet.

Sabean, D. W. (1990) *Property, Production and Family in Neckarhausen,* Cambridge: Cambridge University Press.

Schulze, W. (ed.) (1996) *Ego-Dokumente. Annährung an den Menschen in der Geschichte,* Berlin: Akademie.

Theibault, J. (1993) The Rhetoric of Death and Destruction in the Thirty Years War, *Journal of Social History* 27, 271–90.

Theibault, J. (1997) The Demography of the Thirty Years War Revisited, *German History* 15, 1–21.

Theibault, J. (1998) Landfrauen, Soldataen und Vergewaltigungen während des Dreißigjährigen Krieges, *Werkstatt Geschichte* 19, 25–39.

Ulbrich, C., Jarzebowski, C. and Hohkamp, M. (eds) (2005) *Gewalt in der Frühen Neuzeit,* Munich: Duncker und Humblot.

Ulbricht, O. (2004) The Experience of Violence During the Thirty Years War: A Look at the Civilian Victims', in Canning, J., Lehmann, H. and Winter, J. (eds), *Power, Violence and Mass Death in Pre-Modern and Modern Times,* Aldershot: Ashgate, 97–127.

Vitzthum von Eckstädt, C. (1881) Der Feldzug der sächsischen Armee durch die Mark Brandenburg im Jahre 1635 und 1636, *Märkische Forschungen* 16, 303–86.

Weber, J. (2006) Strassburg, 1605: The Origins of the Newspaper in Europe, *German History* 24, 387–41.

Wilson, P. H. (2008) Dynasty, Constitution and Confession: The Role of Religion in the Thirty Years War, *International History Review* 30, 173 514.

Wilson, P. H. (2009) *Europe's Tragedy. A History of the Thirty Years War*, London: Allen Lane.

Wilson, P. H. (2011a) Atrocities in the Thirty Years War, in Ohlmeyer, J. and O'Siochru, M. (eds), *Plantation and Reaction: the 1641 Rebellion*, Manchester: Manchester University Press, forthcoming.

Wilson (2011b) *The Holy Roman Empire 1495–1806*, 2nd edn, Basingstoke: Palgrave.

Woodford, C. (2002), *Nuns as Historians in Early Modern Germany*, Oxford: Oxford University Press.

3 Patrick Pécherot, eugenics and the Occupation of France

Angela Kimyongür

Introduction

The late 1960s and early 1970s in France marked the beginning of a period of sustained re-examination of the 'années noires', the dark years of the German occupation of France during the Second World War. The Liberation of Paris in August 1944 from four years of foreign occupation was not the straightforward occasion for joy and celebration that might have been expected. Rather, the Liberation was a time when continuing divisions in French society which had, to a certain extent, been camouflaged during the Occupation, were exposed anew and risked plunging the country into civil war. The post-war emergence of a reassuring myth of a France unified in its resistance to the German occupation was a means of avoiding such a catastrophe, and was promoted by Charles de Gaulle, the very embodiment of 'la France résistante'. While what became known as the 'mythe résistancialiste' responded to the political exigencies of the period, it also obscured what had been a much murkier and more complex war-time reality, and it effectively delayed the wider recognition of that reality until years later. Although the immediate post-war years saw the appearance of numerous films and books about the Occupation, focusing mainly on the Resistance, it was not until the early 1970s, with the release of films such as Marcel Ophüls's *Le Chagrin et la Pitié* and Louis Malle's *Lacombe Lucien* that the radical, public re-evaluation of occupied France, and particularly of the Vichy regime began.[1] Serious academic historical research into the period began in the late 1960s, with Robert Paxton's study *Vichy France: Old Guard and New Order, 1940–1944*, published in 1972, the first substantial work on Vichy to appear.[2] Accounts of the daily realities of collaboration, the extent of *attentisme*[3] on the part of substantial parts of the French population, as well as the extent of Vichy's complicity in the deportations of Jewish citizens, continued to emerge in subsequent years. This process of remembering was not limited to professional historians. Alternative memories of the Occupation, challenging the dominant Gaullist memory of the period as one of heroic resistance, have continued to emerge in contemporary French culture, to the extent that historian Henry Rousso characterised the period from 1974 onwards as 'a phase of obsession' and one in which the 'reawakening of Jewish memory [would] serve as a touchstone' (Rousso 1991: 10, 132). That obsession with the dark years continues today in film, literature and popular culture.

More specifically, the genre of crime fiction has, in recent years, offered novelists a fertile format for the exploration of the period. A favoured narrative strategy involves the investigation of an act of criminal violence that is found to have its roots in an act of wartime violence. Thus, the need to investigate the past in order to understand the present can lead to the discovery of a hitherto unacknowledged or forgotten truth about war. Didier Daeninckx's *Meurtres pour mémoire* (1984) is perhaps the best known example of this. In this novel the investigation of the apparently random murders of a father and son, 20 years apart, leads to revelations of the complicity of the Vichy authorities, and specifically of Paris *préfet de police* Maurice Papon, in the deportations of French Jews during the Occupation. Other novels by Daeninckx have sustained this focus on the continuing repercussions of the Occupation: *La mort n'oublie personne* (1989) and *Itinéraire d'un salaud ordinaire* (2006), while in *Le Bourreau et son double* (1986) he focuses on echoes of the Algerian war in present-day France. Crime writer Thierry Jonquet uses a similar technique in *Les Orpailleurs* (1993), where the detective has to investigate past violence, the Holocaust in this case, in order to understand a present-day crime. Müller and Ruoff comment in their analysis of the French *polar*[4] on the tendency of recent crime fiction to focus in this way, on the victims of war and on unpunished perpetrators of violence (Müller and Ruoff 2002: 36).

Novelist Patrick Pécherot continues this appropriation of the detective genre, in order to cast new light on forgotten victims of wartime violence in his 2005 novel *Boulevard des Branques*,[5] albeit in a rather different way. There is no shifting between past and present, as in the novels cited above, since the novel is set entirely during the Occupation. However, there is a keen sense of the author's desire for a just recognition of the victims of war and an identification of the perpetrators. His construction of memories of the conflict operates on two distinct levels: historical and cultural. On a historical level, he offers a reconstruction of day-to-day life in Paris during the Occupation, offering a particular focus on the treatment of vulnerable minorities such as Jews, foreign nationals and the mentally ill in wartime France. On a cultural level, *Boulevard des Branques* offers a recreation of a familiar figure in French popular culture, Nestor Burma, the protagonist of a long series of crime novels written in the 1940s and 1950s by Léo Malet. *Boulevard des Branques* is the third and final novel in Pécherot's Burma series. Given its setting during the Occupation in Paris and aspects of its narrative structure, the novel invites particular comparisons with Malet's first Nestor Burma novel, *120 rue de la Gare*, also set in Paris during the Occupation and published in 1943.

What I intend to do in the course of this chapter is, first, to explore the ways in which Pécherot calls on a cultural memory of the Occupation through his adoption of Malet's fictional hero and through narrative parallels with *120 rue de la Gare*, and second, to examine the ways in which Pécherot goes beyond the kind of analysis of the Occupation which was open to Malet, writing in 1943, and uses the genre of crime fiction, coupled with his retrospective access to knowledge, to explore difficult truths about the Occupation period, and to offer a more complex historical memory of the period.

Patrick Pécherot

Pécherot is one of a number of prominent crime writers in France whose works tackle political or social themes, reflecting his own active involvement in politics. The publicity blurb on the reverse of those of Pécherot's novels, which have appeared in the Folio Policier edition, explicitly identifies him as being, together with Daeninckx and Jean Amila, a committed writer 'in the tradition of those tellers of necessary tales'.[6] Pécherot himself has a background of activity in trade unionism and his novels all have a political or ideological slant to them. His first novel *Tiuraï* (1996) is about nuclear testing in the French Pacific. *Terminus Nuit* (1999) is set during a transport strike. The two first novels of the Burma trilogy are *Les Brouillards de la Butte* (2001), which presents interwar Paris from an anarchist standpoint and *Belleville-Barcelone* (2003), which is characterised by sympathy for the Spanish Republican cause. *Soleil Noir* (2007) has as its historical backdrop the situation of Polish immigrants to France during the 1930s, while *Tranchecaille* (2008) is set during the First World War. *Les Brouillards de la Butte* won the prestigious *Grand Prix de Littérature Policière* in 2002.

Pécherot's decision to resurrect Malet's detective Nestor Burma is clearly one motivated by affection, admiration, and political sympathy, at least for Malet in the earlier part of his life. In his early years, Malet was an avant-garde figure, who associated with anarchist and surrealist groups. However, in later life, he moved to the right of the political spectrum, becoming something of a xenophobe. Pécherot prefers the younger Malet and has said so:

> Through his relentless cocky humour, he overstepped the mark. His version of popular France isn't exactly multicultural. Is Malet racist? It's been said. He has said and written as much. I've no time for that Léo. I prefer the other one. The poet of the streets and of exquisite cadavers. The real Léo.
>
> (Pécherot 2007b: n.p.)[7]

This view of Malet, 'Le vrai Léo', is one which emerges through the character of Nestor Burma, who in Pécherot's novels resembles Malet in various details of his biography. This similarity is particularly evident in the first two novels of the Burma trilogy. *Les Brouillards de la Dalle,* follows the traces of the impecunious young detective, known in this novel only as Pipette, in his anarchist and surrealist days in 1920s Paris, while *Belleville-Barcelone* is set in the Paris of the Popular Front, with the main story line focusing on the political divisions amongst supporters of the Republicans in the Spanish Civil War. Pécherot's tribute to Malet and his decision to appeal to a shared cultural memory of the original Burma novels can be seen in various structural and narrative parallels. In both series, Nestor Burma is the pipe-smoking private detective, following a path through a complex series of events, inevitably falling unconscious at crucial moments in the narrative, either through a blow to the head or another attack on his person as he comes too close to the perpetrator of the crime. In *Belleville-Barcelone* and *Boulevard des Branques* he is ably assisted by Yvette, who, like Burma's secretary Hélène Châtelain in the original novels, is a feisty individual, demonstrating insights not always shared or appreciated by her boss. Burma's opposite number in the police force, Inspector Faroux in Malet's novels, has become Inspector Bailly, equally exasperated by, but ultimately sympathetic, towards the wayward Burma and his unconventional methods. Paris, its streets and *quartiers,* particularly celebrated in Malet's series of novels *Les Nouveaux mystères de Paris* is also a constant reference point in Pécherot's novels.

Pécherot's rewriting of *120 rue de la Gare*

There are numerous narrative similarities, which point to a specific Malet novel, *120 rue de la Gare,* as being an obvious intertextual reference point to the informed reader of *Boulevard des Branques.* Most obviously, both are set in German-occupied Paris. Consequently, there are plentiful references in each novel to the shortages of food, fuel and other basic necessities, which made the appellation 'dark years' as apt on the referential as on the more abstract level. Paris is dark and cold, and Parisians are perennially hungry. In both novels, a mysterious stranger acts as the catalyst to the drama, passing on an apparently impenetrable message, which the detective must decode. In *120 rue de la Gare,* the mysterious stranger is known as La Globule, prisoner 60202, and is an amnesiac whom Burma meets while both are prisoners of war in a German prisoner of war camp. Just before he dies, La Globule passes on to Nestor the cryptic message: 'Tell Hélène, Station Road' (Malet 2006a: 311).[8] A similar narrative strategy is used in *Boulevard des Branques.* Cut off in Chartres by the exodus from Paris, Yvette, Burma's secretary, witnesses the arrival of a train carrying inmates from a mental asylum. One of them approaches her, but appears unable to speak. A piece of paper falls from his pocket. The paper contains a message which, by an extraordinary coincidence, is addressed to Burma. It comes from an old friend of his, Luka, asking for his help: 'My old friend Nes, if this message reaches you, get me out of here, I beg you' (Pécherot 2005: 41).[9] Both of these mysterious strangers suffer from conditions which can be seen as traumatic responses to wartime experiences: one has lost his memory, unable to remember anything before his capture, while the other has lost the power of speech. Both narratives are driven in part by a search for lost treasure of a kind: in *120 rue de la Gare*, pearls belonging to jewel thief Jo Tour Eiffel and, in *Boulevard des Branques*, part of a haul of gold lost during the Spanish Civil War, on its way from Spanish republicans to the Soviet Union in payment for weapons. Both novels are complex, full of twists and turns and any number of red herrings.

While there are obvious narrative similarities between the novels, they are very different in their presentation of the Occupation. Naturally enough, *120 rue de la Gare*, which was written and published during the Occupation, lacks any explicit criticism either of the German occupation itself or of the Vichy government's political collaboration with the occupiers though, as Gorrara has commented, Malet's novel does highlight the disruption to ordinary life caused by the German occupation and offers an indirect opposition to the invasion, articulated through a range of French linguistic and literary references in the novel (Gorrara 2003: 30). It would, of course, have been impractical for Malet to have indulged in explicit criticism, since German censorship would have prevented publication of his book. In any case, his perspective on the Occupation at the time of writing was limited since the novel was published well before the end of the war. In *Boulevard des Branques*, however, Pécherot is able to engage in a more critical evaluation of the Occupation, both because he is at liberty to speak openly where Malet was not but, more importantly, because he has access to information about and interpretations of the reality of the period which were not available to Malet in 1943. Not least, Pécherot has been a witness to the ongoing reassessments of the Occupation period and of Vichy through historiography, the trials of various Vichy officials and through film and literature. Consequently, despite its surface similarities with *120 rue de la Gare*, *Boulevard des Branques* has more in common with a novel like Daeninckx's *Meurtres pour mémoire* in its ideologically driven unearthing of painful truths and hidden memories of the war.

We have already seen that there is much in common between Malet's *120 rue de la Gare* and Pécherot's *Boulevard des Branques*, in terms of an evocation of the Occupation as a dark, cold and hungry time for Parisians. However, even on the level of everyday detail Pécherot is able, by virtue of his retrospective knowledge of the period, to emphasise details which the contemporary reader will know have taken on added resonance, or which Malet did not see fit to mention. References to the treatment of ethnic minorities and of the Jews in particular are a case in point. Such references demonstrate an implicit sympathy for these groups on the part of Pécherot's Burma as narrator. In the early pages of the novel, Burma witnesses the breaking of the windows of shops believed to belong to Jews. A very visual juxtaposition is made between a shop owner clearing up the debris on the Champs Elysées and the Swastika floating on the Arc de Triomphe in the background. There is no need for authorial comment on cause and effect: 'A big guy in shirtsleeves was sweeping the pavement in front of a shop. Looking haggard, he stopped to look at the Arc de Triomphe where the swastika was flying' (Pécherot 2005: 69).[10] A passing reference to a cinema showing the anti-Semitic propaganda film *Le Juif Süss*, first screened in Paris in Feburary 1941, is accompanied by a quotation from a review of the film in *Au Pilori*. Its aggressively racist language needs no commentary from the narrator: 'Jews are not humans, they are stinking beasts. We get rid of lice, we fight epidemics. We defend ourselves against Jews just like we defend ourselves against evil. Death to all that is false, negroid, mongrel, Jewish' (Pécherot 2005: 260).[11] Pécherot has taken the opportunity to change the name of the detective agency for which Burma works. In Malet's novels it was called *Fiat Lux*, an optimistic commentary on the agency's ability to cast light on difficult cases. In Pécherot's novels it has become *Agence Bohman, enquêtes, recherches et surveillance*. The change of name enables Pécherot to foreground the vulnerability both of the Jewish owner of the agency, Bohman and, by extension, of the agency itself. We learn at the very beginning of the novel that Bohman, whose cousin Samuel was a victim of Kristallnacht[12] in Berlin, has realised the coming dangers and has left the capital: 'Octave Bohman had preferred the green of the countryside to German uniforms in the capital. Behind the tanks crossing the Rhine, he could feel the great nightmare approaching. "It's all in *Mein Kampf*, Nestor, all of it. Hitler will do exactly what he wrote"' (Pécherot 2005: 15).[13] The final scene of the novel shows Burma returning to the office to see a freshly posted sign on the wall outside, identifying the agency as a 'Jewish business' (Pécherot 2005: 293).[14] The agency has also undergone a change of location. In Malet's novels the agency is in the second arrondissement of Paris, known as a centre for clothing and tailoring, while Pécherot has moved it to Belleville, a working-class area inhabited by various immigrant groups.

Furthermore, the presence in the novel of characters of different nationalities and political persuasions gives Pécherot the opportunity to shift the emphasis and demonstrate that minority groups, other than the Jewish residents of France, are also being singled out for discriminatory treatment under Vichy. Republicans who sought refuge in France after the Spanish Civil War are no longer welcome. We discover that Max Fehcker, the mute who passed on Luka's message to Yvette, fled Hitler's Germany, fought in the Spanish Civil War, and after Franco's victory fled to France where he discovered in 1939 that immigrants were no longer welcome: 'the laws of hospitality had changed' (Pécherot 2005: 158–9).[15] He is interned in a series of different camps, before gradually losing his grip on sanity. Burma's German friend Luka, the author of the message passed on by Max Fehcker, had been resident in France for 15 years. Seeing the changing circumstances, he feigned insanity, preferring the prospect of internment as a patient in an asylum to feared deportation to a camp: 'When war broke out, they started hunting down foreign nationals. With my German passport, I was headed for the camp. Have you seen how Pétain and Laval offloaded my countrymen onto the Nazis?' (Pécherot 2005: 245)[16] This, as we shall see, is a heavily ironic choice. Burma's friendship with Armenian café owner, Gopian, whose establishment was the object of aggression by right-wing groups in *Belleville-Barcelone*, also demonstrates that Pécherot's Burma is a man comfortable in his relationships with other ethnic groups. Burma makes ironic reference to the police surveillance of communists, another vulnerable minority group in the wake of the proscription of the French Communist Party in September 1939, asking inspector Bailly if he hasn't got enough work on his hands with this: 'Haven't you enough to do keeping an eye on the commies?' (Pécherot 2005: 25).[17] A later reference to La Santé prison points out that it is full, not just of common criminals, but of political prisoners, including communists (Pécherot 2005: 146). There are fleeting references to a spirit of resistance to the Occupation, though in the case of Burma, this is fairly superficial and, in 1940–41, somewhat premature. His response to a written instruction posted by the occupying authorities only to walk on the right-hand pavement is to walk in the gutter, (Pécherot 2005: 121), and he offers a disparaging comment about the singer of a version of *Maréchal nous voilà*[18] heard on the radio (Pécherot 2005: 133). However, his secretary Yvette is clearly taking opposition to the Germans a little more seriously since, having early in the novel picked up a leaflet with instructions about passive resistance, she narrowly escapes being caught by a German patrol with a number of such leaflets in her handbag towards the end of the novel.

While details such as these fill in a number of gaps left by Malet in his evocation of the everyday reality of the Occupation, the main narrative focus in *Boulevard des Branques* is on the apparent suicide of eminent psychiatrist, Antoine Griffart. A suicide note plausibly enough attributes his decision to end his days to despair at the disastrous military defeat of France in June 1940. His death is something of a professional embarrassment to Burma, who had been charged with watching over Griffart by relatives concerned that he was suffering from depression. However, it soon becomes clear that Griffart could not have committed suicide, and the enquiry into his murder leads Burma into an investigation first of the world of French psychiatry during the war, and from there to the links between the fate of mental patients in French psychiatric hospitals during the war, the eugenics debate and the Nazi extermination programme. Burma's enquiry into this area is framed not just by Griffart's death, but also by his search for information about the mysterious mute, Max Fehcker, who passed on Luka's message to Burma and who, it transpires, was being treated by Griffart for partial aphasia. Burma's investigation provides the context for a graphic evocation of the terrible conditions in the mental asylum at Clermont-de-l'Oise. In the original Malet novels, Burma is always in the thick of the action, usually receiving at least one blow to the head, and *Boulevard des Branques* does not deviate from this pattern. After going to the Clermont asylum to challenge Griffart's colleague Delettram, whom Burma suspects of involvement in the former's death, Burma is hit on the head and wakes up an inmate himself, confined in a strait jacket. He experiences at first hand the conditions suffered by inmates of asylums during the Occupation: food deprivation, cold, institutional control of patients by use of ECT and drugs:

> They were filthy, stupefied by sedatives and the crazier ones by electric shock treatment. Their eyes were feverish, and they were skinny too. (…) Food was already rationed out for everyone on the outside. So when it came to subhumans … well, you can imagine.
>
> (Pécherot 2005: 240)[19]

Whilst in the asylum, Burma meets his old friend Luka, the one who had passed on the message to Fehcker, pleading for help to get out of Clermont. Fearing deportation to an internment camp as a foreign national in wartime France, Luka had believed that he would be better off simulating madness in order to be admitted to hospital, but has found that there is actually little difference between asylum and camp and, having played his role as madman too well, is now unable to persuade anyone of his sanity (Pécherot 2005: 244). When Nestor finds him, he is painfully thin, his teeth missing because of the ECT which caused him to clamp his jaws together, and paranoid at the thought of the mysterious waves which can read his mind. While Burma eventually escapes, he is unable to save his friend who dies in the asylum just before Burma can arrange for his transfer back to Paris.

Pécherot's critique of eugenics

While the detective's unexpected stay in the asylum furnishes the pretext for an evocation of the terrible conditions in such institutions during the Occupation, an earlier episode, during which Burma finds in a copy of Breton's *L'Amour fou* a cutting from *La Révolution Surréaliste*, provides a broader intellectual context for Pécherot's critique of asylums and paves the way for its more sinister aspect. The cutting is of an open letter to the medical directors of psychiatric hospitals, which are seen as no better than prisons operating under the guise of science: 'We are opposed to giving men, whether they be narrow-minded or not, the right to sanction their research into the mind by never-ending imprisonment. Asylums are nothing more than horrifying jails' (Pécherot 2005: 143).[20] The professional face of psychiatric institutions is largely represented in the novel by the dead Griffart's colleague Delettram, who is an admirer of the ideas of Alexis Carrel. Carrel was a physician who won the Nobel Prize for Medicine in 1912, but was better known in 1940 for the ideas outlined in his book *L'Homme, cet inconnu* which had been a hugely popular success when published in 1935. In it, he outlined a eugenics agenda, calling for society to 'organise itself with reference to the normal individual', by which he meant that the costs of maintaining the criminally insane, and those of no use to society in prisons and asylums, should not burden 'normal' individuals (Reggiani 2007: 70).

We first learn of Delettram's admiration for Carrel's ideas in a lecture Burma attends at La Salpêtrière hospital.[21] Burma's initial lack of understanding of the implications of what Delettram is saying, including references to the ideas of Carrel, and of Rüdin[22] in Germany, and their currency in a period of national decline, demonstrates the ease with which such ideas could and did propagate in France. It takes the intervention of a Dr Ferdière, whom Burma sees leaving the lecture in disgust, to elucidate for him the notion of racial hygiene and the use to which it is already being put in Germany:

> Racial hygiene advocates eugenics, racial regeneration through the application of biological measures, sterilisation and the systematic internment of the mentally ill and alcoholics. It recommends euthanasia in cases of incurable sickness and insanity, and even its more widespread use for those whose lives are deemed to be worthless…
>
> (Pécherot 2005: 166–67)[23]

Pécherot quotes at length from *L'homme, cet inconnu* in the novel to drive home the point further:

> The feeble-minded and the man of genius must not be equal before the law. Eugenics can have a great influence on the destiny of the civilised races. It will become possible to prevent the propagation of the insane and the feeble-minded.
>
> (Pécherot 2005: 216)[24]

Delettram, like Carrel in real life, is anxious not to promote openly the kind of negative eugenics, involving measures such as sterilisation and euthanasia, already being practised in Germany, but is nonetheless keen to promote a eugenics agenda as a response to the military defeat of 1940, as a new beginning for France. This agenda is to be pursued through a research institute which, we learn, is nearing completion thanks to his good relations with the German occupiers (Pécherot 2005: 168).[25] His colleague Griffart, however, was one of those who, shocked at developments in Nazi Germany, was beginning to distance himself from the eugenics agenda. He had been treating Fehcker, whose mental breakdown had been triggered on learning that his mentally handicapped sister had been killed in Germany. Burma suspects that, having heard that Griffart was about to publish a paper condemning the proponents of 'racial hygiene', Delettram killed his colleague in order to protect his own research (Pécherot 2005: 224).

In fact, Griffart's murderer is revealed to be not, as Burma had suspected, Delettram but Caducée, a hitherto minor character in the plot. Convinced by the stories of lost Republican gold from the Spanish civil war, Caducée believed that the mute Max Fehcker knew of the gold's location. Knowing that Fehcker was being treated in Clermont by Griffart, Caducée believed that Fehcker's consultations with the psychiatrist, trying to unlock his silence, might hold the key to the location. One of the few words Fehcker utters is Tigartentras, a name which crops up repeatedly in the narrative as the supposed location, somewhere in Spain, of the lost gold. Caducée administers phenobarbitol to get Griffart to reveal the secret, but only succeeds in killing him. It transpires, however, that the story of the gold is a red herring. The gold never existed, though the name of its supposed location does have a significance, only revealed towards the end of the novel, which ties in with the main storyline of the mental hospitals and the links to eugenics. Fehcker's repetition of the name was misinterpreted. The name he kept saying was not Tigartentras, a name that all who heard it assumed to be Spanish, because of his having fought for the Spanish republicans, but Tiergartenstraße, the name of the street in Berlin which gave its name to the T4 programme which, planned at number 4, led to the extermination of 300,000 mentally ill or handicapped individuals in Germany. Fehcker became fixated on the name when he learnt that his mentally handicapped sister had been killed by the Nazis.

The novel ends with a very brief epilogue in which the first-person narrative of Nestor Burma gives way to an authorial third-person summary, drawing the threads of the narrative together and underlining the author's stance, albeit in very factual terms. Of these facts, three stand out in the light of recent controversies: the promotion of Alexis Carrel to the directorship of the *Fondation française pour l'étude des problèmes humains,* the fact that many streets in France are still named after him and the assertion that 40,000 patients died in French psychiatric hospitals during the Occupation (Pécherot 2005: 295).

To what extent is Pécherot trying to suggest that French mental hospitals under Vichy were complicit in an attempt to exterminate patients whose lives were deemed to be worthless? What are his observations on the role of Carrel in these deaths? These questions have pertinence beyond the novel, since Carrel's ideas, and the deaths of this unexpectedly large number of patients in French mental hospitals during the Occupation, have both been the subject of recent debate in France.

Whilst outside France, Carrel is largely known for the work which gained him the Nobel Prize for Medicine in 1912, memories of his association with a fascist eugenics agenda during the Vichy regime have ensured that in France, 'His name elicits, above all, French society's relationship with its traumatic past' (Reggiani 2007: 1). More specifically, one might say that it is yet another reminder of France's obsessive relationship with its Vichy past. In the 1990s, the appropriation by the *Front National* of Carrel's ideas on 'moral decay' led to a campaign, which gained particular momentum during the trial of Paul Touvier in 1994, for the removal of Carrel's name from the Faculty of Medicine at the University of Lyons and from streets throughout the country. It was not, however, until March 2003, that rue Alexis Carrel in the 15th arrondissement of Paris was renamed rue Jean-Pierre Bloch, after a well-known Resistance fighter (Reggiani 2007: 3–4). Carrel's ideas, and the role that he played in the Vichy regime through his research foundation, were also brought to the fore by allegations made in a 1987 doctoral thesis, entitled *L'Extermination douce*, by a psychiatrist, Max Lafont, about alleged Vichy complicity in the unusually large numbers of patients who died in French psychiatric hospitals between 1940 and 1944.[26] As the title of the thesis suggests, the author establishes a parallel between what happened to these patients in France and the fate of mentally ill patients under the extermination programme in Nazi Germany, claiming that the deaths were the result of a deliberate Vichy policy (Roudinesco 2007). The momentum of these allegations was sustained by the appearance the following year of Pierre Durand's *Le Train des fous* which provided a fictional exploration of the story. The novel's re-publication in 2001, complete with an emotive cover photograph of a group of patients looking like concentration camp survivors, coincided with a petition that appeared in *L'Humanité* in 2001. Provocatively entitled 'How Vichy killed more than 40,000 "lunatics" ',[27] it also suggested that the fate of the 40,000 dead was more or less intentional on the part of Vichy. It made an explicit comparison of these deaths with the extermination of mentally ill patients in Germany and asked for the French state's recognition of Vichy's complicity in the deaths (*L'Humanité* 1 March 2001). Henry Rousso's 1989 review of both Lafont's and Durand's works was a fairly scathing criticism of a lack of solid historical evidence; their conclusions put into doubt by the failure to establish a clear link between historically verifiable facts and Vichy's role in them (Rousso 1989: 156). Regianni also criticises Lafont's failure to 'attempt to distinguish between the material constraints imposed by the occupation and Vichy's own policies' (Regianni 2007: 5).

A subsequent study, Von Bueltzingsloewen's *L'Hécatombe des fous*, which appeared in 2007, attempted to provide a more scholarly assessment of the historical facts and came to the conclusion that while there were indeed some 40,000–45,000 more deaths than would normally have been expected between 1940 and 1944, these deaths were not the result of a deliberate programme of extermination authorised by Vichy, but rather the result of the shortages of food experienced throughout France, and exacerbated by neglect within the asylums. *Boulevard des Branques* was published in 2005 when Pécherot would not have had access to the research presented in von Bueltzingsloewen's book. However, it seems clear that he was not, in any case, one of those accusing the Vichy authorities of a deliberate policy of extermination. His fictional account of conditions in the mental hospital at Clermont-de-l'Oise emphasises the cold and the lack of food, worse than those experienced by the rest of the population, as well as the abuse of drugs and ECT treatment to keep patients under control, but there is no hint that a deliberate policy of elimination was in place. Pécherot's epilogue makes a clear distinction between the '40,000 patients who died in French psychiatric hospitals' and the '300,000 mentally ill and handicapped who were exterminated' in Nazi Germany (Pécherot 2005: 295–6).[28] Pécherot's own comments on Carrel are similarly subdued, though his observation that streets are still named after him (Pécherot 2005: 295), suggests a regret that this is still the case.

Conclusion

While Pécherot does not use the novel to make the kind of allegations of a form of genocide under Vichy that have appeared elsewhere, his depiction of the plight of those who perished in psychiatric institutions at the time is further evidence of the sympathy we have already seen for the various minorities who found life particularly difficult under the Occupation: Jews, foreign nationals of various kinds and anti-fascists. It therefore associates him with the continued desire to set the record straight as regards the realities of life under Vichy.

This sympathy and this desire are what mark Pécherot out most clearly from Malet who, in *120 rue de la Gare*, offers no comment on the Jews, even though by 1943, the enforced wearing of the yellow star by the Jewish population (imposed in the Occupied zone in June 1942), and round ups of both French and foreign Jews (which began as early as May 1941), were in evidence. Indeed, a somewhat anti-Semitic view of Jewish complicity in the deportations has been identified in novels written by Malet in the 1950s.[29] By emphasising the treatment of a number of persecuted or mistreated minorities, Pécherot would seem to be distancing himself from the 'Malet raciste' whose existence he has acknowledged (Pécherot 2007b). Other differences between Malet's and Pécherot's representations of the Occupation are more straightforwardly attributable to the different time periods in which the two novels were written, with Pécherot being in possession of information which Malet could not reasonably be expected to be aware of. As Gorrara has pointed out, the ending of *120 rue de la Gare* is an optimistic one in which the detective's successful solving of the crime underlines 'a belief that French values and ideals would once again reign supreme' (Gorrara 2003: 34). By the beginning of the twenty-first century, such an optimistic view of the war years could no longer be tenable after the series of revelations about the realities of Vichy which emerged from the 1970s onwards. Consequently, the ending of Pécherot's novel is much more subdued. While Griffart's murderer has been identified, he has been killed, thereby escaping justice. The affair has been officially declared closed, thus preventing any further investigation into the involvement of either Delettram, who is left free to pursue his research or Maillebeau, a former policeman, who figures in the narrative at various points. Maillebeau has turned crook, and has friends in high places to protect him. Burma is left with a sense of powerlessness against forces beyond his control: 'No one had deserved all this mess. It had come like those particles of sand swept along by the wind. It had settled there, that's all. What could we do about it?' (Pécherot 2005: 291)[30] This sense of an all-encompassing evil, of a society permeated by criminality, a criminality tolerated, and even protected by the occupying authorities, is associated in the epilogue with collaboration, as the author links Maillebeau and his fellow criminals with the Bonny and Lafont gang of the French Gestapo (Pécherot 2005: 295). Compared to this, Malet's account of the Occupation is a rather more innocent one. The crime in *120 rue de la Gare* takes place against the backdrop of war, but is quite separate from it, whereas in Pécherot's novel crime is inseparable from the realities of the Occupation, not just in the activities of criminal individuals, but on an institutional level in the criminal neglect of vulnerable victims. As *noir* fiction goes, Pécherot's is a much blacker reconstruction of the Occupation and of war-time violence than that of Malet.

Notes

1 Marcel Ophüls's documentary *Le Chagrin et la pitié* was made for television broadcast in 1969, but was judged to be so controversial that it received only a limited cinema release in 1971 and was not broadcast on television until 1981. Louis Malle's feature film *Lacombe Lucien* was released in 1974.
2 Julian Jackson provides a useful outline both of the historiography of Vichy and of the emergence of memories of the Occupation (Jackson 2001: 1–20, 601–32).
3 The term 'attentisme' is used to describe the response of the overwhelming majority of the population who were not involved in resistance activities, but who did not actively collaborate either.
4 'Polar' is a frequently used generic term for crime fiction in France.
5 Boulevard des Branques is the slang name used in the novel for the Boulevard de l'Hôpital in Paris, address of the psychiatric hospital of La Salpêtrière. The slang address translates as Loony Boulevard. The original French title of the novel will be used throughout.
6 'dans la lignée de ces raconteurs d'histoires nécessaires'. Jean Amila is the pseudonym of Jean Meckert. He was one of the first French writers to be published in Gallimard's crime collection, the *Série noire*.

7 'A force de gouailler sans garde-fou, il a franchi la ligne. Sa France popu, n'est pas black-blanc-beur. Malet raciste? On l'a dit. Lui aussi, et écrit. (…) Ce Léo là, je le laisse. Et je prends l'autre. Le poète du trottoir et des cadavres exquis (…). Le vrai Léo.' All translations are the author's own.

8 'Dites à Hélène, 120 rue de la Gare'.

9 'Mon vieux Nes, si ce mot te parvient, je t'en supplie, sors-moi de là'.

10 'Devant une boutique, un gros type en chemise balayait le trottoir. La mine défaite, il s'est arrêté pour contempler l'arc de triomphe où flottait l'oriflamme à croix gammée'.

11 'Le Juif n'est pas un homme, c'est une bête puante. On se débarrasse des poux, on combat les épidémies. On se défend contre le mal, donc contre les Juifs. Mort à tout ce qui est faux, négroïde, métissé, juif'. *Au Pilori* was an anti-Semitic newspaper published during the Occupation.

12 Kristallnacht is the name given to the night of 9 November 1938 when the German government sanctioned reprisals against Jews for the killing of a German diplomat, by a Jewish student, in Paris. The reprisals involved the ransacking and destruction of Jewish homes and synagogues, and the breaking of thousands of Jewish shop windows. Some 90 Jews were killed.

13 'Octave Bohman avait préféré le vert de la campagne au vert-de-gris. Derrière les chars qui franchissaient le Rhin il sentait se pointer le grand cauchemar: – Tout est dans Mein Kampf, Nestor, tout. Hitler fera ce qu'il a écrit'.

14 'entreprise juive/jüdisches geschäft'. The singling out of Bohman's agency would have been to enable implementation of an ordinance passed by the Germans on 18 October 1940, 'requiring all Jewish enterprises in the Occupied Zone to be placed under trusteeship as a preliminary to "Aryanization"' (Jackson 2001: 356).

15 'les lois de l'hospitalité avaient changé'.

16 'Quand la guerre a éclaté, ils se sont mis à faire la chasse aux ressortissants étrangers. Avec mon passeport allemand, j'étais bon pour le camp. (…) T'as vu comment Pétain et Laval les ont refourgués aux nazis, mes compatriotes?' Luka's fears were well founded. According to Jackson, 'At the end of 1940 the internment camp population stood at about 55,000–60,000, consisting largely of foreign Jewish refugees, former members of the International Brigades, and French Communists' (Jackson 2001: 151).

17 'Vous n'avez pas assez de boulot avec les cocos à surveiller?'

18 'Maréchal nous voilà' was a popular anthem in support of Pétain.

19 'Crades, abrutis de calmants et d'électrochocs pour les plus mal barrés. Les yeux fiévreux. Et maigres, avec ça. (…) A l'extérieur, la bouffe était déjà comptée pour tout un chacun. Alors, les sous-hommes … fallait pas rêver'.

20 'Nous nous élevons contre le droit attribué à des hommes, bornés ou non, de sanctionner par l'incarcération perpétuelle leurs investigations dans le domaine de l'esprit. Les asiles sont d'effroyables geôles'. The open letter 'Lettre aux médecins-chefs des asiles de fous' was in a number of *La Révolution surréaliste* edited by Antonin Artaud, himself interned in various asylums between 1937 and 1943.

21 Although a generalist hospital now, La Salpêtrière became famous as a psychiatric hospital under neurologist Jean-Martin Charcot in the nineteenth century.

22 Ernst Rüdin was a Swiss psychiatrist who directed research into eugenics in Munich during the war.

23 '[L'hygiène raciale] prône l'eugénisme, la régénération de la race à travers l'application de mesures biologiques. La stérilisation et l'internement systématiques des malades mentaux et des alcooliques. Elle préconise l'euthanasie en cas de maladie incurable, d'aliénation, voire sa généralisation à ceux dont la vie est jugée sans valeur…' Dr Gaston Ferdière was the psychiatrist who treated

Artaud in Rodez, and Pécherot has pointed out that his presence in the novel is intended as a homage to the real life Ferdière: 'un militant des droits de l'homme et un antimilitariste convaincu' ('A human rights militant and a convinced anti-militarist.') (Pécherot 2007b).

24 'Le faible d'esprit et l'homme de génie ne doivent pas être égaux devant la loi (…). L'eugénisme peut exercer une grande influence sur la destinée des races civilisées. (…) il deviendra possible d'empêcher la propagation des fous et des faibles d'esprit'.

25 Delettram's research institution is a thinly veiled reference to the institute created by Carrel in Vichy France, called the *Fondation française pour l'étude des problèmes humains*.

26 The figure of 40,000 is not the total number of those patients who actually died during the war. This is estimated to be some 76,000. The 40,000 represents the number of deaths over and above that which would normally have been expected (Riglet 2007).

27 'Comment Vichy a tué plus de 40 000 "fous"'.

28 'quarante mille (…) malades qui trouvèrent la mort dans les hôpitaux psychiatriques français', 'trois cent mille malades mentaux et handicapés [qui] furent exterminés'.

29 David Fraser has argued that in *Des Kilomètres de linceuls* (1955) and *Du rebecca, rue des Rosiers* (1957) Malet depicts Jews fulfilling certain stereotypes and as complicitous in the fate of their fellow Jews under the Occupation (Fraser 2005).

30 'Toute cette saleté, personne l'avait méritée. Elle était venue comme ces poussières de sable que le vent charrie. Elle s'était déposée là, voilà tout. On y pouvait quoi, nous autres?'

References

Carrel, A. (1935) *L'Homme, cet inconnu*, Paris: Plon.

Daeninckx, D. (1984) *Meurtres pour mémoire*, Paris: Gallimard.

Daeninckx, D. (1989) *La mort n'oublie personne*, Paris: Denoël.

Daeninckx, D. (2006) *Itinéraire d'un salaud ordinaire*, Paris: Gallimard.

Durand, P. (1988) *Le Train des fous, 1939–1945. Le génocide des malades mentaux en France*, Paris: Messidor.

Fraser, D. (2005) Polarcauste: Law, Justice and the Shoah in French Detective Fiction, *International Journal of Law in Context*, 1.3: 237–60.

Gorrara, C. (2003) *The Roman Noir in Post-War French Culture. Dark Fictions*, Oxford: Oxford University Press.

L'Humanité (2001) *Comment Vichy a tué plus de 40,000 'fous'*, www.humanite. fr/2001–03–01 (accessed 3 July 2007).

Jackson, J. (2001) *France. The Dark Years 1940–1944*, Oxford: Oxford University Press.

Jonquet, T. (1993) *Les Orpailleurs*, Paris: Gallimard.

Lafont, M. (1987) *L'Extermination douce. La mort de 40,000 malades mentaux dans les hôpitaux psychiatriques en France sous le Régime de Vichy*, Ligné: Editions de l'AREFPPI.

Malet, L. (2006a) *Nestor Burma. Premières Enquêtes*, Paris: Robert Laffont.

Malet, L. (2006b) *Nestor Burma. Les Nouveaux Mystères de Paris*, vols I and II, Paris: Robert Laffont.

Müller, E. and Ruoff, A. (2002) *Le Polar français. Crime et histoire*, trans. J.-F. Poirier, Paris: Editions La Fabrique.

Pécherot, P. (1996) *Tiuraï*, Paris: Gallimard.

Pécherot, P. (1999) *Terminus nuit*, Paris: Gallimard.

Pécherot, P. (2001) *Les Brouillards de la Butte*, Paris: Gallimard.

Pécherot, P. (2003) *Belleville-Barcelone*, Paris: Gallimard.

Pécherot, P. (2005) *Boulevard des Branques*, Paris: Gallimard.

Pécherot, P. (2007a) *Soleil noir*, Paris: Gallimard.

Pécherot, P. (2007b) www.pecherot.com/rubrique.php3?id_rubrique=11 (accessed 18 April 2007)

Pécherot, P. (2008) *Tranchecaille*, Paris: Gallimard.

Reggiani, A. H. (2007) *God's Eugenicist. Alexis Carrel and the Sociobiology of Decline*, Oxford: Berghahn.

Riglet, M. (2007) *L'Hécatombe des fous. La famine dans les hôpitaux psychiatriques français sous l'Occupation*, www.tv5org/TV5Site/litterature/ (accessed 3 July 2007).

Roudinesco, E. (2007) Dans les asiles des affamés de Vichy, *Le Monde des livres*, 23 février 2007. http://editionsbdl.com/extermination.html (accessed 3 July 2007).

Rousso, H. (1989) Review of Max Lafont's *L'Extermination Douce* and Pierre Durand, *Le Train des fous*, *Vingtième Siècle, Revue d'histoire*, 21.1: 156–7.

Rousso, H. (1991) *The Vichy Syndrome: History and Memory in France since 1944*; trans. Arthur Goldhammer, Cambridge, Mass.: Harvard University Press.

von Bueltzingsloewen, I. (2007) *L'Hécatombe des fous. La famine dans les hôpitaux psychiatriques français sous l'Occupation*, Paris: Aubier.

4 United States Army chaplains and magazines

Censorship in World War II

Jenel Virden

Introduction

United States Army chaplains of World War II grappled with numerous problems associated with their work as religious counsellors to American GIs. Among other things their duties often included trying to control influences on the GIs that could potentially lead to moral confusion or degeneracy. However, not all chaplains agreed on what constituted immoral behaviour or immoral influences during time of war. While they might agree on big issues such as the immorality of prostitution or extramarital relations, when it came to other instances the road forward was less clear. For instance, some chaplains complained of behaviour or influences that might be seen as minor concerns by other chaplains. These could include lewd or sexually suggestive United Service Organization (USO) shows or drinking and gambling. While some turned a blind eye, other chaplains waged their own war against such practices. One area that exercised some concern on the part of numerous chaplains falls under the category of indecent literature. From lone chaplains at bases across the American continent and the rest of world to the office of the Chief of Chaplains there was a decided move toward trying to censor what literature GIs were exposed to.

The Chief of Chaplains office in Washington, DC oversaw the work of US Army chaplains throughout the war period. The files of the Chief of Chaplains include reports and correspondence related to what was termed 'indecent literature'. Literature, in the sense used in the Chief of Chaplains files, was very broadly defined and included books, newspapers and magazines, but also cartoons and pin-ups. All of these genres inspired some chaplains to write to the Chief of Chaplains with complaints. These complaints ranged from concerns about pin-ups in barracks and mess halls, to the depiction of the female form in GI newspapers like *Stars and Stripes*, novels that appeared on reading lists or in camps, as well as distasteful cartoons with indecent or immoral themes. The complaints were raised in the Chaplains Corps by chaplains in the pre-war Civilian Conservation Corps (CCC) camps in the late 1930s and chaplains serving at military establishments around the world throughout World War II.

As early as 1938, chaplains were reporting a 'crusade against indecent literature'. Chaplain David Sullivan of Boston reported the launching of a campaign calling chaplains to action by suggesting that chaplains visiting CCC camps should act to arouse 'the boys against ... indecent literature, [hold] a public bonfire of all indecent magazines, [put out a] series of news releases for the camp paper and [gather] volunteer pledge cards' signed by the men against indecent literature. Sullivan asked, in his correspondence with the Chief of Chaplains, if this should be a national campaign (Sullivan 1938).

The question of indecent literature was taken very seriously by the Chief of Chaplains himself, Brigadier General Chaplain William Arnold. As early as 1938 he was including statements about indecent literature in his circular letters. He urged 'all chaplains to survey carefully the literature circulated in their posts, camps and stations; and further, to organise, wherever possible, groups, clubs and societies to combat indecent literature.' He noted that 'indecent literature and profanity are first cousins' (Arnold 1938).

Forms of indecent publications

As noted, the archival files labelled with reference to indecent literature encompassed a broad range of topics that expand the usual understanding of what is termed literature. For example, Arnold's files included complaints sent to him on topics as far removed from literature as nose art on airplanes, which showed semi-naked images of women. One concerned civilian woman, Miss Martin, wrote to Chief of Chaplains Arnold in 1944 noting that in a recent newsreel she had seen images of 'unclothed women' on airplanes that had been labelled morale boosters, to her distaste. She noted that America was fighting for freedom not for license and hoped the chaplains would do much to counteract these 'pagan standards'. Arnold responded to Miss Martin by noting that he had raised the issue with a representative of the air corps and suggested that this imagery was produced by a minority of the men, but that the civilian press liked a good story and 'pick out the unusual and sensational cases for publication'. He reassured her most of 'the boys' were decent (Martin 1944; Arnold 4 August 1944).

Chaplains also fought in the campaign against what they considered to be indecent images by, for instance, taking down pictures they found objectionable in officers' or enlisted men's clubs. In one case, Chaplain William Chapple was written to by the Adjutant General of Camp Sutton on 9 August 1943 because Chapple, apparently, 'on or about 6 August 1943 did tear down and wilfully destroy certain property belonging to the Officers' Club'. He was asked to give his reasons for doing this and 'to make restitution'. When Chapple replied to the Commanding Officer of the Depot on 19 August he explained what took place. He claimed that he took down two pictures of naked women put up in the Officers' Club and that he did not know that the property belonged to the club itself. He stated that as the 'Depot Chaplain, I feel that it is my duty to have removed all such literature and posters that are destructive to the morals of this Command.' He also noted that in his 17 years of experience he knew that such pictures can lead men to immoral actions and that he took down the pictures 'to keep the thoughts and acts of these men pure and clean'.

Chapple then suggested that the Commanding Officer (CO) objected to 'a public place being decorated with such vulgar scenes'. Apparently, Chapple had asked an orderly to take down the pictures, which he did, but the pictures were put back up the next day, so he took them down himself. He was unhappy that the CO had 'seen fit to order me to replace these obscene posters which are contrary to my Christian ideals.' As it transpired, he did not have to do this because the order commanding him to put the pictures back up was delayed by 10 days by which time the officers had 'completely decorated the Officers' Club with such obscene posters of nude women' that now there were 'several' of the offending posters. On 26 August Chappel was written to by the Chief of Chaplains Assistant Edmund Weber acknowledging the original memo to Chapple and his reply. The letter to Chapple from the Chief of Chaplains office says little other than 'it is hoped that the matter ... may be settled to the satisfaction of all concerned' (Coppedge 1943; Chapple 1943; Weber 1943).

The use of pin-ups and nude photographs was of concern to many chaplains serving throughout the war and in most theatres. In June 1944 a different Chaplain Sullivan, Otho, wrote to Arnold complaining about the proliferation of nude photographs 'found almost everywhere.' He claimed these photos were 'passion arousing' and that chaplains have very little impact on getting them removed from clubs and mess halls. He was, essentially, asking the Chief of Chaplains office to provide 'some instruction'. He noted that 'George Washington did not wipe out cursing with his Order Against Profanity but he did inform his officers that it was wicked'. Sullivan suggested that the Chief of Staff could issue a similar order with regard to 'Improper Illustrations'. If nothing else, this order would mean that 'Chaplains would not be asked to approve of filth in fancy frames'. He ended by appealing to Arnold's 'conscience for action and to your wisdom for advice' (Sullivan 1944). No response from Arnold is recorded, but clearly chaplains were concerned that indecent images could lead the weaker men to immoral and unchristian behaviour.

While it might seem odd to include pin-ups and nude photographs in documentation about indecent literature, a more familiar concept of what constituted literature was reflected in chaplains' references to books they came across while carrying out their duties. One District Chaplain in a CCC camp in the Nebraska–Kansas district wrote to the Chief of Chaplains in October 1939 complaining about the book *Dove Creek Rodeo*. The particular excerpt from this novel that perturbed him had to do with a seduction scene in a cabin where the protagonist laid a young woman on a bed and proceeded to 'make love to her'. In the excerpt that he pulled out of the book and sent to the Chief of Chaplains office we read that:

> She pulled his face down to her and kissed him. He lay beside her on the bed and pressed close to her. She was breathing hard and clutching him. He reached for the bottom of her dress. 'No' she said. 'Yes' he said. She closed her eyes and kissed him, her arms about his neck.

But in the next chapter we learn that 'The Kid was fighting mad. He was mad because he had discovered that he was not the first.' Illicit sexual behaviour had occurred and the chaplain objected to the blatant reference to what he deemed to be immoral behaviour. Chaplain Brandon noted that he had taken the book from the reading room in the camp at Blair, Nebraska and that it was 'book number 97' in the travelling library. He then asked Arnold what could be the best and fastest way to get it removed from 'all travelling libraries in … the CCC because of its utter filth.' He further complained that this type of indecent literature made the chaplain's job of encouraging 'clean thinking' more difficult (Brandon 1939).

As was the case with many of the protests from chaplains, this one led directly to censorship. The Chief of Chaplains replied on 18 October informing Brandon that as a result of this inquiry the book would be 'removed and destroyed from all travelling CCC libraries.' Somehow this book had slipped through the selection process, allegedly, by being recommended by 'someone whose moral and religious ideals were sordid and debased, or it was accepted on recommendation without a reading'. Chief of Chaplains Arnold went a step further and noted that no more action was needed on the part of the chaplain, but encouraged him to 'further emasculate this and any other book in any way you possibly can' (Arnold 1939).

During the war literature in all its guises was circulated among GIs in a variety of ways. For instance, there was an Armed Services edition of popular books known as pocket-sized novels. These consisted of everything 'from classics to rip-roaring westerns', as the armed services newspaper *Stars and Stripes* reported in May 1944. This was not a small-scale operation. The reporter noted that three million books a month were being sent to servicemen and were issued free of charge. Each month saw 30 new titles released, with the titles being picked by an advisory board to the War and Navy Departments. They cost as little as 4 cents for the War Department to purchase and an estimated 35 million were to be in circulation by the end of 1944 according to a previous *Stars and Stripes* article from June 1943. Distributed by the Council on Books in Wartime, the first list included approved books such as Franz Werfel's *Song of Bernadette*, William Saroyan's *The Human Comedy*, Captain Ted Lawson's forthcoming *Thirty Seconds*

Over Tokyo, Mark Twain's *Tom Sawyer* and Hervey Allen's *The Forest and the Fort.* (*Stars and Stripes* 8 June 1943 and 2 May 1944)

On the other hand, a book titled *The Sound of an American* by David Ormsbee was criticised in December 1942 by one chaplain from Boston. He noted that 'the author from start to finish revels in vivid pictures of sexual affairs and makes the pursuit of women and the love of liquor the normal life.' Chaplain Hickey had been asked to read and comment on the suitability of this novel for 'reading among soldiers.' Apparently the book had received a favourable review in the Chief of Chaplains Bulletin of 1 November 1942 with Hickey suggesting that the reviewer must not have actually read the book. The Chief of Chaplains Assistant Albert Corpening responded to Hickey and also wrote to the publisher, E. P. Dutton. Corpening concluded that the book was 'designed to pander to the obscene, the lewd, and the indecent'. He further suggested that 'according to the standards of this book women whose husbands are in the Army are expected to give marriage privileges to soldiers who are off to the wars and single girls are to give similar comfort to the "poor Abners" who are about to go on duty or who return from leave'. He informed the publisher that the Chief of Chaplains' office regretted that the book was ever published in the first place (Hickey 1942; Corpening 1942).

It was not just the dime novel or current books that caused concern among some chaplains. One chaplain even complained that Leo Tolstoy's *The Resurrection* included 'stupid slander on the military life'. Chaplain Lynch complained that a particular offending passage noted that 'military life in general depraves men' and asked the Chief of Chaplains whether this type of book would 'aid the war effort and help bolster obedience and inspire confidence in leadership'. Yet in some cases, as in this one, common sense prevailed. While there is no typed, official response to this letter of concern in the record, there was a hand-written memo from someone with initials RJH suggesting that the offending passage from *The Resurrection* was 'perhaps ... not a bad picture of life in the standing army of imperial Russia half a century ago when the book was written'. He further notes that 'for these reasons I question the necessity of any objection to its inclusion in the camp libraries' (Lynch n.d.).

Yet complaints about novels came from other sources as well. In March 1943 Senator Claude Pepper forwarded a letter to Chief of Chaplains Arnold which had been sent to him by a concerned citizen regarding Sinclair Lewis' novel *Elmer Gantry*. Arnold followed up this complaint and discovered that the book was part of material available through the United Service Organization (USO) over which his office had no jurisdiction. He did, however, write to the USO office whose Director of Field Operations responded on 7 April noting that he would investigate the matter as the USO 'does not want to encourage the type of criticisms of religious leadership in which the writer of the book indulges' (Rising 1943; Pepper 1943; Arnold 3 April 1943; Johns 1943).

Chaplains' concerns about indecent literature could and did include smaller publications such as camp newspapers. The content of these publications worried some chaplains partly because the circulation of these papers could extend beyond the men in uniform. Some copies of camp newspapers or *Stars and Stripes* were sent by soldiers to their homes, which meant they were also read by parents and relations. In this context the content of the papers elicited much comment by chaplains. As noted earlier, indecent literature was deemed to encompass not only written, but also visual forms with one area of importance, at least to the chaplains, the publication of cartoons of a suggestive nature. The number of cartoons that caused chaplains to write to the Chief of Chaplains was significant and a general pattern is discernable. For example, a chaplain at Chicopee Falls, Massachusetts, in February 1943, noted that in the camp newspaper there was a comic strip that depicted a row of sketches of nearly naked women with various captions reading 'heats up fast', 'manual control necessary', 'fuselage construction good for observation', 'responds to pressure', 'flutter in tail' and 'best performance when landing gear retracted'. Chaplain Orr noted that he had canvassed opinion among enlisted men and discovered that 'most men thought [this cartoon] was going too far' but admitted that the comics were popular with 'many men.' Chaplain Orr believed, however, that the consequences of publishing these types of cartoons were obvious. He noted that 'if the WAACS were sent here dressed in brassieres and tights, that would be popular too; and a rapid rise of the VD rate would be the inevitable outcome' (Orr, 1943). The need for censorship then was not just because of prudery, but had a very real function to perform – the moral uplift of the men and the curtailment of physical depravity.

Another chaplain noted of a cartoon of a similar nature that 'instead of building morale, it breaks down morals'. Chaplain Orr had also proposed, however, that it required the Chief of Chaplains to take action because 'the voice of a minor Chaplain is like one crying in the wilderness' (ibid.). As Chaplain Batten at Walla Walla Army Air Field noted in October 1944, with reference to a Sad Sack cartoon depicting a visit to a prophylaxis station, 'it is difficult for an occasional sex morality talk by the chaplain to counteract the constant pressure' of these images. Chaplains were contesting not just prudish images and behaviour but wider sexual urges to which the men were exposed. Arnold concurred and noted that 'a soldier has enough of the seamy side of life about him without semi-official Army publications keeping it before him', noting that people will doubt the 'War Department's sincerity in its avowed effort to keep planes, periodicals and performances clean' (Batten 1944; Arnold 1944).

While the War Department had directives about what was allowable in military publications, these instructions were often worded in a rather vague way, for example the instruction to avoid lewd and lascivious language could be interpreted differently by different people. Colonel David

Tully, a defender of the *Stars and Stripes* newspaper, noted that it was edited on the basis of War Department Pamphlet 20–3 *Guide to the Use of Information Materials*. He pointed out that, despite the fact that:

> obscenity and lewdness are barred by editorial policy ... humor is not barred. It is appreciated that humor may at times be vulgar in the discretionary sense of the word ... however, Stars and Stripes is written for the great majority of the soldiers in the theater.

He went on to point out that none of the three surveys already done by May 1945 on the issue of the content of *Stars and Stripes*, had ever 'elicited criticism on the score of obscenity, lewdness, filth or indecency' from the readerships. He also noted that 'bathing beauty art' is used at the discretion of the editor and that those stationed in the continental United States could already get their 'bathing beauty art' readily elsewhere (Tully 1945).

Pulp magazines

While all of these complaints about nose art, cartoons, novels and pin-ups were part of the Chief of Chaplains' concerns about indecent literature, the main area of protest and success in censorship had to do with pulp magazines. By far the largest collection of information in the archive relates to these commercially produced magazines and it was the attempt to ban these publications from sale in Army exchanges that occupied much of Chief of Chaplain Arnold's time throughout 1942. As noted earlier, in a circular letter sent by Chaplain Arnold in September 1938, he quoted an article that appeared in the *Washington Post* that reported how some newsstands had begun banning 'filthy publications' voluntarily. Arnold called these troublesome magazines 'sex literature and crime-provoking stuff', believing that the sale of such literature catered 'especially to depraved tastes' (Arnold 1938).

By mid-war the Chaplains Corps was helped along in its campaign against indecent literature by the United States Post Office Department. As early as July 1942 the US postal service began revoking second-class mailing privileges of certain magazines deemed to be indecent. Postmaster General Frank C. Walker issued a series of press releases outlining the rules and regulations governing postal privileges and informing the public of which pulp magazines the Post Office was charging with violation of these rules in order to revoke their second-class mailing privileges. From the Post Office point of view second-class mailing privileges implied governmental approval of the material being posted, meaning it would be seen as 'a publication fitting and proper for unrestricted circulation by and in the United States mails ... [the second-class postage was] a badge of merit, a certificate of good moral character of the publication' (Walker 1942).

Congress had established the regulations for postal charges and divided post into four categories. These were outlined in the press release as. 'First, written; Second, periodical publications; Third, miscellaneous printed matter ... not exceeding eight ounces; and Fourth, merchandise ... weighing not less than 8 ounces.' According to the Post Office, the second-class, privileged rate operated at a loss for the Post Office, but the loss was set aside in order 'to secure to the public the benefits to result from "the wide dissemination of intelligence as to current events"' stipulating that the material needed to be 'of a public character, or devoted to literature, the sciences, arts or some special industry' (ibid.).

A further restriction to second-class material was that it had to be what was known as 'mailable matter'. The government also believed that, closely linked to all of this, there was a need to understand that second-class mailing rates were a privilege, which had to be earned, and *not* a right. As the Postmaster General pointed out in July 1942, government regulation Title 18, Section 334 of the United States Code stated that 'every obscene, lewd or lascivious,... book pamphlet, picture, paper, letter, writing, print,... is hereby declared nonmailable matter'. The Supreme Court had upheld this restriction, noting that its purpose was to oversee the mail to avoid 'the use of the mails [*sic*] to circulate or deliver matter to corrupt the morals of the people ... [especially] that form of immorality which has relation to sexual impurity' (ibid.).

The statutes, according to the Postmaster General, were not meant to stop *all* publications dealing with issues of sex or sexual instruction. On the contrary, serious information was allowed. What the Post Office hoped to stop was the circulation of material, which could be determined that, 'taken as a whole, has a libidinous effect'. For further clarity, the Post Office pointed out that obscenity was banned 'irrespective of whether the matter is portrayed under the guise of art, fiction, humor, or sex education, or whether it appears in stories purporting to be detailed factual accounts of actual sex crimes' (ibid.). This latter point helps to explain why so many of the banned or challenged magazines related to the detective genre of pulp magazines. These magazines had used the concept of 'true' storytelling to publish articles about sex and sexual deviancy. As with other areas of censorship, however, the issue quickly became one of how to define what was libidinous in order to calculate the decency level of a publication. The criterion for the decision was whether or not the publication was likely to 'arouse the salacity of the reader' (ibid.). The Postmaster General was quick to point out that these regulations and statutes did *not* contravene the rights of free speech or freedom of the press.

The press release noted above related to the revoking of second-class mailing privileges of the magazines entitled *College Humor, Headline Detective,* and *Front Page Detective.* The method by which the Post Office determined the standing of a publication in relation to obscenity statutes included instituting proceedings to analyse the evidence. The Post Office stressed that these were not criminal proceedings and that it was not 'the acts of the owner, publisher, or editor' that were in question. Rather, the only question was whether the publication itself 'meets the conditions set out by the Congress in respect of its use of its second-class mailing permit' (ibid.). In other words, was the publication 'mailable' as defined by the obscenity statutes noted above?

While the actions of the Post Office are 'subject to review by the courts' (ibid.), it was also the case that the Post Office was not obliged to take the word of the publisher at face value. Hence, proceedings to revoke second-class mailing privileges took place before a panel of three Assistant Post-master Generals. For example, in the case of *College Humor* the Postmaster General issued an order to the publisher on 29 May 1942 asking him to attend a hearing on 10 June to answer the question 'why the second-class mailing privileges enjoyed by "College Humor" should not be suspended, annulled, or revoked' (ibid.). It was at this point that the Postmaster General gave specific reasons for instituting the hearing and these revolved around the content of the magazine over the course of several issues and usually entailed listing the titles of the articles that caused offence or, more accurately, were thought to violate the statutes.

The Postmaster General stated that the mailing status was to be revoked on 'the following grounds: That it is nonmailable [sic] within the meaning of 35 Stat. 1129 (18 U.S.C. 334), in that issues since Winter, 1941, have contained matters described and portrayed as Dream Majorette, Background Places Her in Forefront, Fun is Free for Co-Eds Spending Day at Lake Resort, Outdoor Girls Initiated Indoors, Blond Bomber Banks on Curves, Collegiana: It Happened Here and There, College Humor Swing Fraternity, accompanied by photographs and drawings of an obscene, lewd and lascivious character; and other matters of a similar or related nature' (ibid.).

With this evidence the hearing took place where the editor 'made an oral answer, and represented the publication in person. Testimony was given and exhibits were introduced. The publication by its editor ... was provided an opportunity to examine all exhibits and evidence on the publication's behalf' (ibid.). After looking at the evidence, briefs submitted by both sides and hearing the arguments, the panel put forward their findings to the Postmaster General. At this point he found *College Humor* to be in violation of the statutes and that the publication's articles were 'not isolated or casual incidents but were "no more than appeals to the salaciously disposed." ' Although the editor claimed that the magazine reflected 'the customs the habits, the modes, the manners of college life and college people' the Postmaster General determined that the articles and pictures as well as photographs within the magazine did not bear out this claim (ibid.). As a result, the 'authorisation of admission of "College Humor" to the second class of mail matter, and the accordance of "College Humor" of second-class mail privileges under the Act of 3 March 1879, as amended' was revoked. However, the publication was free to reapply for second-class mailing status 'whenever the publication does not violate the laws of the United States' (ibid.). The rest of the press release went on to give a similar, though much briefer account of the proceedings against *Headline Detective*. This was done in consolidation with the hearing for *Front Page Detective*, as they were published by the same firm.

Magazines sometimes made counterclaims, however, in their editorials. For example, as Mark Gabor has noted in *The Illustrated History of the Girlie Magazine*, in October 1937 *Candid Confessions* tried to explain the content of its magazine by asking:

> How many lives have been wrecked through some girl's trusting igno-
> rance? How many young men have had their hopes of youth blasted
> by indiscretions? These conditions will go on as long as men are men
> and women are women – as long as sex is the bogey man which is
> hidden like a skeleton in a closet.
>   ...because we feel that the experiences of others will be of help and
> interest, we have asked those whose lives have been affected by their
> stepping over the line of discretion to tell you their life stories.
>
> (Gabor 1984)

All of the work of the Post Office in revoking second-class mailing privi-leges of pulp magazines relates to the United States Army Chaplains Corps because the work of the Postmaster General was quickly seized upon by the Chief of Chaplains in his censorship campaign. He had at his disposal, over the course of the next few years, documentary proof of the indecency of certain publications. Arnold was quick to realise, as well, that he could use this information to good effect in the Army post exchanges by getting the military to ban the sale of magazines which the government itself had determined to be immoral. On 5 August 1942 Arnold penned a draft letter to be sent to all chaplains informing them of the ongoing campaign by the Post Office to eliminate the second-class mailing privileges of maga-zines deemed to be indecent. He noted that 'the type of magazines sold in post exchanges is a matter of concern both to the general public and to us'. He then outlined what the Postmaster General had done by way of revoking or denying second-class mailing status and listed the magazines that were denied second-class status or had their status revoked. He ended by noting 'in view of the above action by the Post Office Department, it is believed that commanding officers will eliminate from their post exchanges all these publications, non-mailable because of an editorial policy of pandering to the obscene, lewd, and indecent, if the list is brought to their attention. It is the desire of the Chief of Chaplains that this information be brought to their attention' (Arnold 1942).

While the above letter by Arnold was not sent out to all chaplains, Arnold did make his views widely known. On 2 November 1942 the Chief of Chaplains issued a statement outlining his belief that 'any magazine that cannot use the second-class postal permit because of the policy of sustained and systematic appeals to lascivious curiosity or ... pandering to the obscene, lewd or indecent should not be sold by any agency on a military reservation'. Arnold also noted that, when confronted with this information, the Chief of Administrative Services, SOS, stated 'it is not thought that any service or post commander would intentionally permit the sale of unmailable literature' and 'if and when chaplains, in their duties, observe any transgressions of decency or propriety on the part of the post exchanges they should bring that to the attention of the local post commander'. Arnold's views were outlined in an Army Service Forces Bulletin with the added note that 'the Commanding General, First Service Command, fully concurs in the policy outlined by the Chief of Chaplains' (Army Service Forces 1943).

Feeling that Post Commanders would respond favourably if lists of banned magazines were brought to their attention, the Chief of Chaplains asked all chaplains to report the appearance of any banned magazine to the base commander. Some chaplains in the field needed little more encouragement to go off in pursuit of these immoral publications. Chaplain Dux at Fort Knox sent a memo to the Post Chaplain in spring 1943 declaring that he had found for sale at the main post exchange magazines which had been deemed to violate the National Organization for Decent Literature (NODL) Code. This very long list included: *Complete Detective, Crack Detective, Feature Detective, Gags, Gayety, Keep 'Em Laughing, National Detective Cases, Pack 'o Fun, Ranch Romances, Scoop Detective* and *Secret Detective Cases.* Objections were noted over the articles within these publications as recorded in the press releases of the Postmaster General (Dux 1943).

Chaplain Dux's reference to the NODL demonstrates the extent of censorship that was taking place in the United States with reference to pulp magazines. The NODL publicised its judgements about magazines it deemed indecent in various formats, but most notably for the Chief of Chaplains, listed 'banned' publications in the *Acolyte.* In the November 1942 issue there was a full page list of 'Magazines Disapproved by the National Organization for Decent Literature'. The NODL noted that 'this list is neither complete nor permanent. Additional periodicals will be added as they are found to offend against our code, and magazines now listed will be removed as soon as they are made to conform to our standards. Understand we do not attach the "immoral" charge to all these magazines. They are on our list because they offend against one or more of a five point Code adopted by the NODL.' The five ways for a publication to cause offense included magazines that: 'glorify crime or the criminal; are predominately "sexy"; feature illicit love; carry illustrations indecent or suggestive, and advertise wares for the prurient minded.' The list that followed included publications that 'offend against one or more provisions of the above code. The reading contents of many of them deal with lust and passion in the name of love'. The list included 149 magazines that were deemed to be 'procurable in most places' with an additional 41 titles that 'are not distributed everywhere' (Perlow 1942).

A magazine title that brought together the work of the Post Office in revoking second-class postal privileges, that of NODL in publicising indecent magazines and the Chief of Chaplains' campaign to ban publications from Post Exchanges was the *National Police Gazette* (later named simply *Police Gazette*). While the magazine was banned from the United States second-class post in 1942, by the end of the year the *Police Gazette* had been deemed to have improved its content enough to have its second-class postal privileges re-instated. Mr N. K. Perlow of the *National Police Gazette* wrote to Chief of Chaplains Arnold on 25 November 1942 as a follow-up to a telephone conversation they had prior to that date. Perlow sent Arnold a copy of the Post Office letter re-instating their postal privileges and a copy of a page from the *Acolyte*, which indicated that the December issue of the *Police Gazette* was deemed to be unobjectionable. What prompted Perlow to write to Arnold was the fact that the editors 'have been deludged [sic] with cancellations from Army camps, and would therefore, appreciate your immediate attention in sending a release to the Post Exchange Offices, withdrawing your objections to the sale of *Police Gazette*' (Perlow 1942).

Arnold was determined to remove what he considered indecent literature from the reach of men in uniform whom his office was designed to protect from immoral influences. Whether or not Arnold sent a release to the Post Exchange Offices as requested by Perlow is doubtful. In April 1943 Arnold was contacted by the War Department Service of Supply asking him for comments with regard to the *Police Gazette*. Arnold responded on 1 May 1943 to the request for information in a two-page memo to the Adjutant General (AG). The Chief of Chaplains outlined the course of action that he had undertaken with regard to removing magazines that had been banned from the second-class postal rate from sale in post exchanges. He also quoted information that went out in several circular letters to chaplains with regard to this subject, which included information on magazines that had re-applied for postal privileges and were no longer on the banned list, including the *National Police Gazette*. He assured the AG that 'everything possible has been done to inform all Chaplains through the medium of the circular letter that the *National Police Gazette* has again been granted second-class mailing privileges by the Post Office Department'. The archival record also indicates that Arnold's draft memo differed substantially in the last paragraph from what appeared in the final memo sent to the AG. In his draft Arnold stated that 'it appears that the publisher of the *National Police Gazette* hopes to force this office into making a statement to chaplains which could then be used as an indorsement [*sic*] of the magazine'. What was actually sent to the AG, instead, was a less direct attack on the magazine that noted 'the circular letter is mailed

monthly to chaplains. It contains no orders or directions but only information that is considered helpful to a chaplain in the performance of his
duties' (Adjutant General's Office 1943; Arnold 1 May 1943).

While the controversy over the banning of pulp magazines eventually
occupied less of the Chief of Chaplains' time, the issue never truly went
away. In January 1944 Chaplain Ott reported to the Chief of Chaplains
office that he had noted copies of *Esquire* at the local Post Exchange. The
non-commissioned officer in charge agreed not to display the issue and to
send the unsold copies back to the distributor. When the Lieutenant in
charge of the Exchange discovered this he ordered the magazine to be
sold. When Chaplain Ott approached him on the subject Ott was told to
refer it up to the Major. He did this and reported to the Chief of Chaplains that 'the Major maintains that he can see nothing wrong with the
magazine (he is a doctor in private life) and that in his opinion, the
morales [sic] of the men are not thereby corrupted. He tells me I have fulfilled my obligation.... As a chaplain I happen to know that these kinds of
magazines are at least a contributing cause in the deterioration of the
morales [*sic*] of the men.' He was advised by the Chief of Chaplains' office
to make no further protest until the status of the magazine was clarified
(Ott 1944).

Apparently there was an ongoing debate about the magazine itself.
Esquire had been around since the 1930s and had a targeted audience of
men from the beginning. By the time the war broke out the magazine was
distributed widely to men in the armed service. In 1943 the Post Office
had challenged *Esquire* under its censorship campaign and tried to remove
its mailing privileges. However, *Esquire* was able to hold off this threat by
'proving in court that it performed a public service by advancing its suggestive, but nonprurient, pictures in the context of a broad-based socially
redeemable men's magazine'. The publisher brought forward witnesses to
testify including clergymen, psychiatrists, and university professors. The
government's witnesses tended to be moral crusaders. In the end *Esquire*
was let off and the courts decreed that there was no evidence of 'lewd and
lascivious' material. This was to demonstrate to other girlie and pulp magazines that pictures of women in erotic poses were acceptable as long as
there was other material in the magazine, both visual and written, that was
non-sexual (Gabor 1984).

Another source of concern for chaplains with regard to these magazines
was not just the magazine articles' content, but the advertisements in the
back of the magazines. In May 1945 Chaplain Raymond Brock wrote to
Arnold regarding advertising that appeared in the back of the magazine
Army Times. The letter had very little comment, but was attached to several
enclosures. Brock had apparently spotted an ad for 'Girlie Photos' available
by sending $1 to the Charm Photo Co. of New York. The ad promised 'the
world's most beautiful women the way you like to see them. Posed to thrill
you.' It promised that the photos would be 'sent in plain wrapper,' which

they were. Brock helpfully sent along the five black and white photos of women to the Chief of Chaplains to illustrate their indecency. All of the women were clothed, however they appeared in various revealing costumes or poses. The Charm Photo Co. also sent a generic letter thanking the purchaser for sending in the order and offering further collections of photographs that included: 'The Outdoor Set,' 'The Variety Set,' and 'The Bedroom Set'. The Bedroom Set cost $2. Or you could purchase all 23 photos for $3. It was signed 'Very truly yours, Charm Photo Co.'. The response from Arnold's office was sent to Brock on 1 June 1945. In it the Acting Chief of Chaplains Henry Simpson noted that they had contacted various military agencies with regard to this type of advertising but had discovered that 'ARMY TIMES is a commercial publication and that such does not come under the jurisdiction of the Information and Education Division, ASF [American Service Forces]' (Brock 1945). Therefore, there was nothing the Chief of Chaplains office could do with regard to this publication or to the commercial advertisements it contained.

Not all chaplains' complaints prompted positive responses however. In another case, the office of the Chief of Chaplains counselled a chaplain who had complained about a picture used in a camp newspaper, to avoid being overzealous. Suggesting that he needed a sense of proportion, Chaplain Elsam was informed that:

> your attitude in this matter seems very judicious and intelligent. The understanding chaplain wishes to exert the maximum influence against whatever he believes to be pernicious or harmful to the contentment, morale, or morals of the men. He will see things of minor importance which he cannot approve fully but will not wish to gain the reputation of being a complainer about small matters in case something of a serious character should arise about which he should speak out positively. If we cry 'Wolf!' every time we see a rat, we will have nothing convincing to say if the wolf actually comes. The chaplain's judgment and sense of proportion must be his guide in this particular.
>
> (Honeywell 1944)

Conclusion

During the war, according to the official *Report on the Army Chaplain in the European Theater of Operations* 'the degree to which the chaplain was utilised as a consultant in moral issues depended to a great extent upon local circumstances and upon the personalities of the chaplain and commanding officer' (War Department 1946). Some chaplains took a very active role in issues of morality, attempting to lead the way, as it were, in safeguarding the men in their care from corrupting influences. Equally, some chaplains felt more at ease in dealing with the spiritual and pastoral needs of their men than with bigger and broader behavioural or moral issues. In other words the extent of a common policy towards the material was vague and highly personal.

More liberal, progressive chaplains recognised that they worked with a group of young men in close proximity who would do what young men do from a certain age, class and background. So their message suggested that a little bit of license was allowed to satisfy morale. But more immoral behaviour introduced the question of religious doctrine, sin and morality at a higher level. On the other hand there were chaplains who were looking to ban any, and all, material at any point, on whatever pretext. World War II chaplains faced the problem of a changing and increasingly culturally exposed world where talk, discussion, imagery and awareness of issues, especially sexual issues, were more widespread and certainly more commonly imbibed than in any previous era. Chaplains dealt with a variety of issues in this changing social context such as drinking and gambling.

Nevertheless, as self-selected men of the cloth they all, more or less, came to the job with firm convictions about what constituted morality and sin. The widespread protest of chaplains from all theatres against the establishment of brothels and the issuance of prophylactics gives a good illustration of the unanimity of purpose in the Chaplains Corps. The Chief of Chaplains himself stands out as a crusader for men's morals as witnessed in his campaign against indecent magazines. For Arnold, America was at war with 'pagans, atheists and Satan himself' (Gushwa 1977). Clearly, Arnold had a great deal of influence, as illustrated by the number and frequency of the correspondence he received about indecent literature from everyone from publishers of magazines to Senators to ordinary citizens.

There can be no doubt that chaplains had a profound effect on the development of United States Army regulations and policies. In a post-war survey 93 per cent of chaplains said that they felt their service had been valued. At the end of the war the report on the chaplains went on to recommend that instructions to chaplains and special service officers in the future 'be changed to direct the close cooperation of both sections at every level of command in the production of entertainment for military personnel, with a view *to eliminating morally objectionable and offensive material*' (ibid.). In the future the role of chaplains in safeguarding service personnel from morally corrupting influences was to be explicit rather than implicit.

References

Adjutant General's Office (1943) Memo to Chief of Chaplains, 22 April. RG 247, Folder 250.1, Box 195, NARA, Washington, DC.
Army Service Forces (1943) Information Bulletin No. 26, 21 June. RG 247, Folder 250.1, Box 195, NARA, Washington, DC.

Arnold, William (1938) Circular Letter No. 191, 22 September. RG 247, Folder 250.1, Box 195, NARA, Washington, DC.

Arnold, William (1939) Letter to Rev. Charles M. Brandon, 18 October. RG 247, Folder 250.1, Box 195, NARA, Washington, DC.

Arnold, William (1942) Draft letter to 'Dear Chaplain', 15 August. RG 247, Folder 250.1, Box 195, NARA, Washington, DC.

Arnold, William (1943) Letter to Henry Rising, 3 April. RG 247, Folder 250.1, Box 195, NARA, Washington, DC.

Arnold, William (1943) Letter to Adjutant General, 1 May. RG 247, Folder 250.1, Box 195, NARA, Washington, DC.

Arnold, William (1944) Letter to Miss Janet Martin, 4 August. RG 247, Folder 250.1, Box 194, NARA, Washington, DC.

Arnold, William (1944) Letter to Director of Personnel, Army Service Forces, 27 October. RG 247, Folder 250.1, Box 194, NARA, Washington, DC.

Batten, Augustus (1944) Letter to Chief of Chaplains, 5 October. RG 247, Folder 250.1, Box 194, NARA, Washington, DC.

Brandon, C.M. (1939) Memo to Chief of Chaplains, 14 October. RG 247, Folder 250.1, Box 195, NARA, Washington, DC.

Brock, Raymond E. (1945) Letter to Chief of Chaplains, 16 May. RG 247, Folder 250.1, Box 194, NARA, Washington, DC.

Chapple, William C. (1943) Memo to Commanding Officer 12th Replacement Depot, 19 August. RG 247, Folder 250.1, Box 195, NARA, Washington, DC.

Coppedge, McCoy O. (1943) Memo to William Chapple, 9 August. RG 247, Folder 250.1, Box 195, NARA, Washington, DC.

Corpening, Albert N. (1942) Letter to Chaplain David H. Hickey, 30 December. RG 247, Folder 250.1, Box 195, NARA, Washington, DC.

Corpening, Albert N. (1942) Letter to E.P. Dutton and Company, Inc., 30 December. RG 247, Folder 250.1, Box 195, NARA, Washington, DC.

Dux, Victor L. (1943) Memo to Post Chaplain, n.d. RG 247, Folder 250.1, Box 195, NARA, Washington, DC.

Gabor, Mark (1984) *The Illustrated History of Girlie Magazines: From National Police Gazette to the Present.* London: Futura.

Gushwa, Robert L. (1977) *The Best and Worst of Times: The United States Army Chaplaincy 1920–1945*, Honolulu, Hawaii: University Press of the Pacific.

Hickey, David H. (1942) Letter to Chief of Chaplains, 23 December. RG 247, Folder 250.1, Box 195, NARA, Washington, DC.

Honeywell, Roy J. (1944) Letter to Chaplain Elsam, 1 August. RG 247, Folder 250.1, Box 194, NARA, Washington, DC.

Johns, Ray (1943) Letter to Chaplain A. R. Arnold, 7 April. RG 247, Folder, 250.1, Box 195, NARA, Washington, DC.

Lynch, Laurence E. n.d. Letter to Chief of Chaplains, n.d. RG 247, Folder 250.1, Box 195, NARA, Washington, DC.

Martin, Janet (1944) Letter to William Arnold, 22 July. RG 247, Folder 250.1, Box 195, NARA, Washington, DC.

Orr, J. Edwin (1943) Letter to Brig. General W. R. Arnold, 25 February. RG 247, Folder 250.1, Box 195, NARA, Washington, DC.

Ott, Roman J. (1944) Letter to Chief of Chaplains, 13 January. RG 247, Folder 250.1, Box 194, NARA, Washington, DC.

Pepper, Claude (1943) Letter to Brig. General William Arnold, 29 March. RG 247, Folder 250.1, Box 195, NARA, Washington, DC.

Perlow, N.K. (1942) Letter to Brigadier General Arnold, plus attachment, 25 November. RG 247, Box 195, NARA, Washington, DC.

Rising, Henry (1943) Letter to Claude Pepper, 4 March. RG 247, Folder 250.1, Box 195, NARA, Washington, DC.

Stars and Stripes (8 June 1943) *35 Million Books*

Stars and Stripes (2 May 1944) Article *Pocket-Sized Novels*

Sullivan, David (1938) Letter to Chief of Chaplains, 10 May, RG 247, Folder 250.1, Box 195, NARA, Washington, DC.

Sullivan, Otho L. (1944) Letter to Chief of Chaplains, 9 June. RG 247, Folder 250.1, Box 194, NARA, Washington, DC.

Tully, David (1945) Letter to Carter, May. RG 247, Folder 250.1, Box 194, NARA, Washington, DC.

Walker, Frank C. (1942) Press release, 16 July. RG 247, Folder 250.1, Box 195, NARA, Washington, DC.

War Department (1946) Report on the Army Chaplain in the European Theater of Operations, study number 68, 15 May.

Weber, Edmund (1943) Letter to William E. Chapple, 26 August. RG 247, Folder 250.1, Box 195, NARA, Washington, DC.

Part II
Through the cultural lens

5 Hidden conflict, visible world

Keith Tester

Introduction

The question was posed by Edouard Manet in *The Execution of Emperor Maximilian* now in the Mannheim Kunsthalle. In the bottom right hand corner of the canvas there is a shadow, but whose? Within the narrative of the painting it might belong to a soldier who is loading his rifle just like the one to whom the shadow points. But that doesn't seem to be quite right, because the shape of the shadow is of an onlooker on the scene. It is, in fact, the shadow of the spectator. It is mine and yours. It is the shadow of Manet and everyone who will stand before the canvas in the future. Put another way, it is the shadow of someone who is a bystander, neither victim nor perpetrator. Manet's painting is asking questions about what it means to see and know about the torment and humiliation of others from whom the spectator is distant and, apart from the knowledge of their hurt, about whom the spectator is quite ignorant and possibly completely indifferent.

Manet was certainly sure what the question meant for his own activity, and the answer is given by the existence of the painting. For Manet, it was not enough to be a bystander. He took it as an obligation to impress the human face of a political execution upon those who, like him, had not been there. Manet's eyes were not turned away, and his painting tried to ensure the eyes of his viewers would not be either. For Manet once the human face of conflict is known it needs to be pulled into the light of publicity, it has to be turned into a quality of the human world by being made real to those who were not there. Consequently even if future outrages might not be halted at least the victim's suffering and their face might never be forgotten, and at least the damage caused by the perpetrator and their identity will never be allowed to be hidden.

But *The Execution of Emperor Maximilian* is not a documentary work. Paradoxically, given the status of the painting as an attempt to make the execution real, it is a work of *imagination*. It is about *real effects not realism*. Maximilian and two generals were executed on 19 June 1867 by a firing squad under the control of Benito Juárez, as the final act in the failure of

Napoleon III's attempt to replace the Mexican government with his own clients. The news reached Paris on 1 July, and Manet's work was inspired by the stream of accounts coming from Mexico and his longstanding hostility to Napoleon III (Elderfield 2006). Consequently, even as the painting directs a question to its viewer, two questions can be directed towards Manet himself. These are two questions revolving around how the affair of the execution had become visible to Manet. First of all, Manet worked on the basis of newspaper reports and illustrations, yet this work of imagination – which involved him in filtering the contemporary news through the aesthetic prism of Goya – was only possible because he was in Paris, at the centre of global flows of information and therefore *able* to know these things. Second, this particular event was taken by Manet to be especially outrageous because of the context of reading established by his political commitments. Even before the news of the execution came through, Manet was opposed to Napoleon III and this is likely to have caused him to be especially attentive to what happened to the hapless Maximilian in the service of Bonapartist hubris.

So there are three points to pull out of this little case study. *First* of all Manet is asking the viewer what representations of the hurt caused to others mean to those who are not themselves suffering, who are bystanders ensconced in relatively safe European homes. *Second*, Manet is able to pose the question to his viewer and himself alike because the media now make it possible to be aware of destruction far away, on a global range. In this way the issue of moral responsibility running through the first question is put into a context stretching far beyond the local, far beyond the spheres in which the viewer is her or himself an actor. After all, because of their spatial and temporal distance from the execution Manet and his viewers could be outraged, but they were most certainly not victims themselves, nor were they perpetrators. They were bystanders upon an incident from the past (however recent it might have been), which was however put into their present by the immediacy of the news and thereafter Manet's painting (as is the viewer today). This leads to the *third* point arising from the painting: the event it shows, the execution of Maximilian, is offensive and important enough to be the subject of Manet's work because it is contextualised by what might be called an *imaginary* establishing what *ought* to go on between us all. If Manet had not been the subject of a certain imaginary – in other words, if he had not understood the world and its events and affairs in a certain way involving a mix of moral, cultural and political 'oughts' – the execution would not have been relevant to him and, quite simply, the painting would not exist.

In the context of these three points, conflict and the suffering it causes cannot be *assumed* to be visible. Visibility is dependent, contingent. The destruction caused by conflict is only visible if two conditions obtain, and the conflict is hidden where they do not so obtain. These conditions are first, *mediation*. Conflict and more importantly the hurts and humiliations it causes is only visible if it appears in the media. But mere visibility is not enough. Going back to the example of Manet, there had to be something else, some added ingredient, making the news from Mexico so offensive he felt compelled to imagine it in paint. This first condition then is *necessary but not sufficient*. Second, what appears in the media has to be *understood* as relevant and, indeed, *as* offensive else the news from Mexico, or more recently Gaza, will simply lack relevance. The news has to be interpreted in a certain way. The work of interpretation is carried out by and within the imaginary in which the viewer is located. This is the second *sufficient but nevertheless dependent* condition of conflict and its hurts being visible.

This chapter develops these points. The first part of the chapter will explore the two aspects of visibility – mediation and imaginary – and it will also explain precisely what visibility means when it is about something more than simple ocular presence. The second part of the chapter looks in the opposite direction: if visibility is contingent upon mediation and imaginary, conflict can also be hidden when these conditions do not obtain. How might they not so obtain?

Visible world

According to Hannah Arendt, 'it is the function of the public realm to throw light on the affairs of men by providing a space of appearances in which they can show in deed and word, for better and worse, who they are and what they can do' (Arendt 1973a: 8). When light is thrown on deeds and events in this way they are made common to all of us. Such are the stakes of Manet's painting. Arendt also wrote, 'everything that appears in public can be seen and heard by everybody and has the widest possible publicity. For us, appearance – something that is being seen and heard by others as well as by ourselves – constitutes reality' (Arendt 1958: 45). Furthermore:

> the term 'public' signifies the world itself, in so far as it is common to all of us.... To live together in the world means essentially that a world of things is between those who have it in common, as a table is located between those who sit around it.
>
> (Arendt 1958: 46)

In Arendt's terms then, a conflict or any of the other 'affairs of men' is pulled into the light of publicity, and made visible, when it is inserted into a space of appearances. This space is not physical in the sense of an art gallery, rather it is established and enacted through the ability of 'everybody' to see, hear and deliberate about what appears in it. Once this happens, what appears becomes part of the reality we share with one another. It becomes common to all of us and an aspect – a reality – of our world. A conflict is visible in the world when, like a table, we might all sit around it and enter into discussion with one another about what it might mean to us.

Arendt offers important normative arguments, which can act as a baseline to judge what actually happens in the world, but a very simple sociological question is left dangling, a question implied by the story of Manet and Maximilian. *How* can 'the affairs of men' appear in a public realm which is logically distinct from the times and places in which those 'affairs' are of themselves located? Roger Silverstone offers one answer with his concept of the *mediapolis*. According to him, events and occurrences are inserted into public debate because in contemporary relationships the media are openly accessible spaces of appearance and are therefore also the dominant space in which affairs are discussed. According to Silverstone the media constitute our reality. They are the mechanisms making the world we have in common. This is what his neologism *mediapolis* tries to grasp (Silverstone 2007). But still the question remains: *how* do Arendt's 'affairs of men' appear in this mediapolis?

The answer is very simple. They only appear because media institutions have spread throughout the spaces and places in which the 'affairs of men' take place. As Silverstone saw, the world is constituted in and through the media, and as the media are able to penetrate into the times and places of the 'affairs of men' which were previously outside of its purview, so the extent of the world as something between us, as something around which we can all sit like a table, expands. This is one dimension of globalisation. Where the media rely on expensive technology this expansion is dependent upon capitalist investment in technology and the search for profit through the opening up of new markets (here it is important to remember that media institutions are for the most part capitalist organisations or run according to market criteria of effectiveness; media institutions are not philanthropic bodies, existing purely on account of the good will of their financiers). Consequently, these media institutions are likely to report only those 'affairs of men' which will appeal to, or attract, target audiences capable in their turn of being sold to advertisers or regulatory bodies upholding market definitions of 'value for money'. These are the dominant media through which the 'affairs of men' become visible, and they are the institutions through which a public realm operating on a national, or even international scale, might be created. Consequently affairs can only become public if they occur in times and places penetrated by media institutions. In the *first* instance affairs have to take place in front of a camera, or a reporter, technologically capable of transmitting the information back to the metropolitan centres in which the media institutions have their headquarters and where editorial decisions are made. In the *second* instance, these editorial decisions are in their turn made according to a variety of criteria potentially pointing in absolutely different directions; the originality of the affair in question, its pertinence to the specific national mediapolis in which the institution is based; the appeal of the affair to target audiences.

But what is the *basis* of appeal to target audiences? It is about considerably more than the formal properties of media reports, representations or genre. The appeal of an affair is more complex and it is derived from how the decision-making processes of media institutions relate it to how target audiences understand the world, with their understandings about what happens and what ought not to happen. Here the discussion turns to the idea of an *imaginary*. The concept comes from Charles Taylor, and it refers to how men and women, 'imagine their social existence, how they fit together with others, how things go on between them and their fellows, the expectations which are normally met, and the deeper normative notions and images which underlie these expectations' (Taylor 2007: 171). Taylor says: 'we have a sense of how things usually go, but this is interwoven with an idea of how they ought to go' (Taylor 2007: 172. For an examination of Taylor's use of the 'we', see Tester 2010a). The imaginary gives us our taken for granted 'background' knowledge about how things do and ought to go on; it's the set of understandings through which we make sense of the world and our place in it, the set of understandings making it possible for us to do anything together and which also guides us in what ought to be done. An affair appeals when the imaginary makes it understandable as something, which ought, or ought not, to happen. If it cannot be made understandable by the imaginary, it is likely to be simply ignored. Furthermore, an affair becomes visible when it leads to the reality of practices in the public realm, the practices of sharing the affair in common.

Yet why is conflict in particular so central to media reports? At one level the answer to the question is completely obvious: conflict is covered so relentlessly in the media, and it is frequently visible in the public sphere, because the trails of destruction it leaves are so overwhelming both quantitatively and qualitatively. Conflict is visible simply because it is unavoidable. But conflict is only unavoidable for those who understand the world in the terms of an imaginary making it unavoidable. Where the media do not report conflict, or where the suffering is ambiguous in the terms of the imaginary, then it is very avoidable. An interesting example of this situation is the lack of sustained media coverage about what has been happening to Christian communities in Iraq. Iraq sits in the Western imaginary as being Islamic, and consequently the presence of an indigenous Christian community does not fit what 'Iraq' is taken to mean and involve. Consequently, there is no imaginary space in which the destruction of the Christian community can be reported. The public visibility of the human consequences of conflict is not at all inevitable and neither is it intrinsic to the quantity, or quality, of the affair itself. Here the defining case is the lack of visibility in the West of the human consequences of the long-term conflicts in central Africa. Despite the huge number of deaths and the terrifying atrocities, all of this suffering has little, or no, profile for the simple reason of the absence of media institutions (and they are doubtless absent precisely because of the danger). Conflict and its consequences are only visible when the *necessary* condition of presence to media institutions is met alongside the *sufficient* condition of fit with the imaginary expectations of what ought and ought not to go on between humans.

These are abstract points and they need bringing down to earth. The question they raise is one about the content of this imaginary. What are the dominant social and cultural expectations through which affairs are understood? Arendt links them to what she calls the *social question*. The social question arose in Europe in the eighteenth century and identified poverty as an offence to what men and women might expect. This position understands human being in the modern world as being about the struggle to achieve potential, the struggle to be distinctive from the natural constraints implied by the body. These are the terms in which poverty is offensive and this is because it forces its victims always to think about physical need. The social question as imaginary demands the overcoming of material need, through revolution if necessary (Arendt 1973b). To put this into Taylor's terms, poverty is out of kilter with a background norm about what it means to be human, a norm stressing the human ability to change circumstances in the world. These are the terms in which political struggle against poverty becomes part of the repertoire of action available to the men and women who are the subjects of this imaginary. The struggle is contingent upon an imaginary stressing the social question and, without such an imaginary, poverty and its sufferings would be simply the way things are. They would be understood as being beyond human intervention. (For a sustained discussion of the warps of this imaginary when it is applied by the West to suffering in the African continent, see Tester 2010b).

Implicit within the imaginary of the social question is compassion for the downtrodden, although of course the exact political practices following from the compassion can vary enormously, ranging from communism to 'trickle down' economics. In the course of the twentieth century the sphere of compassion expanded beyond poverty to include suffering as such, leading in turn to a condemnation of all those who perpetrate suffering. Today the social question means compassion for all of those who are victims of suffering and who are, more precisely, the victims of conflict. This is the core of the contemporary emphasis on post-traumatic stress and humanitarian disasters alike; both of these forms of suffering are constructed (correctly) as offensive in terms of the normative imaginary expectations, which tie the human condition to potentiality as opposed to restriction.

If the strands of this part of the argument are pulled together, I am contending that visibility is not reducible to ocular presence whether it be immediate or, dominantly, mediated. Visibility means presence in the public realm and this is only possible when an affair like conflict and its human consequences is, first, before media institutions and capable of being reported or broadcast and, second, when the media coverage has an appeal to audiences because it is rendered mutually understandable by the background assumptions of the imaginary through which we share things in common, things like the news of conflict and the damage it does. Media institutions are able to create coverage of just this order because their practitioners are subjects of the imaginary too and because the competitive struggle for profit of media institutions as capitalist organisations has tied the appeal of the imaginary to a series of predictable devices, tricks. In other words, visibility is a *possibility* and, because its visibility *is only ever a possibility*, conflict can also be hidden. Conflict can remain hidden when it is not mediated or understood and – more strongly – it can be *deliberately hidden away*.

Hidden conflict

When Arendt talks about the light of the public realm she does so in the context of a discussion of what she calls 'dark times'. These are times of offences without outrage, times when the light of publicity is extinguished by 'credibility gaps' and 'invisible government', by speech that does not disclose what is but sweeps it under the carpet, by exhortations, moral and otherwise, that, under the pretext of upholding old truths, degrade all truth to meaningless triviality (Arendt 1973a: 8). There is darkness when the light is prevented from falling onto certain affairs. There are three clusters of ways in which affairs such as conflict are either kept or pushed into the darkness, so they might remain hidden from the light of the public realm.

The *first cluster* involves lack of mediation. Here then, there is a failure of the necessary condition of the appearance of an 'affair of men' in the public realm. One set of reasons for the lack of mediation is obvious; the simple absence of media institutions from the time and place of a specific 'affair of men'. Even if McLuhan had a point when he spoke about the 'global village', nevertheless some places in the village are more able to appear in the public sphere than others. The global village has its squires and peasants. The difference is made by a mixture of the frequently imperial history of institutional ties between the metropolitan homes of media institutions and the peripheries, as well as the involvement of places in global economic flows and exchanges. Quite simply, if there is no history continuing in one form or another in the present or profit to be exploited, it is unlikely that media institutions will be present in a place. Therefore the affairs in such a place will not be subjected to the light of the public realm. The affairs might, possibly, appear locally but they will not appear before media audiences distant from those places. Consequently those affairs will remain hidden from view. But the lack of mediation can be deliberate; affairs can be *made to be* hidden. This happens in a variety of ways: imposed censorship, what Orwell called 'self-censorship' which is voluntary and performed by media institutions on themselves so as not to upset the powerful or co-optation (Orwell 2000). The last of these forms of something being hidden involves making media institutions dependent upon state actors and the best example of this is the strategy which the American and British military introduced in 2003 during the Iraq War of 'embedding' journalists in the armed forces so their own well-being became dependent upon that of the units upon whom they were reporting.

Of course, with the development of campaigning groups upholding the imaginary's social question of opposition to suffering, combined with cheap hand-held technologies and the internet, censorship is harder than before. States might well wish to keep certain affairs hidden from the public realm, states might well wish to consign some affairs to absolute darkness, but success cannot be guaranteed. On the one hand there is now a multiplicity of groups with access to news gathering and communication sources of their own and, secondly, the technologically enabled emergence of 'citizen journalists' has punctured the monopoly on access to information once enjoyed by accredited professionals. But even in these circumstances, when an affair ceases to be hidden there can still be darkness. This is the core of the second cluster of ways how the light of the public realm can be darkened.

In this *second cluster*, if an affair is pulled into the light it is possible to create what Arendt calls 'credibility gaps' around the meaning of what appears and this can be done through the spread of interpretive confusion. For example, in May 2004 a series of photographs appeared evidently showing a British soldier urinating on and then kicking a hooded Iraqi prisoner. It was immediately conceded by the British authorities that what the photographs showed was indeed terrible, *if* the photographs truly showed what they appeared to show. The terms of the debate then quickly shifted from the abuse of prisoners of war to very technical questions about veracity. In fairly quick time the British press was publishing articles about how British soldiers lace their boots and how rifles get scratched in combat. The visibility of the photographs in the public realm was unsettled because they were made to be confusing. In the end, it was announced that the photographs could be proved to be fake because the incidents they show take place in a kind of truck that was not in Iraq at that time (the point being that nobody can possibly contradict this contention). Another argument was floated: the photographs show a hooded man being beaten, but the British army has banned hooding, therefore it does not have hoods to put over prisoner's heads, therefore the photographs can only possibly show the actions of a few rogue elements in the army (Tester 2005; Watt and Norton-Taylor 2004). Either way nothing is exactly what it appears to be and so precisely what we are discussing becomes unstable and uncertain.

This little story of Iraqi prisoners being beaten – or not – by British troops is an example of the broader processes of what the sociologist Stanley Cohen has called *denial*. Through the 1990s Cohen worked with human rights groups in Israel and played an important role in bringing to light human rights abuses perpetrated by the Israeli security forces. He helped publicise testimonies, wrote reports and ensured they all got public attention. But what happened was not what Cohen expected. In terms of the normative political theory of the public realm, the information about human rights abuses ought to have caused outrage and the application of considerable pressure on the Israeli state. What happened instead was widespread *denial*. Looking back on the experience of the groups with which he worked Cohen said: 'we were immediately thrown into the politics of denial. The official and mainstream response was venomous: *outright denial* (it doesn't happen); *discrediting* (the organisation was biased, manipulated or gullible); renaming (yes, something does happen, but it is not torture); and *justification* (anyway, it was morally justified). Liberals were uneasy and concerned. Yet there was no outrage' (Cohen 2000: xi).

This is precisely the kind of situation Arendt calls 'dark times' and through Cohen it is possible to see where these times lead. They lead to silence; even if an affair is present in the public realm, it remains hidden because it is not transformed into something we share in common. Quite simply when the meaning of the affair is confused through either complications of interpretation, or denial of the sorts Cohen talks about, what becomes visible is the uncertainty about what the affair is, means or entails, and what the affair actually involves (for example human rights abuses) becomes sidelined. 'Soon a tone of acceptance began to be heard. Abuses were intrinsic to the situation: there was nothing to be done till a political solution was found; something like torture might even be necessary sometimes; anyway, we don't want to keep being told about this all the time' (Cohen 2000: xi). If Cohen is right, it is necessary for us to put ourselves back into the picture, just as Manet pushes his viewer into the frame. If these are indeed dark times in which the light fails to fall on certain affairs, and if therefore it is possible for conflict and its human consequences to remain or be hidden away, we need to think about our personal and individual responsibility for allowing such a situation to prevail. More precisely we need honestly to think about whether we are more concerned with an easy life than a human world.

The return to Manet's question points to the *third* cluster of ways in which affairs might be kept in the dark. Now the situation is more complex because it is necessary to wonder whether affairs might be hidden all the more they are pulled into the light. It is the kind of problem explored by Edgar Allen Poe in his story *The Purloined Letter*, which shows how the most effective way of hiding something is to put it where everyone can see it. For example, Manet's painting of the execution of Maximilian is so well known it is actually incredibly easy to miss the shadow in the bottom right or, if it is noticed, to think of it purely as a formal property of the representation, there to serve some aesthetic purpose alone. The painting is so familiar it's interrogation of the viewer can be missed even as Manet wants it to scream out.

Something similar can happen to news of conflict. Much of the coverage tends to be generic, and consequently the specificity of the conflict and its consequences can be ignored, hidden. In terms of narrative this is one product of changes within media institutions and in particular the replacement of local with thematic expertise. Much of the time media professionals are sent to a conflict zone with little or no deep background knowledge, and inevitably therefore they tend to draw on conventional narrative or representational methods. This leads to the situation in which famine reports, for example, tend to follow a conventional 'morality play' narrative, moving from the initial disaster through the failure of local relief efforts to the success against the odds of Western aid agencies (Hammock and Charny 1996). Consequently, however visible the report might be and however much it is discussed, the specificity of the affair can be hidden. One sign of this is the extent to which there is a media category of 'Africa' as a place which is internally homogeneous and wrecked by conflict, poverty and famine, a category actually as out of kilter with what goes on in the continent as talk of 'Europe' would be unable to capture the differences between, say, the United Kingdom and Holland. Yet charity campaigns make this 'Africa' very visible, thus effectively hiding away Nigeria or Mozambique or wherever. The tendency is exacerbated by the extent to which this media coverage tends to reinforce morality play narratives with generic representation. For example, it is only necessary to think of the phrase 'African famine' to picture in one's mind a range of conventional representations which, once again, serve to hide even as they make visible. The conventional repertoire of images hides the affair in two ways. First of all they are so familiar they communicate in advance what they mean and therefore the specific details need never be considered. Second, because the repertoire has become so generic it implies a certain naturalness about what it purports to show (it is 'natural' for African children to have flies round their eyes), and therefore there is a short-circuiting of the chance of political engagement with the affair itself. The very obviousness of the narratives and representations, their very predictability, makes it possible for conflict to be shared in common, for conflict to be encountered as a reality of the world, without needing to attend to *this* suffering or *that* conflict. *This* suffering, and *that* conflict, become just aspects of how things are, things about which nothing can be done.

In this third cluster then, affairs like conflict and their consequences are hidden away even as they are extremely visible. Like Poe's stolen letter they are hidden, even as – or perhaps it is better to say *precisely because* – they are right in front of us all of the time.

Conclusion

Is this all a counsel of despair? Is the affair of conflict and its human consequences *fated* to be hidden, even as it might be extremely visible? Is the situation one in which an affair does not need to be hidden away because its very illumination casts it into darkness? Not necessarily.

An earlier version of this paper was prepared for a seminar at the Noorderlicht 'Human Conditions' Photofestival in Groningen in 2009. The festival is an annual event, and a major world forum for the presentation and discussion of documentary photography. In 2009 the focus of the exhibition was on the conflicts in the world which remain hidden from Western concern either because they do not fit the 'imaginary' or because they are hidden away. The curators set themselves an ambitious task: 'it is possible to address our understanding and our humanity by making photography personal and providing access to the agony people experience on an everyday level'. They hoped: 'In this way the viewer is brought into contact with the "other", in a manner which underscores that the other is just as much a human being as the viewer is' (Broekhuis *et al.* 2009: 9). The exhibitions succeeded because they consistently focused on individual humans who are marginalised because of their 'otherness', who are forced to suffer the trauma of war, live in slums, work in the sex industries. Throughout there was a focus on the eyes of these men, women and children, a focus on the human in its socially constructed environment. Somehow the photographs managed to convey the gulf between the human condition of these people, and their equally human hopes and aspirations. In this way they spoke to affluent Western viewers in a way guaranteed to hit home. The photographs in the Festival did what Manet's painting did. They posed a question to the viewer about whether we who were not there, we who are not implicated directly in these affairs, we who are bystanders, will make these conflict part of our world and thus prevent them from being hidden. The photographs threw down the challenge in a number of ways.

First of all, there was an emphasis upon situation within conflict zones. The camera operator is literally put into the picture to show what would otherwise be hidden away by censorship and denial; we can see that children and not 'insurgents' are destroyed by aerial bombardments. The contingency of this showing is highlighted by the ubiquity of the destruction contextualising it.

Second, the photographs showed how suffering is scratched into the faces of its victims long after conflict has ended, indeed even if there has been no obvious affair of conflict likely to enter into the public realm. Suffering lasts longer than its media coverage. It demands reparation over a time frame longer than the media allow.[1]

Third, to be human is to be social, it is to share with others and be together with them. The more togetherness, the more humanity in the world. But what if the need to share and be together is rejected? What if the hand held out in need or friendship is spurned because it does not fit with social expectations? The exhibition showed the human face of rejection, making the viewer wonder about personal culpability for this turning away from the humanity of others and, thereby, the diminishing of the humanity of one's self.

Fourth, both visibility and hiding presuppose there is something to be visible or hidden. But what if conflict means complete absence? What if the human face of suffering is, in the final instance, the effacement of the face? What does absence mean and is presence itself utterly contingent on tides and times, which can sweep over the face of suffering without taking it into account?

Finally, in view of the extent to which we in this room are beneficiaries of military hardware, which ensure conflict never comes here, never visits our European homes as it has visited homes in Gaza, do we need to stop thinking of ourselves as bystanders? Is it just an easy excuse to call ourselves bystanders? Do we need instead to accept the dreadful reality of our profit from – and complicity in – conflict? Yet what does complicity mean this these circumstances? Is this the ultimate absurdity confronting the enthusiastic upholders of an imaginary establishing the offensiveness of affairs of conflict and their human consequences?

These are some of the questions, which the 2009 Noorderlicht Photo-festival raised. This is how the exhibition made photography personal. Thinking through the challenge of these questions is the first step towards illumination: illumination of conflict, its human face and, finally, what we are going to do about making the suffering of others visible *and* real.

Note

1 However, this point raises a wider question beyond the scope of this chapter. Photographs endure over time and certainly they endure relative to more fleeting television coverage. But does this consign photographs to a status of being 'instant history' which can be viewed and then filed away by the viewer as 'from the past'? Furthermore, if photographs are going to be able to endure they need to be put in an archival space, which will allow for their permanence. If the space is the gallery then a problem arises because galleries are more likely to be used by some social groups than others and consequently their status as things between us is constructed by a very limited if not self-selecting 'us'. If the space is the Internet the photographs are unable to compel their viewing and they become just one more possibility available to the individualised cyberspace traveller. So a final point emerges here: since the viewers of photographs are also the viewers of television, do they possess the ability to engage with a still photograph over time? Has the act of viewing been 'de-skilled' in a culture characteriSed by the quick passage of images?

References

Arendt, Hannah (1958) *The Human Condition*, New York: Doubleday.
Arendt, Hannah (1973a) *Men in Dark Times*, Harmondsworth: Penguin.

Arendt, Hannah (1973b) *On Revolution*, Harmondsworth: Penguin.

Broekhuis, T., Wim, M., Irene, K. and Gerben, B. (2009) *Human Conditions*, Groningen: Stichting Aurora Borealis and the Noorderlicht Photography Foundation.

Cohen, Stanley (2000) *States of Denial: Knowing About Atrrocities and Suffering*, Cambridge: Polity.

Elderfield, John (2006) *Manet and the Execution of Maximilian*, New York: Museum of Modern Art.

Hammock, J. C. and Joel, R. C, (1996) Emergency Response as Morality Play: The Media, the Relief Agencies, and the Need for Capacity Building in Rotberg, R. I. and Weiss, T. G. (eds) *From Massacres to Genocide: The Media, Public Policy, and Humanitarian Crises*, Washington, DC: Brookings Institution.

Orwell, George (2000) 'Preface' in *Animal Farm*, Harmondsworth: Penguin.

Silverstone, Roger (2007) *Media and Morality: On the Rise of the Mediapolis*, Cambridge: Polity.

Taylor, Charles (2007) *A Secular Age*, Cambridge Mass: Harvard University Press.

Tester, Keith (2005) Reflections on the Abu Ghraib Photographs, *Journal of Human Rights*, 4(1), 137–44.

Tester, Keith (2010a) Multiculturalism, Catholicism and Us, *New Blackfriars*, vol. 91, no. 1036, 665–76.

Tester, Keith (2010b) *Humanitarianism and Modern Culture*, University Park: Penn State University Press.

Watt, N. and Richard, N.-T. (2004) Troops broke the law, admits Hoon, *Guardian*, 11 May.

6 The ethics of remembering

Little Big Man and the exoneration of American guilt

James Aston

Introduction: the Western as American history

Andre Bazin reinvigorated the cultural form of the Western by declaring that it was 'the American cinema par excellence' (Lovell 1976: 166). For Bazin, the Western expressed 'evocations of the birth of the United States of America' (Bazin 1973: 14) that forged not only a worldwide appreciation of its composition, but also articulated the core elements of cinema in an epic form that spoke persuasively about American identity, memory of the past and the embattled and protean nature of American national and political consciousness. Therefore, the West, or more specifically the Western Frontier, acted as a metaphorical terrain that situated the new personality and character of the American pioneer within the divine providence of a new land, whose symbolic function it was to forge a 'new' nation unfettered by the shackles of the 'old' history of Europe. Thus, the frontier encapsulated this new America with its vast untamed and savage wilderness, suggesting the freedom of an untapped and virgin land, in which the crucible of a new civilisation could be formed.

Primarily, this mission lay with the solipsistic individuality of the frontiersman, an amalgamation of various archetypes[1] whose common attributes of heroism, patriotism, independence, self-governance, honour and integrity were underlined with a powerful association of a regenerative and redemptive violence that ensured the twin precepts of progress and success were enabled, and upheld in the conquering and settlement of the West.

Hollywood quickly utilised the potential that the West held in terms of articulating strong and clear notions of a desirable American identity and of forwarding a sanctified and mythologised American past. Westerns, such as *Stagecoach* (1939), *Dodge City* (1939), *Santa Fe Trail* (1940) and *They Died with Their Boots On* (1941), all portrayed a romantic, idealised society replete with technological expertise, military might and an agrarian American pastoral inhabited with a range of individuals from General Custer to Jesse James who underlined the 'Americanised' individual as one of ingenuity, resolve, honour and heroism. The mythic and idealised notion of a typical American identity mapped out in these early archetypal films was further ossified in subsequent Westerns such as *High Noon* (1952), *Shane (1953)* and *The Magnificent Seven* (1960), which provided audiences with recurring generic codes and conventions that advanced powerful and deeply held socio-political values that centred on traditional concepts of what constituted a typical American individual.

However, due to the tumultuous socio-political landscape of America in the 1960s that was characterised by political assassinations, the Civil Rights Movement, domestic unrest and the war in Vietnam, the traditional and dominant cultural expressions of a desirable American identity became untenable. The strict Manichean borders between good and evil, and the Self and the Other, that were previously applied to cultural representations began to break down in the wake of Martin Luther King's and Robert Kennedy's assassination in 1968, reports of atrocities being committed by US soldiers in Vietnam and the growing distrust over leaders such as Lyndon Johnson and Richard Nixon. The result was a crisis in confidence over cultural forms that enabled alternative representational strategies to emerge. One such outlet was New Hollywood[2] which, in the studios attempt to reconnect with an ever disillusioned younger audience, permitted narratives of not only a more sexual and violent nature to be realised, but also enabled alternative cultural representations to be forwarded. In many ways this characterised a revisionist cinema in that dominate narratives and cherished myths were undermined in a range of genres from the war film to the film noir and the gangster film. It was, however, the Western that best encapsulated the revisionist form in its dismantling of dominant images and narratives set by Hollywood and which resonated powerfully within the American popular consciousness.

A key example of New Hollywood's revisionist Western cinema was *Little Big Man*, in that the film both undermined traditional and dominant cultural expressions and pointedly addressed the socio-political landscape of America in the late 1960s and early 1970s. That is to say, central to *Little Big Man*'s representational strategies is an interrogation of American identity that was under threat in both cultural and political realms at the time. Therefore, the film serves as a useful example, with which to examine, how cultural texts respond to traumatic historical events, and how the resultant narratives make sense of complex, contested and controversial understandings of the American past, and notions of American identity that are being articulated at the time. In particular, this article will analyse how American identity is depicted in the film, in terms of how it acts as a mechanism to critique both the United States Cavalry's treatment of the Native American and the US Army's actions in Vietnam, while conterminously exonerating a 'typical' white American identity from guilt or complicity in the actions of either. Or, to put it another way, how in portraying the genocide of the Native American as a lamentation on their disappearance from the American West *Little Big Man* exculpates white America's

guilt and burden of that history, while conterminously forging direct associations with the war in Vietnam and the huge loss of life experienced by
the indigenous populations of South-East Asia. Both these elements of
Little Big Man have important repercussions, in judging, how effective revisionist or alternative historical narratives were, in challenging dominant
cultural forms, and their usefulness in shaping socio-political discourse in
late 1960s and early 1970s American society.

The road to Vietnam

Traditionally the Western was associated with conservative cultural and
political values that particularly in post-World War II America combined
the historical with the mythical to meld 'discussions of imperialism onto
assertions of the power and sanctity of the individual' (Corkin 2004:3) that
legitimised a nationalist sentiment with regards to unsettled and potentially threatening foreign lands. Films such as *The Magnificent Seven*, *The
Alamo* (both 1960), and to an extent the pre-1960 films of John Ford, ideologically adjusted to the new concepts of national definition in order to
account for the United States emergent role as a superpower during the
era of the Cold War with the former Soviet Russia. Thus, the Western promoted 'particular constructions of national identity in a period marked by
intense chauvinism and broad acceptance of a kind of economic and cultural hegemony' (Corkin 2004:5) that produced, however speculatively, a
conservative and traditional representation of the West and the American
individual. If the road to Vietnam was indeed a long, winding path on the
American cultural landscape, prefigured by films such as *Broken Arrow*
(1950), *Apache* (1954), *Cheyenne Autumn* (1964) and *Major Dundee* (1965),
that deliberately sought a re-negotiation with the mythological imagining
of the West, in terms of its frontier history and the merits of conquest and
progress, it was not until the late 1960s that this articulation was given full
form and meaning in a series of films labelled revisionist, anti, or Vietnam
Westerns.

The culmination of political violence and divisiveness over Vietnam
reached its nadir in 1970 with Nixon's televised announcement in April
that US forces had invaded Cambodia contradicting the former de-
escalation pledge of the government. The invasion and widespread
bombing of Cambodia, enforced with a political and nationalist rhetoric
that singled out America, as a 'great institution', emblazoned with freedom
and democracy that was being threatened from 'within and without'
(Hoberman 2003: 273) explicitly stated that it was in the national purpose
and character of the 'true' and 'real' America to prevail. Nixon articulated
Cambodia as an arena that America must emerge from victorious, otherwise both the position of the United States as 'the world's most powerful
nation' and its 'proud hundred-and-ninety-year history' (Hoberman 2003:
274) was at threat. Nowhere, before or after, in the Vietnam War was the

national definition of the United States so forcibly elucidated. Although it would be misleading to claim that a majority of the population reneged on Nixon's nationalist direction and consciousness, there was a rejection of Nixon's assertion of a proud, uncomplicated and self-serving history with a moral and noble crusade in South-East Asia in America's universities, and it found cultural expression through the Hollywood Western. The campus revolts of 1970 stand as a bloody testament to the dissent and divisiveness waged on the political battlefield between students, the counterculture, the New Left, and increasing numbers of unlikely protesters found among the ranks of soldiers and housewives with the dominant social and political institutions of America. Although this rebellion, that culminated in the Kent State shootings in May instigating the shutdown of 536 campuses nationwide and initiating various mass attended demonstrations, has been credited with curtailing the government's mission in South-East Asia by such writers as Tom Wells (1994) and Todd Gitlin (1987), the concurrent production of revisionist cultural forms, of which the Western was one of its more prevalent expressions, is a less unequivocal and positive outcome.

If the Vietnam War had rendered impossible any representation of American history in terms of a simple, natural triumph, then the Western addressed this crisis in representation through the central theme of the Native American. The dominant view of pre-1960s Westerns that situated the Native American as 'irreconcilable savages whose destruction was perhaps unfortunate but in any case unavoidable' (Worland and Countryman 1998:187) was inverted as a justification for the inevitable formation of American civilisation toward a more sympathetic and positive view of the Native American that segued, in the ambiguous and contested era of the Vietnam conflict, into a critique of 'everything imperialistic and genocidal about America' (Worland & Countryman 1998:187). The revisionist Western, according to Armando José Prats in his book *Invisible Natives*, is a 'near-doctrinal system of iconography and ideology, of narrative tropes and generic types that articulates the *reaction against* the Myth of Conquest' (Prats 2002: 127). Prats' understanding of the Myth of Conquest draws upon Slotkin's Myth of the Frontier that views white America's confrontations with Indian barbarism and lack of civilisation as a natural and inevitable predication of frontier experience and progress (Slotkin 1998). These events, which acted as the 'historical' foundation of the pre-1960s Indian Western, have come to stand in for the very experiences and accounts of frontier history themselves. Rather than blithely accepting or dismissing such representations, especially those originating from Hollywood, Prats instead suggests that the evocation of the Myth of Conquest be analysed in terms of what it articulates about the American frontier history, the 'vanishment' of the Indian as judgment on white culture, the typical American identity, and how and what it communicates to the present about traumatic events. The importance of Prats' work and his engagement with the mythical constructs of the Western, especially with regard to the binarism of 'white' versus 'red', is that he offers a framework with which to analyse the construction of white identity. For Prats, a revisionist Western like *Little Big Man* should not egregiously be seen as a 'good' alternative to the 'bad' history of the Indian Western, but a continuation of America's struggle to delineate a desirable and useable archetype of American individualism and identity in the face of the burden and guilt of its past, and conflicts and crises in the present.

Little Big Man and the revisioning of the West

The novel *Little Big Man* written by Thomas Berger and published in 1964 is one of many literary adaptations to form the revisionist canon of Indian films in the late 1960s and early 1970s that continued unabated regardless of the ideological orientation and political motivations of the films. The book follows the picaresque travails of Jack Crabb, a 111-year-old man who claims to be the only white survivor from the Battle of Little Big Horn in 1876 where General Custer's 7th Cavalry were massacred by Cheyenne and Sioux warriors. During the course of the book Crabb becomes a surrogate Cheyenne and continually switches between this life and that of white civilization, where he assumes a number of roles including gunslinger, mule-skinner, gambler and drunkard. The Cheyenne life is presented throughout with a violent denouement, as if to suggest a way of life that is in a continual state of disappearance or extinction, while Crabb's encounters with the white world introduce to him the untenability of realising a decent quality of life and finally discouraging him from finding a 'decent and honourable solution to the conflict between the Indian and white' (Hitt 1990: 103).

Arthur Penn's cinematic adaptation of the book, written by *Paths Of Glory* (1957) and *The Graduate* (1967) screenwriter Calder Willingham, is in many ways adherent to the book's general thematic concerns bar two important and distinct areas. First, Penn's portrayal of the Cheyenne is less ambiguous and 'purer' than in the novel, so as to heighten the parallels 'with the treatment by the United States government of the American Indian with [the US] government's involvement in the Vietnam War,' as well strengthening the film's condemnation of the 'forces that caused that way of life to vanish – racial intolerance, capitalism, [and] environmental plunder' (Kasdan and Tavernetti 1998: 131). The representation of the Native Americans speaks to the present in another way also, in that they 'represent the fashions and mores of the 1960s counterculture, practices that included a return to the land, experimentation with alternative lifestyles, communal living, sexual freedom and search for peace and harmony' (Slotkin 1998: 631). The Cheyenne thus become a visual 'fulfillment of the counterculture's vision of a sexually, spiritually, and (consequently) politically liberated society' (Slotkin 1998: 631). The second connected point to the representation of the Cheyenne is how it is contrasted to that of white civilisation. Although in the novel white society is seen as flawed, and the white man as destructive rather than a beneficial presence on the West, in the film this animus is further buttressed by caricaturing the entire structures of white society as 'disordered, hypocritical, self-seeking, nihilistic; people [who] live in constant fear and tension and project their hatreds and insecurity on to their enemies' (French 1971: 102). In the film life among the whites is portrayed as deceitful and synthetic by pointedly contrasting them against the Cheyenne, who in both the novel and film refer to themselves as 'human beings' and are consistently seen as natural and kind with a strong moral and spiritual outlook. But perhaps the most drastic alteration of a white figure in the film is that of General George Armstrong Custer. Berger's novel presents him as a man of 'splendid paradoxes – compassionate yet odious, brilliant yet vain, impatient yet magnanimous, rational yet cruel' (Hitt 1990: 106). Conversely, the film dispenses with any discrepancy to present Custer as a comic, one dimensional, vainglorious, semi-crazed, fully fledged psychotic who sees a victory at the Battle of Little Big Horn as his ascension to the presidency of the United States. The ensuing defeat and his death is seen as wholly justified on past actions against the Indian of which the massacre of Cheyenne at Washita (1868) stands as his most ignoble and cruel 'victory'.

The first half of the film is a picaresque vaudeville featuring episodic comedic vignettes that deconstruct the typical Western hero. Jack's adventures with the Cheyenne and white society provide an almost Zelig[3] like character at once removed from his surroundings and yet an infallible commentator on the history of the West. In these early travails, Penn sets up established and dominant themes of the mythology of the West, in order to succinctly dismantle and undermine their centrality as foundational elements of the Frontier, national direction and American identity. Critiquing Puritanical Christianity, entrepreneurial and capitalist adventurism, and the legend of the gunfighter, Penn assuredly, and comically, positions alternative representations that instil within the viewer the idea that the conventions, iconography, and values that have been enmeshed within the cinematic narratives of the Hollywood Western are, if not outright fabrications, certainly not as straightforward or as affirmative, as the cultural heritage of the Western have previously specified.

Thus, *Little Big Man*'s first half is a miasmic indictment of many of the originating and sustaining myths of the American past and identity that have formed through cultural sites such as literature, movies and the museum. These unlived and indirectly experienced memories have, for Penn, become a debilitating understanding on both the present and past America. In this section of the film, *Little Big Man* constructs a recognisable view of the tenets of the American frontier and the people who inhabited it only then to depict them as deeply flawed or fallacious representations that Hollywood has to a large extent fortified and repeated, so that they take on the countenance of an actual lived experience or definable reality. For Penn, their mythical construction is not to say that they did not happen at all – they do reveal an underlying and timeless significance of an event or person, and are thus not outright falsifications, but a mythical development of reality that has come to stand in for any accurate or authentic representation of the West. Thus, Penn explores the past interpreted through Western films as a popular expression of the time in which they were made, demonstrating that in an age marked by political assassination, the civil rights struggle, inner-city riots, anti-war demonstrations, generational conflict and the war in Vietnam, these previously held and cherished representations are no longer tenable. It is with the introduction of General Custer and the ensuing three massacre sequences in the second half of the film, that Penn's treatise on the American frontier and individualism is taken to its conclusion. However, rather than expand on his playful retelling of the West, Penn turns toward a more angry and cynical examination of the treatment of the Cheyenne at the hands of the white man that adheres to a simple and crass binarism of 'good' versus 'bad', which undermines the deconstruction of American identity and foundational myths undertaken in the first half of the film. Instead, Penn resituates a superior white American identity and the twin myths of progress and conquest. This, in turn, has a detrimental effect on the critique of the genocidal practises of Custer's 7th Cavalry that *Little Big Man* posits in the second half.

The tone of *Little Big Man* shifts profoundly in its second hour from a ribald and comic adventurism to a bitter indictment of American imperialism and the genocidal tactics of the United States Cavalry. The shift in tone is marked by three massacre sequences, the first of which follows Jack's first experience with the Cavalry after he is hired by Custer as a mule skinner. Jack's ulterior motive is to search for his Swedish wife Olga who has been captured by the Pawnee and under this covert mission he accompanies the Cavalry on an attack on a Pawnee tribe. It is in this sequence that Jack, and the audience, becomes explicitly aware that *Little Big Man*'s cavalry is not the Fordian image of a benevolent and heroic force that has been inculcated within American popular culture but a racist, bloodthirsty and vengeful gang. The scene deliberately sets up a binary between an uncontrolled and marauding violence perpetuated by the soldiers and the indigenous, peaceful and natural existence of the Indian. A binary that continues to Custer's defeat at Little Big Horn and provides a problematic representational strategy in that the Indians assume the role of a passive cipher whereby they 'stand-in' for some other group or concern that the film seems intent of making; in this instance, the indigenous Vietnamese people and American military involvement in South-East Asia.

Richard Maltby described this functioning of the Native American in the Hollywood Western as that of an 'empty signifier' (Maltby, 1996: 49)

that excludes them from any discourse on matters contingent with historical and social configurations. Steve Neale presciently points out that other
ethnic groups do not act as stand-ins for other marginalised races or cultures, such as the Japanese and African-Americans in Hollywood films of
the 1940s, 1950s and early 1960s. Neale posits an explanation predicated
on the 'pastness' of films representing the Indian that precludes any contemporary analysis both of the Indians themselves, and their relationship
and interaction with white America. Prats expands on Neale's position by
stating that the Indian is at once an 'imminent presence and a virtual
absence' (Prats 2002: 11), in that the Hollywood Western represents the
Indian, and yet does not *present* him as an autonomous subject capable of
articulating his own cultural heritage, history and identity, so that it is left
to the 'white man's remembrance' (Prats 2002: 131) to give form to, and
understanding of the Indian. Prats comments that this is axiomatic in a
revisionist Western like *Little Big Man* and has the consequence of solicit-
ing an "exemption of its white hero," in this case Jack Crabb, whose 'self-
proclaimed Otherness demands a compensatory dispensation from the
guilt of Conquest' (Prats 2002: 131–2). Prats' notion of the Myth of Conquest is evidenced most pertinently in the second massacre sequence,
which features the Battle of Washita in 1868 in which Custer's 7th Cavalry
attacked a Cheyenne settlement. This particular scene highlights the
Indian as stand-in and the white hero's removal from the atrocity committed by the cavalry by validating Jack's views and actions as the 'true' path
of white America. The scene also draws direct parallels with Mylai that not
only exculpates guilt over American atrocities committed in Vietnam, but
repositions the 'typical' American so central to the shaping of American
identity.

The Mylai/Washita massacres and the exoneration of American guilt

The details of Mylai were made public in November 1969, when investigative journalist Seymour Hersh uncovered an internal Army investigation
into an incident in March 1968, where an American infantry division
'deliberately wiped out nearly an entire village, including old men, women
and children' (Slotkin 1998: 581). Photographs of the massacre taken by
company photographer Ronald Haeberle were published by *Life* magazine, producing a powerful psychic impact on American popular consciousness that resulted in instilling a crisis of meaning surrounding the
war in Vietnam. The mythology of the Frontier had been applied to
Vietnam, with its tenets of providing freedom and democracy for the
South Vietnamese people, and utilised the conquest myth to legitimise the
notion of creating an 'Americanised' civilisation, similar in theory to that
of the West becoming untenable in the face of the realisation, and that
atrocities may have been committed by the protectors and liberators,

which the American troops were positioned as endorsing. *Life*'s presentation of the story serves as an instructive comparison with the Washita sequence in *Little Big Man*, primarily because it was the first mass mediated exposure of the atrocity, and was thus the first experiential site with which Americans engaged with the issue. Slotkin also describes the 'quasi-cinematic narrative' of the article, that through the positioning and order of the photographs taken by Haeberle and the adjoining text that offers no authoritative or 'omniscient narrator' (Slotkin 1998: 582), strongly situates the reader as constructer of the article, whereupon the meaning is derived from a reader/text interface, as it does generally in cinematic narratives. For Slotkin, the outcome of this arrangement is to make the 'reader feel responsible for and implicated in the outcome' (Slotkin 1998: 582) of the atrocity committed in Mylai. Therefore, by designing the narrative thus, the effect is to inflect and influence one's subjective reasoning of the event that pointedly locates the reader as complicit in the action. In doing so the Myth of Conquest is inverted. The notion of a just and noble 'typical' American, as both rescuer and protector is rendered obsolete, as *Life*'s climactic segment of its atrocity narrative reaches its conclusion, stating unequivocally that the actions of American soldiers at Mylai 'crossed-over' in their indiscriminate killings of women and children to that of the 'savage'. Mylai symbolically altered the terrain of the Myth of Conquest and through the media's representation of the event inverted the normative expectations held about American soldiers and, by extension, if the power of *Life*'s article is not to be diminished, 'typical' American people, so that attributes of heroism, self-governance, honour and integrity, combined with a regenerative and redemptive violence, that acted as precepts in the conquering and settlement of the West, were now thrown into a crisis of (mythological) representation. After Mylai, Slotkin highlights that the Myth of the Frontier had to be reformulated, so as to identify '*ourselves* as Indian' whereby the 'mission now became one of rescuing Vietnam from "us," or (better) of rescuing us from ourselves, by finding a "cure" for the "American Madness"' (Slotkin 1998: 582) that the atrocity at Mylai had evoked.

The Massacre at Washita in *Little Big Man* draws explicit visual connections to Mylai as Penn used extras in the scene of a Vietnamese and Chinese origin. For some, the verisimilitude of the scene provided a stark connection with the conflict in South-East Asia, with the Hollywood Reporter declaring that it looked 'like the 6 P.M. news footage from Vietnam' (Cook 2002: 74–5). Jack is firmly identified as an 'Indian' in this scene that shows him as a trusted member of the tribe, as well as focusing on his duties as a father and husband to his Indian bride and child. The action is predominantly shown through Jack's point of view, as he escapes with Old Lodge Skins and watches the massacre unfold from a position removed from the immediacy of the violence on the other side of a river. Jack watches impotently as the indiscriminate killing committed by

Custer's 7th Cavalry culminates in the brutal murder of his wife Sunshine and their daughter. If *Life*'s article sought to instill a sense of complicity within the reader, in order to evoke a sense of disillusionment over the war in Vietnam and anger at the violence and killing done in the name of all Americans, then this sequence of *Little Big Man* seeks to reconstitute the 'typical' American rent asunder by Mylai and, albeit implicitly, forward a just and valorous Myth of Conquest. Although Jack becomes an 'Indian' he is never truly one of them during the film and in the Washita scene he is separated and distanced from the villages. Jack's position, while suggesting privilege, also signifies exemption, both toward the barbaric action of the Cavalry, and from the 'already vestigial, ephemeral, vanished' (Prats 2002: 155) Indian. Jack is not so much the last Indian but the first American, a newly formed Adam, absolved from the national conscience by being presented as the 'definitive and irrecusable *American*, fully and uniquely so, because he has been somehow cleansed of sins committed against the Indian *in the name of America*' (Prats 2002: 136). The fact that Jack has to swim through the river to escape is symbolic of his rebirth, his baptism as a new 'typical' American. America can now begin in him 'not again or anew but *absolutely*, as if without a past' (Prats 2002: 247). This is explicitly voiced through Jack's indictment of the savagery of the American military, and thus the 'bad' American, when he shouts at Old Lodge Skins 'Do you hate *them* now?'

If Jack's new identity is formed through the dehistorised placement of the Native American as a vessel for another race and through a representation of history as one in which the Native American is defined by its disappearance, then it is exacerbated by the binary opposition that Custer, as symbolic figure of the 'old' identity, inhabits. Custer first appears in *Little Big Man* in a broadly comic vignette featuring Jack and his first wife Olga. Custer's presence is informative in this scene, as Penn frames him from below as he sits upon his horse with the glow of the sun behind him to demonstrate a heroic and authoritative figure, the halo caused by the sun signifying Custer, as a preordained leader of the people here, both to assure a safe passage, and to tame and make safe the uncivilised land of the Frontier. In the next scene Penn immediately contradicts this established and popular figure of Custer as a positive legacy and superior force in the epic saga of the West by having him pompously declare to a distraught and inconsolable Olga that she has 'nothing to fear from the Indians; I give you my personal guarantee'. Needless to say, in the next scene, in a parody of John Ford's *Stagecoach*, she is captured by the Pawnee. Jack's insistence on finding his wife initiates a juxtaposition to his life with the Cheyenne, as similarly Jack joins and leaves Custer's army until he finds himself giving advice to Custer on how to approach the battle of Little Big Horn.

The third massacre sequence comprises the last major scene of the film and is a purposefully disorientating segment in which geographical and spatial boundaries are disrupted, less to convey the immediacy of battle, than to highlight the iconicity of the last stand, made famous by Custer at Little Big Horn. The image of the last stand, of an ever diminishing band of soldiers huddled together against the vast numbers of the enemy, is jettisoned, not in favour of a heroic defeat or sacrifice, but more as a plot device to depict the mental breakdown of Custer, as his men and his dreams are finally crushed and defeated. In the scene, as his men are massacred around him, Custer address Jack, who he thinks is President Ulysses S. Grant and whom he berates for being impervious to the military needs of the 7th Cavalry. The scene shows Custer as a caricature, a madman and self-obsessed butcher who has himself finally 'crossed over' into madness and savagery, much as the soldiers at Mylai did. That *Little Big Man* personifies the 'bad' American, as the one dimensional form of General Custer acts to exonerate the reconstituted 'typical' American, inhabited by the character of Jack, from the traumatic burdens of history, by clearly marking him as separate from the actions, behaviour and identity of Custer. In doing so, *Little Big Man* finally declares that there is in fact a distinct and desirable white American individual, which allows the audience to position themselves in the present as a typical American, but also allows them to remove and exonerate themselves from the burden of guilt over American atrocities toward the Native American, as well as toward the policies and actions in Vietnam.

Conclusion

The construction of a 'typical' American is forcibly elucidated in this final massacre sequence and relates back at once to both the concepts of American identity formed in response to the threat of Fascism and Communism during, and after, the Second World War. That is, a positive, heroic and patriotic rediscovery of a typical American identity promoted in direct opposition of the radical politics, ideology and character of Fascism and Communism that threatened to breach the mainstream political and social arena of America. Similarly, in the case of *Little Big Man* and the war in Vietnam, rather than using the identity of the Native American or the Vietnamese, as a thematic device to suggest and acknowledge how 'other' races and cultures contribute to white America's sense of itself, or at least its 'typical' individual, the film eschews any radical power or political potential over questions of identity and nationhood by situating Jack as a separate, superior and idealised white American. The audience forgets one history, that of violence, conquest and genocide in favour of another less controversial past, which exculpates them from any guilt and wrongdoing. Though this cinematically applied history may not be forced and uniform to the extent that it was applied to an immigrant identity in America during the beginning of the twentieth century it appears, through the film's reassertion of a dominant and oppressive white American identity, to be closer in complexion to Nixon's ideal of a 'true' and 'real' American than any radical politics of identity, history and national direction that was being waged within the university campuses at the time that *Little Big Man* was released (Lovell 1976). In this respect, the film also smoothes over and renders less traumatic and controversial the war in Vietnam and the domestic unrest in America that was reinforced by critical responses at the time of the film's release. For example, of the major magazine and newspaper critics who reviewed *Little Big Man* in 1970 only two, Pauline Kael and Paul Zimmerman of *Newsweek*, drew direct comparisons with the treatment of the Cheyenne in the 1860s and the Vietnamese in the 1960s by the respective US forces of the cavalry and the army. Whether this omission is due to not wanting to provide a connection that would 'expose' the trauma, anxiety and crisis such a relationship would engender or simply because critics were blind to the relationship, remains open to contestation, depending on how one views the cogency of Penn's critique or if indeed the war in Vietnam provided any kind of thematic possibility that could be culturally mined and expressed through the narrative of *Little Big Man*.

As the film ends, Old Lodge Skins prepares to die passing on the code and ways of the Cheyenne culture to Jack saying, that 'there is no other way to deal with the white man. Whatever else you say about them it must be admitted: You cannot get rid of them'. Jack realises that this is true of him also and as Old Lodge Skins lays himself out to die, the film positions Jack as the logical successor to the chief, a man whose experiences with the Indian have enriched and bettered his life, so that he can now go forward, as a central agent in the foundation of a new and just society, with the wisdom he has gleaned from the Cheyenne. In a marked contrast to the book, whereby Old Lodge Skins dies, in the film he is unable to will himself into the afterlife resignedly saying, that 'sometimes the magic works, sometimes it doesn't'. However, despite *Little Big Man*'s sympathetic and pivotal role of the Native American and the intimation at the end that the white man is inextricably bound to the 'other' in the formation of his identity, because the Indian is 'foremost a metaphor' in *Little Big Man* he is thus 'manipulated to address in narratively conventionalised terms' not only the 'shifting historical circumstances, problems and values of dominant white culture' (Worland and Countryman 1998: 188), but to be understood 'according to the [filmmakers] own artistic needs and moral values, rather than in terms of the outlook and desires of the people they profess to know and depict' (Berkhofer, 1979: 103). The film *Little Big Man* also cannot seem to 'get rid of the white man' and in not doing so restores, despite the film's overt myth-debunking, a 'typical' white American identity that it originally sought to examine and undermine.

Notes

1 These include the cowboy, gunfighter, rancher and farmer.
2 New Hollywood cinema is a notoriously difficult term to adequately define. Therefore, in the context of this essay it is confined to the period of Hollywood

filmmaking from 1967–74 that provided alternative industrial, economic, aesthetic and social strategies to dominant Hollywood practices that were in place during the classical period of Hollywood filmmaking.

3 Written and directed by Woody Allen in 1983, *Zelig* is a pseudo-documentary featuring a chameleon-like character who, similar to Forrest Gump, bears witness to many of the major events of the twentieth century.

References

Aldrich, R. (1954) *Apache*. Hecht-Lancaster Productions. USA.

Bazin, A. (1972) *What is Cinema, Volume II*. University of California Press, (1971 1st Printing).

Berkhofer, R. (1979) *The White Man's Indian*. New York: Vintage Books.

Cook, D. (2002) *History of the American Cinema: Volume Nine, Lost Illusions, American Cinema in the Shadow of Watergate and Vietnam, 1970–1979*, University of California Press, 74–5.

Corkin, S. (2004) *Cowboys as Cold Warriors: The Western and U.S. History*, Temple University Press: Philadelphia.

Curtiz, M. (1939) *Dodge City*. Warner Bros. Pictures. USA.

Curtiz, M. (1940) *Santa Fe Trail*. Warner Bros. Pictures. USA

Daves, D. (1950) *Broken Arrow*. Twentieth Century Fox Film Corporation. USA.

Ford, J. (1939) *Stagecoach*. Walter Wangner Productions. USA.

Ford, J. (1964) *Cheyenne Autumn*. Warner Bros. Pictures. USA.

French, P. (1971) 'Review: *Little Big Man*', *Sight and Sound*, Vol. 40, no. 2.

Gitlin, T. (1987) *The Sixties: Years of Hope, Days of Rage*, London: Bantam Books.

Hitt, J. (1990) *The American West from Fiction (1823–1976) into Film (1909–1986)*, London: McFarland & Company, Inc.

Hoberman, J. (2003) *The Dream Life: Movies, Media, and the Mythology of the Sixties*, The New Press: New York.

Kael, P. (1973) Epic and Crumbcrusher, *Deeper into Movies*, Boston: Atlantic Little.

Kasdan, M. and Tavernetti, S. (1998) Native Americans in a Revisionist Western, in Rollins, P. and O'Conner, J. (eds) (1998) *Hollywood's Indian: The Portrayal of the Native American in Film*. University Press of Kentucky.

Lovell, A. (1976) The Western, in *Movies and Methods* [Vol. 1], Nichols, B. (ed.). University of California Press.

Maltby, R. A Better Sense of History: John Ford and the Indians in Cameron I. and Pye D. (eds) (1996) *The Movie Book of the Western*, London: Studio Vista.

Kubrick, S. (1957) *Paths Of Glory*. Harris-Kubrick Productions. USA.

Nichols, M. (1967) *The Graduate*. Embassy Pictures Corporation. USA.

Peckinpah, S. (1965) *Major Dundee*. Columbia Pictures Corporation. USA.

Penn, A. (1970) *Little Big Man*. Cinema Centre Films. USA.

Prats, J. A. (2002) *Invisible Natives: Myth and Identity in the American Western*. Cornell University Press.

Ryan, M. and Kellner, D. (1990) *Camera Politica: The Politics and Ideology of Contemporary Hollywood Film*, Indiana Hollywood Press, p. 19.

Slotkin, R. (1998) *Gunfighter Nation: The Myth of the Frontier in Twentieth-Century America*. University of Oklahoma Press.

Sturges, J. (1960) *The Magnificent Seven*. The Mirisch Corporation. USA.

Walsh, R. (1941) *They Died with Their Boots On*. Warner Bros. Pictures. USA.

Wayne, J. (1960) *The Alamo.* Batjac Productions. USA.

Wells, T. (1994) *The War Within: America's Battle Over Vietnam,* University of California Press.

Worland, R. and Countryman, E. (1998) The New Western American Historiography and the Emergence of the New American Westerns, in Buscombe, E. and Pearson, R. (eds) *Back in the Saddle Again: New Essays on the Western.* London: BFI Publishing.

Zimmerman, P. (1970) How the West Was Lost, *Newsweek.*

7 Loving violence?

The ambiguities of SM imagery in contemporary popular culture

Sarah Harper and Majid Yar

Introduction

It has been noted by numerous commentators that a significant element of contemporary popular culture has been the apparent 'mainstreaming' of explicit sexual imagery and discourse. An integral element within this development is the popular proliferation of imagery using the motifs of Bondage Domination Sadism and Masochism (BDSM). Fashion, advertising, music and the movies have all brought into the cultural mainstream a kind of aestheticised recoding of sex, in which the play of domination and submission take a key role. This would suggest, *prima facie*, that a previously marginalised and stigmatised form of sexual practice has been 'rehabilitated' and brought into the cultural mainstream. However, through an analysis of recent media imagery, it is argued that these popular representations risk blurring the normative boundaries between consensual BDSM 'play' and coercive violence/violation. For example, *Vogue Italia*'s controversial 2006 photospread entitled 'State of Emergency' combines 'BDSM chic' with post 9/11 signifiers of terror and torture, thereby potentially re-inscribing BDSM as a socially and morally dangerous activity.

Mainstream imagery therefore tends to consistently gloss over the centrality of consent in BDSM culture, thereby reinforcing negative stereotypes about the practices and their practitioners. Moreover, we hold that these media representations cannot be understood in isolation. Rather, they inter-connect in a relation of reciprocal influence with other discourses around 'deviant' sexuality, especially the medico-moral and legal discourses. Working together, they perpetuate a confusion of sexual consent and violence, which serves to fuel wider public anxieties about SM as 'deviant' and 'perverted', and supports moves to censor BDSM imagery, such as the recent prohibition on the possession of 'extreme violent pornography' introduced by the UK government.

In the first part of this chapter, we consider the ways in which popular media has of late mobilised SM imagery, across diverse field including film, fashion photography, advertising and music. In the second part, we explore how these media representations intersect with medico-moral and legal discourses, and might thereby work in concert to reproduce the supposed 'deviance' (and, indeed, 'criminality') of BDSM practitioners. However, we also note the ways certain practitioners actively embrace the status and symbolism associated with deviance, as an integral element in the production of a desired social and sexual identity.

The mainstreaming of sex and the rise of 'BDSM chic'

Recent scholarship across fields such as gender studies, media and cultural studies, film, literature and sociology has carefully mapped the sexualisation of culture in Western liberal societies in the past couple of decades (see McNair 2002; Paasonen *et al.* 2007; Sarracino and Scott 2008). If we take the UK as a lens for these cultural and attitudinal changes, the dramatic shift in social sensibilities is all too apparent. Some 30 years ago, explicit sexual representation was largely consigned to the category of pornography, and was available through a limited number of legitimate outlets, each carrying with it varying degrees of social stigma. Consumers could purchase so-called 'top shelf' magazines in news agents, which contained a fairly predictable diet of photographic spreads depicting women in full-frontal nudity. Images of a more explicit kind, such as representations of penetrative sex, were prohibited under the prevalent obscenity laws, whose enforcement was undertaken rigorously by specialist police units such as the Metropolitan Police's so-called 'Vice Squad'.

Even consumption of this most innocuous form of pornographic material was widely seen as unsavoury and shameful. The fact that such publications were commonly referred to as 'dirty magazines' is telling in itself – as the anthropologist Mary Douglas (2002) famously pointed out, the language of 'dirt' functions as a powerful social metaphor for moral contamination, and is habitually used as a means of policing social boundaries and enforcing the normative prescriptions of a social group. Other avenues for accessing pornography were, if anything, even more negatively charged, such as the 'licensed sex shop' and the 'adult cinema'. As Attwood (2007) notes, the prevalent social stereotype of the pornography consumer was that of the 'dirty man in a Mac', lurking around in dark corners, while no doubt enjoying masturbatory self-gratification hidden under his full-length raincoat.

The cultural terrain today is very far removed from that above. First, we must note how the kinds of consumption activities above have lost their associations with 'dirtiness', 'filth' and prurience, and become not only widely accepted, but also celebrated. The UK now has, for example, a whole slew of 'men's lifestyle' magazines where sexualised imagery does not live a kind shameful half-life, discreetly hidden away, but on the contrary proclaims itself with a brash self-confidence. The likes of *Zoo* and *Nuts* magazines are replete with 'soft core' pictorials of models who themselves have become household names. The apotheosis of this valorisation of a career in pornography is perhaps the case of 'Jordan' (real name Katie Price) who has on the basis of her modelling built a formidable career, including production of three best-selling novels, three volumes of autobiography and two children's books; a range of branded products including hair care, perfume, lingerie, swimwear and household decor; fitness DVDs; and a successful 'fly on the wall' television series following her turbulent personal life.

However, the 'mainstreaming' of sexual representation – what has also been referred to as the 'pornification' of contemporary culture and the rise of 'striptease culture' – goes far beyond this. So-called 'hardcore' pornographic production has now become a part of the mainstream culture industry; the public consumes their output in record amounts – the world-wide revenue of the industry from video sales alone is placed at US$20 billion, and to this we must add income from magazines, website subscriptions, pay-per-view services and so on (Lane 2001; IFT 2004). Mainstream cultural production also increasingly borrows the tropes and motifs of pornographic discourse, incorporating them within popular cultural goods (so-called 'porn chic'), and has also made the pornography industry itself the subject of sympathetic representations, such as the film *Boogie Nights* (1997), which was nominated for three Oscars and won a further 21 awards from film critics and festivals.

However, equally striking is the way in which it is increasingly acceptable, not only to enjoy, *but to be seen to enjoy and admit enjoying,* such cultural representations. There has been, in the words of Angela McRobbie, 'a kind of fulsome rehabilitation of porn' (McRobbie 2 January 2004). Perhaps the most notable element of this 'rehabilitation' has been the way in which it has crossed its long-entrenched gender divide and come to be embraced by young *women,* as well as young men. Again, in McRobbie's words:

> The pervasiveness of the 'full frontal', the 'back-view shot' and 'girl-on-girl action' in our increasingly frank and uncensored sexual culture means that it is now absolutely normal for TV presenters and actresses on prime-time soap operas to appear in centrefolds in these poses. Indeed, to be asked is the ultimate accolade. The same holds true for 'pole dancing' – with supermodel Kate Moss (who certainly doesn't need to do it for the money) appearing in the recent White Stripes pop video 'scantily clad' and writhing round a pole.
>
> (ibid.)

This embrace of pornography has now come to claim a prominent place in the traditionally feminised world of fashion. For example, the Porn Star clothing label now markets everything from T-Shirts and thongs to baseball caps for women, emblazoned with logos declaiming 'Do You Wanna F*ck Me?' and 'Eager Beaver'. Playboy, with its easily recognisable 'Bunny' logo, now offers young women branded merchandise including hand bags and jewellery, crop tops, make-up bags and pencil cases, perfumes and pillow cases, mobile phone covers and body care set (Beckmann 2009: 160).

An integral element in this process has been the emergence into the cultural mainstream of 'perverse' sexual imagery (Attwood 2002: 94), long associated with the dangerous, unpalatable and unacceptable. The 'kinky' and 'fetishistic' now abound in consumer culture (Beckmann 2001), spanning everything from 'beginner's guides' to 'kinky sex' through paraphernalia, such as 'fetish boots', blindfolds and handcuffs available for purchase on the high street. The seeming normalisation of the 'perverse' in popular culture is no more striking than in the case of sadomasochism. The very term, owing its name in part to the notorious fantasies of sexual violation, torture and murder penned by De Sade, was for a period of over two centuries associated with one of the ultimate forms of sexual transgression. It sits in a seemingly antithetical relationship to what is widely construed as 'normal' and 'healthy' sexuality: with its conflation of pain and pleasure, and its fantastic embrace of coercion and force, it runs counter to dominant norms that purport to regulate sexual desire. Consequently, cultural representations of sadomasochism have been widely seen as continuous with the perpetration and depiction of violence, and been subject to concerted prohibition. Yet recent decades have seen a remarkable cultural turn-around in this respect. As Wilkinson (2009: 182) notes, 'since the 1990s we have seen a proliferation of SM images in western cultures', and these have come to span the discourses of advertising, pop music, film and fashion.

Probably one of the most widely discussed instances of this phenomenon was the publication in 1992 of Madonna's 'coffee table book' entitled *Sex*. This lavish 124-page pictorial edition featured images not only of Madonna herself, but also of famous actors, models, musicians and other celebrities. The photographs, by Steven Meisel, included depictions of simulated sex (both gay and straight), and those intimating or suggesting analingus, 'water sports' and masturbation. However, for present purposes, most noteworthy are those with clear BDSM themes. These include: a photograph of Madonna tied to a chair and being 'pleasured' by two women, one of whom holds a knife to Madonna's throat; a montage of 15 images featuring these same three and again depicting Madonna is various scenarios of bondage and restraint; a woman in a PVC dress being restrained by a man in a kneeling position on chair, while Madonna whips the woman's backside; and Madonna in a 'peep hole' PVC bra, and sporting restraint cuffs and a blindfold mask. The book apparently sold 1.5 million copies (absolutemadonna 2009), and is now a collectors' item commanding high prices.

In the wake of *Sex*, BDSM themes began to appear regularly in the pictorial repertoire of advertising culture. For example, a campaign for fashion brand *Sisley* has featured a series of photographs depicting SM scenarios including: a man on all-fours, wearing a saddle, and being 'ridden' by a woman and a naked man draped over a woman's lap, as she prepares to spank him with a shoe. The men's fashion brand *Duncan Quinn* has sold its wares with an advert featuring a be-suited man holding a woman by a tie around her throat, as she lies supine on her back on the bonnet of a car, dressed only in her underwear. *Dolce & Gabbana* have advertised using an image featuring a woman being pinned down on the floor by a shirtless man, while three other men watch this scenario unfold. These are just a small selection of the kinds of fashion advertising that now regularly use themes of bondage, domination, masochism and sexual coercion in their glossy campaigns.

BDSM themes have also percolated into other domains of popular culture beyond the spheres of 'art house' photography and fashion advertising. For example, the critically acclaimed hit film *Secretary* (2002) is a BDSM themed romantic comedy-drama which centres on a story about an emotionally repressed lawyer and his self-harming secretary, a lonely pair who discover love and intimacy through a sadomasochistic sexual relationship. Advertising for the film featured its stocking-clad female lead (played by Maggie Gyllenhaal) bending over, alongside the tag-line: 'Assume The Position'. *Walk All Over Me* (2007) is a crime thriller that features as its protagonists a professional dominatrix and her friend who is drawn into the world of sexual domination. Again, the promotional material utilises familiar BDSM themes: one poster shows the two female leads in PVC 'fetish gear', with tag-line reading 'Love. Latex. Larceny'; another features a man on his knees in a cage, alongside the female stars, both of whom are dressed in dominatrix outfits complete with whips. Other films exploring BDSM sexuality include *The Night Porter* (1973), *Maitresse* (1976), *9½ Weeks* (1986), *Bitter Moon* (1992), *Of Freaks and Men* (1998), *The Piano Teacher* (2001) and *The Notorious Bettie Page* (2006). BDSM themes have also become increasingly apparent in popular fiction. For example, Anne Rice (perhaps best known for her best seller *Interview With The Vampire* and its sequels) has also written a series of BDSM themed romances, starting with *Exit to Eden* (1985); other BDSM novels by popular writers include Alasdair Gray's *Something Leather* (1990).

Interpretive ambiguities: BDSM and the renegotiation of the boundaries of the normal and abnormal

How ought we to interpret the aforementioned shifts in regimes of sexual representation in popular culture? It is important not to assume that what we have seen is the emergence of a discursive space in which 'sex speaks' and is spoken about, where previously silence reigned. As Foucault famously noted, 'what is peculiar to modern societies, in fact, is not that they consigned sex to a shadow existence, but that they dedicated themselves to speaking of it *ad infinitum*, while exploiting it as *the* secret' (Foucault 1998: 35). In other words, an incessant discursive preoccupation with sex and sexuality is nothing new. However, we can suggest that what *has* changed in recent times is a significant shift in the tenor and content of such 'sex talk'. It was once dominated by a medico-moral focus upon sex as a *problem* to be analysed, categorised, regulated and managed through social and expert interventions. Increasingly, however, it features in our culture as a prescription to unconstrained pleasure, as fun and leisure, as self-expression and self-realisation. For some commentators, the increasing prominence of sex in popular culture can be read as a progressive development, through which our sexual subjectivities can find a legitimate space for public articulation.

McNair (2002: 11–12) writes of the new sexualised culture as the harbinger of a 'democratisation of desire' which 'on the one hand, expanded popular access to all the means of sexual expression, mediated and otherwise ... and on the other, the emergence of a more diverse and pluralistic sexual culture than has traditionally been accommodated within patriarchal capitalism'. Others have explored these developments as part of the emergence of a new 'sexual citizenship', one in which private desires become the basis of very public claims for recognition, legitimacy and equality of esteem (see for example Weeks 1998; Plummer 1994). Such claims have, of course, proven controversial, not least for feminist writers who see in the new sexual culture a reassertion of sexist codes that objectify women (see for example Levy 2006; Walter 2010). While an undoubtedly important debate, our focus here falls on more specific questions: Does the new culture of sexual explicitness mark a wider shift, in which previously marginalised and pathologised sexualities are increasingly normalised and deemed acceptable in the societal mainstream? Does the rise of BDSM imagery in popular culture mark a decisive shift in sensibilities, such that it has been relieved of its associations with perversion and violence?

At one level, the consolidation of BDSM imagery in popular culture does indeed appear to indicate a greater acceptance of heretofore 'deviant' and 'dangerous' sexualities. Important here would be, not just the textual presence of BDSM practices, styles, and paraphernalia, but also the *contextual* narration of these elements. Thus, for example, the narrative of *Secretary* apparently recodes BDSM encounters, showing them as a legitimate and desirable avenue for establishing meaningful, tender and loving inter-personal relations. *The New York Times* film critic Stephen Holden, in a not atypical reception of the film, concludes that: 'In today's post-Freudian, do-your-own-thing era of free sexual expression, the movie stands to be a wholesome self-help fable about the unlocking of shame and its magical transformation into pleasure and personal liberation' (Holden 2002). In a more restricted, but nevertheless significant manner, the imagery used in *Sex* and other photo-visual representations may be

taken to stake a claim for BDSM as having a place in the socially sanctioned repertoire of 'normal' sexuality, thus rendering it an acceptable
element within the range of Western culture's 'liberated' fantasies and
pleasures. The widespread availability and consumption of BDSM accou-
trements – outfits, whips, handcuffs, restraints and the like – would
support the contention that not only is it now far more acceptable to
produce and consume BDSM imagery, but it is also far more acceptable to
engage and experiment with the associated practices as part of one's
normal sexual 'diet'.

However, a closer examination of these cultural texts in fact leads us to
reconsider any sanguine claims about normalisation and wider acceptance
of BDSM, as either imagery or practice. As Wilkinson (2009: 182) pointedly puts it: 'We should ask what form of SM is being portrayed and for
what purposes. What existing narratives are these images framed within?
Do these images challenge the sexual status quo, or do they reinforce SM's
otherness?' Weiss (2006) offers, for example, an alternative reading of the
text of *Secretary* and of the terms in which it frames acceptance and understanding of BDSM. She argues that the film in fact offers some clearly
defined terms upon which the mainstream (non BDSM practitioner) audience is invited to come to terms with BDSM as a form of sexual preference
and behaviour. First, she argues, the film offers its audience a 'palatable'
version of BDSM by domesticating it within dominant ideological constructions of 'normal' sexuality: the relationship depicted in the film and
its BDSM characteristic notwithstanding is resolutely hetero-normative,
monogamous and suburban. The final scene of the film can be seen to
recuperate sexual dissidence/difference into the most conservative of
American ideologies: a married suburban couple, with a domesticated wife
who keeps the home fires burning and a professional husband who goes
'out to work' daily, complete with briefcase, suit and tie. Thus, when all is
said and done, BDSM is rendered acceptable by reducing it to a little
'kinky flavoured icing' on a resolutely 'vanilla cake' of middle-class,
middle-American, heterosexuality.

The second mode offered to viewers, Weiss (2006: 119) argues, is that
of 'understanding via pathologising'. By this she means that the film
enables its viewers to comprehend the protagonists' sexual predilections,
by explaining them as the product of psychological abnormalities. It is
indeed striking, that both the male and female leads of *Secretary* are represented as 'weird', 'troubled' and 'damaged': Edward is sexually repressed,
emotionally inexpressive and has a failed marriage behind him, while Lee
is the self-harming daughter of an alcoholic father and a neurotic, over-
bearing mother – at the start of the film Lee has just been released from a
psychiatric hospital because her self-harming with a knife was read as a
suicide attempt. Lee's harming of herself, through cutting and self-
mutilation, is given equivalence with the 'harms' that Edward 'inflicts'
upon her in the form of spankings and humiliations. Consequently, the

film effectively reduces BDSM to a warped sexual orientation that arises out of distinctly 'abnormal' experiences, circumstances and personality traits. Far from normalising BDSM, this film re-inscribes it within the space of deviance.

The kind of critical reading of mainstream representations offered by Weiss impels us to ask a fundamental question: in these commercially-oriented cultural goods, just what is being sold to consumers? What is it about BDSM that is marked-out as distinctive, exciting, erotically charged or sexually stimulating? We would suggest that what is being marketed here is *BDSM as kink, as transgression, danger and perversion*. It is precisely as the abnormal, violent 'other' of 'normal' sexuality that it is packaged and sold for the titillation of an outsider audience looking in. In doing so, these representations tend to misconstrue the features of BDSM, as practised by those invested in the 'scene' and instead conflate it with coercion, violence, and even torture, so as to invest it with a transgressive charge.

The problematic encodings in mainstream use of BDSM motifs is exemplified, we would argue, by the pictorial spread entitled 'State of Emergency', which featured in the Italian edition of *Vogue* magazine in September 2006. Photographed by Stephen Meisel, who shot Madonna's *Sex* book, the spread features female fashion models in a number of 'war on terror' themed scenarios. The images include a woman being strip-searched by airport security personnel; being led handcuffed into police riot vans; being pressed face-first into a car windscreen by riot police; being forced to kneel with hands behind the head, as a barking attack dog strains against its leash; lying supine on the street with a riot policeman's boot pressing down on her neck; and being pinned face-down on the concrete, wrists tied behind the back, as a policeman twists her head around by the hair. The spread can be read in a number of ways.

Appearing five years to the month since the 9/11 attacks on New York and Washington, DC, some take it to be a pointed critique of then President George W. Bush's 'war on terror' and the use of force against civilians it has entailed. The juxtaposition of slender, young and beautiful models, and brutal, black-uniformed, truncheon- and gun-wielding security personnel is certainly striking and evokes a sense of violation and vulnerability in the face of state-military power. However, the pictorial is also highly sexualised, with the models' expressions more akin to those associated with coital bliss, than the suffering of police brutality. The signifiers popularly associated with BDSM, fetishism and 'kinky sex' are all too apparent: handcuffs, restraints, subjection and humiliation. The images therefore invite a reading that takes pleasure in the association of sex with war, terror and the violation of rights. As one online viewer tellingly opines, with reference to the aforementioned photograph of a woman being choked under a policeman's boot: 'this girl is smoking hot'. These associations take on an additional resonance with the abuse scandal at Abu Ghraib prison, which came to light in the period before the publication of the *Vogue* pictorial. Most striking is the fact that US military personnel photographed the torture, sexual abuse and humiliation that they inflicted upon their prisoners, producing a kind of 'torture porn' that took sadomasochistic *fantasies* as a repertoire for genuine acts of terrible abuse. As Apel (2005: 89) suggests, the photographic recording of abuse has long provided a way of 'reliving the erotic thrills of torture and mutilation'. Our concern here is that popular uses of BDSM imagery conflate such sexuality with genuine acts of violence, thereby recuperating it within a normative construction of the perverted and wicked. Moynihan (2009) decries the rise in recent fashion and advertising of what amounts to a 'torture chic', which glorifies 'inhumane, sadistic behaviour'. Insofar as such imagery confuses BDSM with torture, it risks pathologising, rather than normalising those who favour such a BDSM sexual orientation.

BDSM representation: conveniently commercial?

A question, which needs to be asked, is whether practitioners of BDSM fetishise genuine torture and perhaps even more importantly a removal of rights, or whether this view merely perpetuates misconceptions surrounding BDSM?

Before entering this discussion, it is important to locate exactly what is meant by the term BDSM community. There are many people who do not associate with 'the scene', who may nonetheless engage with what is termed BDSM activity. Therefore, for the purpose of this discussion, we will be drawing on research, which predominantly focuses on people who self-define as BDSM practitioners, asides from some cases which will be specifically noted as they arise. These cases are drawn primarily from studies these researchers conducted through contacting BDSM mailing lists and engaging with practitioners who frequent BDSM clubs or locations known to be associated with such activity.

The view of the psychiatric community has long been that people engaging in BDSM suffer from a mental illness. Indeed, the most recent revision of the *Diagnostic and Statistical Manual of Mental Disorders* classifies Sexual Sadism and Sexual Masochism as psychiatric disorders (APA 2000). Whilst the *DSM* states that deviant sexual behaviour cannot in itself be classed as a psychiatric disorder, the definitions still remain, in spite of a lack of evidence that either of the two conditions, which need to be met to be diagnosed, have been fulfilled or even tested (Cross and Matheson 2006; Klein and Moser 2006). The *International Classification of Diseases (ICD)* manual highlights sadomasochism as a 'Disorder of sexual preference' alongside fetishism and fetishistic transvestitism (WHO 2007). The overall characterisation of a person engaging in BDSM activity is one of someone mentally unstable and in some way ill.

Such views of BDSM practitioners as mentally unbalanced inevitably filter into the mainstream and have had an impact on not just the legal process, but also the media (Barrett 2007; Yost 2010). The reification of the 'expert' creates a culture of reliance on certain individuals, such as psychiatric professionals, in defining what is an acceptable deviation from the norm and what is classified as an 'illness' (Foucault 1991, 1998). This categorisation of normality, as opposed to the pathological, has framed discussions of mental illness in connection with crime, in numerous TV series, such as *Dexter*, a show about a psychopath killer who kills murderers, which has in fact been suggested as a motivation for a real life murder (WLWT.com 4 December 2009). Similar links have been described suggesting BDSM motivations for crimes such as rape and domestic violence, and the theme of BDSM as pathological has been exploited for consumer titillation through advertising, television and film, as detailed above (Brownmiller 1975). The trend for fashionable use of deviance has been well documented by writers such as Beckmann (2009), as has been the normalisation of BDSM, in an effort to mitigate the effects of the viewer empathising with the protagonists in films, such as *Secretary* (Wright 2006). The outcome of the capitalist driven consumer market is one, which is indebted to a Foucauldian power-pleasure spiral, whereby the very act of defining a practice as deviant signifies it as a new pleasure to be tapped into and therefore becomes a valuable commodity.

Mentally ill?

A critique of the DSM and ICD suggests that such claims about BDSM being driven by mental illness are fallacious. A study of 164 males across two clubs in Finland, found problematic the claim that BDSM practitioners are incapable of handling the real world (Sandnabba *et al.* 1999). It has been discovered that in the sample group studied, the majority held white collar jobs and usually had slightly above average earnings when compared with the general population. Furthermore, a significantly higher percentage of BDSM practitioners hold university or college level degrees, when compared with the rest of the population. This suggests that the people contacted were well-adjusted and able to function in a 'normal' and acceptable way with society (Sandnabba *et al.* 1999).

In a study conducted by Cross and Matheson (2006), the psychoanalytic, psychopathology/medical model, radical feminist and escape-from-self perspectives were tested, thereby examining both psychoanalytic and socially oriented models. This work further supported the view of many people studying the BDSM scene that there is no significant connection with these models. The psychopathological view suggests, that the desire for the harm of the self, reflects 'significant mental disorder', which results in the desire for masochistic activity, whilst the psychoanalytic view states that masochism is due to sexual guilt: both stances were apparently incorrect based on the results of this study (Cross and Matheson 2006: 140). Through using The Stress subscale (amongst others) of the Differential Personality Questionnaire (DPQ), the Neuroticism subscale of the Eysenck Personality Inventory and the Rosenburg Self-Esteem Scale to name but four of the battery of tests used, the mental health of those involved in the study was tested in line with the assumptions made by these theories. To test the radical feminist view, the Feminist Attitudes Scale and Spanos Attitudes Towards Women Scale were implemented. To examine the escape-from-reality hypothesis, another battery of tests was used, including the Danger-Seeking subscale of the DPQ, the Desirability of Control Inventory and the Locus of Control Scale (Cross and Matheson 2006).

The findings revealed that concerning the psychoanalytic view, there was no support for the assertion that masochists are guilt ridden. For the psychopathological view, there was no support for the assertion that masochists are 'more prone to psychological distress or mental instability, than the control group used in the study' (Cross and Matheson 2006: 145). When examining the radical feminist view, it was found that those involved in the study were not only not anti-feminist, but their beliefs and attitudes in general were highly consistent with those held by feminists. Finally, the testing of the escape-from-reality viewpoint showed that through the various methods used to analyse it, none resulted in an agreement with the initial hypothesis.

Power or violence?

There have been studies conducted which attempt to elicit the views of those engaged in BDSM activity and there have also been works created by non-academics in the 'scene' themselves. The extent to which commercially driven representations capture the lived experience of BDSM must be carefully assessed. There have been numerous studies which have engaged with practitioners of BDSM, in an attempt to elucidate the link between violence and the consensual activities which delineate BDSM as a separate phenomenon. The prevailing results are two-fold: BDSM as theatricality clearly separated from 'real life' and power, as the most important factor in scenes, as opposed to pain itself. Both of these aspects are strongly associated with consent in all studies of the lived experience of BDSM practitioners.

As numerous studies cited in this chapter show, the prevailing interpretation of BDSM scenes, amongst participants was that these practices partake of a 'fantastic' performance that is kept apart from 'actual real life'. Communication and trust are ranked highly in importance in BDSM relationships ranging from long-term, through to online short-term negotiation, in terms of what is wanted by both parties, not just the dominant person (Cross and Matheson 2006; Cutler 2003). Taylor and Ussher

(2001) conducted a particularly pertinent study relating to the views held by sadomasochists through using interviews. One respondent explained that 'It's putting your trust into someone so completely, they could kill you if they wanted, I mean I never really think they will, but I guess that's the fantasy ... that they could...' (G cited in Taylor and Ussher 2001). Some made the link with consent, in a much more direct way: 'SM is about consent ... if there's no consent it's not SM ... it's sexual violence ... it's as simple as that' (R cited in Taylor and Ussher 2001). One of the most common themes in the study was that the scenes conducted are completely separate from real life and that this is the only way in which BDSM can work – with both people entering into an explicit agreement about limits and boundaries (Cutler 2003 covers similar issues).

In her autobiographical work, focusing on her discovery of her spanking fetish, through to her eventual involvement in the BDSM porn industry, Niki Flynn echoed such sentiments many times: 'Consent has to exist in reality, but not in the fantasy' (Flynn 2007: 23). A leading website, used for social networking by BDSM practitioners in the UK, shows by its very name the importance of consent in scenes implemented. Informed Consent has a dictionary section where people can find out more about procedures classed as 'safe, sane and consensual' and much of what is discussed on the website hinges on ways of ensuring the safety, both physical and mental, of all involved (Informed Consent, n.d.). In a study of a magazine produced by a sadomasochism club, it was displayed that there was heavy emphasis on safety: 'The only 'cardinal' rules which the Club's membership insists each member should uphold are that all S/M activities must be consensual, non-exploitative and safe' (Houldberg 2010: 168). The magazine is described as being a conduit for information to be filtered out from the Club's clientele to people outside, as a means of demystifying the BDSM community it represents and serves. This is not the only reason for the magazine's existence, as it also provides a forum in which members of the community can provide information and support for each other, but it is a strong enough part of the magazine's identity to warrant a mention in the Club's purpose statement (Houldberg 2010). This shows the way in which the community itself is highly aware of the representations of the community circulating in the mainstream and that it feels the need to contradict this image.

The impact of media messages on the judicial process

The resulting situation, created by the messages conferred by the media and lawmakers, compared with the views held by the BDSM practitioners themselves, is generally one in which the practitioners feel excluded from this discourse. Furthermore, aside from the general feeling of stigmatisation arising from this situation, the impact can be severe for those whose stigma becomes known to people outside the scene (Goffman 1968). That

Goffman's notions on stigma are readily applicable to the situation of BDSM practitioners has been noted by others writing on the issue (Plante 2006). His application of the theory to such cases is apparent, when he includes 'domineering or unnatural passions' as aspects of a person's life, which may result in their being stigmatised (Goffman 1968: 14). When people are stigmatised in the wider community, the effects can be more than just psychological – they can have a severe impact on some people's life chances.

The *Roe* v. *Brown* case, also referred to as the Spanner trials (the police operation was code named Spanner) is the most regularly cited example of litigation against BDSM practitioners, which led to not only the dominants in the scenes being convicted, but also the submissives, who were claimed to be abetting assault (McArdle 1995; White 2006). This case involved a group of men who engaged in BDSM activity including flogging, the use of a spiked glove in holding another's genitals, striking the penis with a ruler and other activities. All of the activity was done on a consensual basis and some of it was filmed. The court ruled that even though consent had been given and no hospital treatment was required, 'one cannot consent to the infliction of injury upon oneself in the course of homosexual sadomasochistic activities' (McArdle 1995: 109; also Bibbings and Alldridge 1993). It has been further discussed that when taking place in the marital home, BDSM activity is viewed in a very different way in the eyes of the law, being accepted as a private act between two people which the law has no right to interfere with (Russell *et al.* 1996). Furthermore, asides from such direct legal proceedings, child custody cases can be heavily affected by one partner disclosing that the other has an active interest in BDSM, even if the child has no knowledge of this interest (Wright 2006; Yost 2010).

In the wake of the well publicised case of the murder of Jane Longhurst in 2003 by a man judged as being 'obsessed with violent internet porn', a campaign was fought to ban pornography deemed as being violent (BBC News 30 August 2006). This campaign was successful and resulted in the creation of the Criminal Justice and Immigration Bill – Part 6, in which the possession of 'extreme pornographic images' is criminalised (House Commons of 2007). Amongst other things, an extreme image is defined as 'an act which results in or appears to result (or be likely to result) in serious injury to a person's anus, breasts or genitals' (ibid.). This judgement therefore eliminates the role of consent in the process and disregards any notion of fantastical elements. It should be noted that violence on screen is still by and large accepted in the media and it is only in the realm of pornography that this distinction is being made. BDSM has essentially become a criminalised practise and it is clear that, whilst people are in certain circumstances permitted to engage in these activities, they must not be allowed to produce pornography, as others can, when they have a particular sexual preference. BDSM is thus further demonised in a society where media influenced campaigns and erroneous information has begun to influence the judicial process.

In a piece of research studying the implementation of the recently devised Attitudes about Sadomasochism Scale (ASMS), Yost (2010) discovered a clear link between participation in BDSM activities and having friends who did so and more positive attitudes towards BDSM. This is suggestive of the fact that knowledge of BDSM as a lived experience demystifies the processes involved, providing further knowledge of the mechanisms involved in creating such an exchange. When people have no access to such direct knowledge they instead rely on messages received through the media, feminist theory and news articles. These alternate sources of information are most often divorced from the context of consent and therefore do not provide a clear picture of the negotiation involved in BDSM scenes. It can therefore be seen that increased levels of documentation of the vital role of consent in BDSM could greatly support moves towards the acceptance of BDSM as a sexual taste, which would in future mean a decrease in prejudicial judgements being made towards those who practise it.

BDSM and the media – subtle differences?

It is apparent that messages in the media influence mainstream thought in spite of research suggesting that the actuality of BDSM practise is very different to the way in which it is represented. It is understandable that such confusion takes place, as the representations linking sexuality with brutal military regimes are often very similar to roles played in BDSM scenarios. One key example is that of Niki Flynn (2007) who has engaged in scenes based around Stalinist brutality, which few would regard as residing in anything like a normal type of sexuality.

However, once one scratches the surface, one finds essential differences in the image presented by the community as a whole in the case of BDSM and the suggestions made in the media. If one makes but a brief enquiry into BDSM online, there is a plethora of information to teach those interested, not just how to be physically safe when doing so, but how to negotiate the route towards a psychologically safe relationship with BDSM (Informed Consent 2, n.d.; Fetlife, n.d.). Once one uses the 'deviant' image of BDSM as a sales technique, the notions of consent, mutuality and safety get lost, and are replaced by titillation only, as the viewer revels in voyeurism of the 'other', whilst maintaining a safe distance – even if this 'other' is in some sense imaginary. The media retains a strong link between actual violence and BDSM which problematises the community, not only by creating a psychological stigma, but also by in turn influencing the attitudes of lawmakers, as happened in the Spanner trials (White 2006). Indeed some people feel actively dissuaded from associating as being interested in BDSM: 'For a long time I would have described myself as kinky, but not into BDSM, and that is probably largely due to the way BDSM is portrayed in the media' (Cutler 2003: 18).

Although it is clear that the media representations can have a severely negative effect for some participating in BDSM, it is less clear whether the effect could be perceived as *wholly* negative for the community. As referenced previously, the act of defining an act, particularly as deviant and 'taboo' can be involved in the creation of new pleasures. The Foucauldian power-pleasure spiral is in effect in this location of BDSM as one of these taboo sexualities, whereby the very nature of a sexual act being declared as wrong, in some way makes it all the more appealing for those who are, or may, become involved. As one person describing the allure of BDSM puts it, 'It's in yer face perversion ... I suppose I like outraging people ... upsetting the balance, you know girls are supposed to be like this, or sex is supposed to be like that' (P cited in Taylor and Ussher 2001).

It can therefore be questioned whether as in Foucault's analysis, 'experts' such as psychiatrists could be unwittingly creating new pleasures which the patient can use, enjoy and participate in; perhaps so too can the media. Media representations could be reinforcing the deviance and therefore the pleasure gained from engaging in BDSM. Violence is prohibited in our society and is punishable through strict sentencing – could this link, blurring the boundaries heighten the perceived joys felt by the BDSM community? The paradox that the exclusion from society created by the label of 'deviant' can itself amplify the pleasures felt through these exchanges, perhaps provides a further explanation for the limited impact of attempts at clarification by people fighting for the rights of those demonised by society or the law due to their sexual practises.

Conclusion

We have here examined the media portrayals of BDSM highlighting the broad spectrum of influence that this niche sexual taste has had on popular culture. The public has a complex relationship with these images, appearing to reify the 'other' at the same time as pathologising and criminalising it. The capitalist need, to find a sexual selling point for a wide array of objects and services, has resulted in the use of titillation and the sale of deviant imagery to provide a safe form of danger which consumers can enjoy in the comfort and safety of their own homes. Sexuality has long been a subject of controversy in the media and some steps have been taken (such as in the film *Secretary*) to explain, at least through pathologising, the dynamics behind what can appear as dangerous sexualities. Normalising, pathologising and criminalising such unknowns can be a useful mitigating technique for a fearful and intrigued audience, yet it leaves the BDSM practitioner in an unusual position.

Normalisation tends toward a greater social acceptance and destigmatisation of heretofore marginalised sexual identities and practices (we might draw analogies here with the increasing social acceptance of gay sexual imagery and its role in attenuating homophobia). However, the 'domestication' of BDSM in mainstream culture threatens to deprive it of the very 'otherness' through which aficionados construct their identities as sexual 'dissidents' who are engaged in an alternative to hegemonic sexuality. Conversely, the tendency to pathologise BDSM (by culturally reproducing associations with danger and transgression) serves to underpin laws restricting the range of legitimate sexual practices and their associated representations. In short, media representations matters because they not only shape wider public understandings of what constitutes 'normal' and 'abnormal' sexuality, but also because these normative understandings play a role in shaping the frameworks of social and legal regulations that impinge upon people's sexual lives.

A move towards disseminating the conclusions of critical research in this field to more mainstream media could be beneficial in reducing the prejudice against this marginalised sexual group. With more inclusivity provided for the role of consent, therapists, psychologists and the judiciary may begin to change their stances towards BDSM. It is only once this has happened that we could begin to see a reduction of life-chance inhibiting judgements in areas such as child custody and employee rights. This shift in the judgement of those considered as experts would work alongside the media in reducing the social stigma currently prevalent. However, it remains to be seen whether this potential shift in status would dampen some people's enthusiasm for BDSM or whether it would merely enable people to be accepted for who they feel they are.

References

Absolutemadonna (2009) The Sex Book 4th edn, 2000) *Diagnostic and Statistical Manual of Psychiatric Disorders – Text Revision*, Washington, D.C.

Apel, D. (2005) Torture Culture: Lynching Photographs and the Images of Abu Ghraib, *Art Journal*, 64(2): 88–100.

Attwood, F. (2002) Reading Porn: The Paradigm Shift in Pornography Research, *Sexualities*, 5(1): 91–105.

Attwood, F. (2007) 'Other' or 'One of Us'?: The Porn User in Public Academic Discourse, *Particip@tions* 4(1), online at: www.participations.org/Volume%204/Issue%201/4_01_attwood.htm.

Barrett, J. (2007) 'You've Made Mistress Very, Very Angry': Displeasure and Pleasure in Media Representations of BDSM, *Particip@tions*, 4(1), online at: www.participations.org/Volume%204/Issue%201/4_01_barrett.htm.

BBC News (30 August 2006) Mother wins Ban On Violent Porn. Available at http://news.bbc.co.uk/1/hi/england/berkshire/5297600.stm (accessed 16 February 2011).

Beckmann, A. (2001) Deconstructing Myths: The Social Construction of 'Sadomasochism' Versus 'Subjugated Knowledges' of Practitioners of Consensual 'SM', *Journal of Criminal Justice and Popular Culture*, 8(2): 66–95.

Beckmann, A. (2009) *The Social Construction of Sexuality and Perversion: Deconstructing Sadomasochism*, Basingstoke: Palgrave Macmillan.

Bibbings, L. and Alldridge, P. (1993) Sexual Expression, Body Alteration and the Defence of Consent, *Journal of Law and Society*, 20(3): 356–70.

Brownmiller, S. (1975) *Against Our Will: Men, Women and Rape*, London: Secher & Walburg.

Cross, P. and Matheson, A. (2006) Understanding Sadomasochism: An Empirical Examination in Four Perspectives in Kleinplatz, P. and Moser, C. (eds), *Sadomasochism: Powerful Pleasures*, Binghampton NY: Harrington Park Press.

Cutler, B. (2003) Partner Selection, Power Dynamics, and Sexual Bargaining in Self-Defined BDSM Couples, submitted in partial fulfilment of the requirements for the degree of Doctor of Philosophy. The Institute for Advanced Study of Human Sexuality: San Francisco.

Douglas, M. (2002) *Purity and Danger*, London: Routledge.

Fetlife (n.d.) 'Fetlife', online at: http://fetlife.com/ (accessed 16 February 2011).

Flynn, N. (2007), *Dances With Werewolves*, Croydon: Virgin Books.

Foucault, M. (1991), *Discipline and Punish: The Birth of the Prison*, London: Penguin.

Foucault, M. (1998) *The History of Sexuality, Vol. 1: The Will to Knowledge*, London: Penguin.

Goffman, E. (1968) *Stigma: Notes on the Management of Spoiled Identity*, London: Penguin.

Greer, C. (2003) *Sex Crime and the Media: Sex Offending and the Press in a Divided Society*, Cullompton: Willan.

Holden, S. (2002) An Office Disciplinarian Gets His Way in the End, *The New York Times*, 20th September.

Houldberg, R. (2010) The Magazine of a Sadomasochistic Club: The Tie that Binds, *The Journal of Homosexuality*, 21(1): 167–84.

House of Commons (2007) Criminal Justice and Immigration Bill – Part 6, online at: www.publications.parliament.uk/pa/cm200607/cmbills/130/07130.43–46.html.

IFT (Internet Filter Review) (2004) 'Internet Pornography Statistics', at http://internet-filter-review.toptenreviews.com/internet-pornography-statistics.html.

Informed Consent (n.d.) Safe, sane and consensual, online at: www.informedconsent.co.uk/dictionary/Safe,_sane,_and_consensual/ (accessed 16 February 2011).

Informed Consent 2 (n.d.) Informed Consent, online at: www.informedconsent.co.uk (accessed 16 February 2011).

Jeffreys, S. (2005) *Beauty and Misogyny: Harmful Cultural Practices in the West*, London: Routledge.

Klein, M. and Moser, C. (2006) SM (Sadomasochistic) Interests as an Issue in a Child Custody Proceeding in Kleinplatz, P. and Moser, C. (eds), *Sadomasochism: Powerful Pleasures*, Binghampton NY: Harrington Park Press.

Lane, F. (2001) *Obscene Profits: The Entrepreneurs of Pornography in the Cyber Age*, London/New York: Routledge.

Levy, A. (2006) *Female Chauvinist Pigs: Woman and the Rise of Raunch Culture*, London: Pocket Books.

Mackinnon, C. (1993) *Only Words*, Cambridge, Mass: Harvard UP.

McArdle, D. (1995) A Few Hard Cases? Sport, Sadomasochism and Public Policy in the English Courts, *Canadian Journal of Law and Society*, 10(2): 109–18.

McNair, B. (2002) *Striptease Culture*, London: Routledge.

McRobbie, A. (2 January 2004) The Rise and Rise of Porn Chic. Times Higher Education. Available: www.timeshighereducation.co.uk/story.asp?storyCode=18 5827&sectioncode=26 (accessed 16 February 2011).

Moynihan, M. (2009) Torture Chic: Why Is the Media Glorifying Inhumane, Sadistic Behavior? Available: www.alternet.org/media/124739 (accessed 16 February 2011).

Passonen, S. *et al.* (eds) (2007) *Pornification: Sex and Sexuality in Media Culture*, Oxford: Berg.

Plante, R. (2006) Sexual Spanking, the Self, and the Construction of Deviance, in Kleinplatz, P. and Moser, C. (eds), (2006) *Sadomasochism: Powerful Pleasures*. USA: Harrington Park Press.

Plummer, K. (1994) *Telling Sexual Stories: Power, Change and Social Worlds*, London: Routledge.

Russell, L., Bracewell, J. and Stoyen, J. (1996) Right to Private and Family Life, *Journal of Civil Liberties*, 1(1): 158–61.

Sandnabba, N., Santtila, P. and Nordling, N. (1999) Sexual Behaviour and Social Adaptation among Sadomasochistically-Oriented Males, *The Journal of Sex Research*, 36(3): 273–82.

Sarracino, C. and Scott, K. (2008) *The Porning of America*, Boston, MA: Beacon Press.

Taylor, G.W and Ussher, J.M. Making Sense of S&M: A Discourse Analytic Account, *Sexualities*, August 2001 vol. 4 no. 3 293–314

Walter, N. (2010) *Living Dolls: The Return of Sexism*, London: Virago.

Weeks, J. (1998) The Sexual Citizen, *Theory, Culture & Society*, 15(3): 35–52.

Weiss, D. (2006) Mainstreaming Kink: The Politics of BDSM Representation in U.S. Popular Media' in Kleinplatz, P. and Moser, C. (eds), *Sadomasochism: Powerful Pleasures*, USA: Harrington Park Press.

White, C. (2006) The Spanner Trials and the Changing Law on Sadomasochism in the UK in Kleinplatz, P. and Moser, C. (eds), *Sadomasochism: Powerful Pleasures*, Binghampton NY: Harrington Park Press.

WHO (2007) International Statistical Classification of Diseases and Related Health Problems 10th Revision Version for 2007. Available: http://apps.who.int/classifi-cations/apps/icd/icd10online/ (accessed 16 February 2011).

Wilkinson, E. (2009) Perverting Visual Pleasure: Representing Sadomasochism, *Sexualities*, 12(2): 181–98.

WLWT.com (4 December 2009) Prosecutors: Ind. Teen Felt Hunger To Kill – Teen Charged With Murder In Brother's Death, 4 December. Available: www.wlwt.com/news/21799757/detail.html (accessed 16 February 2011).

Wright, S. (2006) Discrimination of SM-Identified Individuals' in Kleinplatz, P. and Moser, C. (ed.), *Sadomasochism: Powerful Pleasures*, USA: Harrington Park Press.

Yost, M. (2010) Development and Validation of the Attitudes about Sadomaso-chism Scale, *The Journal of Sex Research*, 47(1): 79–91.

Part III

Through the sociological lens

8 Defining the victims of terrorism

Competing frames around victim compensation and commemoration post-9/11 New York City and 3/11 Madrid

Cristina Flesher Fominaya and Rosemary Barberet[1]

Introduction

What does it mean to be a victim? How does the definition of victimhood and victim status influence the attention and resources victims receive? How does it shape the claims and demands they can make or that others can make on their behalf? The emerging literature on the politics of victimhood highlights the ways in which victims are instrumentalised in political struggles and shows how the very different amounts of moral legitimacy or worthiness attributed to the victims of particular trauma events affects the relative resources they receive (Albrecht and Kichling 2007; Biner 2006; Barker 2007; Ochs 2006), and whether they are included or excluded from the sphere of moral concern (Zeruvabel 1991; Robinson 2009). The politics of victimhood has real consequences, and political and public discourse about victims has political effects (Ochs 2006; Flesher Fominaya and Barberet, forthcoming; Humphrey 2003 cited in Ochs 2006).

Certain victims are more ideal than others, as Christie (1986) argues. The ideal victim, to paraphrase his classic model, is one that is (1) weak (2) carrying out a respectable activity, (3) somewhere they could not be blamed for being, (4) whose offender/perpetrator is 'big and bad' and (5) unknown to the victim. Victims derive moral legitimacy to the extent to which they adhere to this model. But in order to obtain redress, victims often need to engage in the politics of victimhood and make certain demands. The more active and demanding, the less they satisfy the first criteria 'weakness'. Victims, therefore, are caught in a dilemma between conforming to an ideal type in order to garner as much support as possible and rejecting the passivity expected of them in order to fight for more resources and attention when they are not automatically forthcoming.

But it is not only the nature of the *victim* that determines their worthiness, but the nature of the crime itself. In the case of September 11, it has been noted that the victims were attributed with higher status (measured in terms of institutional attention and compensation), than those of the Oklahoma City attacks (see, for example, Shapo 2005: 139–40). As victims of a transnational terrorist attack, as opposed to a home grown one, these victims become symbolic carriers of national sovereignty in a way the Oklahoma City victims do not. Victims of transnational terrorism become endowed with state-like attributes, they 'stand in' for the state (Ochs 2006). Vázquez Valverde (2005) shows from a clinical psychological perspective that response to victims of terrorism is often dictated by political agendas, rather than scientifically based assessments of their needs.

Undoubtedly, the media worthiness of the trauma event also contributes to the salience and importance victims acquire in the public imagination. The spectacular nature of the September 11 attack, for example, provided shocking images that were replayed endlessly on all major media outlets. Following national traumas different carrier groups make competing claims about how traumatic events and their victims should be remembered, compensated, represented or otherwise attended to (Alexander 2004; Smelser 2004; Tota 2005). Victims of national traumas and of political crimes are inevitably caught up in struggles between different carrier groups who vie with each other to have their interpretation of the event, their definition of the worthy victims, and their demands on behalf of those victims become dominant and therefore successful (see Robinson 2008, 2009; Biner 2006). These struggles are played out in the media.

Victims' needs are rarely automatically met, meaning that victims or people working on their behalf need to mobilise and make certain claims and demands to address these needs. Political discourses of victimhood are mobilised strategically 'in self-conscious and tactical ways' (Ochs 2006: 359). The framing literature leads us to believe that those demands and claims that are framed in such a way as to resonate with core cultural narratives and values are more likely to be successful (Snow and Benford 1988; Benford and Snow 2000). While victims associations undoubtedly engage in strategic framing in an attempt to maximise benefits for the victims, not all claims and demands are formulated in an explicit strategic way. The first victims' need in many cases is to be recognised as a legitimate victim. The fight for recognition plays out through public discourses and through legal and institutional mechanisms. Victims who are recognised in one arena may not be in another. In compensation claims, for example, the burden of proof is on the victim and many victims need to struggle with administrations or courts who deny them the status or level of 'victimhood' they believe they deserve. Distinctions between victims and comparisons to other victims inevitably emerge.

This chapter presents a cross national comparative analysis of competing victim frames emerging after the terrorist attacks of September 11, 2001 in New York, in which some 2,752 people died and a further 2,594 were injured (Feinberg 2004)[2] and March 11, 2004 in Madrid, in which 192 people lost their lives and 1,847 were injured. The literature on victimhood in political conflicts shows that often the determination and definition of the victims is an ambiguous and highly contested process. In many cases, there is ambiguity between victims and perpetrator (Borer 2003). Internecine conflicts are rife with disputes over victim 'purity' or victim legitimacy and as victims of different sides compete for recognition and other forms of satisfaction, victim taxonomies and hierarchies of worth and blame emerge (see Smyth 1998; Borer 2003; Porter 2007). While the literature leads us to expect to find competing hierarchies of worth between victims of internecine conflicts, what is more surprising is to find, as we do here, that victims are stratified into competing hierarchies in cases where there is a clear consensus and differentiation between perpetrators and victims. In both Madrid and New York there is no ambiguity about victim-perpetrator identity, that is, the victims are not seen as having brought the crime on themselves in any way.[3] As such, they conform closely to Christie's ideal victim status. While there was initial confusion about who exactly the perpetrators were in the case of 3/11, no one doubted that they were the 'bad guys', whoever they were. Nevertheless, to a greater or lesser degree, multiple competing hierarchies of victim stratification emerged in both 9/11 and 3/11. Victim classification, or status attribution, was then linked to claims about what victims were entitled to, be it commemoration, compensation, charitable donations, representation or medical and psychological treatment. In what follows we analyse how cultural and political understandings of victimhood shaped claims making around two key areas: *commemoration* and *compensation* in the cases of 9/11 and 3/11.

While victims in both contexts satisfy Christie's criteria for ideal victimhood, there were nevertheless key differences in the way that victimhood was understood culturally and politically, which then influenced the competing hierarchies formulated about victimhood, the demands made as a result of the way victims were framed and the satisfaction of those demands on the part of state and institutional agencies. These cases provide a cross national comparison that allows us to see how victim definitions are shaped by political cultural narratives in each case, how nationally situated cultural scripts are used to lend moral authority and weight to their claims or to challenge them and the implications this has for victim commemoration and compensation.

Methods

We used Factiva database to conduct our searches, encompassing a five-year period from the date of the attacks, up to 31 December of the fifth year. For New York, major publications in New York and New Jersey were selected: the *Record*, the *Star-Ledger*, the *New York Daily News*, the *New York Observer*, The *New York Post*, the *New York Sun*, the *New York Times*, *Newsday*, the *Wall Street Journal* and *USA Today*, New York version. We searched on the terms (9/11 or Ground Zero or Twin Towers or WTC or terrorist attacks or September 11th) and (victim* or survivor* or rescue or first responder* or family or neighbor* or resident* or employee* or volunteer* or worker*) and (compensa* or claim* or assistance or help or health care or medical or suffer or aid or dona* or pay* or injur* or service* or harm* or fund* or repar* or relief* or charity* or dollar* or loss* or sick* or Feinberg or resource* or lawsuit* or coverage), limiting the search to when the terms appear in the headline or first paragraph of the article. This generated 2,384 articles.

For Madrid, we used Factiva to search in *El País*, Spain's centre-left national newspaper and in *ABC*, the centre-right national newspaper, using the terms '11-M', víctim* and (compensa* or indemni* or AVT or ayud* or benef* or dona* or pag* or dañ* or prestac* or subsan* or perjuic* or repar* or alivi* or atenua* or subsana* or póstumo or enm* or euros) and (homenaj*, conmem*, recuerdo, record*, monument, olvid*) which generated 1,949 and 2,474 articles respectively.

We used frame analysis and qualitative textual content analysis, systematically coding each news article, developing a classification of themes relating to our research questions: how the victims are defined, how they are classified into taxonomies of worth and how these definitions of the victims are linked to claims made about their right to commemoration and compensation, and what form these should take.

Who is defined as a victim?

The first key difference between the cases lies in who is considered a victim of the attacks and who claims to be a victim. We find that the understanding of victimhood is much more broad and elastic in the case of the United States than Spain. In the United States, victimhood status is progressively extended to encompass a broader set of people. News coverage shows a snowballing of victimhood is evident from the day of the attacks, to the rescue efforts and then to coverage of the broadening impact of the attacks. Thus, victims come to include not only those who died in the Twin Towers, including employees, visitors and rescue workers, but also all of those impacted by the attacks (physically, economically, psychologically), such as bystanders, displaced neighbourhood residents, business owners who suffered damages, employees who lost their jobs, citizens who volunteered their time in the rescue effort, relief workers, hospital staff and even the dogs who searched through the smoldering ruins, some of whom were injured. We attribute this elastic and ever broadening definition of victimhood to be related to (1) the nature of the attacks, which generated extensive damage and required a prolonged clean-up effort, (2) the response of the media, ever searching for human interest stories and (3) the positive connotations of victimhood in the United States, and the litigious nature of society, where claims to loss or injury are often a precursor to a lawsuit, compensation, or recognition.

In sharp contrast to the case of New York and 9/11, bystanders and even first responders of 3/11 were not considered victims and did not claim to be victims. In Spain, victim status was attributed only to those who died or were injured in the attack and their families.[4] However, not all those who fell into this description were always accorded victim status automatically. Within a narrative binary opposition of victims/perpetrators that defined the perpetrators as Islamic fundamentalists, Muslim victims were sometimes denied victim status. Such was the case of Yamila Ben Salah, a Moroccan woman who lost her teenage daughter in the attacks. While she was attending the trial against the surviving perpetrators she was verbally abused by another woman in the court room and again by another woman in the restroom during a break. Another 3/11 victim came to her defense and 'explained' to the aggressor that Ben Salah was also a victim of 3/11 (Jiménez Barca 20 February 2007). As a Muslim Moroccan she was automatically thrust into the perpetrator category. If an ideal victim is one that is clearly differentiated from their attackers, then Muslim victims like Ben Salah 'muddy' those clear distinctions and need to work to be accorded the moral legitimacy automatically extended to the other 'Spanish' or 'non-Muslim' victims. In a cultural context where victimhood does not carry the positive associations nor reap the financial benefits it does in the United States, 3/11 victims were much more narrowly defined than 9/11 victims. Therefore, those victims falling outside the narrow parameters of the accepted understanding of victims (whether in reality or in perception as with Ben Salah) had to work much harder for recognition as legitimate victims. The differences in cultural narratives between the two cases become clearer as we look at specific claims made by victims or those claiming to speak for them.

Victim taxonomies of worth and legitimacy

Among victims, who is more of a victim? We now turn to how the worthiness and legitimacy attributed to victims is linked to claims about two key victim issues: commemoration and compensation.

Competing victim frames around commemoration of 9/11

Who should be remembered and how? Although commemoration of 9/11 victims was highly pluralistic and individualistic (see Flesher Fominaya and Barberet, forthcoming), there were three key ways in which victims were stratified into hierarchies of worth.

A salient distinction was made between victims considered to be heroic victims of 9/11, a status attributed to rescue workers, and non-hero victims (everyone else). Contested hero status manifested itself in the controversy over the 'Heroes of 2001' commemorative US postage stamp. Rep. Gary Ackerman of New York, who wrote the legislation behind the heroes stamp, worried about whether to have the stamp pay tribute to all who died or just rescue workers: 'It was a tough call. But there are always going to be victims. People are killed in horrible ways all the time, whether in

terrorist attacks or car accidents.' (Zaslow 5 September 2002). Some
victims bitterly resented this distinction and argued that the heroic frame
should be extended to encompass all who died. Jennifer Jacobs, the widow
of a worker for Fiduciary Trust Co. International, said, 'My husband had a
uniform, too. It was a shirt and tie.... The postage stamp is a slap in the
face ... Everyone in their own way acted heroically' (Zaslow 5 September
2002). Her comment highlights attempts to reject a recurrent 9/11 victim
binary between uniformed and non-uniformed victims.

In addition to conflict over hero attribution, throughout the years of
negotiation on rebuilding Ground Zero, including agreements on a memorial design, there was intense discussion on how to order the names of the
deceased at the memorial itself and a strong push to list the deceased not
only by where they were employed in the Twin Towers, and by whom, but
also by position or rank and age, thus clearly stratifying the dead by occupational category. The centrality of the importance of occupation to victim
identity is striking and echoes US cultural narratives around work and identity. But the debates over the ordering of the names came up against memorial design conventions, upheld by the designers, that names be
alphabetised. At the continued insistence of family members of the deceased
that alphabetised ordering of the names would be meaningless victims'
names were finally grouped by workplace and a system of adjacencies was
worked out using an algorithm that would allow victims' names to be placed
in proximity to other victims with whom they shared a relationship or with
whom they had died. These debates are striking in the insistence that victims
be individualised, stratified by occupation and endowed with meaning,
reflecting again deeply held US cultural values.

Besides the (contested) attribution of hero status to the rescue workers,
and struggles over the way victims should be ordered and identified in commemoration, a further distinction was made between the deceased and
those that survived. Nearly absent of media attention are those who survived
the Twin Towers attack, including the injured. Survivors' names are not read
at commemoration ceremonies nor are they recognised in any monument
or plaque. They are mentioned only in passing and as we shall see in the
next section, are largely left out of compensation schemes for deceased
victims, especially those survivors who developed after-effects and symptoms
after the immediate aftermath of 9/11. Thus, the media at one point characterise them as 'guilt-ridden survivors', (Pogrebin 15 September 2001) rather
than victims. They clearly are an afterthought to the disaster. Even those
rescue workers who managed to save lives were not attributed hero status as
were their counterparts who perished in the attacks.

Competing victim frames around commemoration of 3/11

In Spain, there was little sense that the victims were heroes (although the
trope that they had died for their country was invoked to a limited degree,

first by President Aznar, who argued shortly after the attacks that they had died 'because they were Spaniards' and then hastily nationalised non-Spaniards posthumously). Hero status was limited to the GEO special forces officer who died trying to capture the bombers some days after the attack in Leganés in the explosion of their suicide bombing. Therefore, there were no struggles over the relative heroicism of the victims or their commemoration.

Instead, conflict over commemoration centred around which victims should be commemorated on 3/11 and in the national monument. At first glance, this issue might make little sense: clearly the victims of the 3/11 attacks (however elastically defined) should be commemorated. But in Spain, the victims of 3/11 were not allowed to claim 'ownership' of that trauma event. Instead, long suffering victims of ETA terrorism, who had no official monument of their own, pushed (through their organisation *Asociación de Víctimas del Terrorismo*, AVT) for commemoration to encompass *all* victims of terrorism. The dispute was further complicated (and attempted to be legitimised) by the fact that some factions of the Popular Party, the party in office at the time of the bombing, had insisted immediately following the attacks and continued to insist five years later, that ETA and not Al-Qaeda were the *true* perpetrators of the attack. Had the ETA/3/11 framing of the event been successful, 3/11 victims would have merely been added to the long roster of ETA victims. This would have raised the issue: why then commemorate some ETA victims and not others? Pushing this commemorative agenda meant attempting to redefine the victims worthy of commemoration in order to advance partisan agendas, linked to the political capital gained by keeping ETA terrorism at the forefront of any national commemoration of 3/11. In this way the victims of 3/11 were drawn into the maelstrom of Spanish national politics and a seemingly straightforward commemorative process was subject to endless debate. Ultimately, the official national memorial monument only commemorates the attack and its dead victims. Initial plans, drawn up and approved by the Minister of Public Works and the Mayor of Madrid, did not include the names of the dead, let alone the survivors. Instead, it consisted of a glass cylinder lined with a membrane on which messages of solidarity from around the world were printed. It was only after the High Commissioner for Victims of Terrorism surveyed the families that the names of the deceased were included in a glass panel at the entrance to the monument. Yet the commemoration of 3/11 has not been confined to remembering those who died in the attacks. At the anniversary ceremonies a wreath is laid for 'All the victims of terrorism', reflecting that the AVT's attempt to widen the victim frame has been partially successful. The European Parliament also made March 11 the European Day of Victims of Terrorism, which paradoxically further dilutes the date's character as a unique event with particular victims, as it extends its meaning to encompass all victims of terrorism. As in the case of 9/11, survivors of the 3/11 attacks are mostly excluded from commemoration.

In Spain, the dead were listed by name only in alphabetical order and without the intervention of the High Commissioner for Victims would have had no permanent mention at all. Furthermore, in sharp contrast to the US case, where there was wrangling over the most appropriate ways to organise the names, there was no distinction made among them by nationality, employer status or any other identity marker. Whereas in the US 9/11 victims were stratified into competing hierarchies of worth and were commemorated in highly individualised ways, 3/11 victims in Spain were treated as a non-differentiated collective actor and commemorative struggles were shaped by the political cleavage between the PP and the PSOE, a dispute which pitted ETA victims against 3/11 victims, via their respective associations, the AVT and the A11MAT (*Asociación 11M Afectados del Terrorismo*). In essence a victim taxonomy of worth emerged between victims of 3/11, who struggled to be commemorated and recognised as victims of that particular attack, and victims of ETA, which the AVT worked tirelessly to push to the forefront of any commemorative effort on behalf of the 3/11 victims. The struggle between victims associations and parties exacted a high price for the 3/11 victims and five years after the attack (2009) there was no official national commemoration of the victims at all. The following comment from A11MAT President Manjón, highlights the anger victims feel at being used as pawns in partisan debates and her understanding that the lack of commemoration in 2009 reflected a truce between parties as a means of resolving their differences, making the victims and their commemoration expendable:

> The victims are worse off than before, the only change is that now there is no photo op (*foto de ocasión*) - we have fallen into the background. I guess that after five years of throwing our dead at each other's feet they [the political parties] have come to a cordial understanding.
>
> (Ximénez de Sandoval 11 March 2009)

Competing frames over compensation of 9/11 victims

Struggles over commemoration are about which victims deserve to be remembered and how. Struggles over *compensation* actually attribute an economic value to victims. Victim compensation through legally approved schemes places a monetary value on suffering and loss that depends on the degree of injury and in the case of the US on the economic worth of the victim. If the way victims are defined in the public imaginary is more or less elastic, who is, or is not, accorded victim status with regards to compensation is legally/juridically determined and therefore less receptive to public discourse, except in the process of creating the legislation or procedures, which is highly political. The moral, legal and political aspects of 9/11 compensation have been well documented (Hadfield 2008; Schneider 2003;

Lascher and Powers 2004; Ackerman 2005; Peck 2003; Rabin 2003; Priest 2003; Shapo 2005; Dixon and Stern, 2004; Final Report of the Special Master of the September 11th Victim Compensation Fund of 2001). In the US the September 11th Victim Compensation Fund was created as part of the Air Transportation Safety and System Stabilization Act, signed by the President on 22 September 2001. A Special Master, Kenneth Feinberg, was appointed to administer the fund and draft its regulations, with input from various sectors, including the public. The regulations were drafted within 90 days of enactment, but finalised in March 2002 and applications to the fund were taken until 22 December 2003. Applying for compensation through the fund placed important limitations on victims' ability to sue the airlines, thus helping to ensure that the airline industry did not collapse, the purpose of the legislation.

If commemorative battles reveal a highly individualised way of defining victims in the US case, the struggles over compensation further underline the degree to which such cultural notions of individualism are manifested in the legal mechanisms established to compensate victims. In the US multiple competing hierarchies emerge around compensation. Three themes emerge in the United States, mostly centered on the New York case, around compensation. The first two are related to the aforementioned theme in commemoration – the idea that some victims are more deserving of recognition than others. The first theme is related to the stratification of loss as determined by the procedures of the Victim Compensation Fund. The fund, in following elements of tort law tradition, established compensation on an individualised basis and based on earnings, and also established minimum payment figures. Under the formula, money is distributed based on a victim's age, number of dependents and earning power (past and estimated future). The average payout was estimated at $1.6 million. Charitable contributions they may have received were not deducted from the award. But contrary to the traditional tort model, claimants had to deduct collateral payments, for example life insurance payments. Charities were finally excluded from deduction. It also prioritised death and physical injury over emotional distress. Victims' complaints about the fund were directed at the compensation scheme. Most of the discourse in the media did not have to do with the fact that a price-tag was being put on a deceased person. Rather, disputes emerged among groups of victims regarding whether they felt they were being disadvantaged by the legislation, i.e. eligible to receive too little. In the case of firefighters and other rescue workers, families of the deceased argued that because of their limited salaries, after deduction of pensions, they were eligible to receive very little. Similarly, families of the more wealthy deceased victims argued that after deduction of life insurance, they were also eligible to receive little compensation and that awards did not increase substantially for the deceased who made salaries over $250,000. Marian Fontana, whose firefighter husband, Dave, was killed, said the public has the incorrect impression the families 'are getting millions. Setting limits on our pain and suffering is a slap in the face to our loved ones' memories' (Sockwell-Mason 7 January 2002). Similarly, Representative King from Long Island said that given that the World Trade Center was a target partly because it was seen as the embodiment of financial success, those who achieved such success should see that reflected in their awards: 'They were the symbols of American capitalism, the symbols of American business and they were murdered because of what they were. Now they shouldn't be deprived of what they're entitled to' (Gootman 6 January 2002).

In response, Feinberg argued that the formula was designed to mini-mise disparity between victims who earned a great deal or very little: 'We want to try and make the gap narrower between higher-end and lower-end claimants' (Sherman 21 December 2001). Only victims killed or injured within 12 hours of the attacks could apply for compensation; rescue workers could apply if they were injured within 96 hours of the attacks. Injury claimants needed to prove a 'verifiable' injury and that they had received treatment within 24 hours of the attacks. New York Governor Spitzer 'criticised that provision as unduly harsh because many injury victims were treated at the scene, where no records were kept, or went home to be with their families without seeking treatment at all' (Geyelin 21 December 2001). But without a doubt this also left out many survivors of 9/11, the residents, business owners, rescue workers and volunteers who months later developed respiratory illnesses and who to this day are lobbying for recognition and treatment.

If families of victims differed over appropriate compensation amounts, they were more unified in their complaint that the compensation scheme did not take emotional distress seriously. Steve Campbell, a New York City police officer whose wife died in the attack, told Mr. Feinberg at a meeting with victims: 'I feel your offer spits on my wife, my mother-in-law and my father-in-law ... I have to watch them pop pills just to get through the day' (Geyelin 23 January 2002). The very nature of the complaints from fami-lies of the deceased generated a backlash: first, from those victims of other terrorist attacks (e.g. Oklahoma, the 1993 twin towers attack and the victims of the embassy bombings in Kenya and Tanzania), and second, from members of the public who felt that they were being greedy: 'We feel your grief, really, I'm just wondering if we have to feel your greed, too' (Geyelin 23 January 2002). The backlash directed against victims' families extended beyond comments made in the public arena, as one victim revealed: 'Whenever I do one of these TV appearances criticising the com-pensation plan, I get hate mail ... They call me a greedy bastard and say I want to profit from my wife's death' (Geyelin 23 January 2002).

The second theme is the 'parallel' source of compensation via the route of charity donations and the controversy surrounding its distribution to the families and survivors of the attacks. The RAND report lists charity as a 'compensation mechanism' and notes that at $2.7 billion, it constituted 7 per cent of the quantified benefits (Dixon and Stern 2004). Indeed, never had such an amount been collected in the history of the United States for one single event. The controversy arose from a variety of problems related to the distribution of funds, including an uncoordinated response (lack of a list of affected persons and lack of coordination among charities to discern who was giving whom how much); a perception that an 'aristocracy of grief' existed whereby uniformed workers were receiving more from charity than other types of victims and families; and concern and resentment from non-9/11 charities that their donations would dwindle because the American public was donating to the 9/11 charities. The RAND report notes the importance of charity donations in terms of responding to the needs of some who could not access other funds – undocumented workers, those who did not qualify for unemployment insurance, small businesses – as well as for providing the quickest emergency and mental health assistance. Charity in many instances was for survivors what compensation would prove not to be.

A woman who lost her husband in the attack said, 'We're not just angry, we're heartbroken about the inequities – that people could value the lives of those men more than they would value the lives of our men.... Nobody got up to the floors where my husband was. ... They died alone. And you have no idea who was helping whom. Don't tell me there weren't people up there trying to do heroic things. They had to be their own heroes and help each other' (Barstow and Henriques 2 December 2001). Her statement reveals the ongoing contestation of hero versus non-hero status, this time linked to compensation, where 'those men' refers to the rescue workers, whose families were receiving a much greater share of the charity donations and 'our' men refers to non-uniformed workers who died in the attack.

The third theme is consistent with our finding with regards to commemoration that survivors are silenced, or at least receive less attention than those who died. In the first two years after 9/11 the compensation claims of families of deceased victims of September 11 emerge as a recurring issue, but 2003 to 2006 marks a change in focus in our media-generated dataset to highlight the increasing problems of those who survived the attacks, yet had lingering injuries or illnesses. Injured survivors had to provide evidence of injury within 12 hours of the attacks, or in the case of rescue workers, 96 hours. But after that time period, many more rescue workers developed respiratory illnesses and were ineligible for compensation. As time evolved, our data shows a struggle on the part of those survivors to achieve recognition of their illness as being related to 9/11, as well as to achieve compensation. This struggle is more arduous than that of families of the deceased and is ongoing.[5] Over 60,000 rescue workers and neighbourhood residents are being treated and monitored for illnesses related to post 9/11 clean-up. In media reports, this population is rarely referred to as 'victim', but rather as residents or rescue workers. In this way these victims are denied recognition of their victim status. Among this group of victims are volunteers, as well as undocumented workers who were hired by clean-up crews as day laborers. An uninsured Columbian immigrant who worked cleaning dust from affected buildings in Wall Street in the months following 9/11 and who now suffers from asthma, headaches and skin rashes, said, 'They lied. They said there was no contamination in the area' (Kadushin and Bode 7 September 2006). Another resident said, 'We were there when the towers fell. We breathed in the air. ... All of us who lived in or worked in the area – Chinese, black, white or Spanish – are suffering' (Kadushin and Bode 7 September 2006).

Competing frames over compensation of 3/11 victims

Unlike the case of 9/11, the bulk of 3/11 victim compensation was determined primarily by the presiding judge in the trial against the surviving perpetrators of the attacks.[6] Judge Gómez Bermúdez charged those found guilty with compensating the victims, but because they were insolvent, the state assumed the financial burden of compensation, as it is legally obliged to do. Under Spanish law, the judgment does not become executable until all appeals have been resolved (29 in the case of the 3/11 sentence) and compensation is delayed until then (an estimated 2–3 years at time of sentencing). However, under the terms of the 1999 Solidarity to Victims of Terrorism Law, victims were able to receive advances on part of the amount and special hardship cases were heard by the Ministry of the Interior. In striking contrast to the US case, victims were compensated solely by degree of loss or injury. The legal heirs of deceased victims received €900.000. The surviving victims are classed into 12 groups depending on the severity of their injuries. Those with the least degree of injury receive a minimum of €30.000, plus €300 for each day of hospitalisation. Those with long lasting effects from their injuries receive an additional €10.000 to €750.000, depending on the severity of their injuries. Group 12 only contained seven victims who were classed as extremely injured. They each receive an additional €900.000. There is one victim who was classed in a group of her own: Laura Vega, who was in a vegetative coma three years after the attacks. Her family received €1 million. An additional €250.000 was established for a fund for her health care, to be administered by a public institution.

Given the egalitarian compensation scheme in Spain, do we find struggles between victims over compensation? In Spain there is no counter discourse that attempts to distinguish between victims according to earning power or other criteria. Instead, we find that some victims have to fight harder to be recognised as legitimate victims by public administrative departments. Victims of 3/11 engage in struggles with the administration around a range of issues regarding burden of proof or eligibility for compensation or treatment. For example, with regards to employment disability, the administration would argue a victim was fit to return to work, the AA11MAT victim association would argue they were not. With regards to the recognition of ongoing need for psychological treatment, the administration would classify a victim as no longer needing treatment or of having abandoned treatment and the victim association would argue they had been switched from one psychologist to the other with no continuity in care. Overall, the burden of proof for victims suffering from psychological trauma was more difficult to satisfy than for physical trauma. Victims of psychological trauma had to work harder to be recognised as 'legitimate victims' than did those who had physical injuries. Distinctions were also made by the administration between immigrant victims from Latin America had rights to dual nationality and those from Eastern Europe who were left in limbo as they had to give up their nationality, but wait to be awarded Spanish nationality. But none of these differences were struggles among victims themselves.

However, once again, there was one area of 'compensation' that was politicised and that made a clear distinction between ETA victims and 3/11 victims. This was the area of victim association funding at the regional autonomous level. The Autonomous Community of Madrid is, and has been, governed by the Popular Party since the time of the attacks. From 2006–09, the President of the Autonomous Community of Madrid did not award any funding to the A11MAT, the organisation that represents the bulk of 3/11 victims (1,200) and whose president has been an outspoken critic of the Popular Party, but did make awards in these years to the AVT and the FVT (Foundation of Victims of Terrorism), both closely aligned with the Popular Party. In this way, a distinction was made between 'good' victims (those who did not criticise the PP) and 'bad' victims (those who did). Because the A11MAT is often the only resource 3/11 victims have in their struggles with the administration (regional and national, irrespective of governing party), this denial of funding constitutes a form of punishment for not having the 'correct' political ideology, despite the fact the A11MAT is avowedly non-partisan and has criticised both major parties. The 'solution' to this problem was itself partisan, with eight socialist party (PSOE) city governments signing agreements to help fund the A11MAT, which also receives funding from the Ministry of the Interior and from anonymous benefactors (*El País* 6 October 2008).

Conclusions: making sense of victim hierarchies in cases of transnational terrorism

The most striking and unexpected finding is the existence of victim taxonomies among victims of transnational as opposed to internecine terrorism. In both cases, despite the absence of debate about the distinction between victims and perpetrators, victim taxonomies of worth emerged. It is clear

from the analysis that three areas were key in determining the victim definition and status, and what they were entitled to as a result of that status:
nationally situated *cultural* narratives about victimhood; the national *legal*
framework; and the *political* arena, in which political and economic
agendas (in the case of 9/11) were also important.

In the US, hierarchies among 9/11 victims and between 9/11 victims
and non-9/11 victims are clearly reflected in commemoration and compensation schemes and the debates they generated. Victim movements
have been very successful in the US in making claims on behalf of victims
and de-stigmatising victimhood (Barker 2007). Therefore, victims of 9/11
were very broadly and elastically defined and received overwhelming
support from the public through charitable donations. 9/11 deceased
victims were also very successfully framed as sacred: symbolic representatives of the nation who were commemorated in grandiose official ceremonies, as well as in a myriad of highly pluralistic and individualistic ways.
9/11 and its victims were framed as unique and unprecedented. This
framing also was reflected in the legislation passed to compensate the
victims, legislation with a clear economic and political agenda. The compensation fund was unique to 9/11 victims, a product of politics and
departed substantially from precedent. There was a clear political and economic agenda behind the compensation scheme and victim compensation
was instrumentalised to save the airline industry from collapse. Victim
compensation was, compared to Spain, highly individualised, and consistent with the common law tort tradition, considered current and future
earnings, as well as the number of dependents of the deceased. It also
clearly defined eligibility and thus circumscribed victimhood to the
physical and temporal immediacy of the individual to the 9/11 attacks.

The uniqueness of the compensation scheme, as well as the anniversary
commemoration, generated resentment on the part of other victims of terrorism on US soil. But even within those groups affected by the Twin Towers
attacks, multiple contested hierarchies emerged, based on (1) occupational
status and 'hero' status (2) struggles over the order in which names should
be listed, centred on employee status and (3) whether the victim was
deceased or had survived. These hierarchies reflect fundamental narratives
in American society that place great importance on occupation and income
as identity markers and esteem indicators (see Flesher Fominaya and Barberet, forthcoming), a preoccupation regarding 'heroism' and again, the
sacred nature of those who died at the hands of terrorists. These distinctions
between victims were codified and reinforced through the legal mechanism
of the compensation fund. Although in the public imagination there were
many legitimate victims of 9/11, the legal restrictions placed on claimants
meant that many of these victims were left out. Surviving victims especially
were made 'invisible' both in the commemorations and denied compensation in many cases. Because of the highly politicised nature of the response
to 9/11, which led to the rapid passage of legislation affecting the victims,

the process did not allow time for victims associations to develop and organise their own claims making, especially around compensation. Trying to fit their needs and demands into a very circumscribed legislation requires them to re-engage the political arena, requesting congress to renew budgetary allowances for ongoing treatment, for example, which is an endeavor that requires significant material and emotional resources.

In Spain, the cultural narratives of victimhood are much less positive than in the US, and victims' movements are much less developed. Victims of 3/11 were certainly viewed with great sympathy, but this did not translate into an abundance of resources from charitable donations. Instead, in keeping with the more developed welfare state in Spain, the state was expected to attend to the victims' needs and claims. Victims were defined very narrowly, both in the public perception and legally, and were compensated according to existing legislation (The Law of Solidarity with Victims of Terrorism) and the result of the trial against the surviving perpetrators. Culturally and legally, then, unlike in the US case, we see little differentiation between victims of 3/11 and they are framed in collective egalitarian terms. It is in the political arena that the strongest taxonomies of worth emerge. 3/11 victims had a harder time being sacralised as representatives of the nation, due to the constant competing frame that they were in truth ETA victims. Although ETA victims are framed by ETA as representatives of the oppressive Spanish state, this definition is not shared by the general Spanish public, who see ETA victims as the outcome of homegrown, rather than transnational terrorism. 3/11 victims therefore had a harder time framing themselves as unique, and were forced into an ongoing partisan struggle that pitted them against ETA victims and denied them autonomy. The salient hierarchy, therefore, was not among different 3/11 victims, but between 3/11 and ETA victims. These struggles shaped commemoration significantly, but had less impact on direct compensation given the less politicised nature of legal compensation in the Spanish framework. However, 3/11 victims, or more specifically the A11MAT victims association that represents the majority of them, suffered significantly. They were 'punished' (through denial of funding) by the PP for refusing to accept ETA's responsibility and for therefore questioning the AVT/PP's narrative that ETA is the most important issue in Spanish politics.

This comparative analysis shows that the politics of victimhood has very real consequences for victims, not only in cases of internecine conflict, but also in cases of transnational terrorism. We have shown that national cultural narratives, legal frameworks and political arenas shape these in very different ways. While a detailed analysis is beyond the scope of this chapter, these findings have implications for ongoing debates about the existence of a 'global' civil society. When it comes to victims of terrorism, even that perpetrated by groups operating 'globally' like Al-Qaeda, it is clear that national contexts continue to shape victims experiences in fundamental ways and with real consequences for the victims.

Notes

1 Cristina Flesher-Fominaya wishes to thank the British Academy for the support that enabled the completion of this research. Rosemary Barberet wishes to acknowledge funding support of PSC CUNY grant 62474–00 40.
2 Dixon and Stern (2004) estimate that 250 persons were seriously injured.
3 We refer here to dominant discourses within domestic public arenas, but see Robinson (2009) for discourses that exclude 9/11 victims from spheres of moral concern in her comparative analysis of online fora.
4 Letschert and Pemberton (2008) show cross national variation among OSCE countries in who is included in the definition of victims, ranging from direct victim only, to families of direct victims, to first responders in a minority of cases.
5 In late 2010 the United States Congress passed the James Zadroga 9/11 Health and Compensation Act, to continue to provide health care and monitoring for tens of thousands of first responders, construction workers and Lower Manhattan residents who were exposed to World Trade Center dust after the attacks.
It also establishes a Victims Compensation Fund that will give monetary awards for to emergency workers and others who fall ill and lose wages as a result of exposure to the dust and to their families in case of death, similar to one set up for people who were killed on 9/11.
6 There were initial compensation payments made by RENFE (the train company) accident insurance, but these were relatively small and determined by the existing insurance policy rather than politically or by the courts.

References

Ackerman, R. M. (2005) The September 11th victim compensation fund: an effective administrative response to national tragedy, *Harvard Negotiation Law Review*, 10: 135–229.

Albrecht, H. J. and Kilchling, M. (2007) Victims of terrorism policies: should victims of terrorism be treated differently?, *European Journal on Criminal Policy and Research*, 13(1–2): 13–31.

Alexander, J. C. (2004) Towards a theory of cultural trauma, in Alexander, J. C. *et al.* (eds) *Cultural Trauma and Collective Identity*, Berkeley: University of California Press.

Barker, V. (2007) The politics of pain: A political institutionalist analysis of crime victims' moral protests, *Law & Society Review*, 41(3): 619–64.

Barstow, D. and Henriques, D. B. (2 December 2001) A nation challenged: the families; gifts to rescuers divide survivors, *New York Times*.

Benford, R. D. and Snow, D. A. (2000) Framing processes and social movements: an overview and assessment, *Annual Review of Sociology*, 26: 11–39.

Biner, Z. Ö. (2006) From terrorist to repentant: who is the victim?, *History and Anthropology*, 17(4): 339–53.

Borer, T. A. (2003) A taxonomy of victims and perpetrators: human rights and reconciliation in South Africa, *Human Rights Quarterly*, 25: 1088–1116.

Christie, N. (1986) The ideal victim, in Fattah, E. A. (ed.) *From Crime Policy to Victim Policy: Reorienting the Justice System*, Houndmills, Basingstoke, Hampshire: Macmillan.

Dixon, L. and Stern, R. K. (2004) *Compensation for the Losses of the 9/11 Attacks*, Santa Monica, CA: RAND Corporation.

El País (6 October 2000) Ocho ayuntamientos socialistas financiarán a la asociación de víctimas de Pilar Manjón, *El País*.

Feinberg, K. R. (2004) *Final Report of the Special Master for the September 11th Victim Compensation Fund of 2001*, Washington, DC: U.S. Department of Justice.

Flesher Fominaya, C. and Barberet, R. (forthcoming) *Surviving the Twin Towers and the Madrid bombings: A cross-national analysis of the politics of victimhood of 9/11 and 3/11*. Manuscript in preparation.

Geyelin, M. (23 January 2002) Criticism of Sept. 11 victims' fund sparks backlash – Families find public considers demands to change terms 'greedy' and unreasonable, *Wall Street Journal*.

Geyelin, M. (21 December 2001) U.S. details payment for attack victims, *Wall Street Journal*.

Gootman, E. (7 January 2002) In last days for comment, victims' fund is under fire, *New York Times*.

Hadfield, G. K. (2008) Framing the choice between cash and the courthouse: experiences with the 9/11 victim compensation fund, *Law & Society Review*, 42(3): 645–682.

Jiménez Barca, A. (20 February 2007) Su hija murió en el tren, su marido fue detenido y ayer le insultaron, *El País*.

Humphrey, C. (2003) Stalin and the blue elephant: paranoia and complicity in post-communist metahistories, in West, H. G and Sanders, T. (eds), *Transparency and Conspiracy*, Durham: Duke University Press.

Kadushin, P. and Bode, N. (7 September 2006) Immigs and locals rally to get aid, *New York Daily News*.

Lascher, E. L. and Powers, M. R. (2004) September 11 victims, random events, and the ethics of compensation, *American Behavioral Scientist*, 48: 281.

Letschert, R. M. and Pemberton, A. (2008) Addressing the needs of victims of terrorism in the OSCE region, *Security and Human Rights*, 19(4): 298–311.

Ochs, J. (2006) The politics of victimhood and its internal exegetes: terror victims in israel, history and anthropology, 17(4): 355–68.

Peck, R. S. (2003) The victim compensation fund: born from a unique confluence of events not likely to be duplicated, *DePaul Law Review*, 53: 209–30.

Pogrebin, R. (15 September 2001) After the attacks: emotional aid; Bellevue psychiatry chief creates action plan to tame a horrendous nightmare, *New York Times*.

Porter, E. (2007) *Peacebuilding: Women in International Perspective*, London and New York: Routledge.

Priest, G. L., (2003) The problematic structure of the September 11th Victim Compensation Fund, *DePaul Law Review*, 53: 527–45.

Rabin, R. L. (2003) The September 11th victim compensation fund: a circumscribed response or an auspicious model?, *DePaul Law Review*, 53: 769–803.

Robinson, L. (2008) The moral accounting of terrorism: competing interpretations of September 11, 2001, *Qualitative Sociology*, 31(3):271–85.

Robinson, L. (2009) Brazilians, French, and Americans debate 9/11: cultural scripts of innocence and culpability, *International Journal of Communication*, 3:652–67.

Schneider, E. M. (2003) Grief, procedure, and justice: the September 11th Victim Compensation Fund, *DePaul Law Review*, 53: 457–500.

Shapo, M. S. (2005) *Compensation for victims of terrorism*, Dobbs Ferry, NY: Oceana Publications.

Sherman, W. (21 December 2001) Feds set payouts to kin of WTC victims, *New York Daily News*.

Smelser, N. J. (2004) Psychological trauma and cultural trauma, in Alexander, J. C. *et al.* (eds) *Cultural Trauma and Collective Identity*, Berkeley: University of California Press.

Smyth, M. (1998) Remembering in Northern Ireland: victims, perpetrators and hierarchies of pain and responsibility, in Hamber, B. *Past Imperfect: Dealing with the Past in Northern Ireland and Societies in Transition*, Derry/Londonderry: INCORE, University of Ulster.

Snow, D. and Benford, R. D. (1988) Ideology, frame resonance and participant mobilization, *International Social Movement Research* 1: 197–219.

Sockwell-Mason, I. (7 January 2002) WTC kin blast comp guidelines, *New York Post*.

Tota, A. L. (2005) Counter-memories of terrorism: the public inscription of a dramatic past, in m. d. and hanrahan, N. W. (eds) *The Blackwell Companion to the Sociology of Culture*, Jacobs, Oxford: Blackwell.

Vázquez Valverde, C. (2005) Stress reactions of the general population after the terrorist attacks of S11, 2001 (USA) and M11, 2004 (Madrid, Spain): myths and realities, *Annuary of Clinical and Health Psychology*, 1: 9–25.

Ximénez de Sandoval, P. (11 March 2009) 'Hay víctimas que no tienen ni para comer.' *El País*.

Zaslow, J. (5 September 2002) Honoring 'heroes' of Sept. 11 stirs a delicate debate – families of plane passengers, office workers want parity for their relatives, *Wall Street Journal*.

Zeruvabel, E. (1991) *The Fine Line: Making Distinctions in Everyday Life*, New York: The Free Press

9 The returns of war

Bodies, images and invented ritual in the war on terror

Michael S. Drake

Introduction

This chapter undertakes a comparative study of the public receptions of the war dead in the UK and the US, using documentation from the public sphere, to produce insights into current conditions of the politics of mourning in relation to the ineffectiveness of the anti-war movements and to remilitarisation processes in these national civic cultural contexts. Judith Butler's work on the 'powers of mourning' after 9/11 was intended to inform critical opposition to the Bush regime's response, but this paper counter-poses to her analysis, the *politics* of mourning outlined by Gillian Rose (1996). The strategy of the anti-war movement, reflected in Butler's argument, produces an impasse of what Rose calls 'aberrated mourning', leaving a vacuum that has been filled by new forms of militarisation.

Debates about embodiment and identity conventionally focus on the living, individuated body, but some bodies are more significant than others in the constitution of collective identities. Because the bodies of the war dead stand in for the body politic in the formation and maintenance of national imaginaries, the repatriation and commemoration of the war dead in forms of representation such as homecoming parades, tributes and ritual burials thus becomes a potential theatre of political contention. This function of the 'culture of commemoration' in the twentieth century has been diversely explored (for example Mosse 1990; Winter 1995; Sebald 2003), but quite separately from that literature, recent work in philosophy has refocused attention on the function of mourning (Rose 1993, 1996; Butler 2006, 2009) drawing insights that can be applied to the current wars of the new global (dis)order.

This chapter looks at the politics of grief in the context of the anti-war movement of 2003–09 in the UK and the US. Judith Butler's (2006) work on the 'powers of mourning' after 9/11 was intended to inform critical responses to the Bush regime's use of violent retaliation. However, comparing Butler's argument to the work of the philosopher Gillian Rose reveals a *politics* of mourning which is overlooked in the simplistic appropriation of grief advocated by Butler and endorsed by the anti-war movement. Butler's anti-war advocacy presents in philosophical form many of the mistakes of the anti-war movement, while Rose's reflections on mourning point toward a politics that does not forsake reason to oppose against it a moralism grounded in immediate affect, but instead engages with the contentiousness of the meaning of grief and its relation to the political. That contention takes place not through the conventional political media of institutional debate or the repertoire of protest, but rather through contemporary cultural forms of mediatisation.

The work of Antigone

In her essay 'Violence, Mourning and Politics', Judith Butler argues that in contrast to the US reassertion of a fantasy of inviolability and security after 9/11, that event of loss 'made a tenuous "we" of us all' (Butler 2006: 20). Butler works through contrasts between the self-determining public body or body politic and the affective, feeling, emotional body. When we represent ourselves politically, Butler argues, we present ourselves as 'bounded beings', 'a community defined by some shared features'. This claim of integrity and self-determination is essential to political movements, but it is confounded by our experience of being 'beside ourselves' with grief (or rage) when we mourn (the concept of grieving is used interchangeably with that of mourning in the essay) because we accept that in the loss we are ourselves undone and thus transformed. 'When we say "we" we ... designate this very problematic. We do not solve it ... this disposition of ourselves outside ourselves seems to follow from bodily life, from its vulnerability and its exposure' (Butler 2006: 24).

Butler thus contrasts the moral to the political, on the grounds of the contrast of the (experiential, emotive, moral) body to the (representational, disembodied, rational) polis. Asking, 'Can this situation of mourning ... supply a perspective by which to begin to apprehend the contemporary global political situation?' (Butler 2006: 28), posits an imaginary community on the basis of this common condition which would produce the perspective of recognition of universal human interdependence, but begs the question of how this 'normative reorientation for politics' could be realised. What would be its medium? How could it be represented?

The polis of the sovereign is conventionally represented in the body of the sacrificial dead and Butler is effectively attempting to establish the discursive conditions for a radical re-engagement with the classical body politic, against its naturalised co-option in modernity as a trope for reaction (Neocleous 2001:137). Butler argues that the state and media operate a repression of affect, a regulation of grief and a demarcation of which lives are grievable (Butler 2009). The public obituary functions performatively 'as an act of nation-building', by its public demarcation of which bodies are grieveable and thus of which bodies are accorded recognition rather than mere 'bare life' (as Agamben would put it) (Butler 2006: 34).

However, Butler's own imaginary community of mourning requires her to project an effective appropriation of the Other dead as a means of reducing otherness, thereby foreclosing the reorientation of politics which she is trying to describe. In formal terms, this can only be imagined as the project of an 'international coalition', the same form of hegemony that produced much of our current global violence. This appeal has to over-look all prior relations of violence and domination on the grounds of a presumed community of affect which implicitly assimilates the death of the Other as our own loss, thus appropriating morality at the same time as ostensibly repudiating the violence of political reason in the form of 'increased sovereign power and hegemonic national unity' (Butler 2006: 46).

Butler's community of grief, is therefore constituted in a one-sided act of agency which reproduces the very inequalities and misrecognitions she wants to repudiate, '...when *we* struggle to find out about the losses that *we* are asked not to mourn, when *we* attempt to name, and thus to bring under the rubric of the human, those whom the United States and its allies have killed' (Butler 2006: 46, emphasis added).

Butler's argument finally collapses back into a simplistic opposition between community and state, the moral and the political, justice and law, emotion and reason, which provides us with no medium through which to imagine, much less begin to realise, the responsibility that must precede reconciliation. In extending this argument, Butler's more recent work further compounds its mistakes, both ethical and political.

A subsequent essay, (Butler 2009) contends that the state and conserva-tive forces obstruct an 'affective response' to the deaths of Others. Butler posits that affect as natural, embodied and spontaneous, as the opposite of repressive forces. Her argument is more concerned with establishing a moral stance to the war than it is with effective strategies, a stance that has characterised much of the anti-war protests in the UK and the US, under the slogan, 'Not in my/our name' – particular, moralist, a refusal of rather than engagement with the political.

Just as those anti-war protests became about petty infringements on our own freedoms, so Butler's essay becomes about securing 'our', 'ability to respond with outrage' (Butler 2009: 54) because she vests moral value in such affect, rather than in the effect of clear, caustic, critical rational anal-ysis. She opposes that moral outrage to 'utilitarian calculus' as though these were the only alternatives available, neglecting rational action just as did the anti-war movement, preferring to secure the conditions of its own moralist disavowal. For Butler, the state is the medium of the social (Butler 2009: 13, 28), which stands between the universal and the individual; the social is merely the shadow the state casts in its relation to the individual as citizen (Butler 2009: 33). The very medium for effective political action today is foreclosed by the requirements of affective moralism. In contrast, Gillian Rose's (1996) elucidation of Hegel's analysis of Antigone shows how this classical figure, rather than providing a simple opposition of private to public, justice to law, emotional to rational, that would require us to repudiate one element in favour of another, provides instead a shift to a higher level of question; in this case, from an either/or to a 'what now?' In this, Rose's analysis completes and also functions as a critique of both Butler's incomplete argument for mourning and the moralism of the anti-war movement, showing how they take up only one side of the equation comprised of the series of dichotomies reason/emotion, justice/law, public/private, etc, repudiating the war by turning their backs on it, abandoning the struggle for political terrain in favour of a moral project which 'perpetuates endless dying and endless tyranny' (Rose 1996: 26).

In Butler, the moral community is counterposed to the state and its politics, but this leaves us stuck, unable to move forward. In her argument, the promise of a politics of mourning is substituted first by a politics of grievability, then by the opposition of the moralised body of community to the rational body politic and finally displaced altogether in favour of an international coalition, which hegemonically appropriates the task of mourning. In contrast, for Rose, it is not the authenticity of the mourner (Antigone) that is significant, but her contextualised action which represents how, 'In these delegitimate acts of tending the dead, these acts of justice, against the current will of the city, women reinvent the political life of the community' (Rose 1996: 35).

For Rose, the work of mourning is work in the Arendtian sense of political action, which is more than an emotional response or labour upon the existing world, which imbues meaning and thus opens the world to new possibilities. This seems to be what Butler also seeks, but fails to reach because of her assumption that mourning proceeds from the emotional experience of bereavement, a response which may be at best transformed into labour, into the construction of oppositions, replicating the corruption of the political which results in miscommunication, in impasse, in war. For the political reorientation that Butler seeks, we need to allow Rose to complete her argument, for us to take up the work of mourning.

Rose says of the ethical stance that is developed from the politics of difference.

> New ethics is waving at the Other who is drowning and dragging his children under with him in his violent, dying gestures. New ethics cares for 'the Other'; but since it refuses any relation to law, it may be merciful, but, equally, it may be merciless. In either case, having renounced principles and intentions, new ethics displays, 'the best intentions' – the intention to get things right this time.
>
> (Rose 1993: 6)

Butler's analysis similarly 'proceeds without taking any account of institutions which are extraneous to its idea, that is, without taking any account of mediation' (Rose 1993: 7). Rose emphasises the work of mourning as the investment of meaning, producing a *politics* of grief rather than a simple opposition between affect and reason. Grief and mourning are contested, challenged and constructed. Mourning is the work of giving (and contesting) meaning, not immediate affect against reason.

> To participate body and soul in our relationships and in our self-identity in the work and in the undoing of the city and yet to be deprived of, or to refuse, the work of mourning has political conse-quences. It tempts us to oppose pure, gratuitous love to the injustice of the world; to see ourselves as suffering but good, and the city as evil.
>
> (Rose 1996: 103)

Rose thus enables us to see how questions about the body of the dead are tied up with questions about the politics of war and the ways that participation in the current war is reshaping our political community.

If the decision to go to war was based on the repression of grief and if a politics of grief could inform the anti-war movement, then this requires us to ask, where are these bodies situated today? How are they represented in our mediated social world? What is the terrain of the struggle over the meaning of the war dead? When we do so, we see that it is in fact not the task of appropriating the death of the Other that must pre-occupy us for a renaissance of politics, but the recognition of the death of those who are purported to represent the body politic, the polis. We can ask how these positions – Butler's moralism in particular, since it reflects the broad anti-war stance since 9/11 – are worked through in actual political practice. The main question that needs to be asked there is how the anti-war move-ment has been so spectacularly ineffective, so unsuccessful that the massive opposition to the invasion of Iraq in 2003's street demonstrations seems to have been reversed in the UK, to the extent that it is now generally consid-ered immoral to publicly oppose the war.

Contending the meaning of the dead

The dead have become contested. The argument that they must not have died in vain provides a morally-charged justification for the continuation of the war, appropriating the dead to the project that killed them. It sus-pends the possibility of mourning, since they cannot be mourned whose function is not yet realised, just as Butler points out President Bush repu-diated mourning for the dead of 9/11 when he announced after only ten days, on 21 September, that it was time for resolute action to take the place of grief (Butler 2006: 29). Bush thus appropriated the dead to his project for a New American Century, for endless war. However, the excul-patory argument that they did not die in our name abandons the fallen dead, rendering those who are mourning doubly bereft and surrendering the political terrain of the meaning of their return. Yet it is exactly here that Rose's work of mourning has to begin. To be a part of a political community means that we have to accept responsibility for all its actions, not only for those that we find morally acceptable.

Furthermore, the anti-war refusal of recognition of the war dead under the rubric 'not in my name' plays into neo-conservative strategy to reinscribe the pre-1968 division of the public from the private sphere, to separate the act of reappropriation of the body by the public state from the mourning of loss, so that the public domain is only increased by these sacrifices, while loss and suffering are consigned to the private sphere as the mere concern of particular individuals rather than issues confronting us as public persons.

In this politics of mourning, it becomes clear that grief cannot be counterposed to the cold reason of politics and the state. The state actually appears as a vast reservoir of sentimentality, a reserve army of emotion that can be brought into play cynically, but none the less affectingly, in ready forms and language of partriotic sentiment which gives shape to the shapeless and undermines any claim to morality on the grounds of immediacy of affect.

Remilitarisation, duty and service: the British case

So what has happened in the current, ongoing conflict? In the UK at least, there has been an apparent reversal of what appeared to be an implicitly anti-militarist and explicitly anti-war public consensus in 2003. Furthermore, there has been a remilitarisation of civic life, public culture and even of society in general, reversing the post-World War II trends towards what the sociologist Martin Shaw called 'post-military society' (Shaw 1991). Military recruitment operates today on University campuses and in schools, alongside militant and politicised protests against rises in tuition fees. On return from active service in Afghanistan and Iraq, British Army regiments are welcomed by large crowds at uniformed homecoming parades. Public subscription and National Lottery funding has raised £7 million to enable the construction of a new National Armed Forces Memorial, the first since 1948 (Hamilton 13 October 2007). The Ministry of Defence has campaigned to renormalise a uniformed military presence in garrison towns, where military personnel had long been advised not to wear uniform off-duty in order to minimise the tensions with local populations, and remilitarisation has extended to attempts to refashion the national image, such as Tony Blair's speech toward the very end of his period of office as Prime Minister, describing Britain as 'a war-making nation', in contrast to the mere peace-keeping role characteristic of contemporary European nation states.

The normalisation of militarism seems pervasive, subtle and arises in some unexpected places. The centre-left *Guardian* newspaper in 2008 published daily for a whole week a series of posters illustrating physical exercises, from a British Army handbook, validating the military as a source of vitality, health and fitness, associated with biopolitical directives through both state policy and popular celebrity culture to improve the fitness of the national population (implicitly, then, through emulation of embodied military virtues) with all the positive moral connotations that those attributes have acquired in a country currently obsessed with the normalisation of body image.

In 2003, at least in the UK, public hegemony *against* the war extended to popular antimilitarism on a scale then unseen since the 1960s. To understand the reversal of this hegemony in such military recuperations of the public sphere, we need to develop some incisive critical and self-critical, reflexive, analysis. I have addressed the theoretical dimensions of that in using Rose to criticise Butler's moralism, but we need to understand how that anti-war stance, and the very grounds of the anti-war movement, left the field open to other forces to construct meaning for the casualties of violence which have such a powerful definitive function.

First, the institution of the British Army itself mounted a concerted campaign from late 2007, almost immediately backed by the *Daily Telegraph*.[1] Using press releases and letters to the press, the Royal British Legion and the Chief of Defence Staff, Sir Jock Stirrup, confronted the government over its neglect of the 'military covenant' in providing inadequate protection and aftercare for service personnel in the context of these new wars. Again through the mass media, the Chief of the General Staff, General Sir Richard Dannatt called publicly for local councils to organise 'homecoming' parades for the regiments returning from Iraq, on the American model (though civic-military relations are very different in the US and the UK for constitutional, historical and cultural reasons). The Telegraph issued a call for response by letter on its website on 22 September and broke the story on 26 September (*Daily Telegraph* 22 September 2007; Adams and Simpson 2007). These parades have exercised the archaic rights granted to the regiments of the army in earlier, more militaristic times, to 'freedom of the city' from which they were recruited. The army seems to be extending this right to bear arms in the streets, to include tanks and artillery pieces (Mack 2009). The parades have attracted large turnouts (Glaze 2007; BBC News 22 November 2007). However, my participant observation of the reception of the parade through Hull by the Royal Yorkshire Regiment suggests that the crowds may have been less than *immediately* patriotic. The flags they waved were supplied by local radio stations. A considerable proportion of the crowd were families of migrant workers attending for free entertainment on their (weekday) day off. Other contingents were young women whose motivations for attending the soldiers' parade seems to have been indicated by their bodily exhibitionism. The parades seem to function as opportunities to participate in spectacle, rather than as patriotic expression.

In Luton, a 'homecoming' parade produced controversy as radical young Muslims protested that the war against terror was being conducted as a war against Islam, in which the soldiers parading had been perpetrators. Those protests provided a pretext for organised violent reaction from the extreme nationalist right. Both sides of this clash were marginalised as 'extremist' by traditional and political authorities. The national effect was to establish a consensus that anti-war protest should be kept distinct from recognition of the performance of military duty, a disjunction that enables remilitarisation and public quiescence over the war to coexist with apparently widespread private anti-war sentiment that extends to service personnel relatives and even into the ranks.

That representation of the war as military role performance provides the key to understanding the outflanking of the anti-war movement in the UK. The renormalisation of the military has underpinned acceptance of the war, substituting the earlier unprecedented public opposition of 2003, with a sense of respect for, and identification with, 'the troops'. Public attitudes have shifted in inverse relation to the duration of the war – the longer it has become and looks to be protracted, the greater the acceptance of the war as actuality.

The military operations in Iraq and Afghanistan have become more publicly acceptable as they have become routinised, reduced to role performance. An appeal for acceptance of the war not in terms of security or ideology, but as the implementation of a responsibility to bring democracy and peace to the rest of the world has found resonance in British national culture suffering post-colonial nostalgia for identification with empire and its self-justification as a force of progress, as the contemporary version of the imperial civilising mission. This contemporary 'mission' is also framed in a particular, self-effacing and yet therefore morally effective form; the term 'duty' figures far more prominently than 'sacrifice' in British rhetoric about the war. Soldiers are seen as doing their duty, no more and no less, circumventing the anti-war contention in whose name they conduct their operations, since that becomes irrelevant. The dominant perspective is that we all have jobs to do and theirs are particularly dangerous, so they are also referred to often as heroes, for instance in the celebrity-supported charity 'Help for Heroes', which has enrolled to represent it the royal family alongside X-factor contestants and David Beckham as other role performers with whom the charitable public might identify. The Help for Heroes website makes explicit the identification of military service with everyday role performance, while disavowing overt support for the war itself, which becomes radically depoliticised as an occupational hazard of the occupation of soldiery:

We believe that anyone who volunteers to serve in time of war, knowing that they may risk all, is a hero. These are ordinary people doing extraordinary things and some of them are living with the consequences of their service for life. We may not be able to prevent our soldiers from being wounded, but together we can help them get better...

(*Help for Heroes*, 'Who are we?' n.d.)

The website reconstructs heroism as non-sacrificial, traumatic, individualised and normalised, simply an exceptional extension of everyday life, evoking solidarity through this inclusion that is also an extension of equivalent status to all contributors, all who share these sentiments. It is not that they have done anything for us, but rather that they are like us and that we are like them, a construction of the heroic that enables the vicarious indulgence in identification with heroism while remaining in its appeal resolutely individualistic, without ever raising the spectre of nationalist, massified identity which characterised the propaganda appeals of earlier wars. It calls, after all, not for commensurate service, or sacrifice; instead, a mere charitable donation is enough to secure identification in the heroic.

It's about the blokes, our men and women of the Armed Forces. It's about Derek, a rugby player who has lost both his legs, it's about Carl whose jaw is wired up so he has been drinking through a straw. It's about Richard who was handed a mobile phone as he lay on the stretcher so he could say goodbye to his wife. It's about Ben, it's about Steven and Andy and Mark, it's about them all. They are just blokes but they are our blokes; they are our heroes. We want to help our heroes.

(*Help for Heroes*, Homepage, n.d.)

Giving, in this sense is an invitation to consume this vicarious identification, offering a consumerism as solidarity, an identification, which resonates between the dreams of post-imperial nostalgia and contemporary imaginaries of consumerist self-actualisation. You too can buy into heroic identification, simply by giving, and even more so by fundraising, the consumerist equivalent of active citizenship, as the page reiterates in repeating the 'it's about' phrase earlier applied to the war-wounded: 'It's about doing your bit, no matter how big or small. Every fundraiser is special to us and can make a real difference, so please keep going!' (*Help for Heroes* Homepage, nd).

In totality, these strategies and effects (since they are not all conspiratorial) wrongfoot the anti-war movement, tackling it on its own ground of moralisation and rendering irrelevant all the questions about the political decision to go to war or even to continue the war. If anything, they strengthen that latter resolve, with the figure of the performing post-ideological cultural multi-tasking in which the actual performance of war fighting becomes of negligible importance in comparison to the emotional, cultural, social and ideological labour of the role, just as for all other labour in the 'new capitalism'. In the UK, the death of service personnel therefore figures as privatised, publicly regrettable, but only potentially controversial on grounds like those of the health and safety criteria that govern everyday life in the consumer-heroic age, while the military labour of the living becomes eulogised as exemplary and identificatory.

Remoralisation, sacrifice and loss: the US case

In the US, remoralisation rather than remilitarisation would describe more accurately the current trends in military-civil relations in public culture, since the US military was not culturally marginalised in the Cold War to the extent that it was in Western Europe from the 1960s on, but retained its status, albeit stigmatised, as a key element of US society. Even ardently anti-war films such as *In the Valley of Elah* (Haggis 2008) have only criticised the conduct of the war by contrasting contemporary conduct to an honourable military-civic tradition, represented in that film by the veteran father of the dead soldier, deeply imbued with stoic values and the honour of the US military-citizen identity and a local woman cop, representing social diversity and self-integrity in public service as the contemporary corollary of the older tradition. Similarly, the US anti-war movement grounds itself politically in its discursive claim to an alternative, true, patriotism, which, like the UK movement, indulges affect by grounding anti-war opposition in moral propriety. Thus, at the end (and only at the end) of Brian de Palma's brutally objective realist film, *Redacted* (2007), we are confronted by real footage of Iraqi war casualties, but with faces censorially obliterated. In that closing footage, De Palma reproduces in cinematic form Butler's discursive failure to represent without appropriating the Other dead, who provide the ethical ground for the film's anti-war posture, a posture that depends on the Other as victim, unable to represent themselves.

US military state policy of Concurrent Return of the bodies of the war dead aims to recover and repatriate all bodies without intermediate burial (Sledge 2005: 41). Remains are identified, prepared for burial and transported in a casket via Fort Dover military airbase for delivery to the next of kin. The bodies are eligible for burial in Arlington national cemetery and are entitled to a military guard of honour if they are given a hometown funeral, preceding which they may be given a civic welcome home with a parade. This public, military-civic ritual round the repatriated US body of the war dead claims it as a sacrifice, but this is not an expenditure or an excess; there is a clear puritan economy about these rituals to ensure that no body should constitute a *loss* in the public domain. Repatriation is not merely spatial, but also symbolic, and the body provides the medium through which rituals 'heal' and even reinvigorate the wounded body politic.

Marvin and Ingle's study, *Blood Sacrifice and the Nation: Totem Rituals and the American Flag* (1999), shows how the body of the war dead functions as a medium for collective self-representation, a cipher through which society expresses itself. In those ritualised mediations, the body of the war dead figures as the sacrificial embodiment of the totem, a *flagbody* which has been symbolically transformed through a sacralisation process, proceeding from the reconstruction of the body in bootcamp, through to its posthumous incorporation into the sacralised community as a blood sacrifice which revives the community by providing a medium for social self-representation. Over the grave containing the body, the next of kin are handed a folded flag in exchange for this sacrifice. When the treatment of the dead was revealed through the censorship of images of the returning coffins (NPR 29 April 2005), revealing the neo-liberal affront to this military-civic ceremonial constitution, the resulting scandal constituted the first crack in the Bush regime's production of a pro-war scenario. However, this owed little to the anti-war protests, but was rather a reaction against the encroachment of neo-liberal rationalisation on the deep cultural constitution of the US republican body politic.

From 2002, the political anthropology of the war dead traced by Marvin and Ingle had been distorted by the very pressures that had marginalised Memorial Days – egoistic individualism, consumerism and the neo-liberal doctrine of primary self-interest. The war dead at that stage were simply treated as baggage to be unceremoniously shipped home from what was expected to be a short war with minimal casualties, maximal profits and tight control over representation, returned from Iraq and Afghanistan as freight via commercial airlines to be unloaded by forklift trucks for warehousing at Fort Dover pending their distribution for burial. In response to this scandal, the previously customary care of the dead was formally instituted in new legislation in 2006, so that the bodies of military personnel killed overseas were repatriated by military transport with an escort and received by a dress uniform honour guard (Levy 2007). The symbolic significance of the dead body thus marked the limit of the commodification of the war process, but also the point at which war casualties became perversely incorporated into processes of legitimation.

Even then the arrival was secret and Defence Department photographs of the caskets were withheld from the media. This ceremonial dimension, open to interpretation, was not for public consumption. The politics of the war dead are after all the politics of meaning, with stakes more complex than the simple opposition between sacrifice and loss. In these photos, the caskets appeared en masse rather than in isolation after their dispersal for individual burial. Draped as they were with US flags, their cumulative symbolic significance rendered the risk of their reinterpretation in the public domain too great (National Public Radio 29 April 2005).

The politics of the images of the caskets was tied up with the issue of numerical representation. The US war department has consistently refused to estimate the numbers of Iraqi dead, but in the UK, in 2007, the Ministry of Defence still refused to release statistics of its own war casualties since the invasions, leading to accusations that they were attempting to cover-up the impact of these conflicts on UK communities. In UK Parliamentary debate, MPs contrasted the muted reception accorded to the war dead in the UK to their civic reception in the US (Brown 23 March 2007). In the US, the civic appropriation of the war dead as sacrifice has also produced a counter-politics in the public domain. On 21 March 2004, the Veterans For Peace held their own ceremony to unveil an 'Iraq War memorial' next to the Vietnam War memorial at California State Capitol, a semi-permanent display featuring names and photos of men and women who had died in Iraq (Bacher 2004). By the time of the Presidential campaigns in September that year, some of the bereaved of the war dead had also begun to exercise what Rose referred to as 'the work of the soul', Cindy Sheehan being the best-known, but others also operating as Real Voices and Military Moms with a Mission (Pleming 2004). However, rather than produce a renaissance of politics, these protests became channelled into the existing politics of personality, attempting to link their cause to a wider movement by backing alternative Presidential candidates in opposition to Bush in the 2004 elections, while Obama's campaign effectively pushed the war issue aside, mobilising on the basis of utopian, almost messianic 'hope' which highlighted economic rather than military aspects of the general crisis of security. Britain's equivalent of Cindy Sheehan, Rose Gentle, was also drawn into electoral politics, which have similarly changed the context of her campaign, imposing a different agenda, directing her toward the question of the war's legality. Just as the anti-war movement in the UK squandered the widespread opposition of 2003 in attempts to broaden the campaign, so these engagements with electoralism by the politicised parents of the bereaved have similarly lost their way, their momentum and their presence on the public stage.

This leaves a critical public vacuum in which civic media and state representation functions largely unchallenged. That representation extends into cyberspace, becoming a hyperbole of remembrance on media websites such as those of the *Washington Post* and *CNN*, which list the names and pictures of the individual dead along with personal tributes, the individualised pages becoming an online monument to each of the dead. This endless repetition of texts and photos and the serial retelling of 'definitive' anecdotes about the individual war dead also normalises loss through violent death, as it becomes reinscribed into social routine and everyday referentiality; so that war and its effects become the continuous backdrop of social experience (or at least for that half-life we all have today, online). Those effects of course are partial, and even partisan, because almost always excluding the far greater numbers of Iraqi and Afghan dead. The presence of war through these sites is packaged, compartmentalised and undeniable, but also distantiated from everyday life, at once its normal accompaniment and, simultaneously, uncontroversial and marginal.

Public bodies and private grief

In the UK, the reception of the war dead is more muted, but also shades into judicial process rather than civic life. Until April 2007, the bodies arrived at RAF Brize Norton, from where they were taken to Oxford for a Coroner's inquest (because the UK officially is not and has not been at war in either Iraq or Afghanistan) before being returned to the next of kin. There is, ostensibly, no 'enemy' whose action could have caused these deaths. While the definition of the death is purely formal, and carefully secured by the Ministry of Defence, the required Coroner's inquest has opened the only space in which there has been effective critical discussion of the conduct of the war, as the context of the death of the deceased, that has challenged official doctrine, invoking a jurisdictional clash over digital and visual information when one inquest required that the US military produce visual data of an incident of friendly-fire in which had resulted in the deaths of British service personnel, a direct clash of jurisdictional competence with US military law, which claims sole prerogative to judge the actions of its own personnel. The inquests of one Oxford coroner, Andrew Walker, proved particularly controversial, and while the inquests have challenged the official accounts of the circumstances of these deaths, those challenges have remained strictly forensic, technical rather than political (Simpson 2008).

This forensic investigative procedure contrasts strongly with Butler's moralistic repudiation, endorsed by the anti-war movement, of the value of these deaths, yet has proved politically and publicly a more effective source of criticism of the UK's involvement in the war. In the Coroner's Reports the dead body itself becomes a triadic element transcending the opposition between sacrificial state and moral community. The body in the Coroner's inquest 'speaks' for itself through the metre of its wounds, the context of its death, rather than becoming re-animated as the totem of sacrificial nation or an object of private loss.

When RAF Lyneham became the single reception point for the return of all the UK's war dead in 2007, another public medium opened in which their deaths are recognised as a public loss, as events in 'the political life of the community' (Rose 1996: 35), through the 'invented tradition' of the townspeople of nearby Wootton Bassett, who stand silently along their High Street to pay their respects to the bodies as they pass in hearses through the town en route to the Coroner. Originating as a contingent and apparently spontaneous response of local civil society, the numbers attending rose with widening media publicity, which focused on the town as the bereaved relatives of each dead soldier began to join this singular, unique, public recognition. However, in the public and localised context of the town's silent, muted ceremony, their expressions of emotional anguish, and the attendant media focus, has proved jarringly anomalous (Jardine and Savill 2009; BBC 14 July 2009). This town's recognition of

the soldier's deaths as loss and its silent expression of public grief is deter-
minedly apolitical, producing a fragile sense of local distinctiveness but
also a radical pluralism, suspending contention and enabling all viewpoints to participate and in so doing, to articulate their public grief
without ascribing any binding meaning to either the dead or the ceremony. As media attention mounted through 2009, the town's civic leaders
were compelled to articulate this delicate fragility of the condition of
public memorialisation in a context of contention through public letters
and media interviews (Gray *et al.* 2009; Morris 2009). The event remains
difficult, awkwardly public in the form of self-imposed restraint, with no
partisan symbols other than those borne by the local veterans association
which originally initiated the event.

The diversion of the UK war dead from Iraq into these extra-political
theatres around the body plays its part in muting propagandistic tendencies to heroic representation of the war dead as sacrifice, in line with wider
cultural differences. Most UK communities lack the kind of democratic
civic life of the US, characterised by archetypal town meetings, shared
values and collective conscience. UK soldier's funerals are thus distinc-
tively private events at which even uniformed soldiers acting as coffin-
bearers do so as the friends of the fallen, in personal honour to their
individual comrade, rather than as part of a symbolic exchange. There is
no homecoming civic parade for the war dead in the UK, no mediated
event articulating the death as sacrifice (the civic leaders of Wootton
Bassett reject the attribution that they 'stand for the nation'). The relation
between the regiment and the bereaved civil family does not pass through
the public domain, with the effect that mourning is privatised, that there
is no public appropriation, but also no public recognition of the war dead.
Even where the protraction of the conflict has led to the appearance of
UK media websites listing the current war dead, these tend to be further
removed from the home pages, requiring multiple clicks to access them,
in contrast to the US, where online memorialisation is more usually accessible direct from the websites' home page. One online gallery proclaims
itself part of the Palace Barracks Memorial Gardens, Holywood, Northern
Ireland, its coverage long-predating the current wars, which figure as just
another theatre of operations, a sub-section of post-1945 conflicts in which
UK forces have taken casualties, the site itself, in its own words, 'has to be
set in the context of the Troubles of Northern Ireland' (Palace Barracks
Memorial Garden, n.d.).

Conclusion

Cultural differences also shape the ways that the military operations are
represented in the US and the UK, illustrating distinct civil-military constitutions and distinct bodies politic, and even, therefore, quite different
wars. Rather than representing the war dead as ideological warriors, the

eulogies on UK websites and in the media more generally represent them as dutiful professionals. However, rather than opening those deaths to political contention, this representation simply appropriates the dead to a different kind of military state, reflecting different military-civil histories and constitutions. UK eulogies for the dead perform the same function of incorporation, albeit it into the UK version of the 'war on terror' project, as a technical necessity of government which requires military war service as role performance. In the US, commemoration in the premise that 'they did not die in vain', but in pursuit of some greater cause, appropriates the dead as sacrifice and thereby precludes public mourning of loss, instead investing their sacrificial value in further war. In the UK, eulogising the dead as good professionals 'just doing their job', simply does the same for a different, but no less endless, project. Similar pitfalls apply to any attempts to appropriate the dead on the grounds of their death, even in the name of universal humanism.

Butler (2006, 2009) assumes that mourning follows from bereavement itself, without ceremony, as a 'knowing' without remembrance, mistaking affect for task. However, mourning is not merely a reflex of the affective body, but involves the investment of meaning. At most, Butler provides the condition that we must give a name and a face to the dead, but that does not invest the dead with a life lived; rather, it marks death as a merely the end of 'bare life', the condition for the appropriation of the dead of the Other, who are stripped of the meanings they may have for their bereaved and become instead a sacrificial salve to our conscience. As did Walter Benjamin after World War I (Jay 2003), Butler seeks to forestall the premature closure of mourning which would fix the meaning of the dead as sacrifice, but like Benjamin, her positional assertion offers no prospect of moving beyond that and indeed closes off the construction of meaning altogether, eclipsing political reason with an assumed immediate solidarity of affect.

In Rose's terms, Butler's strategy produces only the impasse of *aberrated* mourning, 'the stasis of desertion' which is transfixed by its own affective reaction to injustice, unable to pass through this to the inaugurated mourning which would produce a new meaning (Rose 1993: 209). A radical politics of mourning consists not in its affective immediacy, as grieving (or grievance) but in the work of mourning as a process of making meaningful, so any counter-politics of war demands engagement in a struggle for the public meaning of the war dead.

Note

1 With its subsequent revelations of MPs scandalous expenses claims, this appears in retrospect as the first stage in the strategic re-establishment of the *Daily Telegraph*, as an active element of the public sphere, after its long decline into relic status through the 1980s and 1990s.

References

Adams, S. and Simpson, A. (2007) 'Parade snub for Britain's returning soldiers', *The Daily Telegraph*, 26 September 2007, at: www.telegraph.co.uk/news/main. jhtml?xml=/news/2007/09/26/narmy126.xml, accessed 12 December 2007.

Bacher, D. (2004) 'Memorial wall for Iraq's war dead and wounded', *Counterpunch*, 25 March 2004, at: www.counterpunch.org/bacher03252004.html, accessed 3 March 2008.

BBC News (2007) 'Hundreds turn out to see Anglians', 22 November 2007, at: http://news.bbc.co.uk/1/hi/england/7107898.stm, accessed 12 December 2007.

BBC News (2009) 'Wootton Bassett's military tradition', 14 July 2009, at: http://news.bbc.co.uk/1/hi/uk/8149081.stm, accessed 05 September 2009.

Brown, C. (2007) 'Ministers finally admit full scale of war casualties', *Independent*, 23 March 2007, at: www.independent.co.uk/news/uk/politics/ministers-finally-admit-full-scale-of-war-casualties-441494.html, accessed 26 March 2008.

Butler, J. (2006) *Precarious Life: The Powers of Mourning and Violence*, London: Verso.

Butler, J. (2009) *Frames of War: When is Life Grievable?*, London: Verso.

Daily Telegraph (2007) 'Do British troops need "homecoming parades"?', 22 September 2007, at: www.telegraph.co.uk/news/yourview/1563858/Do-British-troops-need-homecoming-parades.html, accessed 30 June 2009.

Glaze, B. (2007) 'Welcome back for our brave Iraq heroes', *The South Wales Echo*, 11 December 2007, at: http://icwales.icnetwork.co.uk/news/wales-news/2007/12/11/welcome-back-for-our-brave-iraq-war-heroes-91466–20233861/, accessed 12 December 2007.

Gray, J. *et al.* (2009) 'Wootton Bassett's silent tribute', *Guardian*, 16 July 2009 (letters), at: www.guardian.co.uk/uk/2009/jul/16/wootton-bassett-letter, accessed 5 September 2009.

Haggis, P. (director) *In the Valley of Elah*, Warner Bros, 2008.

Hamilton, A. (2007) 'A monument at last for the fallen of modern times', *The Times*, 13 October 2007, at: www.timesonline.co.uk/tol/news/uk/article2648622.ece, accessed 30 June 2009.

Help for Heroes, at: www.helpforheroes.org.uk/.

Jardine, C. and Savill, R. (2009) 'Wootton Bassett: A very British way of mourning', *Daily Telegraph*, 7 July 2009, at: www.telegraph.co.uk/comment/personal-view/5771032/Wootton-Bassett-A-very-British-way-of-mourning.html, accessed 5 September 2009.

Jay, M. (2003) *Refractions of Violence*, New York: Routledge.

Levy, M. (2007) 'A brief military history and civilian guide to Arlington national cemetery: Iraq dead ahead', *Counterpunch*, June 2/3 2007, at: www.counterpunch.org/levy06022007.html, accessed 05 March 2008.

Mack, T. (2009) 'Tanks in street for homecoming parade', *Leicester Mercury*, 2 March 2009, at: www.thisisleicestershire.co.uk/news/Tanks-city-streets-homecoming-parade/article-736974-detail/article.html, accessed 30 June 2009.

Marvin, C. and Ingle, D. W. (1999) *Blood Sacrifice and the Nation: Totem Rituals and the American Flag*, Cambridge University Press.

Morris, S. (2009) 'The myth of heroes' highway', *Guardian*, 19 July 2009, at: www.guardian.co.uk/uk/2009/jul/18/wootton-bassett-journalists-afghanistan, accessed 5 September 2009.

Mosse, G. (1990) *Fallen Soldiers: reshaping the Memory of the World Wars*, Oxford University Press.

National Public Radio, 'Photos of caskets bearing war dead released', 29 April, 2005, at: www.npr.org/templates/story/story.php?storyId=4625212, accessed 26 March 2008.

Neocleous, M. (2001) The fate of the body politic, *Radical Philiosophy* 108, July–August 2001.

Palace Barracks Memorial Garden, at: www.palacebarracksmemorialgarden.org/, accessed 20 March 2008.

de Palma, B. (director) *Redacted*, Magnolia Pictures, 2008.

Pleming, S. (2004) 'Families of Iraq war dead target Bush in ads', Reuters, 29 September 2004, at: www.commondreams.org/headlines04/0929–02.htm, accessed 3 March 2008.

Rose, G. (1993) *Judaism and Modernity: Philosophical Essays*, Oxford: Blackwell.

Rose, G. (1996) *Mourning Becomes the Law: Philosophy and Representation*, Cambridge University Press.

Sebald, W. G. (2003) *On the Natural History of Destruction*, London: Penguin.

Shaw, M. (1991) *Post-Military Society: Militarism, Demilitarization and War at the End of the Twentieth Century*, Cambridge: Polity Press.

Simpson, A. (2008) 'Andrew Walker: The coroner who is a thorn in the side of the Ministry of Defence', *Daily Telegraph*, 17 October 2008, at: www.telegraph.co.uk/news/newstopics/lawreports/3217682/Andrew-Walker-The-coroner-who-is-a-thorn-in-the-side-of-the-Ministry-of-Defence.html, accessed 5 September 2009.

Sledge, M. (2005) *Soldier Dead: How we Recover, Identify, Bury and Honour our Military Fallen*, New York: Columbia University Press.

Winter, J. (1995) *Sites of Memory, Sites of Mourning: the Great War in European Cultural Memory*, Cambridge University Press.

10 Frames, forums and Facebook

Interpreting British Muslim understandings of post-7/7 militarist media narratives

Lucy Michael

> The war against terrorism is indeed a war, but of a different sort to the ones we are used to. Its outcome, however, is as important as any we have fought before.
>
> (Tony Blair quoted in the *Daily Telegraph*, 15 October 2002)

Introduction

This chapter examines the creation and manipulation of specific frames by Muslims in the UK in order to understand and respond to dominant media narratives, in the period after the London bombings of 2005. Personal contributions to virtual discussion spaces illustrate the ways in which the process of 'framing' (Gamson 1992) is both an act of rejecting alternative understandings and an emotional attachment to distant concepts and experiences. Here, contributions by and between Muslims in a range of open and in ethno-religious-specific virtual spaces reveal a variety of different frames through which new and changing media narratives could be understood and addressed. These are explored further using ethnographic and interview data collected over a period of four years in two British cities. It is suggested that a significant context for the framing process in relation to post 7/7 narratives of militarism and conflict is that of the city. In this respect, key frames are reviewed in light of contemporary local narratives of inter- and intra-ethnic conflict, and developing organised and transitory responses to images of war and conflict by Muslims within these cities.

It is now widely recognised that many of the frames utilised by international news media outlets to make sense of the Iraq war and 'war on terror' have long continuities with previous militarising and diplomatic frames. There are a considerable number of studies conducted of these frames and the ways in which they have set out a problem of 'new terrorism', some of which I will explore in the next section. Cumulatively, they examine the ways that these frames promote military narratives around domestic, as well as international, events, policy agendas emphasising a new culture of fear and need for national unity in times of crisis, and Islamophobic discourses echoing Cold War ideological divides. Chermak, writing in relation to the representation of terrorism after 2001, points out the significance of these frames relies on a recognition that they are selected, sponsored and promoted by the media and their sources as preferred means of interpreting events, and it is this, with the rejection of other interpretations that gives framing its 'inherent ideological power' (2003: 10).

From 2001, media frames appeared to follow purposive framing by US and British governments to tie together the ideological elements of the anticipated attack on Western democracies. Bush and Blair simultaneously spoke to a narrative of a 'war on two fronts' to promote support for the invasion of Iraq: 'Both, though different in means, are the same in nature. Both are the new threats facing the post-Cold War world, threats from people or state who have no compunction about killing the innocent' (Blair quoted in the *Daily Telegraph* 15 October 2002).

The onset of the war in Iraq prompted a considerable body of academic work examining the militarised frames within which contemporary news media content has been constructed. Those studies have, however, focused largely on dominant frames in the US context or comparative work across 'Western' mainstream media outlets and with attention paid to, either, the currency of military narratives or to Islamophobic frames employed in relation to international and domestic news. In the US, Ryan (2004) has argued that political framing of events in terms of the 'war on terror' has been adopted almost uncritically by US media outlets. Reynolds and Barnett (2003) similarly note the extensiveness with which war and military responses featured in the dominant frame covering all CNN news stories in the aftermath of the 9/11 attacks, alongside American unity and justification. In this, the frame employed by the broadcaster very sharply mirrored the dominant frame of official discourse.

Militarising narratives in this period emphasised national unity, terrorist attacks as 'acts of war' (arguably perceiving the enemy as powerful and unified, rather than relatively powerless and disparate) and included specific attempts to characterise 'the enemy' (often, as Reynolds and Barnett (2003) note, as 'cowards' and 'madmen'). The effect of ongoing military operations on dominant media frames is, however, not uniform across the global media reporting on those operations and on the policy agendas attending to them. Thus Papacharissi and Olivieira (2008), for example, examining military narratives, found these to be more prevalent in US coverage of terrorism than in the UK. They have argued that as British frames emphasised diplomacy, evidently there was a substantial alignment between news frames and national policies. Nonetheless, following Ruigrok and van Atteveldt (2006), it may be too simplistic to carve up the world in this way. In their study, investigating whether international coverage of terrorist attacks was framed in local or global terms after 9/11, they found that although proximity is still a strong determinant of attention for events in the British, American and Dutch press, the framing of these events was more affected by the global event of 9/11 than by local considerations. Thus global frames were much more significant for terror events post 9/11 than local frames. It is in this light that the present chapter re-examines the ways in which frames commonly used by British media outlets can be interpreted as militarising frames by diverse audiences, even as they reflect a more 'diplomatic' perspective than those in the American press and elsewhere.

Framing the problem

Framing is key to understanding about communications, not just from official sources and the media, but also in the public sphere. This is because of its function as an aide to decision-making in times where information about a problem seems to come from disparate sources. Media stories exemplifying an episodic or thematic frame can draw on an established understanding of a problem and give coherence to an audience's appreciation of the larger issues at play behind separate events and processes. Iyengar and Kinder (1987) argue that this has important consequences for how audiences attribute causes, and solutions, to difficult social problems like crime and poverty. Thus, a media organisation, or indeed a range of media outlets, can give coherence to a political issue or public controversy by drawing on shared frames (Gamson 1992). Alternative frames can therefore shape the formulations of a problem and the potential responses (Carroll and Johnson 1990).

Dominant and 'demonising'?

Framing in the war on terror has up to now been approached predominantly in terms of the dominant themes as seen from a majority point of view. This is despite numerous alternative frames being mobilised specifically in relation to the Iraq war and a context in which there was, Karatzogianni notes, a 'media environment ripe for alternative reporting of the conflict' (2006: 178). However, the powerful discourses of demonisation, which exist simultaneously, beg examination of the responses to the dominant frames and alternative frames employed by the demonised. Saied Raza Ameli, in a series of research projects, has shown British Muslims to feel the media to be one of the main factors causing discrimination and misunderstanding between themselves and the rest of society, as well as one of the specific reasons that leads Muslims to feel either neutral or negative about British citizenship and questions of integration (Ameli *et al.* 2004; Ameli and Merali 2004). The cumulative findings of these and other studies led Ameli *et al.* (2007), writing for the Islamic Human Rights Commission, to conclude that:

> [t]he prevalence of domination in the discourse produced demonisation regardless of intention, and this is of great significance in that demonisation as an ideology no longer needs to be the result of a conspiracy or project or the accumulation of deliberate malice – domination of the majority now necessarily means demonisation of the minority Other.
>
> (2007: 34)

As a result, South Asian Muslims in Britain have sought to engage much more closely with Muslim media, in order to access alternative frames and discourses which allow them to understand world events and to articulate their position in relation to them (Ahmed 2005). Yet academic studies examining these demonising frames from a 'minority' perspective have largely emphasised the presence and growth of Islamophobic discourses and narratives in the global media. From the mid-1990s, academics have recognised the potency of these discourses, and the ways in which they are fed by a range of media coverage of domestic and international news events, as well as ongoing concerns about migration, secularism and human rights. The Commission on British Muslims and Islamophobia (1997) identified a series of what it called 'closed' and 'open' views on Islam, further refined by post-2001 studies of the British press, including Richardson's (2007) examination of the extent to which 'dominant' narratives outweigh 'alternative' narratives on Muslims in Europe. These narratives include assumptions about diversity amongst Muslims, difference to non-Muslims, inferiority of Muslims, Islam and Muslims as threatening and the possibility for cooperation between Muslims and non-Muslims.

Much of the research on dominant frames in, and before, this period has been conducted via content and image analyses of news stories in particular and media coverage more widely. Thus the Runnymede Trust (1997), Allen (2004), Richardson (Commission on British Muslims and Islamophobia, 2004) and Moore, Mason and Lewis (2008) have each discovered, and examined, Islamophobic narratives in the British press through content analysis of news stories mentioning Islam or Muslims. Riddell and Yasmeen (2009) employed a similar methodology to examine the employment of those narratives by non-Muslim audiences. Complementary research has looked at how Muslims perceive their own identities, or relate their sense of security, to such narratives and, simultaneously, the changing social, political and legal context. However, the difficulties in knowing how the association is translated from media to audience are already well established (Ruigrok and van Atteveldt 2006). Few studies have comprehensively examined framing from the point of view of (re) articulation, the reassembling of elements in different construction.

To do this, it is necessary to fully examine the ways in which British Muslims explicitly recognise, identify and accept (or reject) such narratives. Aly (2007), doing so in the Australian context, has noted the strategic disengagement with popular media by some, particularly younger Muslims. Such a strategy 'does not shift the perception of media discourse but means that this discourse is no longer used as a basis for constructing identity or for developing a perception of the dominant public opinion' (2007: 37). Muslim participants in her study reported that this also allowed them to move beyond thinking about themselves as victimised by Islamophobic discourses and find alternative narratives of belonging. One way of moving further towards an understanding of how those alternative narratives are discovered and constructed, I suggest, is by identifying the key frames through which Muslims engage with public discourses.

British Muslims: a critical audience

As a well-connected diaspora, Muslims in Britain have long been critical viewers of a wide range of global and regional media outlets, from CNN, Fox, Sky, BBC, BBC World and Al-Jazeera to more distinctly local outlets, including local TV and radio stations which are city-based. Nevertheless, they are keenly aware of the impact of news media on public opinion faced, as they are, with a keen understanding of its behavioural impact on their friends and neighbours in times of crisis. Audiences differ in the respect to which they are immediately influenced by 'priming' effects of mass media, depending on how well-informed they are about an issue, how interested in it they are and how well exposed to news media (Graber 2004). Arguably, therefore, an audience which regularly consumes news and social programming from a range of alternative media sources will be better placed to, first, recognise, and second, be critical of, dominant frames at play.

The participants in the study informing this paper are such a critical audience. This work draws on interviews and observations conducted across Muslim communities in Manchester and Stoke-on-Trent (UK) between 2005 and 2008 and latterly on interviews, focus groups and web forum discussions conducted online between 2007 and 2010. Participants cited in this paper ranged in age from 16 to 54 years old, and all had been resident in the UK for at least 15 years. Participants under the age of 40 were all British-born and the majority of these described themselves as 'third' genderation (i.e. with one British-born parent). Regardless of age, all were daily viewers of a range of satellite news channels, as well as con-sumers of national and local news media via newspapers and radio. However, the younger participants (the under 35s), whose narratives are reproduced here, were also keenly engaged with internet-based media, which was seen as essential in acquiring valuable information and having access to multiple sources of information which could then be assessed in relation to one another.

The inter-connectedness of the lives of young Muslims due to identity ascriptions which are often negative, gives them a particularly interesting perspective on the dominant frames at play. Regardless of individual or collective choice, the identities of young Muslims in Britain are inter-twined with one another (Ramji 2005) and they therefore have a direct impact upon how one another is perceived by the wider society. Moreover, although there may be sharp divisions between young people in terms of class and affluence, they participate in the same or similar counter-publics, which makes them aware of one another's position in relation to the his-torical events around them, and of their common position in terms of gen-erational distance from migration and the development of a national Muslim community in Britain. Thus, they are particularly well-placed to comment on articulations (Hall 1980), which make no sense to them and on frames which reject the agency of the individual in their social, politi-cal and religious lives.

Media usage and consumption is, as for British non-Muslims, connected to the usefulness of this in relation to other daily activities. Young Muslims in both Manchester and Stoke-on-Trent exhibited large networks of friends, both in the neighbourhood and in the institutions with which they were most engaged; schools, colleges and, optionally, faith or youth organ-isations. They used mobile and particularly internet technology to keep in touch with one another and to organise their social activities. Personal web-pages and online diaries ('blogs') were popular amongst this cohort generally and allowed creative identifications around their Muslim and South Asian identities. Users were visibly identified within formal and informal networks through personal networking websites like Facebook or MySpace and were adventurous in their interactions with others in these virtual spaces. Young leader figures were able to use this Internet technol-ogy, with instant access to established groups, to publicise events and draw in non-members to one-off organisational activities, since multiple affilia-tions to organisations with lower levels of commitment to each were more common than deep involvement in, or commitment to, one organisation (Michael 2008).

In Stoke-on-Trent, it was the movement of young people from engagement in youth clubs to activities at the city's colleges that prompted engagement with wider forums in order to access informa-tion from outside the city. This was at least partly in response to a per-ception by young people that the city's Muslim population was particularly closed bounded in its ethnic and religious activities. In Man-chester, a wider range of local media outlets, both mainstream and ethnic-specific, facilitated ongoing engagement with discussion of the position of Muslims in the UK, not least because of the high-profile activity of Greater Manchester Police in counter-terror activities and the city's history of debate around racial equality. Participants reported engaging on a daily basis with national media debates, as well as using Facebook to organise events and receive information from organisations at home and abroad.

With the commencement of Shariah TV on Channel 4 in 2004, and the accompanying web forums, it was possible to see that there was a diverse and engaged audience amongst its British Muslim viewers. Similar forums were launched by Muslim media and political organisations. These, however (and somewhat unexpectedly), drew a much wider audience, as non-Muslims sought out spaces within which to engage in discussion around issues of Islam in Britain. This peaked in particular directly after the London attacks of 2005, when web forums hosted by Muslim media were inundated with messages primarily of condemnation but also of sympathy and support, later cited by mainstream media outlets. Web forums were thus seen to have an additional advantage, of conveying the Muslim voice in all of its diversity to (at least) the national press.

But one of the most cited reasons for engaging with new media was the importance of having 'truthful' information about the situation of Muslims worldwide. This was particularly the case in relation to issues around which Muslim communities in Britain were vilified: the 2001 '9/11' attacks and the war on terror. They were happy to express their opinions through online forums while using the Internet and were a voracious audience for all programmes on Muslims on mainstream TV channels, as well as regular viewers of satellite channels.

Therefore, rather than focusing on disengagement with popular media, as Aly (2007) does, I want to focus on this engagement with mass and new media, to understand how Muslim participants in my studies identified, interpreted and sought to unsettle the dominant frames of this period, as they saw them. Data analysed is sourced, therefore, from everyday communications made by participants on open and closed web forums and restricted access social networking sites (arguably resembling Fraser's 'co-existing public spheres of diverse counterpublics' (1992). There are compelling reasons to undertake such a methodological approach. As Aly and Green (2008) note, an enforced silence is observable amongst Muslims who fear reprisal or labelling, even for sharing opinions similar to non-Muslims citizens critical of government policy or media coverage of terrorism. Thus, it is necessary to look into closed spheres of discussion for such personal reflections. There are, however, ethical constraints on the use of such material and comments are therefore described rather than quoted directly where there is a risk of loss of the anonymity assured to participants. It is worth noting too that no claims to accuracy are made for the information on which participants have drawn in their interpretations. Rather, this paper aims to emphasise that the information which we draw upon as citizens in thinking and making decisions about our engagement with fellow citizens is always partial and shifting.

Identifying the dominant frames

The gradual repositioning of Muslim communities, as a body of risk to social order from 2001 (Michael 2009), has arguably formed the backdrop for the identification of dominant frames in this period. With the intensification of media interest in risk conflicts, risk issues are 'socially explode[d]' by media where they would otherwise be secreted from the public (Beck 1992). This, Mythen and Walklate (2008) have argued, has opened up the possibility for a visible moral dimension to be put into play in dominant (re)presentations of the terrorist risk. The danger in this is that it facilitates a misalignment between 'mass endorsement of morality' and the potential degree of harm from the terrorist risk. The 'moral charge' (Cottle 2005) that ripples outwards further facilitates the connection between terrorist attacks and the wider cultural, social, political and economic processes which are looked to provide meaning. The centrality of media engagement to New Labour governance (the 'constant campaign') brings this moral charge into close proximity to the then government's new policy ventures. It is unsurprising therefore, to find that the dominant frames are so closely related to the British policy agenda of the period. Yet to describe these frames as largely 'diplomatic' (Papacharissi and Olivieira 2008), understates the extent to which the politics of the Iraq war spill into other areas. Since the frames investigated below relate so closely to the position of society, the state and the citizen *whilst at war*, and all of which relate to the *ongoing* nature of the war, it is suggested that these are militarising, rather than militarised, frames.

Three major frames are identifiable from the data. I will briefly outline these before investigating in depth the ways in which these have been identified and responded to by the participants in this study. The first frame identified is that of the 'war at home'. Britain took several steps not taken by other countries to deal with the terror threat after 2001, including the introduction of the *Anti-terrorism Crime and Security Act 2001*, which allowed internment without charge or trial for foreign nationals in Britain suspected of 'links' with international terrorism (the 'Belmarsh' policy) (Liberty 2010). The passing of this legislation marked a period in which the government considered the powers to be justifiable due to a state of emergency, followed as it was by the *Criminal Justice Act 2003*, which increased seven days pre-charge detention in terrorism cases to 14 days, and the *Civil Contingencies Bill 2004* delegating extensive powers to the executive in the event of an emergency, including a terrorist emergency. This was the initial restriction in a series of restrictions on British and foreign nationals suspected of terrorist activities requiring minimal evidence or accountability on the part of the agencies implementing them and set the tone for a perception that if there was a war on, then it was only Muslims who would feel it at home in Britain.

The unique position of the state as arbiter of knowledge and rights characterises the second frame identifiable from the data. In this frame, the establishment of the state as having unique access to knowledge, because of cross-border intelligence, experience in dealing with terrorism, powers of surveillance and a unique position in relation to considering the rights of citizens, allows all other parties to be depicted as weaker, less knowing and less authoritative. Further, the depiction of errors in counter-terrorist operations as specifically connected to individuals reinforces the position of the state as above the citizen, regardless of past errors. The emphasis on the 'newness' of the *type* of terror threat underpins this.

The third frame observable in the data relates to the identification of the 'enemy within'. Insofar as it relies on the connection of Muslims at home and abroad, and reflects a misunderstanding of Muslim connections between counter-terror operations in Britain, Afghanistan and Iraq, it is the most militarising frame of the three. This frame, which draws together many of the Islamophobic narratives identified elsewhere, is made coherent by virtue of an internal hierarchy: first, who is an identifiable suspect population, but virtue of not being British, pro-British or 'western'; second, who are sympathising populations (knowingly or otherwise) facilitating the actual enemy; and third, to what extent do suspect populations share important characteristics which facilitate the enemy's activities through, for example, secrecy, insularity and obfuscation?

The war at home: a particularly British 'state of emergency'

The 'war at home' constitutes the first, and most important, frame in this study. From Blair's comparison of the nature of the Iraq war and counter-terrorism operations in 2002 (*Daily Telegraph* quoted above), Bush's simultaneous statements about fighting 'a war on two fronts', to the 2005 bombings in London, there could have been little doubt about the connection between the two sets of operations in the public mindset. Yet after 2005, with Blair's outright rejection of claims that the London bombings had been prompted by the British presence in Iraq, talk of 'war' was effectively disappeared from British soil. The 'Contest' report on counterterrorism (Home Office 2006), for example, gives just two brief mentions to 'action in Iraq' (pp. 10, 15), once references the 'international coalition' in Iraq (p. 16) and gives no mention at all to the word 'war'. Further, the word 'conflict' is only used to describe issues of segregation and cohesion in local areas in Britain (p. 11). What evidence was there, then, of Britain being at war at all? Despite the geographical distance between the war in Iraq and England, for Muslims, the distance was too small. Faced in 2005 with Labour MP Hazel Blears' comments that Muslims would have to accept as a 'reality' that they would be disproportionately stopped and searched by police, it was clear that at least for some of the population, the war would not only be played out an their TV screens at night. This seemed almost totally at odds with the state's refusal to talk about the impact of the war on Britain except in the most abstract terms. Abbas (2009) notes the general impression given by media coverage that the criminal justice system is successfully prosecuting Muslim terrorists as a result of disproportionate stop-and-search.

For young Muslims in Manchester and Stoke-on-Trent, the war was visible on the streets via the increased Islamophobia directed at them and their families. Participants chose to discuss particular attacks both in public forums and in the local papers, where coverage of the events had already appeared. Yet in Stoke-on-Trent, more than in Manchester, Islamophobic events connected to the politics of the Iraq war were explained within local media as part of the continuing race relations problems of the city. Few received coverage outside the city. In Manchester, with a strong and vocal ethnic minority press, as well as large Islamic organisations with a key interest in flagging up incidents of Islamophobia, the city's daily newspaper (as well as the national media) gave some coverage to such incidents. In both cities, the incidents were discussed within youth groups, mosques and schools, as well as via social networking sites (Facebook being the most popular after 2006). Such discussions were, however, episodic rather than lengthy. More abstract statements, like that by Blears, had greater currency for the long-term since, unlike individual events which carried little evidence of a connection to war, as minister of a government at war, Blears' statement appeared to evidence that connection to a greater extent.

The depiction of Muslims as having a natural relationship with conflict is, however, one of the narratives that underpins this frame. With media explanations for 'conflict' at home generally referencing 'Muslim-related tensions' (*Sunday Times* 8 October 2006), it was hard to unpick Islamophobia from a wider frame which sought to re-racialise the discourses of cohesion which pervaded discussion of almost all social issues at the local level. One *Sunday Times* article (8 October 2006) caused particular consternation amongst participants since it described the response of some Muslim groups to Labour MP Jack Straw's comments on the veil (*burqa* or *niqab*) in a regional newspaper (*Lancashire Evening Telegraph* 5 October 2006) as 'silly'. The article visually drew upon this frame by juxtaposing images of the veil row with those of a Muslim policeman excused from guarding the Israeli embassy in London and a violent clash between Asian and white young people in Windsor, with the caption 'Just a few examples last week of what seem to be rising Muslim-related tensions' (8 October 2006).

The insertion of Straw's comments into a context of wider societal conflict shocked the participants in my study. For the young women, it suggested an unspoken continuity between Muslim women in Britain and abroad, underpinned by an idea that they were all victims of their own people's determination to maintain tradition at all costs, even if it brought conflict. They compared it to the arguments about operations in

Afghanistan to free women from the virtual everyday imprisonment imposed by the Taliban. Having previously been vocal about the choice for women to wear the *hijab* (which doesn't cover the face) if they made the decision independently, some spoke about their fear of how they would be perceived now. With widespread ignorance about what constituted the 'veil' and a perceived loss of face in front of others who would see them as weak and submissive to traditions they (and their parents) had already abandoned, they moved discussions about veiling into private spaces. Facebook pages were filled with jokes about who had chosen (or not) to wear the hijab. In these spaces, the discussion became more gendered than ever, as girls found that their perspective on this debate differed significantly from that of their male friends and relatives. Fears for safety were not top of the agenda, as they were for young men, but a concern that the veil would come to signify cultural 'problems' incorporating the whole group. Straw's comments (*Lancashire Evening Telegraph* 5 October 2006), reported widely in the national media, had drawn vociferous responses from Muslim groups across the country, as well as lengthy discussions in the web forums and mosque study circles attended by this study's participants. A spate of veil-focused assaults on Muslims in the streets of at least six British cities (including Manchester) immediately following his comments put 'war on the streets' firmly in the minds of Muslim respondents, as well as, presumably, non-Muslim readers of the *Sunday Times*.

Earlier that year, under criticism for following up so few of the recommendations from the 2005 Preventing Extremism Together groups, Prime Minister Tony Blair had firmly declared that the real problems underpinning extremism lay with Muslims themselves. Situating the state as an inappropriate party to root out extremism from Muslim communities, he established the Muslim community as a distinct (if not entirely homogenous) group who needed its own political leaders to understand its need, force it to face its own problems and, by extension, reduce conflicts more widely. This seemed to suggest, Malik has argued, that 'the aims and aspirations of Muslims were so different from those of non-Muslims that he could not connect with them' (2009: 122). When the publication of Demos' (2006) *Bringing it home* report later argued for the government to put communities at the heart of the counter-terror approach, it did by resurrecting the 2004 Whitehall plan 'to win hearts and minds', evident in a speech by Labour MP Ed Balls in 2007: 'We have got to win the battle of hearts and minds and persuade people *in communities* in Britain and around the world that values of fairness, stability and opportunity and turning away from extremism is the way to go' (*Independent* 15 January 2007). Participants in this study were quick to point to the way that the term 'community' was used only in reference to ethnic or religious communities: 'Of course we're a community, but not that different from any white communities. I don't know most of the people in the Muslim community in Manchester. So to say we're one community. I don't understand it' (Male, 30, interview January 2007).

Worley (2005) has commented on the ways in which the ambiguity around the term 'community', since the advent of New Labour's community cohesion agenda, has allowed slippage in language between community cohesion and national cohesion debates. Talking about communities rather than ethnic groups, she has argued, has allowed for language around integration to be deracialised. However, the use of 'communities' is arguably recoded as referring only to people who have stronger commitment to community than to nation, as the comments above illustrate. Significantly, Worley notes, the assimilationist nature of this language 'ignores how identities can be and are transnational, or forged across and through other aspects of identity such as gender or religion' (2005: 489).

The state as unique arbiter of intelligence and rights

The participants in this study were also concerned with the largely untouched list of recommendations from the Preventing Extremism Together groups. Here was evidence that the government had been given all of the information it could need to tackle any real problem and it refused to do so. As one participant living in an inner-city area of Stoke-on-Trent known for racial conflict, growing extremist groups and crime put it: 'They talk about poverty, they talk about alienation, they talk about *us* and then they don't do anything' (Female, 27).

The distinction between what the state had been *told* by Muslims, and the information it appeared to *use*, suggested to them that there was an important point being made by either government or the media. Put simply, as it was in a lunchtime discussion on causes of extremism: 'We're unimportant. Individual's views and Muslim's views don't count for anything' (Female, 27).

Intelligence, as it is referred to in counter-terror policy documents prior to 2007, is rarely seen to come from sources other than state agencies, police, local authorities and 'the public'. 'Muslim communities' in contrast are perceived as being painted as withholding information. But participants talked in private about the difficulties they know they would face if they had information to give and how they would deal with them. They portrayed, through their discussions of these perceived difficulties, a rational and loyal citizenship far from the disinterested and dislocated picture of groups of young Muslims portrayed in counter-terror documents amongst whom radicalism might flourish. Discussions ranged from distrust of particular police forces to moral problems with the individuals promoting violent ideologies and planning attacks. The rights of the individual were much more in focus than the responsibilities of the citizen, not because they were in doubt, but because they could not be. For that reason, the position of the state as powerful and disinterested was all the more worrying.

News coverage of criticisms by human rights lawyers and organisations like Liberty, and attempts by government to extend pre-charge detention, suggested to them that the state is in an unassailable position when it comes to individual human rights. Not living in London, they were not so concerned about the designation of the entire London area for stop-and-search without suspicion, but jokes about unwitting Muslim suspects are common. When incidents occurred, like the publication of comments by a Greater Manchester Police officer about stopping young Muslim men visiting Rusholme for Eid by positioning machine guns on the motorways (*Manchester Evening News* 20 January 2005), there seemed more reason to be concerned about how seriously the state took the actions of its agents not least because, by 2005, Greater Manchester Police became the first force outside London to create a counter-terrorism unit. Increasing numbers of raids in the Greater Manchester area filled the pages of the *Manchester Evening News* and made headlines on national evening TV news programmes, as well as being broadcast globally on Sky News. At the same time, roadshows launched by Hazel Blears MP to 'listen' to Muslim grievances were dismissed as a ploy to distract Muslims from other pursuing legal and political means of having those grievances addressed. 'What's the point?', asked one Facebook user, 'We know what we're going to say, we know what she's going to say and then we're all going to go home?' (Male, 26). Nonetheless, by 2009, the Government had claimed to be 'addressing grievances exploited by ideologues' to prevent home-grown terrorism. It was unconvincing, given the government's consistent rejection of links between foreign policy and terrorist attacks. A number of Muslim bloggers in Manchester and elsewhere had already dismissed out of hand in 2007 Brown's intentions to wage a 'cultural' war on Muslims (*Telegraph* 8 January 2007). One blogger wrote:

> There can be no 'cultural war' in this age because of … The Internets. All of the people he is talking about are already completely immune from cultural attack … You cannot tell one billion people that their religion is the new Communism that needs to be defeated and then expect to win. Not only is Islam not analogous to Communism, but even if it was, the tools of any 'cultural war' are in the hands of everyone with a cellphone. Every blogger, e-mail writer and text messager is a soldier in this war. There is no way you can defeat that.
>
> (Anonymous, BlogDial January 2007)

Similar sentiments were expressed by participants as links to this and similar material written by personal friends and acquaintances were exchanged. Seeing themselves as empowered, not just by access to the Internet, but also by their fluency in other languages, helped participants to demonstrate, via open web forums and each other's webpages, the level of knowledge that they had and could accumulate from other sources beyond the state. Although much news coverage positioned the state as having best access to the latest technology, intelligence and controls, influenced by an ongoing series of reports on how costly was the additional policing and intelligence of counter-terror operations (as repeated in the 'Contest 2' report (Home Office 2009), this frame had the potential to be neutralised over time. It could be shown that Muslims had knowledge about radicalisation that was valuable to the state and which it could not ignore. The danger of doing so would be the reinforcement of the third dominant frame.

Identifying the 'enemy within'

The final frame positions a series of (dis)qualifying criteria around people who share characteristics with the unknowable enemy. It is important to distinguish the enemy in this frame from the visible and known enemy at war. Rather, in this frame, the enemy is the one (i.e. *any* one) capable of and motivated to facilitate the predicted attacks 'on British citizens and our way of life' (Home Office 2006: 25). With no identified causes for the attacks, and an outright rejection of a link to British foreign operations in Iraq, such attacks on the state could (theoretically) be launched by *any* motivated party. This frame is identifiable from the responses of the participants to three essential narratives in relation to Britishness; sympathy with terrorists and violent ideologues, facilitation (knowing or otherwise) of the spread of violent ideologies or incivilities and the sharing of characteristics with known enemies which should rightly raise suspicions. The debate on the 'Britishness' of British Muslims is discussed at length elsewhere (cf. Vertovec 1998; Werbner 2002; Ameli 2002; Abbas 2005; Hussain and Bagguley 2005; Cesari 2010), and there is little need to explore it in depth here, except to note that it was reflected in its full diversity within the contributions of these particular participants to the range of forums and blogs they regularly visit. Since the range of participants in this study reflect different class, gender and sectarian positions, as well as different migration histories, educational levels and professions, these discussions are linked largely only by a common reference to a particularly South Asian heritage. Yet it is this heritage that was seen as being most problematic in relation to being cast as 'not British', since the wider national debate on Britishness drew on narratives about dual nationalities and related ongoing legal, political and economic links to Pakistan. Questions were positioned within these narratives around the possibility for citizens of dual nationality to be 'properly British'. A large number of participant of Muslim-related web forums, however, rejected strongly the sentiments of posts such as those who suggested that 'Saying British Muslim is like saying halal pork' (Channel 4 2004, see also *The Muslim News* 2004).

In both cities, participants strongly emphasised their local identity over a British one, although those in Manchester felt that this was more of an international identity, given the multicultural nature of the city. This is not an unusual pattern to observe in these debates and, further, the saliency of these localised discourses has been recognised in policy circles recently, with city-based advertising campaigns such as 'I love Burnley'. Despite repeated claims to being and feeling British, however, the majority of participants reported feeling frustrated at their claims never really being accepted (as they saw it). Across a large number of conversations, they queried the terms 'Western', 'non-Muslim' and 'European' as being designed to explicitly exclude them without referencing them as viable other parties. 'If they had to talk about Muslims, they might have to talk to us', commented one male youth leader in Stoke-on-Trent, discussing the impossibility of engaging properly with the media when only one 'Muslim voice' is needed for each article. 'They just don't bother otherwise. We're not worth it'. In his late 20s, he saw the 'Muslim voice' as already being a position filled by a second generation who had access to the media for the first time: 'Our generation won't get a look in until next time' (Male, 26).

Material appearing in the media at this time of most concern amongst the participants, however, was that which questioned the motives and the intelligence of non-Muslims sympathetic to their defence of Islam. From the messages contributed by non-Muslims to websites like that of the Muslim News in the wake of the London bombings, to accusations that the Mayor of London Ken Livingstone and MP George Galloway were 'Islamist sympathisers', there are a range of discourses which connect alliances with Muslims to allegations of sympathising with Islamists and violent extremists. Muslims, however, are those most firmly posited as unwitting sympathisers according to the young men in this study. From 2005, in Stoke-on-Trent, participants noted the emphasis on the responsibility of 'the community' to be watchful of every risky activity and reported at length the visits by local police to their youth club to observe boxing matches, martial arts demonstrations, open days and so on, all at the request of 'community elders'. In Manchester, female young leaders within an Islamic centre decried the acceptance of such responsibility by fellow Muslims, which they saw as a fearful reaction to the allegations of sympathising and facilitating radicalisation by ignorance. Being closer to the young people 'at risk', they saw the acceptance of that responsibility as complicit with government's refusal to move on bigger social justice issues and to recognise real grievances. An ex-city councillor in Manchester echoed their concerns: 'I was horrified when Muslim leaders were asked, "How will you stop them?", and they said, "We'll try harder". How, if you don't know who?' (Male, 40)

Harder to identify, and harder to unsettle, were narratives connecting more abstract characteristics of the enemy. Responses to coverage of social issues like cohesion, education and employment, emphasised discomfort with the depictions of British South Asian Muslims (more often described simply as 'Muslim communities') as being characterised by *insularity, self-reliance, strong internal codes* and *impenetrability*. If the pact between state and Muslim leaders had not already reinforced colonial style political approaches to governance of ethnic communities and discouraged public (rather than civic) engagement with Muslims, increasing depictions of British Muslims in this light might have done the same. These narratives, most of which are already identified by Richardson (2004) as Islamophobic, are of particular interest here not because of their Islamophobic nature, but because they speak to a particular trope about sympathising communities. To that extent, they bear similarity to the narratives used to describe the difficulties of the state to deal with terrorism in Northern Ireland. Moreover, these characteristics can be thought of not simply as having something in common with the enemy, but also recalling the 'enemy' as anyone capable and motivated in facilitating that enemy. Depicted in such a manner, British Muslim communities stand as signifiers of an Open Door to terrorists that the state sought to shut down through the 'Secure Borders, Safe Haven' immigration and border control policy (Home Office 2002), and they are denied that victim identity that Aly (2007) describes.

Language and dual nationality, as we noted above, are already seen as problematic in terms of 'Britishness'. Yet in this, the participants' responses have been sophisticated and rational. Constantly aware of how others seek to view and understand them, there is a possibility for unsettling these ideas. In Manchester, therefore, participants emphasised their international identity as something which had resonance with the city itself, with foreign language and travel not as suspect, but as a cosmopolitan aspect to their identity. One participant tells the story of his revelation of himself as an 'international traveller', during the 'Britishness' debates, as a turning point in his decision to engage more actively with global news and media, regularly consuming information from and contributing to a very diverse range of media outlets: 'I have advantages other British people don't have' (Male, 23).

The success of this strategy was variable for participants, but for some it gave them confidence to build new alliances with non-Muslims through educational or work institutions, and through local political and social organisations.

Conclusion: interrogating 'everyday' spaces online

The discussions presented in this chapter suggest that there are several powerful reasons to interrogate the content of web-based forums and social networking sites. First, the language adopted can be either that of the dominant narrative or an alternative way of enunciating the perspective of the subaltern. It is noticeable that although the dominant frames employed by mass media organisations are rejected, the language adopted is familiar. Further, these are the spaces in which citizenship is played out in the everyday. Citizenship is constructed not only of the relationship between the individual and the state, or even between the individual and fellow citizens at a distance, but in the interactions between the individual and those citizens with whom s/he already interacts on a regular basis, in relationships with varying degrees of exchange, respect, tolerance, familiarity, intimacy and so on. Finally, these discussions are important too, because they illustrate the variety of ways in which people construct and test their public responses to statement by powerful others.

The role of the web forum in conveying and disrupting frames in this period should not be understated. Discussion forums for Muslims, in the period 2005–09, were not just web-based. Since the inception of New Labour's plans for joined-up governance, forums had become part of the policy language of communication. Residents' forums, BME forums, city consultative forums, police forums and ward forums, were all spaces in which issues of risk and liveability were regularly discussed (though rarely in a consistent fashion). Alongside these were created forums supported by a range of religious or ethnic groups to give a common voice and discussion point, such as the Manchester Muslim Forum. Many of the forums without a wider remit were short-lived in their activity. Yet the emergence of forums for discussion on the websites of mainstream media organisations prompted an increased interest in discussions with a wider audience made possible by such open technology.

Militaristic framing of the war on terror is just one type of framing interesting in publications of this period but, as this paper has attempted to demonstrate, where it has been considered previously, the process of framing itself has only occasionally been considered from the perspective of those demonised by it. This study, by examining the frames through which British Muslims have interpreted the media reporting social and political affairs, has sought to address that gap. Here it is shown that Muslims, in the present study, perceived media coverage through three dominant frames; the war at home; the unique (and unassailable) position of the state as arbiter of information and rights, and the identification of an enemy within. These three dominant frames, unlike those employed by British and international mass media, are borne of the local context from which participants viewed the war on terror. Recalling Iyengar and Kinder (1987), we might suggest that where the mass media cannot provide a frame through which difficult problems can be understood, a critical interactive audience may be in a position to substitute their own frames and may have strong reason to do so. There is evidence that adopting a 'victim identity', as recognised by Aly (2007) and others, is not the only strategy available to British Muslims who feel demonised by such militaristic framing. Indeed, these interpretive frames suggest that adopting such an identity appears to be functional only in relation to others in the same 'outsider' group in this case, since 'the enemy' cannot also truly be victim. Yet alternative bases for constructing strong identities that are resistant to demonisation, such as self-reliance, strong internal codes and impenetrability of the social group, are undermined by the identification of those very characteristics as suspicious. What is observable from these personal responses to the dominant media discourses is that often the young Muslims in this study viewed the discourses not as a result of hate, but as a result of fundamental misunderstandings and ignorance. Thus, attachments to foreign languages and international travel are framed not within a cosmopolitan discourse, which might view the prioritisation of these aspects of social life as laudable in a globalising world, or empathy with powerless populations in other countries as humanistic, but within frames which makes these suspect characteristics of a social group. Personal contributions to virtual discussion spaces thus illustrate the ways in which the process of 'framing' is both an act of rejection of alternative understandings and an emotional attachment to distant concepts and experiences.

The success of attempts by British Muslims and sympathetic others to critique and unsettle these and other dominant frames is evident by the publication of 'Contest 2', the UK's counter terrorism strategy (Home Office March 2009). This was one of the most significant in a series of governmental texts seeking to engage the wider public with the issue and to communicate shared responsibility for its success. With an aim no different from that of the 'hearts and minds' strategy in 2004, or from that exemplified by the demarcation of responsibilities between central government and local communities in the Government's publication of *Preventing Violent Extremism: A Strategy for Delivery* in 2008, it nonetheless illustrated a departure from previous approaches to government communications on terror. The language of counter-terrorism, despite significant continuities between these documents, had in the in-between period come to be seen as a crucial weapon against terrorism in itself. So important was it perceived to be following, in particular, the publication of studies such as Demos' (2006) *Bringing it home* report, that the British government sought to examine how the language used in government was being used to radicalise Muslims in the UK and internationally (Armstrong *et al.* 2008). The document sought to significantly re-frame the problem of terrorism and the government's efforts to deal with it. This was at least partly because of the success of other parties in inserting alternative narratives into debates around counter-terror operations and changes in law and policy, as well as the problem of ongoing Iraq-operations as a driver of radicalisation. It was also intended that, although news media could not be forced to adopt new language, over time it was likely that the governments' lead would be followed.

The responses captured in this essay are a reflection of the wider critiques of militarising frames employed in the war on terror, but more particularly, they offer us a way to think sociologically about the interpretation of those frames. The extent to which frames are perceived in differing constructions, assuming within them disparate narratives about citizenship and the state in times of war and terror, direct attention beyond a simplistic reading of frames as Islamophobic or militarised, to an appreciation of the ways in which citizenship is constructed for the individual through their everyday understandings vis-à-vis the significant others with whom they communicate. The city arguably offers, then, the best vantage point from which to view these everyday understandings. With interpretations so influenced by everyday encounters with the representatives of the state, the suspecting and suspected populations, it is essential to ground our understanding of framing effects in that everyday world. The city, the neighbourhood and the street, all influence the decisions made by the young Muslims in this study to engage with one another, with other known, unknown and unknowable citizens and with a wider global audience.

References

Abbas, T. (2009) 'British Islamic Culture after 7/7: Ethnicity, Politics and Radicalisation', in Krause, W. (ed.) *Citizenship, Security and Democracy: Muslim Engagement with the West*, 123–40, London: International Institute of Islamic Thought.

Abbas, T. (ed.) (2005) *Muslim Britain: Communities under Pressure*, London: Zed Books.

Ahmed, T. S. (2005) 'Reading Between the Lines: Muslims and the Media', in Abbas, T. (ed.) *Muslim Britain: Communities under Pressure*, 109–26, London: Zed Books.

Allen, C. (2004) 'Justifying Islamophobia: A Post-9/11Consideration of the European Unionand British Contexts', The American Journal of Islamic Social Sciences, 21:3: 1–25.

Aly, A. (2007) 'Australian Muslim Responses to the Discourse on Terrorism in the Australian Popular Media', *Australian Journal of Social Issues*, 42(1): 27–40.

Aly, A. and Green, A. ' "Moderate Islam": Defining the Good Citizen', *M/C Journal* 11.1 (April 2008), 19 February 2011, at http://journal.media-culture.org.au/index.php/mcjournal/article/view/28, accessed 1 December 2010.

Ameli, S. R. (2002) *Globalization, Americanization and British Muslim identity*, London: Islamic College for Advanced Studies Press.

Ameli, S. R. and Merali, A. (2004) *Dual Citizenship: British, Islamic or Both? Obligation, Recognition, Respect and Belonging*, London: Islamic Human Rights Commission.

Ameli, S. R., Elahi, M. and Merali, A. (2004) *Social Discrimination: Across the Muslim Divide*, London: Islamic Human Rights Commission.

Ameli, S. R., Marandi, S. M., Ahmed, S., Kara, S. and Merali, A. (2007) *British Muslims' Expectations of the Government: The British Media and Muslim Representation: The Ideology of Demonisation*, 26 January 2007, London: Islamic Human Rights Commission, at www.ihrc.org.uk/file/1903718317.pdf, accessed 4 June 1997.

Anonymous (2007) 'Gordon G. Brown will never get it', *BlogDial*, at www.irdial.com/blogdial/?p=554, accessed 14 February 2011.

Armstrong, J., Chin, C. J., and Leventer, U. (2008) *The Language of Counter-Terrorism: When Message Received is Not Message Intended*. Report to the Foreign and Commonwealth Office, April 2008, Camb, MA: John F. Kennedy School of Government, Harvard University.

Beck, U. (1992) *Risk Society: Towards a New Modernity*. New Delhi: Sage.

Carroll, J. S., and Johnson, E. J. (1990) *Decision Research: A Field Guide*, Newbury Park, CA: Sage.

Cesari, J. (2010) *Muslims in the West: Religion*, Law and Politics. London: Routledge.

Channel 4 (2004) 4Community Forum: Shariah TV, April–May 2004, at http://community.channel4.com/, (forum offline since 2008).

Chermak, S. M. (2003) 'Marketing Fear: Representing Terrorism After September 11', *Journal of Crime, Conflict and the Media*, 1(1): 5–22.

Commission on British Muslims and Islamophobia (1997) *Islamophobia: A Challenge for Us All*, London: Runnymede Trust.

Commission on British Muslims and Islamophobia (2004) *Islamophobia: Issues, Challenges, and Action: A Report by the Commission on British Muslims and Islamophobia*, Robin Richardson (ed.), Stoke on Trent, UK: Trentham Books.

Cottle, S. (2005) 'Mediatized Public Crisis and Civil Society Renewal: The Racist Murder of Stephen Lawrence', *Crime, Media and Culture*, 1(1): 49–71.

Daily Telegraph (2002) 'Blair: we must fight terror on both fronts', 15 October 2002.

Daily Telegraph (2007) 'Brown to end Blair's terror strategy', 8 January 2007.

Demos (2006) *Bringing it Home: Community-based Approaches to Counter-Terrorism*, London: Demos.

Fraser, N. (1992) 'Rethinking the Public Sphere: a Contribution to the Critique of Actually Existing Democracy', in Calhoun, C. (ed.) *Habermas and the Public Sphere*, 109–42. Cambridge, MA: MIT Press.

Gamson, W. A. (1992) *Talking Politics*, New York: Cambridge University Press.

Graber, D. (2004) 'Mediated Politics and Citizenship in the Twenty-First Century', *Annual Review of Psychology*, 2004, 55: 545–71.

Hall, S. (1980) 'Race, Articulation, and Societies Structured in Dominance', in UNESCO (ed.) *Sociological Theories: Race and Colonialism*, Paris: UNESCO. Pp. 305–45. ISBN: 9231016350.

Home Office (2002) *Secure Borders, Safe Haven*, London: HM Stationery Office.

Home Office (2006) *Countering International Terrorism: The United Kingdom's Strategy*, Cm 6888, London: HM Stationery Office.

Home Office (2009) *Pursue Prevent Protect Prepare: The United Kingdom's Strategy for Countering International Terrorism*, Cm 7547, London: Home Office.

Hussain, Y. and Bagguley, P. (2005) 'Citizenship, Ethnicity and Identity: British Pakistanis after the 2001 riots', *Sociology*, 39(3): 407–25.

Independent (2007) 'Brown aide admits errors in fight against terror', 15 January 2007.

Iyengar, S. and Kinder, D. (1987) *News That Matters*, Chicago: University of Chicago Press.

Karatzogianni, A. (2006) *Politics of Cyberconflict*, London: Routledge.

Lancashire Evening Telegraph (2006) 'Straw in plea to Muslim women: take off your veils', 5 October 2006.

Liberty (2010) *From 'War' to 'Law': Liberty's Response to the Coalition Government's Review of Counter-Terrorism and Security Powers 2010*, London: Liberty.

Malik, K. (2009) *From Fatwa to Jihad: The Rushdie Affair and its Legacy*, London: Atlantic Books.

Manchester Evening News (2005) 'Festival yobs may have cars snatched', 20 January 2005.

Michael, L. (2008) *Leadership in Transition: Intergenerational Tensions in Two Pakistani Communities in Britain*, PhD Thesis: Keele University.

Michael, L. (2009) 'Securing civic relations in the multicultural city', in Krause W. (ed.) *Citizenship, Security and Democracy: Muslim Engagement with the West*, 164–86. London: International Institute of Islamic Thought.

Moore, K., Mason, P. and Lewis, J. (2008) 'Images of Islam in the UK: The representation of British Muslims in the national print news media 2000–2008'. Report commissioned for Channel 4, 7 July 2008. Cardiff: Cardiff University School of Journalism, Media and Cultural Studies.

Mythen, G. and Walklate, S. (2008) 'Communicating the Terrorist Risk: Harnessing a Culture of Fear?', *Crime, Media and Culture*, 2(2): 123–42.

Papacharissi, Z. and de Fatima Olivieira, M. (2008) 'News frames terrorism: a comparative analysis of frames employed in terrorism coverage in US and UK newspapers', *Press/Politics*, 13(1), 52–74.

Ramji, H. (2005) 'Exploring intersections of employment and ethnicity amongst British Pakistani young men', *Sociological Research Online*, vol. 10, Issue 4, published 31 December 2005, at www.socresonline.org.uk/10/4/ramji.html, accessed 17 November 2006.

Reynolds, A. and Barrett, B. (2003) 'America under attack': CNN's verbal and visual framing of September 11', in Chermak, S., Bailey, F. and. Brown, M. (eds), *Media representations of 9/11*, New York: Greenwood Publishing.

Richardson, J. E. (2004) *(Mis)Representing Islam: the racism and rhetoric of British Broadsheet newspapers*, Amsterdam: John Benjamins.

Richardson, R. (2007) *The Search for Common Ground: Muslims, non-Muslims and the UK Media*, London: Greater London Authority.

Riddell, K. J. and Yasmeen, S. (2009) '"Murderous Little Malcontents" Public narratives of hate and marginalisation: letters to the editor as a site of Muslim social exclusion', *Australian Political Studies Association Annual Conference 2009*, North Ryde, NSW, at www.pol.mq.edu.au/apsa/refereed_papers.html, Accessed 14 July 2010.

Ruigrok, N. and van Atteveldt, W. (2006) 'Global angling with a local angle: how U.S., British and Dutch newspapers frame global and local terrorist attacks', *Harvard International Journal of Press/Politics*, 12(1): 68–90.

Runnymede Trust, The (1997) *Islamophobia: a challenge for us all*, London: Runnymede Trust.

Ryan, M. (2004) 'Framing the war against terrorism: US newspaper editorials and military action in Iraq', *Gazette*, 66(4): 363–82.

The Muslim News (2004) 'Have your say: Explore your British Muslim identity', at http://www.muslimnews.co.uk/yoursay/index.php?ysc_id=3, accessed 19 September 2011.

The Sunday Times (2006) 'Symbols of Separateness', 8 October 2006.

Vertovec, S. (1998) 'Young Muslims in Keighley, West Yorkshire: Cultural identity, context and "community"', in. Vertovec, S and Rogers, A. (eds) *Muslim European Youth: Reproducing Ethnicity, Religion and Culture*, 87–101. Aldershot: Ashgate.

Werbner, P. (2002) *Imagined Diasporas among Manchester Muslims: The Public Performance of Pakistani Transnational Identity Politics*, Oxford: James Currey Publishers.

Worley, C. (2005) 'It's not about race. It's about the community': New Labour and 'community cohesion', *Critical Social Policy*, vol 25, 483.

Part IV

Through the political lens

11 The Israel–Hezbollah War and the Winograd Committee[1]

Raphael Cohen-Almagor and Sharon Haleva-Amir

Introduction

On 12 July 2006, the Hezbollah terrorist organisation attacked two Israeli Defense Forces' armored Hummer jeeps patrolling along the border with gunfire and explosives, in the midst of massive shelling attacks on Israel's north. Three soldiers were killed in the attack and two were taken hostage. Hezbollah leader Sheikh Hassan Nasrallah said: 'No military operation will return the Israeli captured soldiers. ... The prisoners will not be returned except through one way: indirect negotiations and a trade of prisoners' (Al Bawaba News 12 July 2006). Later that day, four Israeli Defense Forces (IDF) soldiers were killed when their tank hit a mine some 6 km inside Lebanese territory.

The IDF began heavy artillery and tank fire. Israel Air Force jets struck roads, bridges and Hezbollah guerrilla positions in southern Lebanon. The air raids were intended to block any escape route for the guerrillas who may be taking the captured IDF soldiers to areas further removed from the border, in order to prevent an Israeli rescue mission. But this was too late. The information about the kidnapping had arrived considerable time after fact, when the abductors were well inside Lebanon. The destructive air-strike could not halt the abductors. It only fueled the escalation.

Prime Minister Ehud Olmert convened the government on Wednesday night, 12 July 2006, in order to decide Israel's reaction. The government agreed that the attack had created a completely new situation on the northern border, that Israel must take steps that will 'exact a price' (Gutkin 13 July 2006) and restore its deterrence. Olmert rejected Hezbollah's demand that Israel redeem the kidnapped soldiers' freedom by releasing Lebanese and Palestinian terrorists jailed in Israel.

That night, Israel responded by bombarding bridges in central Lebanon and attacking Hezbollah positions along the border. Hezbollah did not blink and retaliated on 13 July 2006 with Katyusha rockets across northern Israel. One person was killed and dozens were wounded. In Nahariya, a woman died when a rocket struck her home. Another 29 people were injured, including a number of children. Most of the casualties were lightly wounded; one person sustained serious wounds. At least 11 people were wounded when another barrage of Katyusha rockets fired from Lebanon struck the northern town of Safed.

The Israeli–Hezbollah War ended on 14 August 2006 when the UN Security Council Resolution (no. 1701) entered into force (Security Council SC/8808 2006). In the thirty four days of fighting, 155 Israelis were killed (Ynet 14 August 2006); 36 of them were civilians, killed as a result of the rockets campaign; 119 of them were soldiers, killed in Israel and in Lebanon; 3,970 rockets were fired on Israel (Rofe-Ofir and Grinberg 14 August 2006), an average of 120 rockets a day. Many of those rockets hit buildings, caused damage and cost lives. About 2,000 people were injured; many of them suffered shock and anxieties. The estimated damage was more than five billion shekels. On the Lebanese side, these figures are contested. Hezbollah claims that it had suffered about 250 casualties (*International Herald Tribune* 21 February 2007). Israel had estimated its forces killed 600 Hezbollah fighters (*International Herald Tribune* 21 February 2007). A UN official estimated the deaths at 500 (Bishop 22 August 2006); Lebanese officials had also estimated that up to 500 fighters were killed and another 1,500 were injured (Coughlin 4 August 2006). According to the *Report of the Commission of Inquiry on Lebanon pursuant to Human Rights Council resolution S-2/1*, 1,191 Lebanese citizens were killed during the war and 4,409 citizens were injured (A/HRC/3/2 23 November 2006, p. 3).

During the war, voices of protest were heard in Israel, mainly from reserve service soldiers (Reiss 8 August 2006; Scoop 16 August 2006) and journalists. Distinguished writers such as A. B. Yehoshua, Amos Oz and David Grossman, who had later bereaved his own son, called for the government to avoid the expansion of the military operations and move from the martial arena to the political arena (Horev and Bengal 10 August 2006). After the war, thousands of people have criticised the government's decisions, demanded the establishment of a national inquiry committee to investigate the war events and called for the resignation of the war architects: Prime Minister Ehud Olmert, Minister of Defence Amir Peretz and Chief of Staff Dan Halutz (Sheffer 10 September 2006).

This article criticises the establishment of the committee and the results it reached, arguing that it was a 'sold game': The person under investigation should never be allowed to nominate his judges. This is mockery of justice and travesty of social responsibility.

The Winograd Committee: background, mandate and scope of operation

Soon after the battles were over, Minister of Defense Peretz had established a military review committee led by former Chief of Staff, Amnon Lipkin Shahak. This initiative was immediately criticised by the media and by army officials. On 22 August 2006, only five days after the committee was appointed, it ceased to exist. A few more military and governmental review committees were established during the first weeks after the war, but they had all collapsed. The public and the media called to nominate a state committee of inquiry.

On 17 September 2006, the government had decided, according to article 8a(a) of the Government Law 2001, to appoint a governmental committee of inquiry. The committee had the same mandate as a state committee of inquiry would have, with two notable differences: Its members were not appointed by the Supreme Court and the committee's recommendations, especially with respect to resignations, did not possess the same legal weight. The committee had the capacity to operate autonomously and independently, the authority to subpoena witnesses, the power to recommend prosecution of any Israeli public official whom it found was involved with willful or negligent criminal behavior and to make recommendations that will resonate in the public domain in Israel (Bedein 16 September 2006). On 18 September 2006 Israel's Legal Advisor to the Government Menachem Mazuz stated that while the committee may make its recommendations public, it cannot recommend to the authority who appointed it, Prime Minister Ehud Olmert, to step down (Yoaz 20 September 2006).

The committee's scope of operation was to thoroughly investigate the deployment and the proceeding of the political echelon, as well as the defense system concerning the gamut aspects of the northern battle, which commenced on 12 July 2006 (Winograd Committee 17 September 2006). Retired judge, Dr. Eliyahu Winograd, was appointed to chair the committee. Nahum Admoni, former head of the Israeli Mossad (the Israeli CIA), was due to chair the committee. Admoni had recommended that a retired judge will do so and asked to resign from the committee (Israeli Ministry of Foreign Affairs 14 September 2006). Given that the committee was asked to inquire into the security establishment's role, Admoni and Judge Winograd agreed that a reserve Major General would join the committee in place of the former (Israeli Ministry of Foreign Affairs 14 September 2006). Other members of the committee were Professor Ruth Gavison, a leading figure in the field of constitutional law and a human rights activist; Professor Yehezkel Dror, Israel Prize laureate for his studies on policy making and public administration; Major General (retired) Menachem Einan and Major General (retired) Dr. Haim Nadel (Israeli Ministry of Foreign Affairs 14 September 2006).

The decision to appoint the committee was rightly criticized. The Movement for Quality Government in Israel (a pre-eminent citizen watchdog organisation, which peerlessly advocated for public accountability and the rule of law) and the 'Ometz' (courage in Hebrew) Association (an Israeli NGO that operates to strengthen the moral-ethical values of the governmental systems in Israel, to pursue constitutional equality for all and to eagerly guard human rights and basic freedoms in all aspects of life) had petitioned the High Court of Justice, arguing that this was just another measure in Olmert's continued retreat and delay battle, calling on Judge Winograd to decline the appointment, stating that only a state commission headed by a judge appointed by the Supreme Court was the answer. Those motions were denied (Ben and Yoaz 12 September 2006; HCJ 6728, 7607/06 30 November 2006). In addition, MK Zehava Galon of Meretz (Civil Rights Party) petitioned the High Court of Justice to instruct the committee to hold public hearings and to publish its protocols after each session. The ruling was given after the commission had completed hearing testimonies behind closed doors. The High Court of Justice's decision, written by President Dorit Beinish, held that the Winograd Commission had a duty to expose its proceedings and the evidences which were presented to its members, as long as publicity would not harm Israel's national security interests (HCJ 258/07 6 February 2007). As a result of this ruling, it was decided by the committee to establish a website in which protocols will be published (Winograd Committee 12 February 2007). Of the 75 witnesses who appeared before the committee only 30 testimonials were published, mainly those of governmental officials and executives (Winograd Committee 2007).

The Winograd Interim Report

The much expected Winograd Interim Report was published on 30 April 2007 and caused immediate turmoil. The Report contended that the decision-making process which had lead to the war-opening was flawed, with serious and dangerous deficiencies (Cohen-Almagor May 2007; Levine 2007; Tristam 2008):

a   The decision to respond with an immediate, intensive military strike was not based on a detailed, comprehensive and authorised military plan, nor based on a careful study of the complex characteristics of the Lebanon arena. A meticulous examination of these characteristics would have revealed the following: the ability to achieve military gains having significant political-international weight was limited; an Israeli military strike would inevitably lead to rockets fired on the north of Israel; the effective military response to such rocket attacks was an extensive and prolonged ground operation to capture the areas from which the rockets were fired – which would have entailed a high 'cost'. Such operations did not enjoy broad support. These difficulties were not explicitly raised with the political leaders before it was decided to strike Lebanon from the air.

b   Consequently, in deciding to go to war, the government did not consider the whole range of options in response to the abduction. This failure reflected weakness in strategic thinking, which undercut the response to the violent event.

c   The support in the cabinet for this move was gained, in part, through ambiguity in the presentation of goals and modes of operation, so that ministers with different or even contradictory attitudes could support it. The ministers voted for a vague decision, without understanding and knowing its nature and implications. They authorised commencement of a military campaign without considering how it will be possible to end it.

d   Some of the declared goals of the war were not clear and in part were not achievable by the authorised modes of military action.

e   The IDF did not exhibit creativity in proposing alternative action possibilities, did not alert the political decision-makers to the discrepancy between its own scenarios and the authorised modes of action, and did not demand – as was necessary under its own plans – early mobilisation of the reserves so they could be equipped and trained in case it was decided to launch a ground operation.

f   Even after these facts became known to the political leaders, they failed to adapt the military mode of operation and its goals to the reality on the ground. On the contrary, declared goals were too ambitious and it was publicly stated that fighting would continue till they were achieved. But the authorised military operations did not enable their achievement.

The Winograd Committee concluded that the primary responsibility for these serious failings rested with Prime Minister Olmert, Minister of Defense Peretz and Chief of Staff Dan Halutz. They singled out these three, because it was likely that had any of them acted more prudently the decisions in the relevant period and the ways they were made, as well as the outcome of the war, would have been significantly more positive for Israel. Nevertheless, the Interim Report stopped short of personal recommendations regarding the failed trio.

The Prime Minister 'bears supreme and comprehensive responsibility for the decisions of "his" government and the operations of the army' (Winograd Committee Interim Report April 2007: section 99, 129–30). Olmert also came under criticism for rushed actions at the outset of the war and for failing to consult with either military or non-military experts. 'The Prime Minister made up his mind hastily, despite the fact that no detailed military plan was submitted to him and without asking for one', the Report said (ibid., 135, 135). 'He made his decision without systematic consultation with others, especially outside the IDF, despite not having experience in external-political and military affairs' (ibid., 121, 133). Olmert was also criticised for failing to 'adapt his plans once it became clear that the assumptions and expectations of Israel's actions were not realistic and were not materialising' (ibid., 128, 134). 'All of these', the Report said, 'add up to a serious failure in exercising judgment, responsibility and prudence' (ibid., section 135, 136).

The findings levelled heavy criticism at Defense Minister Amir Peretz for being unaware of the state of the Israel Defense Forces, even though he should have been. Peretz 'did not have knowledge or experience in military, political or governmental matters. He also did not have good knowledge of the basic principles of using military force to achieve political goals' (ibid., 139, 136). Despite these deficiencies, the Report stated, 'he made his decisions during this period without systemic consultations with experienced political and professional experts, including outside the security establishment' (ibid., 158, 140). In fact, the Committee found, 'his serving as minister of defense during the war impaired Israel's ability to respond well to its challenges' (ibid., 161, 140).

Chief of Staff Dan Halutz bore more blame, since Olmert and Peretz were inexperienced in military matters. Halutz reacted impulsively to the kidnapping of the two reserve soldiers. He was criticised for entering the war 'unprepared' (ibid., 174, 142) and for failing to inform the cabinet of the true state of the IDF ahead of the ground operation. According to the Winograd findings, the army and its Chief of Staff 'were not prepared for the event of the abduction despite recurring alerts' (ibid., 16, 116). The Committee also found that Halutz had failed to 'present to the political leaders the internal debates within the IDF concerning the convergence between the stated goals and the authorised modes of actions' (ibid., 188, 143). Winograd said that Halutz displayed lack of professionalism and lack of judgment. Winograd added that, despite his lack of experience, Olmert did not request help or question the plan put to him. Peretz also came under similar criticism for not inspecting the war plan with sufficient care.

The Interim Report had criticised the entire government, by saying that the cabinet voted to go to war without understanding the implications of the decision:

> The government did not consider the whole range of options, including that of continuing the policy of 'containment', or combining political and diplomatic moves with military strikes below the 'escalation level', or military preparations without immediate military action – so as to maintain for Israel the full range of responses to the abduction.
>
> (ibid., 123–5)

In one crucial meeting that lasted two and a half hours, without substantive deliberation, and without examining different alternatives for action, the government had authorised a wide military campaign. This was without knowing how the campaign might progress, without inquiring what would be its aims and without probing the implications for Israeli society (Cohen-Almagor May 2007; Winograd Commission submits Interim Report, April 2007).

Discussion: the Winograd Committee and its final report

The shift from the 'yishuv' to the sovereign state of Israel was manifested by the concept of 'mamlakhtiut' (statehood), meaning legitimate state public authority. The concept was contrasted with 'yishuviut' (inhabitation) and 'tnuatiut' (party-affiliated goals). It accentuated the need to ascribe state activities with unitary character, divorced from partisan political considerations. This need was of paramount importance in the spheres of public administration and services, and in state security (Cohen-Almagor 1995). The salt of the earth people are 'mamlakhtiim'. They are part of the establishment. They are conformist. They know what is expected of them and they deliver the goods. This was also the case with the Winograd Committee.

Eliyahu Winograd is a well-respected judge who sat on many national committees. Ruth Gavison also sat on numerous committees. Like her colleague Winograd, her eye is always open to the government. She is part and parcel of the establishment and likes to remain active in these influential circles. The two army generals, Haim Nadel and Menachem Einan, are highly respected officers who were there to investigate the army's conduct. They also are very 'mamlakhtiim'; always have been. The wild card was Yehezkiel Dror, Israel's foremost scholar on public administration. He usually has an uncompromising voice of conscience and he never cared too much about being 'mamlakhti'. Thus, his nomination was quite a surprise (Cohen-Almagor February 2008).

The criticisms against the establishment of the committee, that it was wrong for the Prime Minister to be able to choose the people who will investigate his actions, proved to be justified. In this respect, the Report, which was published on 30 January 2008, was not surprising. Still, it is interesting how the distinguished committee members were able to take Olmert off the hook. Members of the committee have stated that the manner in which the ground operation was conducted, gave rise to extremely grave questions. They also stated that a profound change is necessary in the patterns of action of the government and military echelons, and that a determined and ongoing effort will be needed to bring about change in the modes of action of the governmental-military system.

The members of the committee explained that they did not wish to include in the Final Report personal conclusions and recommendations. They believed that the primary need for improvements applied to the structural and systemic malfunctioning revealed in the war on all levels. Nonetheless, they stressed, the fact they refrained from imposing personal responsibility did not imply that no such responsibility existed. They did not wish to impose different standards of responsibility on the political and the military echelons, or on persons of different ranks within them. When they imposed responsibility on a system, an echelon or a unit, they did not imply that the responsibility was only or mainly of those who headed it at the time of the war. Often, such responsibility stemmed from a variety of factors outside the control of those at the head. In addition, a significant part of the responsibility for the failures and flaws they have found was with those who had been in charge of preparedness and readiness in the years before the war.

As said, one government meeting preceded the decision to bomb targets in Beirut. The government had no idea that by this they forced the region into war. This is quite disturbing: No checks and balances. No monitoring mechanisms (*New York Times* 30 January 2008). In sum:

- One of its greatest failures, a subject that has also occupied a great deal of time in the Winograd Committee's probe of the war, is the fact that the IDF did not put an end to the short range-rocket attacks. An analysis of testimonies and investigation reports suggest that while the Air Force and the intelligence branches focused on Hezbollah's arsenal of medium and long-range rockets, dealing with Katyushas was neglected. The medium-range Fajr rockets in the Hezbollah arsenal and the longer range, Iranian-made Zilzal rockets, were under careful IDF study since its withdrawal from southern Lebanon in May 2000. This careful preparation resulted in the success of what the IDF had called 'the Fajr night', the 34 minutes during the first night of the war during which the Air Force struck dozens of homes of Hezbollah activists where the rockets were hidden and eliminated that threat (Cohen-Almagor February 2008).
- The committee found serious failings and shortcomings in the decision-making processes and staff-work in the political and the military echelons and their interface.
- The committee found serious failings and flaws in the quality of preparedness, decision-making and performance in the IDF high command, especially in the Army.
- The committee found serious failings and flaws in the lack of strategic thinking and planning, in both the political and the military echelons.
- The committee found severe failings and flaws in the defense of the civilian population and in coping with its being attacked by rockets.
- These weaknesses resulted in part from inadequacies of preparedness and strategic and operative planning which go back long before 2006 (Cohen-Almagor February 2008).

However, the committee stopped short of telling Olmert he had to take responsibility and resign. Olmert behaved irresponsibly when he appointed Amir Peretz to be Minister of Defense. He did this out of partisan political considerations, knowing full well that Peretz was unqualified for this heavy responsibility. By this Olmert abandoned security considerations and drove Israel's enemy to try the inexperienced trio (Olmert, Peretz and Halutz). Halutz was the first Chief of Staff in the history of young Israel who came from the Air Force. He had no experience in commanding ground forces. In his mind, the key for military success is to control the skies. Israel did control the skies as the Hezbollah has no air force, but it was unable to put a stop on the incessant barrages of rockets on northern Israel. When the government opened war, it had knowingly decided to subject one million people to continuous rocket attack, without providing them with adequate shelters and defense.

Much of the public discussion between the Interim Report and the Final Report revolved around the question why Olmert authorised a wide-scale ground operation after the UN declared a ceasefire. To recall, on Friday 11 August 2006 the UN Security Council passed a ceasefire resolution (no. 1701) that was supposed to enter into force on Monday 14 August 2006. Yet Olmert decided on Friday to launch the ground operation. His critics saw this as yet another spin, willing to sacrifice soldiers just to save his face. Olmert explained to the committee that he believed there might be a vacuum between the ceasefire declaration and the actual bolstering of UN Interim Force in Lebanon (UNIFIL) peacekeepers and therefore that Israeli positions would be taken by the Hezbollah militia. As such, Olmert believed he had no other choice, but to approve the ground assault (Makovsky 1 February 2008). The Committee accepted his reasoning that the altered ceasefire terms were disappointing to Israel and therefore left no choice to Olmert, by his own judgment, but to approve the ground assault, partly in order to improve the ceasefire terms.

Yossi Verter concluded that 'The bottom line of the complete Winograd Report is that there is no bottom line' (Verter 1 February 2008a). In another political culture he wrote 'anyone else would have resigned long ago, after the partial report, but not Olmert. He viewed the Final Report as an opportunity to turn over a new leaf' (Verter 1 February 2008a).

Internal politics

Both Chief of Staff Halutz and Minister of Defense Peretz had resigned from office before the Interim Report was published. Halutz succumb to public pressure whereas Peretz lost the internal Labor elections for the party leadership to his arch rival Ehud Barak. Immediately afterwards, Peretz resigned office and Barak, the most decorated soldier in the history of the IDF, took over. Therefore, the main protest was directed towards Prime Minister Olmert. On 3 May 2007, three days after the release of the Interim Report, the Knesset held a special session to debate the Report's findings. Opposition leader Benjamin Netanyahu called for Olmert to resign, but Kadima's MKs supported Olmert and a vote of no-confidence was not held (BBC News 3 May 2007a). Olmert himself had promised he would act upon the committee's Final Report. Later that day, tens of thousands of protesters had gathered at Tel Aviv's main city square, calling upon Olmert and his government to resign (BBC News 3 May 2007b; Observer Reporter 4 May 2007). De facto, not only that Olmert did not leave his position, but Barak's nomination as defense minister, in June 2007, had strengthened the government stability and enabled the continuance of its tenure. Avigdor Yitzhaki was the only Kadima member who tried to evoke an internal rebellion inside Kadima, calling upon his friends to dismiss Olmert from his position (Somfalvi 31 January 2008). His failure had led Yitzhaki to resign his position as the coalition chair, after the Interim Report in May 2007 (Mualem 2 May 2007a) and from the Knesset on 7 February 2008 (Somfalvi 31 January 2008).

After the Final Report's publication, the reserve officers' organisation and bereaved families who called upon Olmert's resignation reduced the intensity of their protest because of the implicit and ambiguous conclusions of the Report (Azoulay 23 January 2008; Galili *et al.* 28 January 2008). Prime Minister Olmert felt great relief that he was exonerated. He described the Report as 'lifting the moral stigma from me' (Galili *et al.* 31 January 2008). His close colleagues said he was 'moved to tears' after reading the Report sections that dealt with the ground operation (Galili *et al.* 31 January 2008). He had no intention of resigning.

Soon after he was elected as chair of the Labor party, Ehud Barak said that he would quit the government if Olmert did not resign following the release of the final conclusions of the Winograd Commission. Alas, after the final report was released, Minister of Defense Barak did not fulfill his promise, claiming the Report was not as grave as it was expected to be. His justification for staying in the government was the heavy responsibility he took upon himself facing the great challenges ahead, namely the Iranian, Hezbollah and Palestinian threats. Barak's advisors concluded that resigning from the government would be irresponsible given that the Defense Minister was the only one who could, and must, correct the inadequacies cited by the Winograd Report.

Some of Barak's colleagues were not convinced: Ophir Pines-Paz resigned his office as the Culture, Science and Sports minister on 30 October 2006 (Somfalvi 30 October 2006); Eitan Cabel, Secretary General of the Labor Party, resigned office as a Minister without Portfolio, immediately after the Interim Report was released, on 1 May 2007, calling upon PM Olmert to do the same (Mualem 2 May 2007b); Shelly Yachimovich and Danny Yatom demanded that the Labor Party pull out of the coalition. On the other hand, other Labour members, ministers in the Olmert government, argued against leaving the coalition. Barak remained in office (Haaretz Service 31 January 2008; Verter and Mualem 1 February 2008d).

Opposition leader, Benjamin Netanyahu, called Olmert an unfit leader and an incompetent Prime Minister. Netanyahu said that Israel's citizens were demanding a new and worthy leader, who would be elected into office (Mualem 1 February 2008).

The Winograd Report did not cause a dramatic change in public opinion regarding Prime Minister Ehud Olmert. According to a public opinion poll conducted on 31 January 2008 not only the political leadership, but also the public, remained indifferent to the Report. A Haaretz-Dialog survey found that most of the public believed Olmert should resign following the Report. But compared to the public's feelings after the release of the Interim Report nine months earlier, support for Olmert had increased (Verter 1 February 2008b). After the Interim Report 68 percent of the public believed that Olmert should resign his office; while nine months later, with the release of the Final Report, only 53 percent of the public thought Olmert should resign (Verter 1 February 2008c; Dialog Survey 1 February 2008). The survey also showed that after the Final Report, only 14 percent of the public thought that Olmert was responsible for the war outcomes, whereas the parallel figures after the Interim Report showed that 36 percent of the public saw Olmert as the main person responsible for the war outcomes (Dialog Survey 1 February 2008).

On 4 February 2008, the Knesset convened for a special session, dedicated to Winograd's Final Report. The session included Olmert's speech as a response to the Report conclusions. Olmert said he 'carries the full responsibilities for the failures' of the war, although he defended the decision to go to war against Hezbollah (Ilan 4 February 2008). He said, 'The unequivocal opinion of the defense establishment before the Second Lebanon War was that in the case of an abduction attempt or rocket attacks, Israel must respond harshly in the entire area in a disproportionate fashion', in order to deal with the Hezbollah threat (Ilan 4 February 2008).

Olmert reminded the plenum of the support that the war initially garnered from the entire political spectrum, the media and the public. He criticised the opposition leader and Likud Chairman Benjamin Netanyahu for calling upon him to resign, saying that Netanyahu was a major supporter of the war effort (Ilan 31 January 2008; Ilan 4 February 2008).

Netanyahu responded that the:

> Second Lebanon War was a failure.... The prime minister is evading responsibility. It won't help to put the responsibility on the people, the opposition, on me personally. We all supported the war, and even today we wouldn't take it back.... But we didn't support the failed management of the war.
>
> (Ilan 4 February 2008)

Meretz MK Zehava Galon addressed Olmert, saying that he should be denounced on the 'public pillory' (Ilan 4 February 2008). 'You won your war of survival, but the state of Israel lost. A state is not a survival plan and therefore you must resign.... You are not fit to move the state in the direction of a peace process. The peace camp is not a sanctuary state. Peace must not become the last refuge of the villainous and corrupt' (Ilan 4 February 2008). Labor MK Eitan Cabel criticised the Prime Minister by saying: 'I was a minister in the government and participated in the decision-making process ... I have no expectations of you ... to get up and leave. Regrettably, I have no expectation that you will set a personal example' (Ilan 4 February 2008).

During the session, bereaved parents started a commotion and shouted at Olmert. 'You are not my Prime Minister. I relinquish my citizenship!', cried Elipaz Baloha, who lost his son during the Israel–Hezbollah War. Baloha was subsequently removed from the Knesset and the other bereaved parents followed him in solidarity (Frykberg 11 February 2008). MKs Uri Ariel and Arieh Eldad of the National Union Party had also left the hall, after a failed attempt to rally other MKs to join them and leave the plenum (Ilan 4 February 2008).

Nevertheless, the Knesset approved, in a majority of 59 versus 53, Olmert's speech in a symbolic vote. Six Coalition members voted against the statement; four Arab MKs, as well as former Defense Minister Amir Peretz did not attend the special session (Ilan 4 February 2008).

International implications

Talkbacks in the Arab nations started referring in a positive manner to the appointment of a Winograd-like committee in Lebanon to investigate the Israel-Hezbollah War and in Egypt to investigate the failing economics. But the Arab leaders did not want to appoint a committee that threatened their thrones. Hassan Nasrallah, leader and General Secretary of the Hezbollah, was quick to endorse the Winograd Report, viewing its conclusions as evidence that his organisation had won the war. Nawaf Musawi, head of international relations for Hezbollah, called the war a 'divine victory' against Israel. He added that 'no one will take us lightly from now on, especially since we have only gained strength of late' (Gulf News 1 May 2007). The Winograd Report had political implications in Lebanon as, according to Musawi, the Report contradicted Beirut officials who claimed that the war had hurt Lebanon and was not won by Hezbollah (Bechor 3 May 2007). The further implications are the weakening of Israel in the eyes of its enemies, as its sophisticated army was unable to win against the Hezbollah militias (Bechor 3 May 2007).

The Final Report also focused on the US-Israel relationship. The committee analysis showed that changing signals from Washington officials, regarding the terms of the ceasefire agreement, during Friday 11 August 2006, were at the center of Olmert's controversial decision to launch a ground assault (Winograd Committee Final Report January 2008: 533–4). According to the Report, the United States allowed the reversal of cautiously negotiated terms, between a draft that the Assistant Secretary of State David Welch, sent to Israeli authorities on 10 August 2006, to a new draft sent by the Under Secretary of State for Political Affairs, Nicholas Burns, later on that same day. The Committee reported that the latter draft included no enforcement for a weapons embargo on Hezbollah and it did not mention the condition, according to which embargo violations would be sanctioned by chapter 7 (The Use of Force Authorization) of the UN Charter (Makovsky 1 February 2008). Later, Israeli government officials argued that they had no idea that the United States would allow carefully negotiated terms to be suddenly reversed.

Conclusions

The Israeli government responded hastily and without much thinking to the Hezbollah attack. Rushing into action without proper examination is irresponsible. Responsible government is required to ponder the consequences of its decisions. The government of Israel should have announced immediately after the kidnapping of the two soldiers that it regarded the Hezbollah attack as a severe breach of international law and that it will respond in the time and manner it sees fit, reassuring the Hezbollah as well as the citizens of Israel that such attack will not pass unnoticed. The way to respond to guerilla warfare is by guerilla warfare. The IDF has several elite platoons that are suitable for the job. There is no need to rush into action and to escalate tensed situations into unnecessary wars. Israel did not retrieve the kidnapped soldiers. Its massive attack on Lebanon brought about large-scale retaliation that subjected more than one million Israeli citizens to continuous rocket attacks, that resulted in hundred of thousands of refugees and hundreds of people killed or maimed. If at all, the war strengthened the Hezbollah in Lebanon and weakened Israeli deterrence.

Prime Minister Olmert who came to office as the person who would bring peace to Israel, and who was willing to bring forward daring ideas that would solve once and for all the Israeli–Palestinian conflict, proved to be a great disappointment. Olmert wanted to annex 6.3 percent of the West Bank to Israel, areas that are home to 75 percent of the Jewish population of the territories. His proposal would have also involved evacuation of dozens of settlements in the Jordan Valley, in the eastern Samarian hills and in the Hebron region. In return for the annexation to Israel of Ma'aleh Adumim, the Gush Etzion bloc of settlements, Ariel, Beit Aryeh and settlements adjacent to Jerusalem, Olmert proposed the transfer of territory to the Palestinians equivalent to 5.8 percent of the area of the West Bank, as well as a safe passage route from Hebron to the Gaza Strip, via a highway that would remain part of the sovereign territory of Israel, but where there would be no Israeli presence. Olmert spoke of the establishment of a Palestinian state with its capital in East Jerusalem and was willing to accept a token number of Palestinian refugees (Ben 17 December 2009; Sackur 2009). However, the person who was elected on a clear and explicit peace plan, who was the Peace Camp's great hope, had led

Israeli Ministry of Foreign Affairs (14 September 2006) 'Establishment of the Winograd committee', at www.mfa.gov.il/MFA/Government/Communiques/2006/Establishment%20of%20the%20Winograd%20Committee%20 14-Sep-2006 (accessed 11 October 2010).

Levine, H. (29 May 2007) 'Behind the headlines on the Winograd commission's interim report', *Center for Defense Information*, at www.cdi.org/friendlyversion/printversion.cfm?documentID=3969 (accessed 23 March 2011).

Makovsky, D. (1 February 2008) 'Winograd part II: Implications for U.S.–Israeli relations', The Washington Institute for Near East Policy: *Policy watch/Peace Watch*, at www.washingtoninstitute.org/templateC05.php?CID=2714 (accessed 11 October 2010).

Mualem, M. (2 May 2007a) 'Yitzhaki quits as coalition chair after ultimatum to Olmert' *Haaretz*, at www.haaretz.com/news/yitzhaki-quits-as-coalition-chair-after-ultimatum-to-olmert-1.219506 (accessed 11 October 2010).

Mualem, M. (2 May 2007b) 'Senior labor minister quits cabinet to demand Olmert's resignation', *Haaretz*, at www.haaretz.com/print-edition/news/senior-labor-minister-quits-cabinet-to-demand-olmert-s-resignation-1.219569 (accessed 11 October 2010).

Mualem, M. (1 February 2008) 'Opposition leader Netanyahu: Olmert is incompetent, unfit to lead', *Haaretz*, at www.haaretz.com/news/opposition-leader-netanyahu-olmert-is-incompetent-unfit-to-lead-1.238410 (accessed 11 October 2010).

New York Times (30 January 2008) 'English summary of the Winograd commission report', *The New York Times*, at www.nytimes.com/2008/01/30/world/middleeast/31winograd-web.html?_r=1&pagewanted=print (accessed 11 October 2010).

Observer Reporter (4 May 2007) 'Protesters call on Israel's Olmert to quit over Lebanon war failures', *Observer Reporter Online, no* longer available online (accessed 9 June 2008).

Reiss, O. (8 August 2006) 'Reserve soldiers reveal: This is how IDF had abandoned us' (Hebrew), *Ynet*, at www.ynet.co.il/articles/0,7340,L-3287879,00.html (accessed 11 October 2010).

Rofe-Ofir, S. and Grinberg, H. (14 August 2006) 'Rear-area headquarters: Returning to normal in all the northern settlements' (Hebrew), *Ynet*, at www.ynet.co.il/articles/0,7340,L-3291201,00.html (accessed 11 October 2010).

Sackur, S. (2009) 'Standing by the Olmert plan', *BBC HARDtalk*, at http://news.bbc.co.uk/2/hi/middle_east/8273336.stm (accessed 23 March 2011).

Scoop (16 August 2006) 'Reserve soldier reports from Lebanon: The naked truth about the war' (Hebrew), *Scoop*, no longer available online (accessed 9 June 2008).

Security Council SC/8808 (11 August 2006) 'Security council calls for end to hostilities between Hizbollah, Israel, Unanimously adopting resolution no. 1701 (2006)', at www.un.org/News/Press/docs/2006/sc8808.doc.htm (accessed 11 October 2010).

Sheffer, H. (10 September 2006) 'Thousands demonstrated in the city circus: "Olmert, go home"' (Hebrew), *NRG*, at www.nrg.co.il/online/1/ART1/476/523.html (accessed 11 October 2010).

Somfalvi, A. (30 October 2006) 'Pines-Paz resigns from government', *Ynet*, at www.ynetnews.com/articles/0,7340,L-3321526,00.html (accessed 11 October 2010).

Somfalvi, A. (31 January 2008) 'Kadima MK Itzhaki quits Knesset over war report', *Ynet*, at www.ynetnews.com/articles/0,7340,L-3501043,00.html (accessed 11 October 2010).

Tristam, P. (2008), 'Analysis: The Winograd commission report on Israel's 2006 war in Lebanon–Criticism and contradictions', *About.com*, at http://middleeast. about.com/od/israel/a/me080130c.htm (accessed 23 March 2011).

Verter, Y. (1 February 2008a) 'Over to you, Ehud!' (Hebrew), *Haaretz*, at www. haaretz.com/print-edition/opinion/over-to-you-ehud-1.238363 (accessed 11 October 2010).

Verter, Y. (1 February 2008b) 'Haaretz–Dialog poll: Third of public calls for Olmert to stay', *Haaretz*, at www.haaretz.com/news/haaretz-dialog-poll-third-of-public-calls-for-olmert-to-stay-1.238421 (accessed 11 October 2010).

Verter, Y. (1 February 2008c) 'Decrease in the demand for Olmert's resignation' (Hebrew), *Haaretz*, at www.haaretz.co.il/hasite/spages/950343.html (accessed 11 October 2010).

Verter, Y. and Mualem, M. (1 February 2008d) 'Senior Labor party sources: Barak expected to stay in office', *Haaretz*, at www.haaretz.com/news/senior-labor-party-sources-barak-expected-to-stay-in-office-1.238423 (accessed 11 October 2010).

Winograd Committee (17 September 2006) 'The commission of inquiry into the events of military engagement in Lebanon 2006–Letter of Appointment' (Hebrew), at www.vaadatwino.co.il/nomination.html (accessed 11 October 2010).

Winograd Committee (12 February 2007) 'Press Releases' (Hebrew), at www.vaadatwino.co.il/press.html#null (accessed 11 October 2010).

Winograd Committee (2007) 'List of witnesses' (Hebrew), at www.vaadatwino.co.il/statements.html#null (accessed 11 October 2010).

Winograd Committee Interim Report (April 2007) (Hebrew), no longer available online (accessed 9 June 2008).

Winograd Committee Final Report (January 2008) (Hebrew), no longer available online (accessed 9 June 2008).

Winograd Commission submits Interim Report (30 April 2007), 'Israel Ministry of Foreign Affairs', at www.mfa.gov.il/MFA/Government/Communiques/2007/Wi nograd+Inquiry+Commission+submits+Interim+Report+30-Apr-2007.htm (accessed 23 March 2011).

Ynet (14 August 2006) '155 Victims of war in the northern war' (Hebrew), *Ynet*, at www.ynet.co.il/articles/0,7340,L-3288289,00.html (accessed 11 October 2010).

Yoaz, Y. (20 September 2006) 'Mazuz: soon I will decide whether or not Olmert will be investigated' (Hebrew), *Walla News*, at http://news.walla.co.il/?w=/1/978184 (11 October 2010).

12 Media actors in war and conflict

Insights from political psychology and the Bosnian war

Maria Touri

Introduction

In the current era of information overload, the diffusion of communications technologies and the availability of multiple sources of information have generated a certain degree of openness and publicity, reducing the ability of political leaders to have complete control over the definition and framing of events (Brown 2005). In the case for conflict and war, the life-and-death risks that conflicts involve makes them hard cases for media effects to occur (Baum and Groeling 2010: 11). However, the same risks can grant conflicts unusual visibility and public attention through the media, reducing leaders' time for deliberation and accelerating decision-making.

The role of the media in foreign policy-making and conflict has been explained by several theories that have illuminated certain dimensions of the interdependence between national news media and governments (Bennett *et al.* 2007; Entman 2004; Hallin 1986; Wolfsfeld 1997), as well as the role of global TV networks on diplomacy and foreign policy (Gilboa 2002; O'Heffernan 1991; Robinson 2002; Strobel 1997). Media influences are often discussed in connection to latent opinion and anticipated public reactions (Robinson 2002; Van Belle 2004; Zaller 2003). Through their perceived power to generate domestic audience costs and the anticipation of public punishment, the media become a potential source of cost for political leaders (Baum 2004a; Fearon 1994; Schultz 2001; Slantchev 2006). In this interaction, violence can play an ambiguous part. International relations theorists have demonstrated the possibility for audience costs to escalate violence. During war and conflict, when governments become locked into their positions, backing down makes them prone to domestic audience costs in the form of credibility loss, which could give them incentive to continue a bloody war. By making conflicts 'public events in which domestic audiences observe and assess the performance of the leadership' (Fearon 1994: 577), the media could be said to contribute in this process. However, at the same time the visibility they give to violence during war and conflict can trigger costs of a different form. The

'CNN effect' debate emphasises the possibility for a strong policy media impact, through the pressure that emotive pictures in humanitarian disaster news reports can put on policy makers to 'do something', in anticipation of the public's reaction. However, having been widely questioned, the theory offers limited insight in the role the media can really play in such situations (Gilboa 2002; Robinson 2002). Although Robinson's (2002) 'policy-media interaction' model and Entman's (2004) model of state–media relations have shed light on the degree of media independence and power, so far little systematic work has been conducted in explaining when and under what conditions the media can contribute to policy-making during war and conflict. This theoretical deficit could be down to the fact that the actual cost of media coverage of war and conflict is not readily visible, but subtle and derives from the power relations that characterise the complex interactions that policymakers develop with each other, with the public and the media.

This chapter makes a first attempt at addressing this deficit through the psychological school of thought. The application of psychology in international relations and decision-making has produced evidence of systematic biases that can distort political leaders' assessments and affect decisions in predictable ways (McDermott, 2004). Media coverage of conflict situations embodies complex interactions that could often trigger such biases. To demonstrate this, I revisit the power relations that underpin the news framing process during conflict through the prism of prospect theory, a theory from the field of political psychology. Concerned with the importance of the political environment in determining decisions, prospect theory can illuminate the media's role as a factor that can influence decision-making through the changes it causes to a leader's domestic environment. The chapter concludes by applying the theory to the US press coverage of the war in Bosnia with an attempt to re-evaluate the media's role in President Clinton's decision-making.

Prospect theory: a brief introduction

Prospect theory is a descriptive psychological theory of human decision-making under conditions of risk, originally developed by Kahneman and Tversky (1979) as a critique of utility theory. In their subsequent development of the theory, Kahneman and Tversky formulated hypotheses that have been generalised and applied to various forms of decisions under risk, especially in politics and international relations.[1] One of the theory's key positions is that individuals evaluate their choices in terms of gains and losses, while they tend to assess the outcomes of these choices with respect to deviations from a given 'reference point', rather to net asset positions. In other words, when individuals face a choice problem, the change that a decision could cause to their current position, matters more than the final outcome of the decision. The theory also posits that, when evaluating outcomes, individuals treat gains differently from losses. Losses tend to loom larger than corresponding gains; so that a person who loses a given amount of money will hurt more than a person who wins the same amount will be satisfied. As a result, when people find themselves in a bad situation they tend to become more willing to take risks to reverse this situation (risk-seeking). On the contrary, when they feel they are in a secure and beneficial situation where things are going well, they become more cautious with their decisions (risk-averse). This pattern, called the 'loss aversion' phenomenon, implies a preference that individuals have for a given reference point (usually defined as the status quo), than the 50/50 possibility that this reference point will change either for the better or the worse (Levy, 1994a). Hence, as individuals, we would prefer the certainty of winning a given amount of money than the 50/50 possibility that we win double the amount or nothing at all.

The differential treatment of gains and losses has drawn attention to how individuals 'frame' a choice problem and more importantly, whether and why they frame choices in terms of gains or losses, as framing tends to determine choice evaluation and risk propensity. The concept of framing has been defined by Tversky and Kahneman (1981) as individuals' processing of information that is based on intrinsic forces, such as their temperament, and defines how they make sense of a given situation. Scholars in the political psychology school have recognised the importance of context in framing situations and decisions (McDermott, 2004), which creates scope to locate the national news media in the political decision-making process as a contextual factor in the leader's domestic environment. What predetermines the framing of a choice problem is a complex aspect of the theory as the frame 'is controlled partly by the formulation of the problem and partly by the norms, habits and personal characteristics of the decision-maker' (Tversky and Kahneman 1981: 453). Prospect theory, and its applicability to real life political behaviour, is often criticised for this vagueness (Boettcher 2004; McDermott 2004; Mercer 2005), which raises questions regarding whether the role of the media [as a potential cause of framing effects] can be isolated from other influential factors. Nevertheless, it is the theory's focus on the importance of the situation in determining people's risk propensity that offers a portal for the news media to be incorporated in the decision-making process in an international conflict. As vehicles of complex power relations between journalists and decision-makers, news frames can turn into signals of domestic gains or losses for the leader, with potential implications on his choices.[2]

Domestic costs and the contest over news framing

Media criticism and opposition to political actions may be considered as an obvious form of media pressure, but the damage the media can cause to a leader's integrity can often be less direct, particularly when news stories are approached as a platform for framing contests where political actors compete by sponsoring their preferred meanings (Carragee and Roefs, 2004).

The essence of the news framing contest lies in the information exchanges that leaders, social and political actors, the media and the public are involved in and the power relations that these exchanges embody. As traders of information, the media will normally strive to maintain the right balance between protecting their sources by preserving leaders' preferred framing on the one hand and responding to the audiences' information needs, on the other (Baum and Potter, 2008). Leaders are aware of journalist's preferences and this allows the former to employ the necessary strategies for advancing interpretations of events, or 'frames', which will gain public approval. These would normally have to resonate with the wider culture of a society, so that they can stimulate similar reactions by elites and the public, minimising domestic opposition; and with the media's political culture and market imperatives, as only then will the market also demand coverage that is consonant with a leader's dominant frame (Baum and Potter 2008; Cook 1989; Entman 2004; Wolfsfeld 1997). Normally, when conflicts arise, leaders enjoy a substantial informational advantage over the news media, which are then expected to retain leaders' frames and 'rally around the flag' (Baker and Oneal 2001; Chapman and Reiter 2004; Zaller and Chiu 2000). This enables elites to dominate the framing of events, at least to the extent that counterframes do not develop beyond the acceptable 'politics as usual' statements.[3] The public's informational disadvantage also makes the media more responsive to leaders' preferences than to those of the public (Baum and Groeling 2007; 2008).

Failure to control the news framing contest is more likely, when the conflict progresses and journalists are able to disclose information from a wider range of sources, enabling the public to update their beliefs about the reliability of the information they gather and learn more about the quality and effectiveness of a policy. To overcome their information disadvantage, members of the public are expected to use heuristic cues and information shortcuts through the news media, relying on the opinions of trusted political elites (Baum and Potter 2008; Iyengar and Kinder 1987; Krosnick and Kinder 1990). The credibility of these opinions depends partly on the belief that the source and the audience share common interests (Crawford and Sobel 1982), but also on how costly a frame is for the speaker. Opposition party endorsements of, or presidential party attacks on the president, for example, are atypical because they represent potentially self-damaging signals, which increase their credibility (Baum and Groelling 2010: 9).[4] In essence, if elite competition over policy framing can disrupt the potential for public acceptance (Masters and Alexander 2008), media coverage that reflects heterogeneous elite discussion could signify a leader's failure to dominate not just the news framing process, but public perceptions as well.

Such failures reveal a discrepancy between 'reality' and a leader's frame and leaders' limited capacity to manipulate the framing of events independently from the true status of those events (Baum and Groeling, 2007: 17). The Iraq War 2003 is a case in point, when Bush's 'war on terror' frame, employed as an effective replacement for the Cold War frame, secured domestic unification behind his decision and avoided resistance by national news media. As American casualties continued, the capacity of the administration to frame the war to their own advantage shrunk, when such frames contradicted the tenor of actual events, paving the way for less uniform and more critical reporting (Baum and Groeling, 2008: 7; 39; Entman, 2004: 112). Signalling a leader's 'unfaithfulness' means that news frames can cause a credibility loss and create conditions for anticipated punishment at the polls.[5] Prospect theory draws attention to the way that failure to dominate the framing contest may affect a leader's perception of a given situation and decisions, through the sense of loss that such failures can activate.

Loss aversion and the media's invisible impact

The loss aversion effect and the psychological implications that losses can inflict are the most famous implications of prospect theory. These are more significant than the simple assumption that no ones likes to lose, as they suggest that individuals take high risks in order to avoid or recoup a loss (Jervis, 2004). For political leaders, loss aversion suggests that the spectre of losing control over the news framing contest could be crucial enough to shape their behaviour in a situation such as an international conflict. Here, news media frames and international outcomes converge in the domestic accountability that leaders are subjected to for foreign policy decisions; and international political issues matter to the degree that the domestic political system translates them into costs and benefits for the leader (Van Belle, 2000: 20–23). So long as the domestic arena becomes the primary source of threats to a leader's incumbency, losses over the news framing contest will matter, turning the media into a conduit for loss aversion. In this context, the loss aversion effect can illuminate a subtle role of the media, which is activated through the fear of a credibility loss that media frames could inflict through public opinion. Their influence occurs not just through current news frames but in anticipation of them.

The loss aversion effect can explain why governments are more concerned to prevent a decline in their reputation [than to increase it by a comparable amount] as reputation affects future utilities and future losses hurt more than future gains gratify (Jervis, 1991; Levy, 1994). The possibility of the *future* loss the media can create is linked to the public's ability to retrospectively assess the reliability of information consumed in the past, based on which a leader's future claims can be assessed. According to

Baum and Groelling, 'retrospective updating may lead to a shift in the balance of previously stored considerations as individuals retag some negatively or positively tagged information based on a retrospective revision of their reliability assessment' (2010: 37). The authors give the example of the Bush administration's investment on the Weapons of Mass Destruction frame to justify the war in Iraq, which was later picked up by critics as an unreliable claim to undermine the administration's credibility in future claims.

Yet, an even more crucial explanatory feature of prospect theory is the impact that a *change* from a current position in the news framing contest may have on a leader's behaviour. As 'the carriers of value ... are *changes* of wealth rather than final asset positions [emphasis added]' (Kahneman and Tversky 1979: 273), change matters more than the final outcome and individuals attach added personal value to the things they already have. People's tendency to overweigh the disadvantages of leaving their current position and the efforts they make to preserve rather than improve their position has been described as the 'status quo bias' effect (Samuelson and Zechauser 1988 in Levy 1994b: 120). The status quo bias draws attention to the efforts a leader could make to avoid a deterioration of his position. In the case of a news framing contest, this could be a leader's effort to maintain the control of the news framing and public interpretations of events that he would normally secure in the early stages of a conflict, when the information gap between politicians and the media is wider.

The need to sustain the status quo position and avoid future domestic losses can induce leaders to incorporate the media's anticipated reaction in the planning of their actions, avoiding choices that could cost them the public support. With the proliferation of new technologies and the growing volume of information, political leaders need to ensure there is consistency between their declarations and actions (Brown 2005: 64). Whether this leads to more carefully designed communication strategies or policy initiatives with greater chances of domestic and international approval, the end result is that, especially in situations such as a conflict, aversion to losses makes the media essential to our understanding of political decision-making.

Media influences on framing one's 'domain'

The input of prospect theory is not confined to explaining latent media influences. In the event of loss of control over the news framing contest, the loss aversion effect can shed light on a more overt media pressure on leaders' international behaviour, as they strive to recoup this domestic loss.

The impact of perceived domestic losses on decision-making in international conflicts was addressed by McDermott and Kugler (2001), in an analysis of the 1991 Gulf War through the prism of prospect theory. The authors suggested that the limited public approval Bush's national policies were receiving at home led the President to believe he was in a vulnerable position and to frame his position, or 'domain' in prospect theory's terms, as one of losses, which was one of the factors that increased his risk propensity in Iraq. Van Belle's (2000) account of the news framing of the US economy at the time adds to this behaviour explanation. US economic problems were particularly harmful to Bush's domestic standing and the news framed his attempt to deal with these as a failure. However, Bush's first threat against Iraq coincided with a significant interruption in the media attention to the economy. If Bush's intentions towards Iraq were designed to also downgrade this negative media attention, he was certainly successful (ibid: 35–36). Prospect theory highlights the possibility that, through the losses the news framing contest can inflict, the media manipulate a leader's reference point, making an identical situation (i.e. international conflict) seem different under circumstances of loss aversion. If by signaling a domestic loss, news frames signal a deterioration of the leader's position, they could push an actor in a position of losses where risk prevails.

Excessive risks could be justified by prospect theory's position that the magnitudes of the losses involved need not be that large to induce risk-seeking behaviour (Levy 1992: 287; 1994b: 123). Consequently, for a leader whose decisions are designed to meet domestic demands for power, the very fact of losing control over the news framing contest could be more important than its size. Recouping this media loss can become a factor relevant to the decisions made in the international realm, what is also called 'the segregation effect', that describes people's tendency to focus on the factors that seem most relevant to the immediate problem when making choices (McDermott and Kugler 2001: 65). Personality and other contextual factors will of course have a critical effect on how a leader defines his reference point and frames his position, and the way the media's role is manifested in the decision-making process is subject to the particularities of a given situation. Along similar lines, the degree of risk an actor is willing to take will obviously vary from one situation to another. Prospect theory could suggest that a leader's loss of power over the struggle to dominate the news framing contest may increase risk propensity in a conflict, but the type of risks will depend on the situation at hand. Although prospect theory cannot predict the policy outcomes that the news framing contest can generate, it offers an alternative view of the potential trajectory through which the media's influence can occur.

The Bosnian war

The Bosnian case represents an international armed conflict in the resolution of which the US contributed actively mostly in the last stages of the war. By general admission a highly complex conflict, the Bosnian war was the product of historical and economic reasons, as well as of the demise of the Communist ideology after the end of the Cold War, which gradually led to the destabilisation of the Federal Republic of Yugoslavia (FRY).[6] With several of the republics, notably Slovenia and Croatia, seeking independence in the early 1990s, fights between supporters of the federal state and those supporting its dissolution quickly turned into one of the bloodiest wars in the region (Gow 1997; Robinson 2002). It was not before the end of 1995 that a peace agreement was finally reached in Dayton, Ohio. The war was characterised by the failure of diplomacy to end the war sooner, due to the reluctance and inability of the international community to use force and the lack of political commitment to follow through on initiatives (Gow 1997: 10). As Gow (1997) explains, the US played a crucial role in the final settlement, but failed to help end the war earlier when the opportunity to implement the Vance Owen peace proposal in 1993 fell through.

Despite recognition of Bosnia, for most of the duration of the war, Clinton chose to defer to the European allies and UN forces in the Balkans. The peacekeeping force UNPROFOR that was deployed by the EU led to the arms embargo policy which disrupted the ability of the Bosnian government to defend itself against the Bosnian Serbs. (Entman 2004; Gow 1997; Hansen 2006; Herring 1997; Robinson 2002). Clinton had contemplated involvement in early 1993, but due to fears of a quagmire and domestic political damage the decision to maintain a military distance prevailed (Entman 2004; Robinson 2002; Zaller 2003). A common observation among communications scholars is that a US policy vacuum enabled news media frames to force the administration to intervene more decisively in the final stages of the war (Robinson 2002; Shaw 1996; Strobel, 1997).

Yet, the role of the media in this intervention has been less than clear-cut. On the one hand, the emotive language and empathy framing of Clinton's 'inaction' and of the failing Western policies evoked emotional public reaction, which is believed to have shaped the timing of the intervention, following the fall of Srebrenica in July 1995 (Entman 2004; Robinson 2002: 80–82). On the other, policy-makers have rejected the media's pressure, as they resisted acting in response to news coverage in the earlier stages, claiming ability to withstand dramatic TV images (Gowing 1994; 1996). I argue that prospect theory can illuminate the media's role through their potential influence on Clinton's articulation of the non-intervention and intervention options, and the sense of loss that Clinton's inability to keep the media's framing under control generated. Even if the media did not trigger the intervention, I posit that their role is pivotal in understanding Clinton's course of action.

'Civil war' vs. 'genocide' frames

Despite the domestic criticism Clinton received for vetoing a unilateral American lifting of the arms embargo (Gow 1997; Hansen 2006), evidence suggests that, until the fall of Srebrenica and the US intervention that culminated in the Dayton Accord, he framed his position as one of gains. In other words, he perceived himself and the country to be in a secure position, facing no particular risks from the situation in Bosnia and feeling no pressure to act. His decision to refrain from a more direct and active involvement demonstrates a cautious and 'risk-averse' behaviour and can be justified by the absence of a direct impact of the war on US interests. According to Nye's (1999) typology of threats to US interests, the Bosnian crisis is best classified as a 'C' list threat (Nye 1999: 26–30). Overlapping with none of America's vital interests meant that involvement in this ethnic war would lead to no gains (Riedlmayer 1993).

This policy line was reinforced by the complex nature of the conflict with the war being framed by officials as a conventional case of ancient hatred and aggression by one state (Serbia) against another (Bosnia) (Gow 1997: 203–207). The war was articulated as a 'civil war', with mutual aggression from all sides, and associated with previous American experiences, such as Vietnam. Officials framed Bosnia as a dangerous foreign involvement in a far away place, for which the West bore no ethical responsibility (Hansen 2006; Herring 1997). This articulation was countered by debates of 'genocide' and of a conflict instigated by Serbian extremists and politicians who saw profit in unleashing forces on the other. This frame emerged later on, after the US administration had began to see Bosnia as the innocent victim of Serbia's aggression (Gow 1997; Herring 1997; Mousavizadeh 1996a: 162 Burns 1992 in Hansen 2006: 113); and it gradually paved the way for Clinton's shift towards a more active involvement and recognition of the international community's responsibility to protect the innocent victims of this war (Herring 1997).

In prospect theory's terms, Clinton's behaviour embodies a departure from his initial reference point [where the war appeared distant and unrelated to US interests] and a change in his perception of the situation. Contrary to the initial stages where Clinton may have been confident that no American interests were at stake and no action was required, as the war progressed, he started to feel less secure and more anxious about the loss that the US and he, personally, could suffer from this situation. Evidence suggests that the prospect of a humiliating UN withdrawal from Bosnia and fears that the Bosnian government would withdraw its support for UNPROFOR for failing to fulfil its mission marked the deterioration of the situation, creating the need for a more decisive policy (Robinson 2002: 84). However, as Robinson explains, these factors could not have accounted for the decision alone. According to Gow (1997), the reports of the war and the pressure to do something affected Clinton personally. In line with prospect theory, this must have placed him in the domain of losses, which translates in his willingness to make decisions that he initially considered as risky and unnecessary, for fear that the situation could deteriorate even further for him and for US interests.

Media challenges of the dominant frame: activating the loss aversion effect

For most of the duration of the conflict, the national media would primarily reflect the official framing of the war that prevailed in the Administration circles, showing no evidence of Clinton's loss of control of the news framing contest. Through a combination of dramatic, but also distanced reporting, the civil war frame was reproduced more widely than questions of genocide and ethnic cleansing. Despite the escalation that followed Bosnia's declaration of independence in March 1992, media coverage, although dramatic, remained distanced and confused (Auerbach and Bloch-Elkon 2005). By repeatedly reproducing frames of old grievances that were re-waken with the end of the Cold War (Campbell 1998: 53–54) and recounting Bosnia's history of ethnic unrest through simplified frames (Myers *et al.* 1996), news reports created emotional distance between the audience and the suffering people (Gowing 2000; Robinson 2002).[7] Such coverage provides limited evidence that the media defied Clinton's position, but with the fall of Srebrenica in July 1995, his approach was challenged in a more forceful manner. The incident triggered extensive media attention that combined the 'failure' frame with images of horrific human suffering and emotive language. It exposed Clinton's failure to manipulate the framing of events and promote non-intervention as the optimal policy (Robinson 2002),[8] reflecting a discrepancy between the official policies and anticipated public interpretations of the situation, which was destined to generate fears of public punishment.[9] As Herring posits, already many people in the West saw the war in Bosnia as a threat to their values and thought that important things were at stake in the area, contrary to what they were told by politicians (1997: 173). Such views could only be amplified by the media's open criticism of a 'half-way house policy', which Clinton himself did not see as entirely moral (Gow 1997: 221).

If we evaluate this evidence in connection to the significance of the news framing contest for a leader's credibility, it can be argued that, after the fall of Srebrenica, the media's framing of the war raised questions of honesty and signaled a potential damage to the credibility of the US as an actor which the international community could rely on. The press portrayed the US as unable to defend the suffering victims and as Schelling (1966) explains, commitments are interdependent; US failure to defend one specific commitment would consequently make future similar instances questionable in the eyes of the national public. What this media coverage reflected was a) a shift to frames of policy failure and b) a change in Clinton's standing in the news framing contest as the media sent signals of negative anticipated public perceptions.[10]

Prospect theory offers a three-fold explanation for why the media could have influenced the US intervention in Bosnia. First, Clinton was in the domain of losses when he decided to take a more forceful action. This is evident in the shift from his belief that the war posed no threat to US interests (domain of gains) to the perception that things were not going well and something had to be done (domain of losses). Second, the shift and deterioration in the media coverage was consistent with, and parallel to, the shift in Clinton's perception about the costs the war which would evoke for his and US interests. As Clinton stated: 'I don't like where we are now ... this policy is doing enormous damage to the United States and to our standing in the world. We look weak ... [it] can only get worse down the road ... we have a war by CNN' (Woodward 1996: 261 in Robinson 2002: 83). All this underlines the media's contribution in creating conditions of domestic pressure under which Clinton was operating and activating the loss aversion effect. In this instance, the loss aversion effect implies that Clinton was prepared to take a greater risk, in order to avoid further deterioration of the situation, both in the war and the media front. Third, the adoption of a more forceful action that put the US army in harm's way was a riskier approach, compared to the initial policy of non-intervention.

With a more direct involvement of US forces, Clinton articulated America's identity as world leader and 'freedom's greatest champion' (Entman 2004; Clinton 1995g in Hansen 2006: 144), and as Zaller (2003) explains, his policy shift was based on his belief that his current policies would prove beneficial at the time of the 1996 election. They would put an end to the disturbing images and restore the Pax Americana, shaping the world situation to which the US public would be responding once the presidential election heated up. Looking at existing evidence of the US press coverage of the Bosnian war and the timing of the US policy shift through the prism of prospect theory, it can be argued that the empathy and critical news framing was one of the factors that manipulated Clinton's reference point. It made Bosnia relevant to his and the US interests and contributed to the sense of deteriorating situation that prompted him to frame his domain as one of losses.

Conclusion

The key objective of this chapter was to underline the need for a more systematic theoretical approach to the media's role in war and conflict, since most relevant debates are grounded on empirical evidence. With the aid of prospect theory, I have drawn attention to the significance of the news media as a source of domestic cost for leaders in the context of an international conflict, with potential implications for their international behaviour. Although there is a rich body of work that explains the impact of domestic institutions on international politics (Bueno de Mesquita and Lalman 1992; Fearon 1994; Milner 1997; Putnam 1988; Schultz 1999), an impact that is often manifested through the domestic cost that certain foreign policy decisions entail, so far there have been no attempts to methodically locate the media as an institution in this interaction between domestic and international politics.

With the employment of prospect theory, I have offered an alternative interpretation of existing knowledge of the interaction between political leaders, the national media and the public in war and conflict. This has offered insight in those instances when the power relations embedded in news framing in a domestic setting can culminate in perceptions of loss and influence a leader's international behaviour. The Bosnian conflict offered a suitable case on which to test this theoretical approach. As media scholars have already recognised the media's potential pressure on Clinton's policy shift, prospect theory has helped illuminate a potential mechanism through which this pressure was activated.

In the case of war and conflict, where violence intensifies and so does public scrutiny, the psychological school offers a constructive theoretical tool to systematically link media coverage, public opinion and political decision-making through the cognitive biases that characterise leaders' judgment. Like with many international relations theories, there are a number of questions to which prospect theory has no real answers. Nevertheless, it manages to delve into psychological biases and heuristics that can explain leaders' misperceptions (Downs and Rocke 1997:13) and which could pave the way for theory development in the area of media effects and international politics.

Notes

1 See McDermott (1992) for an application of prospect theory on the Iranian hostage rescue mission, 1980 and Farnham (1992) for an application of the theory on Roosevelt's decision-making behaviour during the Munich Crisis, 1938.

2 I need to clarify that prospect theory will be approached at the individual level with the government as a unitary actor, which will inevitably lead to simplifications. However, the emphasis here is placed on an alternative route through which the media's role can be understood, rather than the way decision-making is formulated. The analysis is based on the assumption that all members of a government are power-seeking politicians and the damage that news framing could cause carries the same weight for all.

3 Such statements would normally include intra-party praise or cross-party attacks, with limited persuasive power on audiences.

4 'Cheap-talk' is the opposite of costly signals, representing self-serving frames (Baum and Groelling 2010: 27–28) and costless, non-verifiable claims (Farrell and Gibbons 1989).

5 Leaders are judged on how faithfully they represent the citizenry and although citizens do not punish for honest mistakes, what matters to them is whether they would have wanted the policy if they shared the same information with the leader (Downs and Rocke 1997; Slantchev 2006).

6 The FRY consisted of six republics, namely Bosnia and Herzegovina, Croatia, Macedonia, Montenegro, Serbia and Slovenia and two autonomous provinces, namely Kosovo and Vojvodina (Gow 19997: 12–13).

7 Such framing emphasises the complicated aspects of a conflict, targets elites more than it targets masses and can create emotional distance, putting limited pressure on leaders to intervene (Campbell 1998; Robinson 2002).

8 See Robinson (2002) for an analysis of the New York Times, Washington Post and CBS news coverage.

9 Evidence of an attentive American public during the conflict is limited, but public attention did increase in certain instances, such as the Sarajevo market attack, where a peak in media coverage was reported as well. Yet, since June 1995 both media coverage and public attention remained at high levels (Bennett et al., 1997; Burg and Shoup 1999).

10 This anticipation can be explained by the public's view of the role of the US as a superpower, as well as the tendency of domestic publics to punish their leaders more for losses than to reward them for comparable gains (Levy 2000:201).

References

Auerbach, Y. and Bloch-Elkon, Y., (2005) 'Media framing and foreign policy: the elite press vis-à-vis US policy in Bosnia, 1992–95', *Journal of Peace Research* 42 (1): 83–99.

Baker, W. D. and ONeal, J. R. (2001) 'Patriotism or opinion leadership? The nature and origins of the 'rally "round the flag" effect', *Journal of Conflict Resolution* 45 (5): 661–687.

Baum, M. A. (2004a) 'How public opinion constrains the use of force: the case of Operation Restore Hope' *Presidential Studies Quarterly* 34 (2): 187–226.

Baum, M. A. and Groeling, T. J. (2007) 'Iraq and the "Fox effect": An examination of polarizing media and public support for international conflict', paper presented at the annual meeting of the American Political Science Association, Chicago.

Baum, M. A. and Groeling, T. J. (2008) 'Crossing the water's edge: elite rhetoric, media coverage, and the rally-round-the-flag phenomenon', *The Journal of Politics*, 70 (4): 1065–1085.

Baum, M. A. and Potter, P.B.K. (2008) 'The relationships between mass media, public opinion, and foreign policy: toward a theoretical synthesis', *Annual Review of Political Science*, 11: 39–65.

Baum, M. A. and Groeling, T. J. (2010) *War Stories: the Causes and Consequences of Public Views of War*, Princeton, N.J.: Princeton University Press.

Bennett, S. E., Flickinger, R. S. and Rhine, S.L., (1997) 'American public opinion and the civil war in Bosnia', *The Harvard International Journal of Press/Politics* 2 (4): 87–105.

Bennett, W.L., Lawrence, R.G., and Livingston, S. (2007) *When the Press Fails: Political Power and the News Media from Iraq to Katrina*, London: The University of Chicago Press.

Boettcher III, W.A. (2004) 'The prospects for prospect theory. an empirical evaluation of international relations applications of framing and loss aversion' *Political Psychology*, 25 (3): 331–362.

Brown, R. (2005) 'Getting to war: communications and mobilization in the 2002–03 Iraq war' in Seib, P. (eds.) *Media and Conflict in the Twenty-First Century*, NY: Palgrave Macmillan.

Bueno de Mesquita, B. and Lalman, D. (1992) *War and Reason: Domestic and International Imperatives*, New Haven, Conn.: Yale University Press.

Burg, S. L., and Shoup, P. S. (1999) *The War in Bosnia-Herzegovina: Ethnic Conflict and International Intervention*, New York, London: M.E. Sharpe.

Burns, J.F. (1992) 'Bosnia's nightmare', *The New York Times*, 24 May 1992, Section 4, p. 1.

Campbell, D. (1998) *National Deconstruction Violence, Identity, and Justice in Bosnia*, Minneapolis: University of Minnesota Press.

Carragee, K. M. and Roefs, W. (2004) 'The neglect of power in recent framing research', *Journal of Communication*, 54 (2): 214–233.

Chapman, T. L. and Reiter, D. (2004) 'The United Nations Security Council and the rally 'round the flag effect', *Journal of Conflict Resolution* 48 (6): 886–909.

Clinton, W.J. (1999g, April 7) 'Remarks to the United States Institute of Peace', *The public papers of the president*, vol. 1 (pp. 506-511), Washington, D.C.: The United States Government Printing Office.

Cook, T. E. (1989), *Making Laws and Making News: Media Strategies in the U.S. House of Representatives*, Washington, DC: Brookings.

Crawford, V.P. and Sobel, J. (1982) 'Strategic information transmission', *Econometrica*, 50 (6): 1431–1451.

Kahneman, D., and Tversky, A. (1979) 'Prospect theory: an analysis of decision under risk' *Econometrica*, 47 (2): 263–291.

Downs, G.W. and Rocke, D.M. (1997) *Optimal Imperfection? Domestic Uncertainty and Institutions in International Relations*, NJ: Princeton University Press.

Entman, R. M. (2004) *Projections of Power*, Chicago and London: The University of Chicago Press.

Farnham, B. (1992) 'Roosevelt and the Munich crisis: insights from prospect theory', *Political Psychology*, 13 (2): 205–235.

Farrell, J. and Gibbons, R. (1989) 'Cheap talk with two audiences', *American Economic Review*, 79(5): 1214–23.

Fearon, J. D. (1994) 'Domestic political audiences and the escalation of international disputes', *American Political Science Review*, 88(3): 577–592.

Gilboa, E. (2002) 'Global communication and foreign policy', *Journal of Communication*, 52 (4): 731–748.

Gow, J. (1997), *Triumph of the Lack of Will: International Diplomacy and the Yugoslav War*, London: Hurst.

Gowing, N. (1994) 'Real-time television coverage of armed conflicts and diplomatic crises: does it pressure or distort foreign policy decisions?', Cambridge, MA: Joan Shorenstein Barone Center on the Press, Politics, and Public Policy, John F. Kennedy School of Government, Harvard University.

Gowing, N. (1996) 'Real-time TV coverage from war: does it make or break government policy', in Gow J. *et al.* (eds.) *Bosnia by Television*. London: British Film Institute, 81–91.

Gowing, N. (2000) 'Media coverage: help or hindrance in conflict prevention?', in Badsey S. (ed.), *The Media and International Security*, London: Cass, 203–226.

Hallin, D. (1986), *The Uncensored War*, New York: Oxford University Press.

Hansen, L. (2006) *Security as Practice: Discourse Analysis and the Bosnian War*, London: Routledge.

Herring, E. (1997) 'An uneven killing field: the manufacture of consent for the arms embargo on Bosnia-Herzegovnia', in Evans M. D. (ed.), *Aspects of Statehood and Institutionalism in Contemporary Europe*, Aldershot: Dartmouth, 159–82.

Iyengar, S. and Kinder, D. R. (1987) *News That Matters: Television and American Opinion*, Chicago: University of Chicago Press.

Jervis, R. (1991) 'Domino beliefs and strategic behaviour' in Jervis, R. & Snyder, J. (eds.) *Dominoes and Bandwagons: Strategic Beliefs and Great Power Competition in the Eurasian Rimland*, New York: Oxford, 20–50.

Jervis R. (2004) 'The implications of prospect theory for human nature and values', *Political Psychology* 25 (2): 163–76.

Kahneman, D. and Tversky, A. (1979) 'Prospect Theory: An analysis of decision under risk', *Econometrica*, 47: 263–291.

Krosnick, J. A. and Kinder, D. R. (1990) 'Altering the foundations of support for the President through priming', *The American Political Science Review*, 84(2): 497–512.

Levy, J. S. (1992) 'An introduction to prospect theory', *Political Psychology*, 13 (2): 171–186.

Levy, J. S. (1994a) 'An introduction to prospect theory', in Farnham, B. (ed.) *Avoiding Losses/Taking Risks: Prospect Theory and International Conflict*, Michigan: The University of Michigan Press, 7–23.

Levy, J. S. (1994b) 'Prospect theory and international relations: theoretical applications and analytical problems', in Farnham, B. (ed.) *Avoiding Losses/Taking Risks: Prospect Theory and International Conflict*, Michigan: The University of Michigan Press, 119–147.

Levy J. S. (2000) 'Loss aversion, framing effects, and international conflict: perspectives from prospect theory', in Midlarsky, M.I. (ed.), *Handbook of War Studies II*, Ann Arbor: University of Michigan Press, 193–221.

Masters, D. and Alexander, R. M. (2008), 'Prospecting for war: 9/11 and selling the Iraq war', *Contemporary Security Policy*, 29 (3): 434–452.

McDermott, R. (1992) 'The failed rescue mission in Iran: an application of prospect theory', *Political Psychology*, 13 (2): 237–263.

McDermott, R. (2004) 'Prospect theory in political science: gains and losses from the first decade', *Political Psychology* 25(2): 289–312.

McDermott, R. & Kugler, J. (2001) 'Comparing rational choice and prospect theory analyses: The US decision to launch Operation "Desert Storm", January 1991', *Journal of Strategic Studies*, 24(3): 49–85.

Mercer, J. (2005) 'Prospect theory and political science', *Annual Review of Political Science*, 8: 1–21.

Milner, H. V. (1997) *Interests, Institutions and Information*, NJ: Princeton University Press.

Mousavizadeh, N. (1996a) *The Black Book of Bosnia: The Consequences of Appeasement by the Writers and Editors of the New Republic*, New York: Basic Books.

Myers, G., Klak, T., and Koehl, T. (1996) 'The inscription of difference: news coverage of the conflicts in Rwanda and Bosnia', *Political Geography*, 15 (1): 21–46.

Nye, J. (1999) 'Redefining the national interest', *Foreign Affairs*, 78(4): 22–35.

O'Heffernan, P. (1991) *Mass Media and American Foreign Policy: Insider Perspectives on Global Journalism and the Foreign Policy Process*, Westport: Ablex Publishing.

Putnam, R. D. (1988) 'Diplomacy and domestic politics: the logic of two-level games', *International Organization*, 42 (3): 427–460.

Riedlmayer, A. (1993) 'A brief history of Bosnia-Herzegovina. The Bosnian manuscript ingathering project', at www.kakarigi.net/manu/briefhis.htm (accessed July 2010).

Robinson, P. (2002) *The CNN Effect: The Myth of News, Foreign Policy and Intervention*, London: Routledge.

Samuelson, W. and Zeckhauser, R. (1988), 'Status quo bias in decision making', *Journal of Risk and Uncertainty*, 1(1): 7–59.

Schelling, T. (1966) *Arms and Influence*, New Haven, Conn.: Yale University Press.

Schultz, K. A. (1999) 'Do Domestic Institutions Constrain or Inform? Contrasting Two Institutional Perspectives on Democracy and War', International Organization, 52 (2): 233–66.

Schultz, K. A. (2001) *Democracy and Coercive Diplomacy*, Cambridge: Cambridge University Press.

Shaw, M. (1996) *Civil Society and Media in Global Crises*, London: St Martin's Press.

Slantchev, B. L. (2006) 'Politicians, the media, and domestic audience costs', International *Studies Quarterly*, 50 (2): 445–477.

Strobel, W. (1997) *Late Breaking Foreign Policy*, Washington D.C: Institute of Peace.

Tversky, A. and Kahneman D. (1981) 'The framing of decisions and the psychology of choice', *Science*, 211 (4481): 453–458.

Van Belle D. A. (2000) *Press Freedom and Global Politics*, Westport: Praeger.

Van Belle, D. A. (2004) *The Latent Effects of the Media in Foreign Policy Making: The Asskicking, Turbocharged Power of a Free Press*, Paper presented at the 45th Annual ISA Convention, Montreal, Quebec, Canada, March 17–20, 2004.

Wolfsfeld, G. (1997) *Media and Political Conflict: News from the Middle East*, Cambridge: Cambridge University Press.

Woodward, B. (1996) *The Choice*, New York: Simon and Schuster.

Zaller, J. (2003) 'Coming to grips with V.O. key's concept of latent opinion', in MacKuen, M. and Rabinowitz, G. (eds.), *Electoral Democracy*. Ann Arbor: University of Michigan Press, 311–36.

Zaller, J., and Chiu, D. (2000) 'Government's little helper: U.S. press coverage of foreign policy crises, 1946–1999', in Nacos, B., Shapiro, R. and Isernia, P. (Eds.), *Decisionmaking in a glass house*, Lanham, MD: Rowman & Littlefield, 61–84.

13 Virilio and the gaze of the state

Vision machines, new media and resistance

Andy Robinson

This chapter examines various aspects of Paul Virilio's theory of vision. Virilio is a major contemporary theorist whose work has inspired scholars such as James Der Derian, John Armitage and Julian Reid. This chapter will seek to provide an introduction to Virilio's theory of war and the media before relating this theory to new media. Virilio is here viewed as a theorist of domination and oppression, seeking to explain the contours of power by reference to the effects of regimes of vision and distance on ways of seeing. Yet he is also a theorist of resistance, seeking to theorise the possibilities (however marginal) for overcoming this regime of vision. Virilio's theory is based on a pessimistic narrative of historical change viewed in terms of a quasi-class struggle between the military or logistical logic and the civilian population. Historical change has been motivated mainly by the unfolding of the 'essence', or social logic, of the military, as an institution seeking security (Virilio 1990: 13). This is a struggle which, in Virilio's view, is currently being won mainly by the military, although new forms of popular struggle are constantly being recomposed. The media (old and new) fit into his theory mainly as outgrowths of the military regime of vision, as will be explored below. This chapter will question, however, whether certain aspects of the new media are *necessarily* part of a controlling, logistical way of seeing, or whether they are open to reclamation as counter-logistics. It will also explore the implications of his theory for activism, conceived as popular struggle against dominant ways of seeing and their correlates in the control of space.

The politics of vision

One of the major effects of the military logic has been on the production of vision and film is crucial to this reconstruction. According to Virilio, the emergence of artillery removed the cartographic basis of strategy because of the physical destruction of the battlefield (Virilio 1989: 1). Henceforth, film replaced mapping in tracing 'the decomposition and recomposition of an uncertain territory' (ibid. 1989: 99). In contrast to older forms of warfare, today the scope of battles undermines visual organisation, as soldiers respond to orders from outside their field of vision (ibid. 1989: 75). Hand-to-hand combat is similarly replaced by instant interface (1989: 90). People lose sight of local reality (ibid. 1989: 100). In such a battlefield, artificial vision emerges as a way to fix or reconstruct a landscape otherwise undergoing infinite fragmentation (ibid. 1989: 89).

The military field of perception is constantly enlarged (ibid. 1989: 86) and war comes to resemble around-the-clock television (ibid. 1989: 90). War is henceforth about light and waves used as projectiles (Virilio 1989: 95). Direct vision, and hence the vision of civilians, is excluded from the battlefield, which becomes a cinematic 'location' through reconnaisance (ibid. 1989: 15–16). Some pilots are shut off from sensory input from outside the aeroplane, instead relying on radio guidance and signals, accompanied with sexualised emotional support (ibid. 1989: 31). In this way, as in feminist international relations theory (e.g. Enloe 2000), the absent or invisible woman becomes crucial to male activity, interpellated as a logistical spouse with whom mythical exchanges take place (Virilio 1989: 32–3, 54). This is perhaps the reason why few films dare dispense with an often unnecessary romantic sub-plot. For Virilio, this change in military perception, arising from changes in battlefield logistics and effectiveness, reacts back on society, altering people's vision more broadly.

For Virilio, what we see becomes an effect of technologies of vision. Faith in perception is enslaved to faith in the technological sightline (Virilio 1994: 13) and is now disintegrating (ibid. 1994: 16). This has decompository effects. War now 'rests entirely on the de-regulation of time and space' (Virilio 1986: 138), and the result is 'as though our society were sinking into the darkness of a voluntary blindness, its will to digital power finally contaminating the horizon of sight as well as knowledge' (Virilio 1994: 76).

The changed regime of vision also brings about a situation where artificial images have primacy over lived realities. The result has been a 'de-realisation' of war, in which images rather than objects, facts, times and spaces hold sway (Virilio 1989: 1). The functions of attacking and seeing are fused in modern weapons (ibid. 1989: 26). In some cases, projectiles are themselves guided by television pictures, bypassing the combatant (ibid. 1989: 104). Ultimately this is producing the automation of the war-machine (ibid. 1989: 109). Armies themselves are 'routed' and vanish into thin air (Virilio 2000: 33). The apprehension of reality is undermined by its very origin in optical perception, with its retention of outdated images (Virilio 1989: 99). The world becomes a nightmare in which reality has stopped amidst constant crises and catastrophes, with disastrous accidents becoming part of normal life (Virilio 2000: 36, 89). Time is distorted as the gaze is cast forward and back, with response depending on anticipation (Virilio 1989: 76). This has devastating, perception-distorting psychological effects. Combatants come to feel they are being 'watched by invisible stalkers' and are watching themselves from a distance (ibid.

1989: 90). Imprisoned in the closed circuits of electronics, people suffer a kind of possession or hallucinatory state (ibid. 1989: 106). This type of military hallucination is also crucial to Virilio's theory of consumer society, as will be explored below.

Today, the rise of artificial vision is reaching its zenith in the emergence of technologies which entirely replace human sight. So far, soldiers have become reliant on a vision machine which coexists with the war-machine, providing a visual persepctive on military action (ibid. 1989: 2). Today, this machine is making the man behind the camera obsolete (Virilio 1994: 47). There is now a possibility of 'sightless vision' in which computers, not viewers, control cameras and interpret their meanings. This would mean that we are being watched by objects, not people (ibid. 1994: 59), with the vision machine 'capable of seeing in our place' (ibid. 1994: 54). The video system would then 'function like a kind of mechanised imaginary' from which humans are excluded (ibid. 1994: 60). The 'objective perception', or 'how machines might perceive things', is forever inaccessible to humans (ibid. 1994: 73). As a result, 'the automation of perception ... is threatening our understanding' (ibid. 1994: 75). It also poses threats to political power, through the automation of deterrence which leaves little space for decision (Virilio 1986: 140). This vision machine completes the death of reality. The image the computer sees is not reality, but a statistical calculation of pixels, a kind of rational illusion based on 'closed-circuit optics' (Virilio 1994: 75).

The logistical form of perception ultimately colonises the societies which use it. The technologies of total war make possible 'the totalitarian tendencies of the moment' (Virilio 1989: 100). Virilio portrays this colonisation of everyday life as a kind of pollution of the life-size scale of the world (Virilio 2000: 14). Furthermore, it defines local spaces and times as 'other'. The 'virtual vision' of the world time of instantaneity supplants the actuality of 'the vision of the real world around us' (ibid. 2000: 15). The local is now the periphery or outside of a world which, for US military leaders, has the global as its interior, so domestic politics is handled as foreign policy formerly was (2000: 10). The significance of the local-global distinction is crucial here, in that it distinguishes logistical perception radically from various forms of local knowledge. It is important to distinguish human-scale mobilities immanent to local knowledge with this new kind of global gaze. Virilio contrasts the logistical gaze which never looks back to the historical nomad or migrant who turns around to familiarise her/himself with the land (ibid. 2000: 22), in effect relocalising at each point reached. The global gaze is in contrast a death of locality.

The vision machine does not, however, bring an end to logistical war. The reliance on artificial vision-machines to eliminate 'natural' invisibilities reinforces a tendency to produce artificial invisibilities, hence the rise of stealth equipment and an 'aesthetics of disappearance' (Virilio 1989: 5; c.f. 1994: 49). Today, information war has emerged as a strategy to use

'electronics as a hegemonic technology' (Virilio 2000: 132). The information revolution is also a revolution in virtual disinformation (ibid. 2000:
108), special effects are being extended to the battlefield (Virilio 1994:
71), and deception is winning out over real weapons (ibid. 1994: 68) and
over deterrence (ibid. 1994: 72). Outward appearance in military settings
has lost its truth-value 'in a profusion of camouflage, decoys, jamming,
smoke-screens, electronic counter-measures, and so on' (Virilio 1989: 95).
All sides seek to develop 'perfect' weapons invisible, not so much to
humans as to the gaze of other technologies (ibid. 1989: 110). One
example of such a new technology is the centroidal-effect decoy which
produces a signature in electronic systems similar to that of a missile's
target (Virilio 1994: 71). Though Virilio does not reach this conclusion,
such measures might be said to exploit the gap between representation
and reality to confound the former. Since the latter has become impenetrable through the hegemony of artificial perception, this creates a deeply
unpredictable and disconcerting world.

This world of infowar produces resonating effects in politics and war,
creating a range of mutations. One might refer here to a tendency in
nuclear doctrine in lesser powers (India, Israel, Iran, North Korea...)
towards keeping secret whether one has the bomb and if so how many and
where. It is the *possibility*, not the assurance, of retaliation which grounds
such strategies (Bajpai 1998; Hersh 1991; Sigal 1999).

Vision, media and society

The new regime of vision developed for military purposes also tends to
return to societies and hegemonise people's ways of seeing through the
proliferation of techniques and technologies of military origin. In Virilio's
account, the society of spectacle involves the colonisation of leisure-time
by military technologies and their ways of seeing (Wilbur 1994). Consumer
society is itself part of an attempt at logistical management. The aim is
taken to do away with direct repression through a 'social assault' of consumerism which modifies ways of life (Virilio 1986: 26). Television, for
instance, is indicted for putting people into a field of images in which they
are powerless to intervene, effectively imprisoning people in its frame
(Virilio 1994: 64–5). The new means of communication and identification
'become ways of blocking history' through instantaneity (Virilio 1989: 78).
Virilio's account echoes those of Debord (1970) and Marcuse (1991), suggesting that a particular kind of image-oriented, instrumentalist, perceptu-
ally reduced subjectivity arises from exposure to consumer society.

According to Virilio, people in consumer societies are bombarded by
visual technologies with disconnected images intense in detail, but lacking
in breadth, context and relationality. They have a kind of false presence,
simulating an experience of reality without actually having any real reference to a particular locality. In mass culture, 'ghostly images' stolen by the

camera can be sold as enthralling objects (Virilio 1989: 39), arguably creating the base-units for the formation of Barthesian myths (Barthes 2000).
These 'signs, representations and logotypes' have proliferated in the industrial world owing to a 'system of message-intensification' which bombards
with images instead of words and focuses on attention-grabbing phatic
images (Virilio 1994: 14). Such images tend to spread in conditions of least
resistance, such as after military defeat and to be put in the service of political and financial powers (ibid. 1994: 14; 1986: 109). They are thus, maybe,
an effect in the field of culture of 'disaster capitalism', the exploitation of
catastrophe to produce greater systemic incorporation (Klein 2007). A contrast also emerges between images (of war for instance), shown in all their
brutality, and voiceovers which use self-censored, politically correct language – 'soft' language with 'hard' images (Virilio 2000: 69–70).

The unreality of images is for Virilio an effect of their lack of locality.
Images always differ from lived realities and are 'like death', because
whereas lived realities are inimitable (like the situated standpoints of
indigenous knowledge), images are frozen in place and duplicated (Virilio
1989: 45). They thus produce an artificial, simulated experience of the
world. Images and snippets of information are often self-contained, sometimes simulated (they do not require a truth-referent), and they increasingly escape both the need to be understood or read, rather than received
(c.f. Barthes1985: 231) and the possibility of being interpreted. Of course,
as Chomsky and Herman (1988) argue, the dispersed facts are often
meaningless only because something has been left out, because of what is
elsewhere called the lacuna or sanctioned ignorance. Also, the collapse of
dimensions intensifies fears that the Other is already inside, leading to a
plethora of perceived risks (from terrorism to invasive species) well-
documented by Michael Moore in *Bowling for Columbine*.

The de-realisation brought about by artificial vision has effects on perception. The result is a crisis both of dimensions and of representation
(Virilio 1989: 58). Dimensions, or spatial differences, are undermined first
by military then cinematic technologies and, as a result, things and places
are disintegrating (ibid. 1989: 60). This produces a condition of sensory
deprivations, with technological exposure corroding perceptual capacities
(Virilio 2000: 37–8), creating an 'impoverishment of sensory appearances'
and decline or pollution of sensory ecology (ibid. 2000: 114). In this
context, the natural speed and sensitivity of sight are lost to a fixed gaze
(Virilio 1994: 13). This situation causes 'reflex self-mutilations' (Virilio
2000: 40) as people get out of the habit of using their bodies (ibid. 2000:
42) and the range of adaptability of eyesight is lost (Virilio 1994: 10) in a
'eugenics of sight, a pre-emptive abortion of the diversity of mental
images' (ibid. 1994: 12). The elimination of distances and delays pollutes
everyday life (Virilio 2000: 116). Ultimately, only a visual message will
survive (Virilio 1994: 15). Virilio also suggests that speeding-up makes
humanity cease to be diverse (Virilio 1986: 47), echoing Levi-Strauss's

(1966) theory of indigenous societies as 'cold' (or slow) societies and modernity as 'hot' (or rapid). Virilio also stands in a long tradition of theorists who analyse the spectacle as self-referential and tautological, ultimately referring back to its own images (Marcuse 1991; Baudrillard 1998; Negr 2003: 27).

On the other hand, people become dependent on technologies which the system can interrupt at will and which are vulnerable to accidents (Virilio 2000: 141). (This has been used in the case of mobile phone jamming in protest zones and the internet cut-off in Xinjiang.) Orgies of destruction become necessary to provide the excitement people are otherwise unable to feel because of affect-blocking and sensory insensitivity; today, life becomes orgy punctuated by routines, through phenomena such as terrorism scares (Virilio 1990: 68–9). For Marcuse (1988), the absence of intensity in life feeds back, through frustration, into warfare as vicarious aggresion, but the highly mediated nature of the aggression prevents it ever being satisfying, rendering it self-reproducing. It is also reminiscent of the observation that we have now gone past moral panic to a permanent sense of crisis (Muncie, 2009).

In the resultant, de-realised space, inquisitorial perception becomes widespread. Journalism has become complicit in the police-style investigation (Virilio 1994: 35). Fiction, too, reproduces the inquisitorial spirit in forms such as detective novels, with a modality drawn from science (ibid. 1994: 37). Today this culminates in forensic dramas such as *CSI*, celebrating not the hero but the technique. It is also revealing that detective and police dramas are almost unique in surviving the decline of drama in the age of reality television. They express, perhaps, the nodal point of the ideology of today. Graeber (2007) analyses such shows as only able to heroise police by treating them as bearers of constitutive power, of law-creating violence and thus putting creative power symbolically in the hands of its real-world enemies. He also suggests they have replaced the western – a triumph, one might add, of telepresence over identities linked to the past. In police investigation, similarly, the rise of forensics such as fingerprints, and of CCTV evidence, has seen the decline of eyewitness accounts, so that 'the human eye no longer gives signs of recognition, it no longer organises the search for truth' and thought is no longer integrated in an investigation focused on latent remainders (Virilio 1994: 42–3). One result of the reliance on telepresence is that legal representatives become unable to create a reality-effect (ibid. 1994: 44). Of course, it also depends on a process of derivation or representation which is imagined to be far less fallible than it is and which is vulnerable to the same kind of countermeasures as those seen in war: the planting of evidence, the contamination of samples, false positives, identity theft and so on. The illusion that biometrics fix identity (that the watched body betrays the subject) misunderstands the effects of telepresence: a constant field of unstable appearances based on electronic and visual deception.

The ever-present risk of crisis is another feature arising from telepresence in contemporary societies. The reason for crisis is that people are denied the thinking time necessary for rational action (Virilio 2000: 129), becoming vulnerable to contagion effects. Politics and economics are also at risk of crashes arising from high-speed communications (ibid. 2000: 67, 133), a risk which is also used to blackmail nations to comply with neoliberalism (ibid. 2000: 133). The systemic de-regulation of markets is for Virilio connected to the de-regulation of strategic information (ibid. 2000: 144). The risk of crashes is due to the replacement of true and false with actual and virtual in the economy (Virilio 1994: 68). The immediacy and omnipresence of the current system also has to avoid the risks of breaking the connections and symmetries and ending up with pasts and futures (Virilio 2000: 126). Overall, this creates a risk of an 'accident to end all accidents', a global and generalised collapse (ibid. 2000: 134). The Internet brings a systemic risk of a chain reaction from instant effects (ibid. 2000: 107). There is a positive side to this systemic risk. Historically, capitalism has dealt with such problems by means of spatial and temporal fixes, expanding into new territories or new regimes of production. If Virilio is right, capitalism has exceeded the scale where spatial and temporal fixes are possible, making its end a real possibility.

Deterrence, security, war and illusion

The hypnotic effects of artificial vision also produce the power of the state itself. War cannot 'break free from the magical spectacle' because it aims to produce the spectacle, by instilling of fear through images (Virilio 1989: 7–8, 87–8). Ultimately this magic is not designed to be used, but simply to be 'brandished and quantified in public' (ibid. 1989: 9). 'The state's only original existence is a visual hallucination akin to dreaming' (ibid. 1989: 43). State heroes become such by becoming unknown, separated from the 'sense-memory' of kinship and affinity (ibid. 1989: 43–4). Cinema also restores something akin to the mythical time which co-exists with profane time in indigenous cosmology (ibid. 1989: 41). Cinema is a kind of black magic which puts order back into visual chaos, creates a standardised version of mythical space, and homogenises what viewers see and hear (ibid. 1989: 50). One might here view the 'dream factory' of cinema as reproducing in absence the dimension of otherness, which in indigenous cosmology is lived directly through participatory ritual. I would suggest that, in contrast to Virilio's view, this dimension of myth has a dual significance. One might here read Mircea Eliade (1971) with Barthes (2000), but equally with Benjamin's (1974) messianism as dimension of escape and Graeber's observation that a rich fantasy-life, a 'spectral nightworld of sorcerers and witches', correlates with the diffusion of social power (Graeber 2004: 34). It is, Graeber suggests, a function of the displacement of the potential for social war. Myth also finds its reflection in other forms of violence than those of the state. For instance, 'terrorism' throws war back to its 'psychotropic origins in sympathetic magic', the spectacle of death (Virilio 1989: 7). This effectively repeats Baudrillard's (1983) analysis of terrorism as implosion and as the return of symbolic exchange.

There is, however, a difference between the state's type of war and those of other agents. Security, or deterrence, differs from popular defence in seeking this kind of victory in advance. It seeks to pre-emptively win without fighting by scaring the enemy (e.g. Virilio 1989: 74). Logistical war seeks to impose a plan devised in time on the enemy and, in this way, is the origin of totalitarianism which in turn grounds current spatial and temporal changes (Virilio 1986: 117–18). It replaces the power to act, alienated in heightened speeds and technology, with the power to react (Virilio 2000: 123), a 'reduction of power in favor of a better trajectory, life traded for survival' (Virilio 1986: 63). Instead of combat, deterrence seeks to cause material and moral losses which cause the enemy to melt away (ibid. 1986: 39). It is an extension of a total war which aims to destroy the soul, honour, identity or 'mana' (creative power) of the enemy (ibid. 1986: 75). It aims not to kill the enemy but to deter him, which is to say, to 'force him to interrupt his movement' (ibid. 1986: 145). It is equivalent to absence of movement, which today is sought to maintain a 'precarious equilibrium' on the edge of crisis. This suppression of wills corresponds to the suppression of gestures (ibid. 1986: 125). Weapons thus serve to threaten more than to fight (Virilio 1994: 66), with terror depending on the elimination of actual war (ibid. 1994: 67), sapping the enemy's will to fight, or using the 'shock and awe' of overwhelming force. Deterrence is not, however, an end to war, but war transferred from the actual to the virtual (ibid. 1994: 67). Virilio suggests that we are currently suffering the moral and material collapse in Europe (Virilio 1986: 39), with apparent peace really being exhaustion (ibid. 1986: 46). He also views the biodiversity crisis and loss of 'natural' economies as effects of a slow war of depletion which sustains military power (ibid. 1986: 64). The military believes it can save itself by means of engines used as prostheses (ibid. 1986: 94).

The pursuit of security, or control of space in advance to disempower the other, is contrasted to popular defence. The military seeks to eliminate randomness from social relations, including by eliminating dialogue (Virilio 1990: 17–19). It views chance as 'synonymous with disaster and ruin' and seeks to eliminate it through planning (Virilio 1986: 18). This requires the reorganisation of the entire social body around the supposed need for security (Virilio 1990: 62; 1986: 122). Deterrence is related to the 'politics of everyday fear' (Massumi 1993). With the compression of space-time, danger can be lived simultaneously by millions (Virilio 1989: 97). In a threatening world, the army can pose as a protective force (Virilio 1986: 104). The ideology of security replaces the population's legal and political identity, and right to self-defence, effectively putting civilian society under military control (Virilio 1990: 73). Similarly, logistical society implies the disappearance of the commons, the civilian space and the right to space (Virilio 1986: 78). Governments engage in a 'deliberately terroristic manipulation of the need for security', using it as a new 'unanimity of need', an artificially-created feeling of insecurity designed to produce a demand for the mass consumption of protection (ibid. 1986: 122). In this way, people can be induced to pay more to consume less (ibid. 1986: 123).

The various links between film, and other media, and war form a complex texture in Virilio's work. Sci-fi imitates a military look based on the world wars, combining anachronistic components (Virilio 1989: 81). 'Not that it's a B-52 in outer space' (ibid. 1989: 81) ... except in a recent episode of *Doctor Who*, where it literally is. Genres of films are seen to rise and fall with periods of military power; musical comedies, for instance, could not survive demobilisation and deterrence (ibid. 1989: 13). War photos transmute into the 'American dream' and thence into Hollywood (ibid. 1989: 27). The 'fictional worlds' of war and cinema blur into each other in Hollywood fundraisers (ibid. 1989: 66). In some instances, war and film become indistinguishable; Germans plan to re-enact a battle for film, using real warships, but call it off as the British plan a real attack in response (ibid. 1989: 72). Technologies of cameras are copied from those of guns (ibid. 1989: 15, 86). Television, initially a way to expand the range of vision, becomes entertainment (ibid. 1989: 94). Computerised tracking cameras used in filmmaking are descended from pilot training systems (ibid. 1989: 109), instantiating a link between the 1970s economic crisis, the rise of pilot simulators and the take-off of cinematic special-effects. Generals copy tactics from films (ibid. 1989: 79) and technicians switch between army simulation and film set design (ibid. 1989: 81). Commanders put soldiers at the disposal of film-makers (ibid. 1989: 73) and films are suppressed for being too close to reality (1989: 74). Military adversaries seek to undermine charismatic enemies by outdoing them in cinematic technology (ibid. 1989: 74). Military technologies are turned against migrants, with electronic surveillance of borders (ibid. 1989: 107). The body of the film star is fragmented, much like the vision of the military voyeur (ibid. 1989: 33), and so on. The central point behind all the connections is the politics of vision.

One of the effects of cinema is temporal. For Virilio, cinema frees time from linearity (Virilio 2000: 85). Virilio's view of cinema is very different from Deleuze's, in which the freeing of time from linearity is portrayed in affirmative terms, yet they both focus on this effect of modern cinema. Perhaps this expresses the affinities between the two types of war-machine. In Virilio's theory, the war-machine is exclusively associated with the military apparatus of the state, but in Deleuze and Guattari's work, it arises autonomously from nomadic bands and is later captured by the state. Deleuzian cinema could thus be an effect of the nomadic force of the war-machine, just as Virilio's view of cinema relates it to the military. Of course, cinema reacts back on social relations. 9/11 was prefigured in

Hollywood (Roten 2002). Reactive networks take on cinema images as components of identity, as when fighters in Sierra Leone imitate *Rambo* (Richards 1996), or real-world mafias, inheritors of a media-created image (Albini 1993), now take their lead from movies such as *The Godfather*, repeating terms and customs which never existed before (Gambetta 2009). The aftermath of 9/11 was marked by a bizarre controversy over the cancellation of a Spiderman film, because it showed the Twin Towers in the background. Film industry critics slammed the cancellation, arguing that people need escapism in times of crisis, only to be assailed with accusations of failing to recognise what is really important. But why did the sacrifice of a film, like the sacrifice of liberties, become a means to impart 'importance' on an event? This controversy was, perhaps, a quiet recognition that 9/11 was a cinematic event, combined with a vain attempt to insist, through the silencing of film, on its extra-cinematic 'reality'.

Virilio and the Internet

How does Virilio's theory relate to the Internet and other new technologies? The Internet is, of course, a military invention (Virilio 2000: 109), but one which emerges from seeking a *defence against the logistics of the other*, which is perhaps why it is so well-suited to popular defence. It was, as Virilio suggests, designed to forestall accidents affecting strategic communications (ibid. 2000: 142). It emerges from the race of the state-appropriated war-machine (Karatzogianni and Robinson 2010: 103) to stay ahead of other states and of networked war-machines, thus producing new forms of network power which undermine state power. One can thus argue that, even though it came from the state, it is actually a technology of *defence* rather than security and thus can be used as a tool of popular defence. Yet it also reproduces aspects of logistical perception. Increasingly, visual realities are recognised as true ones – the virtual response to tall stories is, 'pics or it didn't happen'. Of course, a great deal happens without pictures being taken (the revolution, the old saying goes, will not be televised and the map is not the territory), but such existences are accessible only through horizontal, local, networked connections unavailable either in the virtual space or to the mass.

Virilio mainly takes a negative view of the Internet, arguing that virtual communities are actually communities of 'tele-present' believers (Virilio 2000: 117). I would argue that he underestimates the possibility for the recomposition of communities within virtual spaces, which reproduce a local time of distances and delays through phenomena of degrees of connection and the cultural insulation of particular virtual lifeworlds. The question here is whether a technology can become a tool, or whether the two categories are forever distinct (Illich 1973). Internet phenomena actually produce a strange kind of duality, on the one hand reproducing aspects of the earlier forms of manipulated massification (e.g. easily identifiable, mass-reproduced images) while partially subverting the control of such forms of logistical power by centralised agencies. This can be 'spun' either as an increase in logistical perception reproducing media-tised power, or a decrease in logistical concentration, diffusing logistical power to a wider range of actors. Internet memes, for instance, reproduce the instantly recognisable images Virilio sees as central to logistical percep-tion, but does so in a way which to an extent 'reclaims' them. The capabil-ity to produce memes is in principle diffused, limited only by others receptivity and each meme is endlessly varied by users; the split between producers and receivers of images disappears. If this is a triumph of logis-tical vision, it is also its subversion through *bricolage* and its diffusion in a war-machine which is no longer under state control.

The Internet is a medium of telepresence, with near-instantaneous communication. It is also, however, a space in which distances and delays are reproduced, for instance in the distance separating nodes in a massive global network, so that something may take many quick clicks to find. Consider the problems in surveillance of a person hiding behind multiple proxies: for each additional level of concealment to be unpacked, time is added to the investigation, rendering it increasingly costly. Speed also arises in the constant conflict between technologies of encryption and decryption, with effective encryption depending on delaying how long a guessing programme takes generating possibilities and speed-ups in guess-ing (such as quantum computing) constantly risking making previous encryption standard obsolete. Another example would be flashmobs and their Internet-aided movement equivalents (Cleaver n.d.). Virilio analyses the 'mob' as an instantaneous and immediate group, mobilising speed in sites of circulation to re-form the nomadic band (Virilio 1986: 4–6). In some ways, the Internet revives this nomadic band in the possibility of instant mobilisation, both in offline settings and in terms of virtual direct action. It can thus associate with war-machines of the nomadic type, rather than exclusively those of the military type.

One area of strong overlap between war and the Internet is the field of gaming, in which many games (from first-person shooters to real-time strategy games) are modelled on warfare. Hence, for instance, the impor-tance Virilio attaches to the rise of combat simulators (Virilio 1989: 107–8). These, in turn, give rise to imitative videogames and logistical sports such as Laser-Tag, even as the sport of shooting becomes suspect. Wargaming is arguably an imitation of an object already ahead of its imita-tion. Wargaming may have its origins in combat simulators (Marcuse 1991: 81–2), but war looked like a video-game long before video-games looked anything like war. This said, there is also a recurring panic over such games, and a fear that logistical power may be diffusing. States, from Germany to Venezuela, attempt to legislate against first-person shooters for their tendency to place logistical power and perception in the wrong hands. More recently, controversy has arisen over the possibility of playing wargames as the Taleban (Poplak 2010), echoing an older accusation that insurgents have their own combat recruitment games (Sutherland 2006; al-Ghoul n.d.). The US military has got in on the game with its own wargame, *America's Army*, designed as a recruiting tool. Yet even in such an obvious case of the subordination of gaming to reality, the military does not avoid the temptation to confuse cheating at the game with real-life treason (Bramwell 2005). There is also a possibility that games have expressive power, which can be used for persuasion against, as well as for dominant relations (Bogost 2007).

The internet diffuses its own logistical power and also increasingly diffuses the logistical power of earlier technologies. Virilio speaks of the directorial suppression of chance in film-making through sound and video editing, reducing the director's role from imagination to foresight (Virilio 1989: 82). This is now undermining the power of directors and studios further, as users can 're-direct' clips extracted from films in their own online videos, such as AMV's. We become, Virilio argues, 'directors of our own reality' (ibid. 1989: 83), as those who watch come to exhibit themselves (ibid. 1989: 84). Virilio argues that 'the commercial distribution of video and audio equipment is destroying the extraordinary technical capacity of the old cinema to shape society through vision, to turn a thousand film-goers into a single spectator' (ibid. 1989: 84). Cinema has been subject to a swift ageing process rendering it obsolete because anyone can make films (Virilio 1994: 51). Today, the monopoly on production of films persists mainly at the level of production and visibility: while anyone can make a film, not everyone has access to Hollywood technologies, budgets or media profile. Cinematic power is concentrated, in typical 'global city' fashion, in Hollywood as agglomeration effects interact with cheap widespread diffusion (Storper and Christopherson 1987). Yet certain genres mysteriously escape the resultant monopoly, notably artistic cinema, soap operas and animation. Film censorship also becomes much more difficult in the age of web video and torrents. Of course, there is also an ongoing conflict over 'intellectual property', which is a struggle over the possession of dreams, reusable images, fragments of the virtual, or mythical archetypes – whether these items, and the affective power they contain, are to be possessed exclusively and hierarchically, or diffused more widely.

In a virtual age, technologies tend to diffuse. The production of video, for instance, is now available to anyone with a cheap camcorder, webcam or phone-cam. As Virilio observes, this expands the field of logistical perception. Nevertheless, it also means that the field of the image does not belong entirely to the state. One example of this diffusion is the ambiguous relationship of the state to journalism. Journalists, Virilio suggests, have periodically been treated as similar to spies by the military (Virilio 1994: 48) and excluded from post-Vietnam warzones by means including murder (ibid. 1994: 56). We might here refer to Sami al-Haj, an al-Jazeera journalist held for six years at Guantanamo Bay, to the bombing of the station's offices in Iraq and Afghanistan and to alleged US plans to bomb the station in neutral Qatar. On the other hand, reporters are also allowed into warfare when it became necessary to mobilise filmgoers (ibid. 1994: 53).

Virilio, popular struggle and activism

Virilio's theory also has relevance in terms of the issue of resisting logistical power. From the view that logistical power works by destroying intensity and local lifeworlds, one can view activism as an attempt to recover intensity and re-localise lifeworlds at the expense of the spectacle. Distinctions must here be made between the recovery of *active* intensities, the terrain of affinity networks and of *reactive* intensities, the terrain of reactive networks. According to Virilio, the main aim of popular defence is to prevent the reduction of the population to being mere resources and slaves, which is what occurs when the situation depends on 'the illegality of armed force' (Virilio 1990: 54). One might say that it aims to ward off abjection, or what Agamben terms *homo sacer* or bare life; Virilio's discussion of Red Brigade captives as 'human commodity' (ibid. 1990: 65) and of slaves and prisoners as 'living dead' (Virilio 1986: 76, 107) mirror Agamben's theory. For Virilio, the whole of what he calls the 'military proletariat' is in this status, along with other beings such as animals (ibid. 1986: 85), occupied by the will of another and distinguished from the beings of Reason (ibid. 1986: 86–7). Today, the worker's body is devalued even more, as it is no longer necessary for the kinetic force of war (ibid. 1986: 98). Activism can be seen as warding-off this kind of abjected position through the pursuit of engaged, rehumanised relations. Black bloc action, for example, is explicitly theorised as denaturalising the cityscape to break the spell of images (Graeber 2007). The challenge is how not to reproduce statist logistics – a challenge leading either to anarcho-pacifism (the negation of logistics) or autonomism (the recovery of popular defence). Virilio's approach tends towards the latter. In effect, he points towards a need for a popular and minoritarian *counter-logistics*.

Virilio has a concept of popular defence or popular struggle, covering a variety of forms of resistance of civilians to the power of the logistical gaze. Such resistance occurs, for instance, in guerrilla war as physiological resilience and control of the choice of the time and place of combat (Virilio 1990: 49–51). It also occurs in ecological struggles which are targeted against the triumph of speed and of non-places such as airports and roads (ibid. 1990: 89). 'From this angle, then, an ecological defense worthy of the name becomes the last truly political stakes of civilian populations' (ibid. 1990: 91). It contests the way in which delocalised, global non-places both occupy more territory than the local and occupy it in a totalitarian way (ibid. 1990: 91–2). This global/logistical versus local struggle has been going on since the Middle Ages, with local groups often prepared to defend the local ecosystem which defines them, to the point of death, rather than become displaced proletarians (Virilio 1986: 78). Virilio discusses as an example the struggle in Larzac by farmers opposed to a land grab to expand a military base, claiming the military violated and damaged the fields because the 'Larzac celebration' frustrated 'their primary function, the power to invade' (ibid. 1986: 104). The war-machine depends on rejection or exclusion as its primary necessity and hence replaces 'sacred ancient hospitality' with 'fortresses' (ibid. 1986: 78). The restoration of hospitality (or abundance), through movements such as 'No Borders', social centres, skipping and squatting, is thus a challenge to the underpinnings of logistical society. Another parallel here is between Graeber's (2007) powers of creation and force, and Virilio's (1986: 89) contrast of the poetic and military potential of populations.

Resistance becomes undefeatable (though not necessarily victorious) if it becomes impossible to terrorise (c.f. Routledge and Simons 1995). Disempowerment or 'deterrence' as we have seen, depends on the all-pervasiveness of anxiety. Hence, the importance of affective techniques designed to ward off anxiety, such as those developed by *La Ruta Pacifica* (Karatzogianni and Robinson 2010: 176–77). Activists in Argentina recount a sense of being too afraid to speak, instilled by the terror of the military regime, which is co-extensive with Virilio's account – people were afraid of their neighbours. This generalised fear was finally broken in the uprising of 2001, by the gesture of speaking the unspeakable (Sitrin 2006: 24). Wars become, as Virilio suggested of Vietnam, dependent on the duration of endurance, particularly of civilians (Virilio 1990: 51). On the military side, it becomes dependent on speed as a basis for morale (Virilio 1986: 55). Yet counter-insurgency terror rarely works; all but the least popular insurgencies are not defeatable in this way (Findley and Young 2007). Somalia was not only not terrorised, but managed to turn the tables, producing images which inverted the spectacle and caused US demoralisation (Debrix 1999). Given the right psychological techniques or conditions, deterrence is thus vulnerable at the level of morale. Another weakness of deterrence is that it is impossible to deter others from inventing and perfecting new weapons (Virilio 1986: 146). This is raised regarding Cold War nuclear deterrence, but also applies to new forms of popular defence. Cost provides yet another weakness: while militaries may have the ability to use massive force, it is so expensive as to rarely be cost-effective (ibid. 1986: 150).

Activism is above all not a publicity stunt, not a performance for the mass or state gaze, but something else, an expressive action, an act *against* or in radical antagonism with the state, imposing costs on it. It is something which restores the existence of popular defence as a logic outside that of the game of images arising from logistics. The irony is that the media remain suspicious of covering activism, because they view its events as staged to be covered and therefore as not being 'real' news – precisely what anarchist protests are not (Graeber 2007). 'Terrorism', on the other hand, *is* a publicity stunt (Virilio 1989: 39). Virilio's discussion of 'terrorism' is actually rather ambiguous as to whether it forms part of logistical power or of popular defence. Virilio treats the Palestinian struggle, including 'suicidal' attacks and attacks on aircraft, as popular resistance driven to desperation by the closure of space. The vulnerability of non-places, as vectors to the media which is the last territory of the globally displaced, is crucial to resistance (Virilio 1990: 56). He also portrays the state of emergency in a city at war, such as Beirut, as a kind of return to the 'open warfare' of the 'native combatant', bringing about fears of popular self-government (Virilio 1986: 120–1). Virilio also observes that terrorists perform a 'role reversal' on the system with their own 'savage documentary genre' of degrading images of hostages (Virilio 1994: 56). On the other hand, terrorist groups are often criticised as extensions or even innovators in the logistical logic. Terrorism reproduces the violence of the state, returning to the state's most basic, mythical level (Virilio 1989: 7). It also produces excuses for repression which link it to the security apparatus (Virilio 1990: 62). Between these two views, Virilio reaches the ambiguous conclusion that 'the Palestinian tragedy ... is the way of the future', but only if considered apart from 'the strange brew of somewhat dubious terrorist factions' (Virilio 1990: 57). This might point towards the distinction between active and reactive resistance: the future is networked resistance, but hopefully without the dubious reactive inscriptions.

Conclusion

Virilio provides an account of the contemporary world, and the place of mass culture within it, which involves a novel, thought-provoking theory of alienation. For Virilio, people are not simply alienated at the site of production, but in the channelling of sensory perception. A condition of 'telepresence' has corroded experiences of the local and created a generalised, mutual surveillance. The power of the state and the force of global markets are largely effects of this regime of telepresence. This contributes to a sense of the enormity of the struggle suggested by any attempt to reconstruct humanised or ecological relations. Yet his account is not entirely pessimistic. His theory of popular defence suggests the possibility of resisting domination. We also have reason to believe his account is too pessimistic: new technologies which are part of the order of telepresence can often be converted into tools of resistance. The boundary between the logistics of power and the counter-logistics of resistance is more porous than Virilio realises. This said, the crucial challenge is to reconstruct ways of seeing which escape the confines of telepresence. This requires a response – an imposition of slownesses or an acceleration beyond the speed of the state – which destroys the grip of telepresence on ways of seeing. The point is not to put on a performance for the gaze of power or its subjects, but to reclaim, in the lived immediacy of local lifeworlds, a site of affective counter-power which at its limits, becomes undeterrable.

http://records.viu.ca/~soules/media301/dromologies.htm

References

Albini, Joseph L. (1993) 'The mafia and the devil: what they have in common', *Journal of Contemporary Criminal Justice* 9 no. 3, 240–50.

al-Ghoul.com (n.d.) 'Digital Jihad', at: www.al-ghoul.com/digital_jihad.htm (accessed 3 September 2010).

Bajpai, Kanti (1998) 'India: modified structuralism', in Muthiah Alagappa (ed.), *Asian Security Practice: Material and Ideational Influences*, Palo Alto, CA: Stanford University Press, 157–97.

Barthes, Roland (1985) [1967] *The Fashion System*, London: Jonathan Cape.

Barthes, Roland (2000) [1957] *Mythologies*, London: Vintage.

Baudrillard, Jean (1983) *In the Shadow of the Silent Majorities and Other Essays*, New York: Semiotext(e).

Baudrillard, Jean (1998) [1970] *The Consumer Society: Myths and Structures*, London: Sage.

Benjamin, Walter (1974) [1930s] 'On the concept of history', at: www.efn. org/~dredmond/Theses_on_History.PDF (accessed 3 September 2010).

Bogost, Ian (2007), *Persuasive Games: The Expressive Power of Videogames*, Cambridge, MA: MIT Press.

Bramwell, Tom (2005) 'FBI, Secret Service to track America's Army cheaters', *Eurogamer*, 13 January 2005, at: www.eurogamer.net/articles/news130105americasarmy, (accessed 3 September 2010).

Chomsky, Noam and Herman, Edward S. *Manufacturing Consent: The Political Economy of the Mass Media*, New York: Pantheon.

Cleaver, Harry (n.d.), 'Computer-linked social movements and the global threat to capitalism', at: www.cseweb.org.uk/downloads/cleaver.pdf, (accessed 3 September 2010).

Debord, Guy (1970) [1967] *Society of the Spectacle*, New York: Black and Red.

Debrix, François (1999) *Re-Envisioning Peacekeeping: The United Nations and the Mobilization of Ideology*, Minneapolis: University of Minnesota Press.

Eliade, Mircea (1971) [1949] *The Myth of the Eternal Return, or, Cosmos and History*, Princeton, NJ: Princeton University Press.

Enloe, Cynthia (2000) *Bananas, Beaches and Bases: Making Feminist Sense of International Relations*, Berkeley, CA: University of California Press.

Findley, M. G. and Young, J. K. (2007) 'Fighting fire with fire? How (not) to neutralize an insurgency' *Civil Wars*, Vol. 9: 4 December, 378–401.

Gambetta, Diego (2009) *Codes of the Underworld: How Criminals Communicate*, Princeton, NJ: Princeton University Press.

Graeber, David (2004) *Fragments of an Anarchist Anthropology*, Chicago, IL: Prickly Paradigm Press.

Graeber, David (2007), 'On the phenomenology of giant puppets: broken windows, imaginary jars of urine and the cosmological role of the police in American culture', at: http://balkansnet.org/zcl/puppets.pdf, (accessed 2 September 2010).

Hersh, Seymour M. (1991) *The Samson Option: Israel's Nuclear Arsenal and American Foreign Policy*, New York: Random House.

Illich, Ivan (1973) *Tools for Conviviality*, New York: Harper and Row.

Karatzogianni, Athina and Andrew Robinson (2010) *Power, Conflict and Resistance in the Contemporary World: Social Movements, Networks and Hierarchies*, London: Routledge.

Klein, Naomi (2007) *The Shock Doctrine: The Rise of Disaster Capitalism*, Toronto: Knopf Canada.

Levi-Strauss, Claude (1966) 'The scope of anthropology', *Current Anthropology* 7 no. 2, 112–23.

Marcuse, Herbert (1988) [1968] 'Aggressiveness in advanced industrial society', in *Negations*, London: Free Association Books, 248–67.

Marcuse, Herbert (1991) [1964] *One Dimensional Man*, Boston, MA: Beacon Press.

Massumi, Brian (ed.) (1993) 'The politics of everyday fear', Minneapolis: University of Minnesota Press.

Muncie, John (2009) *Youth and Crime* (3rd edn), Los Angeles/London: Sage.

Negri, Antonio (2003) *Time for Revolution*, London: Verso.

Poplak, Richard (2010) 'Why it's okay to wage joystick Jihad', *Globe and Mail*, August 27th 2010, at: www.theglobeandmail.com/news/national/why-its-okay-to-wage-joystick-jihad/article1688137/, (accessed 3 September 2010).

Richards, Paul (1996), *Fighting for the Rain Forest: War, Youth and Resources in Sierra Leone*, Oxford: James Currey.

Roten, Robert (2002), 'Is Hollywood responsible for 9–11?', *Laramie Movie Scope*, 15 April 2002, at www.lariat.org/AtTheMovies/essays/moviesand911.html, (accessed 3 November 2010).

Routledge, Paul and Simons, Jon (1995) 'Embodying spirits of resistance', *Environment and Planning D: Society and Space*, 13 no. 4, 471–98.

Sigal, Leon V. (1999) *Disarming Strangers: Nuclear Diplomacy with North Korea*, Princeton: Princeton University Press.

Sitrin, Marina (2006) *Horizontalism*, Edinburgh: AK Press.

Storper, Michael and Christopherson, Susan (1987) 'Flexible specialization and regional industrial agglomerations: The case of the U.S. motion picture industry', *Annals of the Association of American Geographers* 77 no. 1, 104–17.

Sutherland, J. J. (2006) 'Jihad video may be just a game', *National Public Radio*, May 26th 2006, at: www.npr.org/templates/story/story.php?storyId=5430837, (accessed 3 November 2010).

Virilio, Paul (1986) [1977] *Speed and Politics*, New York: Semiotext(e).

Virilio, Paul (1989) [1984] *War and Cinema*, London: Verso.

Virilio, Paul (1990) [1978] *Popular Defense and Ecological Struggles*, New York: Semiotext(e).

Virilio, Paul (1994) [1988] *The Vision Machine*, London: British Film Institute.

Virilio, Paul (2000) [1998] *The Information Bomb*, London: Verso.

Wilbur, Shawn (1994) 'Dromologies: Paul Virilio, speed, cinema, and the end of the political state', at: http://records.viu.ca/~soules/media301/dromologies.htm, (accessed 3 November 2010).

14 Blame it on the Russians

Tracking the portrayal of Russian hackers during cyber conflict incidents[1]

Athina Karatzogianni

Introduction

This chapter tracks the portrayal of Russian hackers in relation to various cyber conflicts and cyber crime incidents. It employs cyber conflict theory (Karatzogianni 2006, 2009a, 2009b, 2010), in order to engage with various aspects of cyber conflicts implicating Russian hackers, such as the cyber conflicts involving Estonia and Georgia. Further, its purpose is to identify and analyse the continuities in the coverage of Russian hackers, and links made in the global media between intelligence, cyber espionage, cyber crime and patriotic hacking, which, eventually and inevitably, also implicated Russian hackers and Russia in the Climategate hack. The selected events and discussion are important in the context of war and violence in culture and the media, as it reveals tensions and pressures in understanding the transfer[2] of physical conflict to cyberspace, essentially lurking in the following plateaus: cultural perceptions of electronic crime, hackers and hacktivism and un-nuanced media representations of such perceptions; difficulties in defining the often subtle or otherwise ideological distinctions behind ad hoc assemblages engaging in cyber conflict, hacktivism, cyber crime and the media portrayal of such events; the overall presence in culture and the media, of a residual, politicised, and ideological discourse, indiscriminately portraying individuals, which nevertheless engage in fundamentally diverse ways, in order to effect change, to protest electronically, to support ethno-national causes or to engage in criminal activities in cyberspace; and the effect of such discourses on diplomacy, global politics and the question of defining and regulating cyber conflict, cyber protest and cyber crime on a global level.

Further to note, that this chapter is not written in defence of Russians or the Russian government. The intention here is to simply demonstrate that although Russians *are* involved in cyber crime and cyber conflict incidents – as are other nationals by participating in cyber crime gangs, ad hoc patriotic assemblages, or even hacking dissident media organisations to reinforce the government line – they are also portrayed by the majority of the global media as *the* perpetrators of everything under the sun (unless the crimes are attributed to China or Chinese hackers).The paper demonstrates that the Russians were accused relentlessly of the Climategate hack under a new Cold War rhetoric spurred on by Russia's energy interests and motivations. In contrast to the overwhelming blame that Russian hackers are made to bear, there are other possible competing explanations: involvement of oppositional bloggers and scientists invested in the Climategate debate, or computer security failure at East Anglia University's network.

The first element of my analysis is mapping the physical events, as well as the environment of cyber conflict, through employing cyber conflict theory to do so (Karatzogianni 2006). The Estonian and Georgian cyber conflicts are of the ethno-national type, revealing also cultural struggles, due to Russia's alleged continuing intervention in the political life of these countries. The hacker groups involved in these conflicts, and their systems of belief and organization, aspire to hierarchical apparatuses (nation, ethnicity, identification with parties and leaders). The Climategate hack case, on the other hand, has socio-political and economic aspects, as it is an issue that is global in nature in terms of content. However, the Climategate case also points to ethnic and national issues in the coverage, as geopolitical narratives involved the main protagonists in the Climategate debate and the actual groups blamed for the hack. In mapping the environment of cyber conflict, the relationships between military and security, politicians and media, and geopolitical dimensions need to be addressed.[3]

In the process of building my argument, I surveyed approximately 130 articles collected between 2007 and 2010. The articles were sampled manually by using the keyword 'Russian hackers' on two different web search engines, Google and Yahoo, while also snowballing to include other items that followed the initial searches. The articles discussed here include sources from mainstream media (online versions of newspapers, magazines and TV outlets, such as the *Guardian, New York Times, Wall Street Journal, The New Scientist*, the *Independent, Le Monde, BBC, AFP, Reuters*); country- and incident-specific media and blogs (such as the *Georgian Times, Russia Today* and climate sceptic blogs); and IT business, security, and military sites and blogs commenting on cyber security and on technical aspects of the cyber conflicts discussed (such as *National Defence Magazine, Wired Magazine, Asian Computers, PC World*, Villeneuve's blog). An effort was made to include an equal number of articles out of these three types of sources.

My analysis is also based on my previous research, where I integrated elements of social movement, conflict and media theories into a single analytical framework of 'cyber conflict', in order to explain the empirical evidence of various cyber conflicts (ibid.). Elements of social movement theory were adopted to discuss socio-political cyber conflicts; conflict theory was used to address ethno-religious cyber conflicts; and media theory was deployed as a component for both, deriving a single integrated analytical framework for understanding cyber conflicts. This framework has been applied when analysing ethno-religious and ethno-national cyber conflicts (i.e. Israeli–Palestinian, pro-Islamic-anti-Islamic conflicts related to the Iraq war, Indian–Pakistani and American–Chinese) and socio-political cyber conflicts (such as anti-globalisation, anti-war movements, dissidents in authoritarian regimes and Internet censorship in different countries (ibid.).[4] Lastly, I have used framework analysis of content, similar to Juyan Zhang and Shahira Fahmy's (2009) approach in their comparative analysis of American and Russian press coverage of political movements in Ukraine, Belarus and Uzbekistan. The authors chose the sourcing, causality and moral judgment frames to apply to their empirical evidence. This type of frame analysis is taken into account, when looking at discourses and analysing the Internet as a medium.

The first section of this article is an overview of cyber attacks; the second discusses the global media coverage of Russian cyber crime; the third explains the connection of cyber crime and politically-motivated cyber attacks in the post-Soviet cyber space; the fourth section looks at cyber security and geopolitics discussions. The last section dwells on the new Cold War rhetoric and the framing of Russians as responsible for the Climategate hack. Although the global media often portrays individuals and groups of Eastern European or post-Soviet origin as a uniform category, the main focus here is focused on the media portrayal of Russia and the Russians.

Cyber conflict events: a brief background

Before I proceed to discuss the ways Russian hackers were represented in the media, I provide a very brief description of the cyber conflict incidents themselves. The Estonia cyber attacks lasted roughly a month (beginning on 27 April 2007) and handicapped Estonian government, media and bank sites. The attacks served as a protest platform for ethnic Russians objecting to the relocation of the Bronze Soldier of Tallinn and included defacement of web sites, 'denial of service' attacks and the use of botnets previously used for spam.

The South Ossetian–Georgian cyber conflict occurred right before and during the actual armed conflict in August 2008 between Georgia and Russia. On 7 August, Georgia launched a military attack in South Ossetia in an attempt to re-establish control of the area.[5] Russia retaliated by bombing and occupying Georgian cities. The war ended after five days; in the aftermath Russia supported the independence of South Ossetia and Abkhazia (another region seeking independence from Georgia), keeping troops in the areas. The cyber conflict began several days before the actual war, when the virtual infrastructures of various South Ossetian, Russian and Georgian organisations were attacked, leading to defacement of web sites, services denied and botnets. According to Internet rumours, the

Russian Business Network (RBN), a well-known cyber crime gang linked to malicious software and hacking, was involved in the attacks, together with the Russian security services. Several governments such as Estonia, Poland and Ukraine offered assistance to Georgia.

In November 2009, the 'Climategate hack', as it was termed by the media, was discovered: thousands of e-mails, files and other communication among scientists at the Climate Research Unit (CRU) at the University of East Anglia were hacked into and the materials posted on a Siberian server. The controversy, which portrayed climate change scientists as manipulating data and the peer-review process, coincided with the Copenhagen summit, where world leaders were meeting to discuss climate change. Three independent inquiries in the UK rejected allegations of wrong-doing by the scientists involved, though it was found there was room for improvement in the CRU's working practices (Gillis 7 July 2010).

Russia portrayed as a nation of unemployed superhackers and as a centre of cyber crime

Many of the online news articles addressed here consistently describe Russian hackers as highly educated and talented people who, upon unemployment, are forced to turn to illegal activities. The examples of this type of explanation are plenty. For instance, a local media outlet in the United States called *Elk Grove Citizen* presented a story, in which special agent LuAnna Harmon of the FBI's Sacramento division visits a high school to talk about cyber crime and frequently mentions Russian cyber crimes as her examples. When asked by the students about the reasons cyber crimes happen in Russia, she blamed the situation on highly educated people who turn to crime since there are few jobs for them (Macdonald 13 April 2010). In another report, by *The Register*, Dmitry Zakharov, director of communications at the Russian Association of Electronic Communications, is quoted saying '[W]e are not able to offer talented technology people jobs. So they get involved in illegal activity' (Leyden 12 April 2010).

Russia is also consistently portrayed as a nation of superhackers, responsible for sophisticated attacks. Various media reports involve interviews with security professionals and Russian hackers about their background and motivations. For example, in the BBC interview with Evgeny Kaspersky, the 'computer security guru' and an owner of Internet security firm Kaspersky Labs, the reporter refers to the Russian city of Tomsk as a centre for producing hackers (Rainsford 11 March 2010). Tomsk is mentioned because the files relating to the Climategate hack were leaked and posted on a server there.[6] In the interview, Kaspersky describes Russia as a nation of 'superhackers' and attributes their abilities to good technical education. The graduates at Tomsk are described in the article as facing a choice of either creating sophisticated information protection systems, or joining the ranks of Russia's hackers for hire. However, this description of unemployment as the main reason for hacking in Russia is not always consistent. For instance, *National Defence Magazine* features a former US intelligence officer's description of Vladimir, who comes from a well educated Russian family and who could be anything he wanted to be, but chose instead to be a cyber thief (Magnuson May 2010).

Another theme in describing Russia as a nation of hackers is the portrayal of Russia and its relationship to its home-grown hackers and cyber crime gangs. Russia is presented as one of the top five countries from where international hacking attacks originate and as a growing centre of cyber crime. Russia is also portrayed as a top cyber security concern in a Cold War style discourse, a topic to which I return below. Typical examples are representations of Russia as the top producer of viruses, Trojans and spyware, ranking second in generating spam (RT 19 February 2008); Russia as the second largest host of malware according to Sophos (Megerisi 22 March 2010); and Russia as a centre for selling private databases, for example, in the Savyolovsky market (Stack 17 March 2010).

Furthermore, reports on cyber crime gangs, exploits and cyber attacks of various kinds frequently mention the RBN, which is described as capable of taking a whole country offline. NATO sees both the RBN and Russian hackers' community as a general threat (RT 8 January 2010). Botnets[7], one of the frequent tools of cyber attacks, are universally mentioned as a trademark technique of RBN and of Russian hackers in general. Botnets distributing spam and controlling millions of computers are also reported in coverage of the Estonian and Georgian cyber conflicts. In 2009, 75 per cent of business structures were reported to have been exposed to various cyber attacks, with Russia being among the top ten countries generating the threat (Secrest 29 April 2010). The reporting of cyber attacks often mentions interviews with experts and statistics of computer security firms, such as Symantec, Sophos and Kaspersky.[8]

Russians are often described as being arrested for, or linked to, the most famous cyber crime incidents of the last five years, such as the Charles Schwab brokerage attack and the Royal Bank of Scotland (RBS), a robbery of £6 million in 12 hours (Hawkins 7 April 2010).

Lastly, there is a recurrent reference to the Russian mafia's cyber capabilities. However, admittedly, the RBS robbery was not technically sophisticated: the gang hacked into the system cloning 44 debit cards, but it was the coordination of cashers (individuals draining ATMs) that helped pull the robbery off in different countries. Nevertheless, the impression is given that the hackers had super cyber capabilities, as they managed to 'blitz more than 2,000 machines in 28 cities worldwide' (Findlay 14 March 2010).[9]

A central issue that comes up in the cyber crime reports of this type is extradition and the difficulty of trying cyber criminals in the United States. The good cooperation between Russian business and the American

Securities and Exchange Commission to fight cyber crime also tends to get coverage (Thomson 22 March 2010). Besides cyber crime activities involving millions of dollars, there are also several Internet safety problems and instances where Russians hackers were selling various personal accounts from Gmail to Facebook and to Twitter (Barratt 25 April 2010; Tynan 26 April 2010). As explained by one of the researchers at Kaspersky Labs, Russia comes second in the numbers of cases of password stealing Trojan viruses, accounting for 12 per cent of all the incidents, with China accounting for 63 per cent (McMillan 29 January 2010).

Inevitably, these stories create a mythology surrounding the abilities of Russian hackers, whereby they emerge as superhackers with astonishing accomplishments. Russia itself appears as a nation of highly capable hackers, a nation that both nurtures its computer specialists (thanks to its reportedly high quality technical education) and fails them by dooming them to unemployment and lack of opportunities, thus 'forcing' them to turn to cyber crime.

Russian cyber crime as 'patriotic' hacking

Another aspect of mediation of Russian hacking is the alleged link between cyber crime networks, cyber espionage and political hacking. The researcher and blogger Nart Villeneuve argues that there is a potential relationship there, as the boundaries between crimeware networks and cyber espionage 'appear to be blurring, making issues of attribution increasingly more complex. It may also indicate that there is an emerging market for sensitive information and/or politically motivated attacks, as crimeware networks seek to monetise such information and capabilities' (Villeneuve 10 April 2010). More importantly, this prompts Villenueve to believe that such attacks demonstrate that botnets involved with criminal activity are being used to conduct both political and apolitical distributed denial-of-service attacks (DDoS) (Villeneuve 10 April 2010).

Examples of this type of activity abound in the Russian and post-Soviet landscape. For instance, the website of the Russian newspaper, *Novaya Gazeta* [New Newspaper], critical of Russian authorities, had experienced six days of downtime due to a hacker attack in 2003 (Periscope it 3 February 2003). In 2010, *The Guardian* reported a more recent attack on *Novaya Gazeta*, in which the newspaper staff described the scale of the attack as comprising more than a million hits a second on the server. This report suggested that the attack was carried out by a 'highly sophisticated' state agency, displeased with the newspaper's editorial direction (Harding 27 January 2010). Other incidents include attacks on the Polish government system, which coincided with the 70th anniversary of the outbreak of World War II and a visit by Russian Prime Minister Vladimir Putin (Leyden 13 October 2009). In Kyrgyzstan in 2009, two of the country's main Internet service providers, ns.kg and domain.kg, came under a massive denial-of-service attack. Some reports stated the assault had shut down 80 per cent of the country's bandwidth. Media descriptions presented this as a case of suspected Russian influence (Weinberger 14 May 2010).

The linking of cyber crime to cyber conflict is explicit in media reports that one of the botnets drafted for the Georgian cyber attack was 'Black Energy', a Trojan horse-hijacked army of PCs thought to have been used to hit Citibank, while 'Black Energy 2' was being used to launch DDoS attacks against Russian banks (Keizer 7 April 2010). The Georgian press also makes the link to cyber conflict explicit by suggesting the involvement of the Russian intelligence service, the Federal Security Service (FSB). According to these reports, the FSB attacked the National Bolshevik Party and moderate opposition groups like 'The Marc of Those Who Disagree', and mainstream media outlets such as *Kommersant* and *Ekho Moskvy*. The reports quote Andrei Soldatov's piece in *Novaya Gazeta*, where he suggests that the FSB did not have to use their own in-house resources, but could simply point the growing community of 'hacker-patriots' in the right direction (Goble 31 May 2007).

In yet another report from an outlet specialising in national defence, Paul Joyal, the National Strategies Inc. managing director for public safety and homeland security, is quoted saying that there is a nexus between cyber crime and state actors: 'You can be a criminal, a member of an intelligence organisation and a businessman all at the same time' (Magnuson May 2010). RBN, he continues, was 'deeply involved in a cyber attack on Georgia that began weeks before Russian forces invaded the nation in 2008' (ibid.).[10]

The reporting of cyber crime, the brilliance of Russian hackers, Russia's portrayal as a centre of cyber crime with the mafia allegedly connected both to government and intelligence services, and patriotic hacking are all mentioned in reports of the Estonian and Georgian cyber conflicts in the global media:

> In Estonia in 2007 and in Georgia during the war in 2008, hackers were able to freeze all Internet activity and crucially deny service to banking and government systems. Many accused the Russian government of orchestrating the cyber attacks – a claim Moscow denies, even though *hacking in Russia has a long and well-established history.*
>
> ((RT 8 January 2010) [my own italics])

The real life event that sparked the cyber conflict in Estonia was the removal of a Soviet war hero statue from Tallinn's square and the subsequent riots that took place in Estonia for several days around 26 April 2007, leading to several casualties. By 20 April 2007, although the real world riots calmed down, the country's digital infrastructure was crumbling from cyber attacks. The statue incident reflected deeper tensions and the cultural conflict between the Estonian state and ethnic Russians in

Estonia, who make up around one-quarter of the Baltic republic's population of 1.34 million.

Estonia is considered to be an Internet success story due to its e-commerce and also has strong e-government presence. The Estonian cyber conflict included denial of service attacks, clogging the country's servers and routers, infiltrating the world with botnets, banding computers together and transforming them into 'zombies' hijacked by viruses to take part in such raids without their owners' knowledge. Multiple sources flowed into the system and the attackers even rented time in botnets. The attacks lasted three weeks. The plans of the attackers were posted in Russian language chat rooms with instructions on how to send disruptive messages and which websites to target. The attacks targeted all levels of the social, political and economic infrastructure: the Estonian presidency and its Parliament, almost all of the country's government ministries and political parties, three of the country's six big news organisations, two of the biggest banks and other firms specialising in communications. Blaming the Russian state for the attacks, the Estonian authorities rapidly mobilised to fight the war, utilising contacts in several countries and requesting NATO and the EU for help.

Although Estonia claimed that the attacks had originated in Russia, and the global press similarly linked the attacks to the Russian government, others claimed that nationalist hackers had done most of the work: 'it had been perpetrated by an impromptu "flashmob" ...' (Slideshare n.d.).[11] The Estonian government was also portrayed as going through a 'panic attack', exaggerating the situation when its networks were attacked in cyber space: 'Faced with DDoS and nationalistic, cross-border hacktivism—nuisances that have plagued the rest of the wired world for the better part of a decade—Estonia's leaders lost perspective' (Poulsen 22 August 2007).

To use the lens of cyber conflict theory, the Estonian case points to ethno-national and cultural elements, with ethnic Russians utilising ICTs to protest their anger at the treatment of Russians in Estonia.[12] The use of patriotic hacking as a facet of hacktivism creates questions, in terms of how the groups were organised, their mobilisation, framing and organisation of the attacks. Similar elements of organising are found in socio-political cyber conflicts. At the same time, wider issues of cultural conflict and geopolitical tensions need to be explored. Article 5 in NATO's charter states that if a NATO ally is the victim of an armed attack, each and every other member of the alliance should consider this act of violence as an armed attack against all members and should take the actions it deems necessary to assist the ally attacked. As NATO does not yet define electronic attacks as military action, it cannot intervene even when the origin of attack can be proven. Also, the use of information communication technologies is a very convenient and cost-effective tool for protest, usually related to hacktivism and the ethical debates surrounding it. Linked to the real life protests and their online incarnation is the uncertainty about the 'enemy within' and the anxiety about the always incomplete project of national purity, as manifested in the lives of the ethnic Russians in Estonia and elsewhere. These cultural struggles are exacerbated by the media and propaganda, with groups defending the purity of their national space using online technologies.[13]

In the case of the Georgian cyber conflict, the circumstances were different, but here, too, patriotic hacking was the main element. It was reported as a 'virtual war' in cyber space accompanying the brief war in the summer of 2008 between Georgia and Russia. Once again, the media accused Russia of orchestrating the cyber attacks, even though it appeared to be due to patriotic hacking by individuals or groups of hackers. Various reports suggested that state organisations provided no support for the cyber attacks during the Georgian cyber conflict.[14]

Tracking the new Cold War rhetoric: espionage, security and crime in cyberspace

Diplomacy, espionage and security in cyberspace were frequently discussed in media narratives of Russia and Russian hackers implicated in cyber conflicts.[15] These issues form part of the narrative which consistently blames Russian hackers for any types of activity involving the use of computers. What emerges here is a new Cold War discourse, often used to discuss together the geopolitics in the region, the role of NATO in maintaining cyber security and the specific cases linked to Russian hackers.

One telling example is the discussion in the global media of cyber espionage perpetrated by Russia and China.[16] It is worth noting here, that cyber espionage is not currently a crime in international law and not usually grounds for war. In a report in UK's *Telegraph* Jonathan Evans, the head of MI5, has warned that Britain faces 'unreconstructed attempts by Russia, China and others' who were using 'sophisticated technical attacks' to try and steal sensitive technology on civilian and military projects, along with political and economic intelligence (Gardham 4 December 2009). In *The Times* Evans is mentioned once again, writing to 300 businesses in 2007 to warn them of Chinese hacking attacks and data theft (Loyd 8 March 2010). Anthony Loyd links the interests of hostile state intelligence agencies and cyber criminal syndicates known as *partnerka* [syndicate, partnership], claiming they lead 'commercial espionage in Europe and are known to have links with Harry and his comrades in the FSB' (ibid.).

Such narratives regarding global security espionage and cyber security are linked in the media to questions about Russia and the participation of countries previously within the Soviet sphere of influence in NATO. This is particularly prevalent in the media debates around the coverage of Estonian and Georgian cyber conflicts, as well as around NATO's cyber security capabilities, doctrine and general regulation of cyber conflict. The problem is viewed in the mainstream media as NATO's need to develop an agreed concept of what constitutes worldwide cyber security (Austin 10 January 2010). Most of the coverage related to Russia and NATO makes extensive use of the Cold War framework. For example, NATO Secretary-General Rasmussen is reported to have understood the special security concerns of East Europeans 'who chafed under Moscow's decades-long domination during the Cold War, and criticised Russia's new military doctrine' (Reuters 12 March 2010).[17]

Questions of cyber security are also embedded in international politics of secession and recognition. For example, the United States Secretary of State Hilary Clinton has stated that they support Georgia and will neither recognise Abkhazia nor South Ossetia (Civil.Ge 5 December 2009). South Ossetia was the reason for the war between Russia and Georgia, with Russia recognising South Ossetia and Abkhazia's quest for independence.[18] As Nikolai Petro explains in an interview, set up by Saylor Company (a US public relations firm employed by the governments of Abkhazia and South Ossetia), these two countries seem to be on quite different trajectories. While Abkhaz leaders have always been clearly focused on obtaining international recognition as a sovereign state, some South Ossetian leaders seem to aspire to some form of integration with North Ossetia, within the Russian Federation (Petro 13 November 2009). Paul Goble, writing in the *Georgian Daily*, mentions the analysis of Anatoly Chekhoyev, a former secretary of the South Ossetian Oblast committee of the Communist Party of the Soviet Union (CPSU), who also served in the USSR Supreme Soviet and Russian Duma. He asked his readers to consider what might have happened if Moscow had not acted as it did; 'if Russia had stayed silent, then one could have shaken loose Daghestan, Chechnya, Ingushetia and all the rest with the wave of a hand' (Goble 28 November 2009).

Besides the international relations aspects of the Russian-Georgian war, there are regional media issues linked to this case. 'The only war we can win against Russia is an information war, so we shouldn't miss our chance', argued the Georgian politician analyst Tornike Sharashenidze (Kiguradze 13 November 2009). The Georgian media environment is described as highly politicised with broadcasters providing either intensely pro-government or pro-opposition view (UNCHR 16 February 2009). In that kind of environment, it is not surprising that there are conflicts beyond what my brief discussion of cyber conflict has shown.[19]

The actual Georgia–South Ossetia cyber conflict started the same day as the military offensive on the 8 August 2008, although attacks were also registered in July. The websites of the president of Georgia, the Georgian Parliament, the ministries of defence and foreign affairs, the National Bank of Georgia and online news agencies were attacked, with the cyber conflict becoming more intense as the real conflict escalated. Images of Hitler were manipulated and juxtaposed on the Georgian President. The Georgian response involved using filters to block Russian IP addresses, moving websites elsewhere, and appealing to Estonia and other countries for help.

Estonia dispatched specialists and Poland provided websites for Georgian use (Heickero March 2010).

Possibly the most fascinating discussion on the Georgian cyber conflict comes in the form of a journal article written by Stephen Korns and Josua Kastenberg and published in *Parameters*. In their article, they re-affirm the view that most security experts have attributed the 2008 DDoS attacks to 'an amalgam of government-incentivised agents, hackers and cyber citizen protestors' (Korns and Kastenberg 2009 66). They give the example of an Internet journalist who accessed a website and downloaded pre-packaged software that would have enabled him, to join in the attacks, had he chosen to do so (Morozov 2008 in Korns and Kastenbeg 2009, 65).

In fact, Korns and Kastenberg make very interesting observations about this cyber conflict. First, they bring up the issue of cyber neutrality: in contrast to Estonia, which experienced cyber attacks, but essentially defended in place, Georgia maneuvered by relocating strategic IP-based cyber capabilities to a private company in the United States (Korns and Kastenberg 2009, 68). Korns and Kastenberg believe that Georgia's unconventional response to the August 2008 DDoS attacks, supported by US private industry, adds a new element of complication for cyber strategists (ibid. 61). Second, they show that since the 2001 Council of Europe Convention on cyber crime, to which the United States is a party, omits any reference to the terms 'cyber attack' or 'cyber weapons', cyber attacks are currently part of cyber *crime* and not cyber *war* as such. From that perspective it would have been Interpol, rather than NATO that would have to respond to Estonia and Georgia (ibid. 64–65).

To push Korns' and Kastenberg's argumentation further, any cyber attack could be framed as cyber crime and prosecuted as such, unless it is part of an armed conflict. This implies that any political hacking could be prosecuted as a (cyber) crime. Indeed one of the patriotic hackers (or a cultural protester, as he was portrayed by some) in the Estonian cyber conflict discussed earlier was convicted and fined for his activities. The ethical debate on hacktivism notwithstanding, this shift could potentially mean that electronic disobedience or hacktivism as we know them, could also be prosecuted as criminal activities, despite their mostly symbolic effects. An additional problem here is the difficulty in determining with certainty the origin of cyber attacks, or establishing whether an attack is a state-sponsored mission or ad hoc initiative. As Korns and Kastenberg put it, 'cyber conflict between nations is a serious concern, but as the Georgian DDoS attacks demonstrate, perhaps of even greater concern is the growing trend of cyber conflict between nations and ad hoc assemblages' (ibid. 70).

The Estonian cyber conflict led to the establishment of a Cooperative Cyber Defence Centre of Excellence[20] by NATO in 2008 in Tallinn (Johnson 16 April 2009). Furthermore, in May 2010, the Secretary of Defence Robert Gates announced the activation of the Pentagon's first comprehensive, multi-service cyber operation, the US Cyber Command (CYBERCOM), with Keith Alexander as its commander. Talking about cyber space as the fifth battle space, transferring soldiers from communications and electronics to an Army Forces cyber command, and wondering on how cyber warriors should be trained, confirms a trend toward militarisation of what was previously a criminal and commercial matter (Rozoff 26 May 2010). With Russia and China frequently depicted as the main suspects, the United States and its NATO allies have had to address cyber warfare questions in its twenty-first century strategic concept. With 120 countries developing cyber capabilities, NATO's Director of Policy Planning Jamie Shea commented that 'there are people in the strategic community who say cyber attacks now will serve the same role in initiating hostilities as air campaigns played in the twentieth century' (ibid.).

NATO will have to eventually create a coherent strategy for cyber warfare. This problem has been addressed by various scholars of Internet security (Central European University 7–8 June 2010). In June 2010, the *Sunday Times* reported that a team of NATO experts led by former USA Secretary of State, Madeleine Albright, prepared a document stating that a cyber attack on the critical infrastructure of a NATO country could equate an armed attack, justifying retaliation (Smith and Warren 6 June 2010). The organisation's lawyers were reported saying, that since the effect of a cyber attack can be similar to an armed assault, there is no need to redraft existing treaties. If an attack on critical infrastructure resulted in casualties and destruction comparable to a military attack, then the mutual defence clause of Article 5 could be invoked. Still, the level of attack is not exactly clear, as the perception of dangers of cyber warfare continues to change.

The new Russian stereotype and the 'Climategate hack'

To conclude the discussion of Russian hackers, let me now turn to the Climategate hack – an incident which was consistently attributed to Russia by the global media. This attribution became particularly clear after several key figures, such as Professor Jean-Pascal Ypersele, the vice chairman of the Inter-governmental Panel on Climate Change, supported the Russian hackers scenario. Here are some typical examples of the narratives that followed: 'Russian hackers illegally obtained ten years of e-mails between the world's top climate change scientists' (Kolasinski 4 December 2009); 'The British media and some UN scientists have suggested that the Russian secret service, the FSB, was complicit in the theft' (Snapple 7 January 2010); 'The guiding hand behind the leaks, the allegation went, was that of the Russian secret services' (Walker 7 December 2009); 'Russia, a major oil exporter, may be trying to undermine calls to reduce carbon emissions' (*Telegraph* 6 December 2009); 'This is not the first time Russian hackers have created global Internet disarray' (MacNicol 7 December 2009); 'Russian computer hackers are suspected of being behind the stolen e-mails' (McCarthy and Owen 6 December 2009). A typical coverage in *The Times* by Tony Halpin sums up all the reasons why Russian hackers and Russia were immediately implicated: Russia's desire to discredit the summit, poor, talented but unemployed hackers, the RBN and the use of patriotic hackers by the FSB. All these were connected together, fitting the overall move to blame Russian hackers – a move already built up by the global media (Halpin 7 December 2009).

Most media representations of the Climategate hack linked the events to other incidents in the past, suggesting a consistent narrative frame which blames the attacks on Russian hackers. Russian hackers were ideal in that respect. Although the Climategate material was uploaded on various servers in Turkey and Saudi Arabia before ending up in Tomsk in Siberia, it was Tomsk that became the key factor in the Russian hackers' story. Reporters interviewed students in Tomsk, where a computer school was located, and stated that 'in 2002 Tomsk students launched a "denial of service" attack at the Kavkaz–Tsentr portal, a site whose reports about Chechnya angered Russian officials' (Stewart and Delgado 6 December 2009; also reported by Merchant 7 December 2009). The FSB office in Tomsk put out a special press release stating that the students' actions had been a legitimate 'expression of their position as citizens, one worthy of respect' (ibid.). Around the same time, the media frequently linked the Georgian and Estonian cyber conflicts, implicating the Russian security service and accusing the Russian police of turning a blind eye to cyber crime (Judge 7 December 2009).

Several reports, some from bloggers, however, began deviating from the general certainty and consensus that attributed the Climategate hack to the Russians. Since hackers used open proxies to mask their identities, they could have originated from anywhere in the world. If Russian hackers were indeed involved, leaving the files at Tomsk would be too obvious. Yet, most reports pointed a finger at Russian hackers. The media repeatedly mentioned Russian hackers' sophistication, linking it to earlier, equally skilful attacks. In the case of the Climategate hack, the impression was given that the hackers selected specific information implicating the scientists of the past 13 years. None of the media reports mentioned that the files titled after freedom of information act might have been collected by someone working at the University of East Anglia. Fred Pearce reported, for example that a number of people claim to have stumbled on non-public files on the UEA server in the months prior to the hack. Among them was David Holland, a British engineer and an amateur climate sceptic, who in December 2008 notified the University that the search engine on their home page was broken and falling through to a directory. In November 2009, Charles Rotter, the moderator of the blog Watts Up With That (http://wattsupwiththat.com/), wrote that in July of that year he had discovered that the university had left station data versions from 2003 and 1996 on its server and that those who knew where to look could find the files available in public access (Pearce 9 February 2010a, b).

There are other reasons why the leak version might be more plausible than an attack by Russia or Russian hackers. Lance Levsen, for example, has argued that if the file was not already collected and stolen, the actual collection of the material and cracking meant a super-sophisticated operation. A reasonable explanation for the archive being in such a state is that the FOI Officer at the University was practicing due diligence and that someone at UEA found the file and released it into the wild. The release of FOIA2009.zip could have occurred not because of a hacker, but because of a leak from UEA by a person with scruples (Levsen 7 December 2009). Also, notably, the 'hackers' made several efforts at disseminating the material before succeeding; this, once again, is not consistent with the pattern of how Russian hackers would operate.[21] Lastly, the fact that the documents were on a server due to computer security failure at UEA, and then 'magically' found their way to climate change bloggers (Pearce 9 February 2010a;b), provides another competing explanation to the Russian hacking scenario. The *Guardian* reported that Norfolk police interviewed climate researcher Paul Dennis, who heads an adjacent laboratory at UEA and had e-mail contact with American bloggers such as McIntyre of the Climategate Audit, Patrick Condon of the Air Vent and Anthony Watts of Watts Up With That. All these bloggers were sent the leaked material. A connection to Russian hackers, indeed, was not proven. Moreover, according to The *Guardian*, Norfolk police has discounted tabloid stories of links to Russian intelligence in this incident (Leigh *et al.* 4 February 2010a).

Conclusion

The way Russian cyber crime gangs and incidents are narrated by global mainstream media, alternative media and bloggers, shapes a very specific portrayal of Russian hackers and their superior abilities in relation to hacking and cyber crime. There is no significant difference between mainstream and independent media and blogs, except that in blogs the bias against Russians is often far more explicit. The hackers are consistently portrayed as having 'incredible' powers to support criminal activities, attack opposition groups' virtual presence or hack for the benefit of the state in time of need. This stereotypical depiction of Russian hackers is reminiscent of Cold War imagery, such as that of the incredibly intelligent Russian spies who are forced to work for their government to survive poor living conditions. At the same time, this depiction creates a consistent narrative frame to explain any international incident as one carried out by this specific ethnic and cultural group. This narrative frame helps explain the certainty with which the 'Climategate hack' was attributed to Russian hackers without any valid proof and based solely on speculation.

The main argument of this chapter is that the ammunition for blaming the Russian hackers for the Climategate hack is to be found in the public discourse that portrays Russians as super hackers and links cyber crime to patriotic hacking, international espionage and global politics. This explains media stories of Russia's government and politico-economic elite allegedly inter-mingling with the Russian mafia and cyber crime gangs to get support during cyber conflicts, in which the Russian state is opposed (cyber attacks against opponents), implicated (Estonia) or is engaged in a brief war, as was the case with Georgia.

The global media have portrayed Russian hackers in a consistent manner, playing up their capabilities (such as, for example, their sophistication) and linking them to cyber crime gangs, robberies and identity thefts. Even if there are indeed individuals from Russia, or elsewhere in the post-Soviet space who are engaged in cyber crime, the assumption of Russian guilt in all cases reinforces the older Cold War portrayal of Russians in the Western world. There is a demonstrated tendency for the global media to look for a Russian hand and geopolitical implications in stories relating to former Soviet countries or countries under Soviet influence in the past. Also, there has been an exaggeration of the sophistication of Russian hackers, primarily because of their use of botnets to conduct attacks previous to the Climategate hack, particularly in patriotic hacking in the cases of Estonia and Georgia. By the time the 'Climategate hack' appeared with a huge impact just before the Copenhagen summit, the scene was set for Russian hackers to be blamed for what under a calmer mindset might have been more plausibly explained differently or at least reported alongside another, competing explanation.

Notes

1 This chapter was originally published in *Digital Icons: Studies in Russian, Eurasian and Central European New Media* (www.digitalicons.org; issue 4, autumn 2010, pp. 127–50, www.digitalicons.org/issue04/athina-karatzogianni/). *Digital Icons* publishes original research on the impact of digital and electronic technologies on politics, economics, society, culture and the arts in Russia, Eurasia and Central Europe. It is republished here, with certain amendments, in order to reach a less specialised audience. I must reiterate my thanks to the guest editor Adi Kuntsman, to the journal's three anonymous reviewers and to Maria Touri who reviewed the article for inclusion in this volume, for their creative suggestions for improvement.

2 For a discussion on the role of affective structures during the transfer from the real to the digital virtual look at my Wikileaks Affects: Ideology, Revolution and the Digital Virtual, in Karatzogianni, A. and Kuntsman, A. (eds) *Digital Cultures and the Politics of Emotion: Feelings, Affect and Technological Change*, Palgrave, forthcoming 2011.

3 For another example of similar types of analysis see Greg Simons's work on the reporting of modern warfare and the Russian war on terrorism (Simons 2010).

4 In socio-political cyber conflicts, I have looked at the impact of ICTs on mobilising structures, framing processes structures of political opportunity and hacktivism. In ethno-religious cyber conflicts I have focused on ethnic/religious affiliations, discourses of inclusion and exclusion, information warfare and conflict resolution.

5 Since the early 1990s South Ossetia was controlled by a Russian-backed government seeking international recognition.
6 In fact, the files were originally uploaded in Turkish and Saudi Arabian servers before Tomsk.
7 Botnet is a collection of automatic software agents, which are frequently associated with distribution of spam and malware.
8 This is in itself problematic, as these companies make profit precisely by selling protection technologies against these types of incidents, thus having vested interests in fuelling anxieties around computer security.
9 A similar report stressed the origin of the cyber criminals: 'A group of Eastern Europeans was charged with hacking into the network of payment processor RBS WorldPay...' (Mills 10 November 2009). Other reports mention the Russian origin of hackers indirectly (Crosley 23 December 2009; Hawkins 7 April 2010; McIntyre 22 December 2009;).
10 This connection, however, has not been proven.
11 Members of Nashi, a private pro-Kremlin youth group, also claimed to have had a hand in launching attacks and state-controlled media were reported to have helped whip up Anti-Estonian fervour that may have aided in recruiting hackers. (Weinberger 14 May 2010). According to *Agence France-Presse*, an ethnic Russian student Dmitri Galushkevic, was convicted of attacks against the website of Estonian Prime Minister, Andrus Ansip (Nichols 25 January 2008).
12 For a further discussion of Estonian cyber conflict, see Karatzogianni 2009a; Belot and Stroobants 17 June 2007.
13 The Estonian cyber conflict is also a reflection of the instability of the EU/ NATO enlargement project, especially in relation to Russia's hegemonic aspirations, energy and weapon disputes (Karatzogianni 2009a, 6–7).
14 Sharon Weinberger cites Project Grey Goose, an open-source intelligence initiative, whose analysts 'concluded that nationalist hackers had honed a cyber-kill chain", which involved recruiting novices by posting patriotic rhetoric and images, publishing and sharing a list of target web sites, discussing malware to use in the attack and evaluating results for follow-on attacks' (Weinberger 14 May 2010). Another report by a non-profit research group, The USA Cyber Consequences Unit, stated that most of the attackers were Russians, but Russian sympathisers in countries such as Ukraine and Latvia were also involved (Goodin 18 August 2009). The same report confirmed that although the cyber attacks were carried out with little, or no, direct involvement from the Russian government or military, the timing of the attacks, launched within hours of the Russian military's invasion, could only have come with a fair amount of cooperation from Russian officials (Goodin 18 August 2009).
15 An interesting example of how new media and web 2.0 are impacting diplomacy is the use of social networking to raise awareness, raise funds, organise for global issues and boost grass roots diplomacy. This use of new media tools takes place on different levels, from influencing official diplomacy, with Russian President Dmitry Medvedev making the tongue-in-cheek suggestion that he and his US counterpart Barack Obama begin conducting diplomacy via text message (Earthtimes 14 April 2010) to 'Twitter diplomacy', with a delegation organised by Washington and sent to Russia (Barry 23 February 2010).
16 For a detailed analysis of Chinese hackers, the Google-China cyber conflict, business and the Sino-American relationship in the global system, see Karatzogiannni 10 March 2010.
17 In terms of the real environment and geopolitics of the Georgian cyber conflict, Russia sees armament in Georgia as a serious problem and it has brought it up in NATO meetings in Brussels after the war. (Petro 13 November 2009). On 4 December 2009, NATO and Russia resumed their political dialogue,

which NATO had broken off after the war in Georgia (Khashig and Ponomarev 13 December 2009).

18 The only other countries recognising them are Venezuela and Nicaragua, Peru and small states like Nauru (*Georgian Times* 14 April 2009). For a detailed discussion of cyber conflict in unrecognised states see Karatzogianni, forthcoming.

19 For instance, there are efforts at operating television channels from both sides of the conflict. In January 2010, the Georgian Public Broadcaster inaugurated its first Russian language television channel, *Pervyi Kavkazskii* [First Caucasian]. When the channel further widened its range of coverage by becoming available on the French-operated satellite provider Eutelsat across almost the entire post-Soviet space, Eutelsat discontinued transmitting the channel, invoking suspicions that the Russian authorities were implicated in the decision. Oleg Panfilov, the Head of the Center for Journalism in Extreme Situations, and a host on First Caucasus, said to *Eurasia Monitor:* 'During the Russian aggression against Georgia in August 2008, ordinary people in various parts of the post-Soviet space could not receive objective information in the Russian language, while the Kremlin enjoyed an information monopoly' (Kvelashvili 5 February 2010). Meanwhile, *Russia Today* reported that as the channel is targeting ethnic minorities in the Caucasus region, it would act as a Georgian propaganda tool (RT 14 November 2009).

20 Known as CCD COE or K5.

21 Paul Hudson, a weatherman and climate change sceptic was sent a sample, a month before the documents were leaked, but did not use it (Leigh *et al.* 4 February 2010b). Matthew Taylor and Charles Arthur explain that a month after Hudson received his sample, someone hacked into the RealClimate website, using a computer in Turkey and uploaded a zip file containing all 4,000 e-mails and documents. At that point, the website's co-founder shut down the site. Then hackers used a computer in Saudi Arabia to post a fresh copy of the zip file, this time stored on the Tomsk server. Then the incident was picked up by blogs and organisations all over the world (Taylor and Arthur 27 November 2009). Eventually the story spread through climate change sceptic sites and then found its way into the mainstream media (Hurlbut 20 November 2009).

References

Karatzogianni, A. *The Real, The Virtual, and the Imaginary State: Cyber Conflict in Small and Unrecognised States*, Media and Cultural Studies, Basingstoke: Palgrave Macmillan (forthcoming).

Karatzogianni, A. 'Wikileaks Affects: Ideology, Revolution and the Digital Virtual, in Karatzogianni, A. and Kuntsman, A. (eds) *Digital Cultures and the Politics of Emotion: Feelings, Affect and Technological Change*, Palgrave, forthcoming 2011.

Karatzogianni, A. (10 March 2010) 'The Thorny Triangle: Cyber Conflict, Business and the Sino-American relationship in the Global system', *e-International Relations*, 10 March 2010. www.e-ir.info/?p=3420 (accessed April 2010).

Karatzogianni, A. (2009a) Introduction: New media and the Reconfiguration of Power in Global Politics', in *Cyber Conflict and Global Politics*, edited by Athina Karatzogianni, Routledge Series Contemporary Security Studies, London and New York: Routledge.

Karatzogianni, A. (2009b) 'How small are small numbers in cyber space? Small, virtual, wannabe "states," minorities and their cyber conflicts', in *Cyber Conflict and Global Politics*, edited by Athina Karatzogianni. Routledge Series Contemporary Security Studies, London and New York: Routledge.

Karatzogianni, A. (2006) *The Politics of Cyber Conflict*, Routledge Research on Internet and Society. London and New York: Routledge.

Simons, G. (2010) *Mass Media and Modern Warfare: Reporting on the Russian War on Terrorism*, Surrey: Ashgate.

Zhang, J. and Fahmy, S. 'Color Revolutions in Colored Lenses: A Comparative Analysis of USA and Russian Press Coverage of Political Movements in Ukraine, Belarus and Uzbekistan', *International Journal of Communication* 3 (2009), 517–39.

Index of internet sources

[All articles were last accessed 10–17 May 2010]

AFP (13 November 2009) EU satellite centre to monitor Georgia rebel zones: official', at www.reliefweb.int/rw/rwb.nsf/db900SID/SNAA-7XU7T9?OpenDocument.

Asia Computers (31 March 2010) 'Russian hackers embarrass Microsoft', at http://asia-computers.com/russian-hackers-embarrass-microsoft/.

Austin, G. (10 January 2010) 'NATO and the 'Evil Cyber Empire': Surprising Futures!' *New Europe*, at www.neurope.eu/articles/98357.php.

Backwell, B. (7 December 2009) 'Pachauri condemns hackers attempt to 'discredit' IPCC', at www.rechargenews.com/business_area/politics/article200932.ece.

Barley, S. (7 December 2009) 'Climategate: Russian secret service blamed for hack'. *New Scientist*, at www.newscientist.com/blogs/shortsharpscience/2009/12/since-over-1000-confidential-e.html.

Barratt, J. (25 April 2010) 'Facebook hacker claims to be in NZ', *New Zealand Herald*, at www.nzherald.co.nz/connect/news/article.cfm?c_id=1501833&objectid=10640757.

Barrett, L. (17 March 2010) 'Russian hackers manipulated stock prices: SEC', at www.internetnews.com/security/article.php/3871201/Russian-Hackers-Manipulated-Stock-Prices-SEC.htm.

Barry, E. (23 February 2010) 'Washington sends delegation to Moscow, via Silicon Valley', *The New York Times*, at www.nytimes.com/2010/02/24/world/europe/24russia.html.

BBC News (14 April 2010) 'No malpractice' by practice', at http://news.bbc.co.uk/1/hi/sci/tech/8618024.stm.

Belot, L. and Stroobants, J.-P. (17 June 2007) 'Les Temps des cyber guerres', *Le Monde*, at www.lemonde.fr/web/article/0,1–0,36–924253,0.html.

Bentley, E. (14 December 2009) 'Were Russians hackers behind Climategate?' *Moscow News*, at www.mn.ru/interview/20091214/55397385.html.

Booker, C. (17 April 2010) 'Climategate: A scandal that won't go away', *Telegraph*, at www.telegraph.co.uk/comment/columnists/christopherbooker/7601929/Climategate-a-scandal-that-wont-go-away.html.

Cavanaugh, T. (26 January 2010) 'Not with a bang but a twitter: Interwebs bring new dark ages', at http://reason.com/blog/2010/01/26/not-with-a-bang-but-a-twitter.

Central European University. Participants' reflections on workshop themes. 'Cyber security: Europe and the Global Society Revisited: Developing a network of scholars and agenda for social science research on cyber security', *Budapest Hungary*, 7–8 June 2010, at http://ww.cmcs.ceu.hu/cybersecurity/main.

Charles the moderator (23 November 2009) 'The CRUtape Letters™, an Alternative Explanation', at http://wattsupwiththat.com/2009/11/23/the-crutape-letters®-an-alternate-explanation/.

Cheek, M. (2 March 2010) 'What is Cyber war anyway? A conversation with Jeff Carr, author of Inside Cyber Warfare', at www.thenewnewinternet. com/2010/03/02/what-is-cyberwar-anyway-a-conversation-with-jeff-carr-author-of-inside-cyber-warfare/.

Civil.Ge. (5 December 2009) 'Lavrov: 'Georgia Armament serious problem', at www.civil.ge/eng/article.php/article.php?id=21754.

Computer Fraud and Abuse Act, 18 U.S.C. 1030, at http://www4.law.cornell.edu/uscode/18/1030.html.

Connor, S. (1 February 2010) 'Climate e-mails hacked by spies', *Independent*, at www.independent.co.uk/environment/climate-change/climate-e-mails-hacked-by-spies-1885147.html.

Cosgrove, M. (10 February 2010) 'The Great Climate debate commits suicide', at www.fleshandstone.net/commentary/1759.html.

Council of Europe. (23 November 2001) Convention on Cyber Crime, Budapest, at http://conventions.coe.int/Treaty/EN/Treaties/Html/185.htm.

Crosley, K. (23 December 2009) 'Did Russian hackers attack Citibank?' *Business Computing World*, at www.businesscomputingworld.co.uk/did-russian-hackers-attack-citibank-also-top-banking-information-security-threats-and-a-great-security-resource/.

Deutsche Presse-Agentur (4 December 2009) 'NATO urges Georgia to improve ties with neighbouring countries', at www.india-server.com/news/nato-urges-georgia-to-improve-ties-with-17329.html.

Earthtimes (14 April 2010) 'Medvedev proposes 'text messages' diplomacy', at www.earthtimes.org/articles/show/318749,medvedev-proposes-text-message-diplomacy–summary.html.

Eshel, D. (10 February 2010) 'Israel adds cyber-attack to IDF', *Military.com*, at www.military.com/features/0,15240,210486,00.html.

Etengoff, A. (21 November 2009) 'Hackers steal confidential global warming data', at www.tgdaily.com/security-features/44763-hackers-steal-confidential-global-warming-data.

EUbusiness (11 December 2009) 'EU calls on Russia to pull out of disputed Georgian village', at www.eubusiness.com/news-eu/georgia-russia.1x3.

Evron, G. (11 August 2008) 'Internet Attacks Against Georgian Websites', *CircleID*, at www.circleid.com/posts/88116_Internet_attacks_georgia.

Freeguide (1 April 2010) 'Windows phone 7 managed to be installed on HTC HD2', at www.freeguide.me/web/windows-phone-7.

Findlay, R. (14 March 2010) 'Royal Bank of Scotland raiders' huge £6m haul in just 12 hours', at www.dailyrecord.co.uk/news/business-news/2010/03/14/royal-bank-of-scotland-raiders-huge-6m-haul-in-12-hours-86908–22110087/.

FoxNews (21 November 2009) 'Climate skeptics see 'smoking gun' in researchers' leaked e-mails', at www.foxnews.com/scitech/2009/11/21/climate-skeptics-smoking-gun-researchers-leaked-e-mails/.

Gardham, D. (4 December 2009) 'Cold war enemies Russia and China launch a cyber attack every day', *Telegraph*, at www.telegraph.co.uk/technology/news/6727100/Cold-war-enemies-Russia-and-China-launch-a-cyber-attack-every-day.html.

Georgian Times (14 April 2009) 'Nauru may recognise South Ossetia's independence', at www.geotimes.ge/index.php?m=home&newsid=19592.

Gillis, Justin. (7 July 2010) 'British Panel Clears Scientists', *New York Times*, at www.nytimes.com/2010/07/08/science/earth/08climate.html?_r=1.

Goble, P. (28 November 2009) 'Moscow might have lost North Caucasus if it hadn't aided South Ossetia, former CPSU official says', at http://georgiandaily. com/index.php?option=com_content&task=view&id=15833&Itemid=65.

Goble, P. (31 May 2007) 'Window on Eurasia: FSB encourages, guides Russia's 'Hacker-Patriots', at http://windowoneurasia.blogspot.com/2007/05/window-on-eurasia-fsb-encourages-guides.html.

Goodin, D. (18 August 2009) 'Georgian cyber attacks launched by Russian crime gangs', *The Register*, at www.theregister.co.uk/2009/08/18/georgian_cyber_ attacks/.

Goodin, D. (25 November 2009) 'Climate change hackers leave breadcrumb trail', at www.theregister.co.uk/2009/11/25/cru_climate_hack_identity/.

Halpin, T. (7 December 2009) 'Is Russia behind the Climategate hackers?', *Times Online*, at www.timesonline.co.uk/tol/news/environment/article6946385.ece.

Harding, L. (27 January 2010) 'Alexander Lebedev sells Aeroflot and air-leasing stakes for $575m', *Guardian*, at www.guardian.co.uk/media/2010/jan/27/lebedev-sells-aeroflot-stake.

Harvey, F. (5 December 2009) 'E-mail scandal dominates debate on rail road to Copenhagen', *Financial Times blogs*, at http://blogs.ft.com/energy-source/2009/ 12/05/email-scandal-dominates-debate-on-rail-road-to-copenhagen/.

Hawkins, A. (7 April 2010) '3 year for hacker who ripped off Charles Schwab accounts', *Forbes blogs*, at http://blogs.forbes.com/moneybuilder/2010/04/07/3-year-sentence-for-hacker-who-ripped-off-charles-schwab-accounts/.

Heickero, R. (March 2010) 'Emerging cyber threats and Russian views on information warfare and information operations', Swedish Defence Research Agency, Defence Analysis, at www.foi.se.

Hickman, L. and Randerson, J. (20 November 2009) 'Climate sceptics leaked emails are evidence of collusion among scientists', *Guardian*, at www.guardian. co.uk/environment/2009/nov/20/climate-sceptics-hackers-leaked-emails.

Hoffman, S. (4 March 2010) 'RSA: Security expert says USA is already engaged in cyber war', *CRN*, at www.crn.com/security/223101637;jsessionid=34XLIZKR4BA 4VQE1GHOSKHWATMY32JVN.

House of Commons (24 March 2010). 'Science and Technology Committee–Eighth Report. The disclosure of climate data from the Climatic Research Unit at the University of East Anglia', at www.publications.parliament.uk/pa/ cm200910/cmselect/cmsctech/387/38702.htm.

Hurlbut, T. (20 November 2009) 'CRU files scandal reaches print media', *The Examiner*, at www.examiner.com/x-28973-Essex-County-Conservative-Examiner~y2009m 11d20-CRU-files-scandal-reaches-print-media.

Immunet (27 April 2010) 'Beware of hackers 'liking your profile too much: Facebook changes call for user vigilance', at http://blog.immunet.com/blog/2010/4/27/ beware-of-hackers-liking-your-profile-too-much-facebook-chan.html.

ITComputerzone (9 August 2009) 'Russian hackers accused mastermind of attacks Twitter', at http://itcomputerzone.com/internet/russian-hackers-accused-mastermind-of-attacks-twitter.html.

Johnson, B. (16 April 2009) 'No one is ready for this', *Guardian*, at www.guardian. co.uk/technology/2009/apr/16/internet-hacking-cyber-war-nato.

Johnson, K. (8 December 2009) 'Climate: Whodunnit?' *Wall Street Journal Blogs*, at http://blogs.wsj.com/environmentalcapital/2009/12/08/climategate-whodunnit/.

Johnson, K. (30 November 2009) 'Climategate: The fallout continues from CRU hacking', at http://blogs.wsj.com/environmentalcapital/2009/11/30/climategate-the-fallout-continues-from-cru-hacking/tab/article/.

Judge, P. (7 December 2009) 'Russia accused of Climategate hack', *E-Week Europe*, at www.eweekeurope.co.uk/news/news-security/russia-accused-of-climategate-hack-2674.

Kaplun, A. (5 March 2010) 'E-Mails Show Scientists Planning Push-Back Against 'McCarthyite' Attacks on Climate Science', *New York Times*, at www.nytimes.com/gwire/2010/03/05/05greenwire-e-mails-show-scientists-planning-push-back-aga-33296.html.

Keizer, G. (7 April 2010) 'Botnets 'the Swiss Army knife of attack tools', at www.computerworld.com/s/article/9174560/Botnets_the_Swiss_Army_knife_of_attack_tools_.

Khashig, R. and Ponomarev, S. (13 December 2009) 'Abkhaz election again pits Russia against Georgia', at www.etaiwannews.com/etn/news_content.php?id=1131528&lang=eng_news&cate_img=logo_world&cate_rss=WORLD_eng.

Kiguradze, T. (13 November 2009) 'Public debates on the war report in Tbilisi', *The Messenger Online*, at www.messenger.com.ge/issues/1982_november_13_2009/1982_temo.html.

Kolasinski, T. 4 (December 2009) 'An inconvenient hoax', *The Daily Evergreen Online*, at www.dailyevergreen.com/story/31800.

Korns, S. W. and Kastenberg, J. E. (2009) 'Georgia's cyber left hook', *Parameters*: 38.4: 60–76, USA Army War College, at www.carlisle.army.mil/usawc/Parameters/08winter/korns.pdf.

Kvelashvili, G. (5 February 2010) 'Georgia's Arduous Attempt to Challenge Moscow's Broadcasting Monopoly', *Eurasia Daily Monitor*, Volume: 7 Issue: 25, at www.jamestown.org/single/?no_cache=1&tx_ttnews%5Btt_news%5D=36017&tx_ttnews%5BbackPid%5D=7&cHash=30ac2d2fad.

Leigh, D., Arthur, C. and Evans, R. (4 February 2010a) 'Detectives question climate change scientist over e-mail leaks', *Guardian*, at www.guardian.co.uk/environment/2010/feb/04/climate-change-email-hacking-leaks.

Leigh, D., Arthur, C. and Evans, R. (4 February 2010b) 'Climate e-mails: were they really hacked or just sitting in cyber space?' *Guardian*, at www.guardian.co.uk/environment/2010/feb/04/climate-change-email-hacker-police-investigation.

Le Page, M. (4 December 2009) 'Why there is no sign of a climate conspiracy in hacked e-mails', *New Scientist*, at www.newscientist.com/article/dn18238-why-theres-no-sign-of-a-climate-conspiracy-in-hacked-emails.html.

Levsen, L. (7 December 2009) 'Comprehensive network analysis shows Climategate likely to be a leak', at http://wattsupwiththat.com/2009/12/07/comprhensive-network-analysis-shows-climategate-likely-to-be-a-leak/.

Leyden, J. (12 April 2010) 'Russian trade body aims to fight cyber crime', *The Register*, at www.theregister.co.uk/2010/04/12/russia_cybercrime_feature/.

Lyden, J. (13 October 2009) 'Polish government cyber attack blamed on Russia', *The Register*, at www.theregister.co.uk/2009/10/13/poland_cyberattacks/.

Loginof.com (18 February 2010) 'Famous researcher talks about Internet in Russia', at http://loginof.com/2010/02/famous-researcher-talks-about-internet-in-russia/.

Loyd, A. (8 March 2010) 'Britain applies military thinking to the growing spectre of cyber war', at http://technology.timesonline.co.uk/tol/news/tech_and_web/article7053270.ece.

Macdonald, C. (13 April 2010) 'FBI agent visits Monterey Trail High', *Elk Grove Citizen*, at www.egcitizen.com/articles/2010/04/13/news/doc4bc4fe6887a 33275902281.txt.

MacNicol, G. (7 December 2009) 'Are Russian hackers responsible for creating Climategate?', at www.mediaite.com/online/are-russian-hackers-responsible-for-creating-climategate/.

Magnuson, S. (May 2010) 'Russian Cyber thief case illustrates security risks for U.S. corporations', at www.nationaldefensemagazine.org/archive/2010/May/Pages/RussianCyberthiefCaseIllustratesSecurityRisks.aspx.

McCarthy, M. and Owen, J. (6 December 2009) 'Climate change conspiracies: Stolen e-mails used to ridicule global warming', *Independent*, at www.independent.co.uk/environment/climate-change/climate-change-conspiracies-stolen-emails-used-to-ridicule-global-warming-1835031.html.

McIntyre, D. (22 December 2009) 'FBI says Russian hackers hit Citigroup for tens of millions', *Daily Finance*, 22 December 2009, at www.dailyfinance.com/story/fbi-says-russian-hackers-hit-citigroup-for-tens-of-millions/19290466/.

McMillan, R. (29 January 2010) 'Stolen Twitter accounts can fetch $1,000', at www.computerworld.com/s/article/9150001/Stolen_Twitter_accounts_can_fetch_1_000.

Megerisi, H. (22 March 2010) 'Russia arrests $9million cash machine hackers', at www.pcpro.co.uk/news/security/356617/russia-arrests-9-million-cash-machine-hackers.

Merchant, B. (7 December 2009) 'Ex-KGB officers may be the hackers behind ClimateGate', *Treehugger*, at www.treehugger.com/files/2009/12/ex-kgb-officers-hackers-climategate.php.

Mills, E. (10 November 2009) 'Eastern Europeans charged in payment processor hack', *CNET News*, at http://news.cnet.com/8301-27080_3-10394558-245.html.

Morozov, E. (14 August 2008) 'An Army of Ones and Zeroes: How I Became a Soldier in the Georgia-Russia Cyber war', *Slate.com*, at www.slate.com/id/2197514.

Newton, P. (11 December 2009) 'Tracking down the 'Climategate' hackers', *CNN*, at. http://edition.cnn.com/2009/WORLD/europe/12/11/hacking.emails.climate.skeptics/index.html.

Nichols, S. (25 January 2008) 'First hacker convicted for Estonia attacks', at www.v3.co.uk/vnunet/news/2208059/first-hacker-convicted-estonia.

Parker, J. (27 November 2009)'Climategate debunked', *The Examiner*, at www.examiner.com/x-29137-Tallahassee-Environmental-News-Examiner~y2009m11d27-Climategate-debunked.

Pearce, F. (24 November 2009) 'Hacked archive provides fodder for climate sceptics', at www.newscientist.com/article/dn18192-hacked-archive-provides-fodder-for-climate-sceptics.html.

Pearce, F. (9 February 2010a) 'Search for hacker may lead police back to East Anglia's climate research unit', *Guardian*, at www.guardian.co.uk/environment/2010/feb/09/hacked-emails-police-investigation.

Pearce, F. (9 February 2010b) 'How the "climategate" scandal is bogus and based on climate sceptics' lies', *Guardian*, at www.guardian.co.uk/environment/2010/feb/09/climategate-bogus-sceptics-lies.

Periscope it. (3 February 2003) 'Hacker attack takes Russian newspaper offline for days', at www.periscopeit.co.uk/website-monitoring-news/article/hacker-attack-takes-russian-newspaper-offline-for-days/594.

Petro, N. (13 November 2009) 'Russia is miscast in the Georgian tragedy', at www. opednews.com/populum/diarypage.php?did=14946 [questions prepared by Saylor Company, a USA public relations firm employed by the governments of Abkhazia and South Ossetia].

PINewswire (12 March 2010) 'New Blackenergy Trojan targeting Russian, Ukrainian banks', at www.pinewswire.net/2010/03/new-blackenergy-trojan-targeting-russian-ukrainian-banks/.

Poulsen, K. (22 August 2007) 'Cyber war' and Estonia's panic attack', *Wired*, at www.wired.com/threatlevel/2007/08/cyber-war-and-e/.

RA-10 Inquiry Report (3 February 2010) 'Concerning the Allegations of Research Misconduct Against Dr. Michael E. Mann', Department of Meteorology, College of Earth and Mineral Sciences, The Pennsylvania State University, at www. research.psu.edu/orp/Findings_Mann_Inquiry.pdf.

Radio New Zealand News (6 December 2009) 'UN defends scientists over leaked e-mails', at www.infowars.com/un-defends-scientists-over-leaked-emails/.

Rainsford, S. (11 March 2010) 'Inside the mind of a Russian hacker', *BBC*, at http://news.bbc.co.uk/1/hi/8561910.stm.

Ravilious, K. (8 December 2009) 'Hacked e-mail climate scientists receive death threats', *The Guardian*, at www.guardian.co.uk/environment/2009/dec/08/hacked-climate-emails-death-threats.

Raywood, D. (9 March 2010) 'Colorado bank locks down debit cards after links made to Heartland breach', *SCMagazine*, at www.scmagazineuk.com/colorado-bank-locks-down-debit-cards-after-links-made-to-heartland-breach/article/165338/.

Reuters (2 December 2009) 'Georgia releases Ossetians in likely prisoner swap', at www.reuters.com/article/idUSATRE5B122Q20091202.

Reuters (12 March 2010) 'NATO chief tries to quell E.Europe's security fears', at www.khaleejtimes.com/DisplayArticle08.asp?xfile=data/international/2010/March/international_March499.xml&section=international.

RiaNovosti (3 December 2009) 'Russian envoy optimistic over joint threat assessment with NATO', at http://en.rian.ru/russia/20091203/157089431.html.

Rozoff, R. (26 May 2010) 'USA Cyber Command: Waging War in World's Fifth Battlespace', at http://rickrozoff.wordpress.com/2010/05/26/u-s-cyber-command-waging-war-in-worlds-fifth-battlespace/.

RT (8 January 2010) 'Global hacker threat comes from Russia?', at http://rt.com/Top_News/2010-01-08/global-hacker-threat-russia.html.

RT (25 November 2009) 'Global Warming: Leaked 'Climate Fraud' e-mails under probe', at http://rt.com/Top_News/2009-11-25/hackers-global-warming-scandal.html.

RT (14 November 2009) 'Anti-Russian propaganda on Georgian TV channel', at http://rt.com/Top_News/2009-11-14/anti-russian-propaganda-georgia.html.

RT (19 February 2008) 'Russia named 'spam superpower', at http://rt.com/Business/2008-02-19/Russia_named_spam_superpower_.html.

Secrest, B. (29 April 2010) 'Cyber Crime: Russian hackers threaten the world', at www.conservativerefocus.com/blog5.php/2010/04/29/cyber-crime-russian-hackers-threaten-the-world.

Shackelford, S. J. 'Estonia two-and-a-half years later: A progress report on combating cyber attacks', *Journal of Internet Law*, forthcoming, at http://papers.ssrn.com/sol3/papers.cfm?abstract_id=1499849.

Sheppard, N. (11 December 2009) 'Scientist uses UN security to stop questions about ClimateGate', at http://newsbusters.org/blogs/noel-sheppard/2009/12/11/climategater-uses-un-security-halt-questions-about-scandal.

Sheppard, N. (26 November 2009) 'CNN FINALLY reports ClimateGate – To downplay it of course', at http://newsbusters.org/blogs/noel-sheppard/2009/11/26/russian-tv-does-better-job-reporting-climategate-cnn.

Simmons, A. (30 April 2010) 'Facebook probes password hackings', *ABC News*, at www.abc.net.au/news/stories/2010/04/30/2887235.htm.

Slideshare. (n.d.) 'Whos Hacking Your Pc?' , at www.slideshare.net/vbdotnetnrew/whos-hacking-your-pc.

Smith, M. and Warren, P. (6 June 2010) 'NATO warns of strike against cyber attackers', *The Sunday Times*, at www.timesonline.co.uk/tol/news/world/article7144856.ece?

Snapple (7 January 2010) 'Tomsk hackers Part III: FBI investigating death threats against global warming scientists', at http://legendofpineridge.blogspot.com/2010/01/tomsk-hackers-part-iii-fbi.html.

Snapple (21 March 2010) 'The BBC interviews of a reformed hacker', at http://legendofpineridge.blogspot.com/2010/03/bbc-interviews-reformed-russian-hacker.html.

Softpedia 'Mastermind Behind the RBS WorldPay Hit Arrested in Russia', at http://news.softpedia.com/news/Mastermind-Behind-the-RBS-WorldPay-Hit-Arrested-in-Russia-138240.shtml.

Spamfighter News (12 March 2010) 'BlackEnergy Trojan attacks Russian, Ukrainian banks on new version', at www.spamfighter.com/News-14021-BlackEnergy-Trojan-Attacks-Russian-Ukrainian-Banks-in-New-Version.htm.

Spamfighter News (5 January 2010) 'Russian hacker could face imprisonment of 17–25 years', at www.spamfighter.com/News-13697-Russian-Hacker-Could-Face-Imprisonment-of-17–25-Years.htm.

Spamfighter News (10 March 2010) 'Legally designed cloud computing used for malicious purposes', at http://spamnews.com/The-News/Latest/Legally-Designed-Cloud-Computing-Used-for-Malicious-Purposes-2010031012686/.

Spamfighter News (16 April 2010) 'Botnets, Hackers' instant attack weapons', at www.spamfighter.com/News-14215-Botnets-Hackers-Instant-Attack-Weapons.htm.

Stack, Megan (17 March 2010) 'Russian secrets for sale, no questions asked', *LA Times*, at http://articles.latimes.com/2010/mar/17/world/la-fg-secrets-for-sale17-2010mar17.

Stewart, W. and Delgado, M. (6 December 2009) 'Were Russian security services behind the leak of "Climategate" e-mails?', at www.climateark.org/shared/reader/welcome.aspx?linkid=144998&keybold=climate%20AND%20%20deal%20AND%20%20post%20AND%20%20Kyoto.

Streetwise Professor (SWP) (8 December 2009) 'In which SWP actually defends the FSB', at http://streetwiseprofessor.com/?p=3022.

Takahashi, D. (17 March 2010) 'SINET event draws feds and security entrepreneurs together', *VentureBeat*, at http://venturebeat.com/2010/03/17/sinet-event-draws-feds-and-security-entrepreneurs-together/.

Taylor, M. and Arthur, C. (27 November 2009) 'Climate e-mail hackers had access for more than a month', *Guardian*, at www.guardian.co.uk/environment/2009/nov/27/climate-email-hackers-access-month.

Telegraph (6 December 2009) 'Climategate: was Russian secret service behind email hacking plot?', at www.telegraph.co.uk/earth/copenhagen-climate-change-confe/6746370/Climategate-was-Russian-secret-service-behind-email-hacking-plot.html.

Thomson, I. (22 March 2010) 'Russia and USA working together to shut down stock hacker', at www.securecomputing.net.au/News/170201,russia-and-us-working-together-to-shut-down-stock-hacker.aspx.

Thomson, I. (27 September 2007) 'Estonia attacks down to online mob', at www.v3.co.uk/vnunet/news/2199732/estonia-attack-online-flashmob.

Tynan, D. (26 April 2010) 'Your Facebook profile may be sold by Russian hacker', at www.pcworld.com/article/195005/your_facebook_profile_may_be_sold_by_russian_hacker.html.

UNCHR. (16 February 2009) 'Attacks on the Press 2009 – Georgia', Refworld, at www.unhcr.org/refworld/country,,,,GEO,,4b7bc2e82d,0.html.

USA Department of State. (29 September 2006) 'United States Joins Council of Europe Convention on Cyber crime', press statement, at www.state.gov/r/pa/prs/ps/2006/73353.htm.

Villeneuve, N. (10 April 2010) 'Blurring the boundaries between cyber crime and politically motivated attacks', at www.nartv.org/2010/04/10/blurring-the-boundaries-between-cybercrime-and-politicaly-motivated-attacks/.

Walker, S. (7 December 2009) 'Was Russian secret service behind leak of climate-change e-mails?' *Independent*, at www.independent.co.uk/news/world/europe/was-russian-secret-service-behind-leak-of-climatechange-emails-1835502.html.

Watts, A. (6 December 2009) 'Media now blaming Russians for Climategate leak', at http://wattsupwiththat.com/2009/12/06/media-now-blaming-russians-for-climategate-leak/.

Weinberger, S. (14 May 2010) 'Hackers are Internet Shock troops', *Aviation Week*, at www.aviationweek.com/aw/generic/story_channel.jsp?channel=defense&id=news/dti/2010/05/01/DT_05_01_2010_p19–218221.xml&headline=Hackers%20Are%20Internet%20Shock%20Troops.

Werz, M. and Manlove, K. (9 December 2009) 'Climate migration will affect the world's security', at www.truthout.org/topstories/120909sg02.

Wilson, R. (7 May 2010) 'Cyber security is a worldwide imperative', *The Bulletin*, at http://thebulletin.us/articles/2010/02/10/business/doc4b72565659bf0979208886.txt.

Yribarren, B. (9 February 2010) 'Status update: College publisher hacked!', at www.coscampusonline.com/status-update-college-publisher-hacked-1.2145417.

Zetter, K. (22 March 2010) 'Russia arrests alleged mastermind of RBS WorldPay hack', *Wired*, at www.wired.com/threatlevel/2010/03/alleged-rbs-hacker-arrested/.

Zimmer, C. (6 December 2009) 'George Will: Uncheckable?' *Discover Magazine blogs*, at http://blogs.discovermagazine.com/loom/2009/12/06/george-will-uncheckable/.

Part V
Through the gender studies lens

15 Making the pain count

Embodied politics in the new age of terror

Gillian Youngs

> ...go to the theatre if you want catharsis, go to literature, don't go to the camps. Nothing comes out of the camps. Nothing.
> (Words of the daughter of a holocaust survivor towards the end of the film
> *The Reader* – Hare 2008)

Introduction: pain and embodied politics

Where does pain go, politically speaking? How does the force of it drain out of the public sphere? How could it be different, and what are the conceptual and theoretical tools that might help it to be so? These are the kinds of questions at the heart of this contribution and the term 'heart' is used here in a deliberate sense. For, as we all know the heart is the symbolic reference for the worlds of feeling, emotion and sentiment; areas it will be argued here that are generally absent from the politics of the public sphere and thus their capacities to engage (or not) with the realm of human pain, its implications, and its links to the darker side of humanity, human interactions and destinies. Analytically, the addressing of an absence is self evidently much more challenging than the addressing of a presence. This discussion aims to shed some light on that problematic.

The title of the piece – making the pain count – sets out a problematic that confronts us in political analysis and one that the war on terror, now perhaps more accurately referred to as the new age of terror, has illuminated from diverse perspectives and standpoints. It is in part this diversity and its reach, socio-economically, culturally and geopolitically, that, I argue, has made it hard to turn away from the theme of pain. For when there are so many, from such extended and contrasting communities and locations, who have suffered and suffer still from the direct and indirect impacts of an amorphous state of terror, and wars and their aftermath related closely and loosely to it, the realities of pain not only seem, to some extent, all encompassing and inescapable, but also insistent and overwhelming. While this is far from a unique state of affairs, in fact quite the reverse, as my opening quote suggests (and more on that below), its ubiquitous relevance in space and time is an intrinsic part of its potency as a subject that demands our attention, that persists no matter how much we might try to ignore it, turn away from it, or leave its absence from mainstream political public sphere preoccupations to endure.

This is where the thread of memory becomes important, because it is a carrier of many connections related to the human experience of time and space. It makes the links between past and present, reminds us of how deeply the past lives in the present, how the present re-shapes the past including as it remembers, re-remembers, distorts, recreates and allows to fade away. While memory is both public and private, comes in many public and private forms, its individual as well as collective components and characteristics are always interacting (Radstone and Schwartz 2010). Memory is embodied literally, not only because of its relationship to lives lived and the direct consciousness of them and their distinctions and significance over time and space, but because while frequently mediated by images and words, by public narratives and representations of different kinds, the translation of all these into an individual's particular memory is a highly personal process (Misztal 2003; Radstone and Hodgkin 2003; Neiger *et al.* forthcoming 2011).

This discussion addresses memory in perhaps an unusual way, in that it is preoccupied with the memory that may or may not be contemporaneously in the making. In some regards, this may seem a contradiction in terms, because how can we know about memory in advance as it were. The hypothesis this exploration considers relates directly to such a point. In looking at the connections across pain, embodied politics and memory and examining how these may be disrupted by the current disembodied state of the public sphere, the analysis that follows probes how memory may be prevented, distorted or restricted. So this is an engagement that looks to the future from the present in the context of memory studies (Grosz 1999). Its points hopefully shed light on what may not be remembered to political effect, why this might be the case and what some of the implications may be.

Three areas are considered. The first relates to the problem of disembodiment in public sphere politics and the many contributions of feminist analysis especially in the field of political studies and international relations to uncovering manifestations and results of this disembodiment. The second considers the relationship of this disembodied state of affairs to the absence of pain as politically meaningful and ways in which this might be addressed. Arguments are presented here that link disembodiment to 'pain as an absence' in public sphere politics, the result being distorted political memory along lines that reflect this absence. The third area focuses on the possibilities for radical transformation of this situation and the importance of the dimension of memory for enabling the revisiting and reclaiming of the past in the interests of a less painful present and future. The multiple threads of pain over space and time and their connections to one another and mirroring of one another are central here.

Disembodied politics and the new age of terror

When we talk about gender in the context of the public sphere the sense of what is being referred to all too frequently degenerates into reductive notions about male and female, men and women. While these binaries of gender are in play in feminist analysis its specific focus operates at complex structural and historically embedded levels (Walby 1990; Pettman 1996; Peterson 2003). It is useful to provide some clarifications on this before specifically addressing the area of disembodiment. When referring to feminist analysis, distinctions can be made across feminist theory, feminist politics and concrete gender inequalities. While many of these distinctions should be obvious, highlighting them can be helpful to achieve a clear starting point.

The first represents a body of theoretical work stretching back in time, which has many dimensions and approaches, crosses many disciplines and subjects, and has its own riches, tensions and complexities. The second area, as it is adopted here, refers largely to the realm of feminist practice in political regards, across different contexts and settings, whether at the individual or collective levels, local, national or global. This again has a long history and many contemporary variants including in global women's movements. There are linkages between feminist theory and feminist politics, and while the latter is likely to be dependent on the former, the former can be assessed for its analytical purchase without necessarily implicating the latter. For example, feminist theory can be applied to help identify the third area, concrete gender inequalities, without necessarily engaging feminist politics to address them. It is worth stressing in relation to this third area that, whether we think in terms of feminist theory or feminist politics or not, it is an area of concrete reality. Those who choose to deny the relevance of feminist theory, or feminist politics, cannot deny the existence of gender inequalities across economic, political and cultural circumstances (Human Rights and Equalities Commission 2008; Walby 2009).

While this chapter relates to all three areas, feminist theory, feminist politics and gender inequalities, its main preoccupation is the first, and to a lesser extent the second. There is a long history of feminist theory addressing the partial nature of the public sphere constructed primarily in terms of masculinist power, identities, discourses and practices. *Public Man, Private Woman* (Elshtain 1993) is the apt and succinct title of a central text tracing the gendered construction of the political public sphere (see also Pateman 1988). The political environment has historically been theorised, articulated and developed in mainstream regards as dominated by male power and influence, and this remains largely the case despite the growing presence and influence of women. The following comment by the Human Rights and Equalities Commission (2008) neatly sums up the picture. 'A snail could crawl the entire length of the Great

Wall of China in 212 years, just slightly longer than the 200 years it will take for women to be equally represented in Parliament.' The lack of female presence and influence remains overwhelming with women holding just 11 per cent of FTSE 100 directorships and the Commission estimating that to achieve equality at the current rate of progress here and in the judiciary and civil service would take 73, 55 and 27 years respectively. Feminist theoretical analysis has focused on the implications of this profound absence of women, and women's influence, and the dominant male-centred theories that have articulated and rationalised it over history through to the present.

As Elshtain's title referred to above suggests, the whole nature of the public and politics has been constructed in a male frame, while the role and identities of women have been located on the opposite of the binary in the private. Thus, masculine and feminine identities have been locked into an oppositional frame, which is fundamentally abstract, and arguably ontologically and epistemologically reductive along specifically gendered lines. Such reductionism results in a disembodied political public sphere by denying humanity that is equally masculine and feminine as intrinsic to it. This is reified further by the mutually reinforcing sets of binaries, through which, masculinist politics operates, for example, man/woman, science/nature, rationality/irrationality, mind/body and intellect/ emotion. As feminist theoretical work has demonstrated, it is essential to probe the deeper gendered infrastructure underpinning the man/woman opposition to understand how gendered politics are configured (Youngs 2000). For, naturally, we are not talking about a static scenario, but one that is constantly in process and full of tensions, challenges and contradictions.

In simple terms, when we remove women and the feminine from the political public sphere as defining forces (alongside men and masculinity), we remove the sides of the binary associated with them – nature, irrationality, body and emotion, to take the illustrations above. The binaries themselves are false constructions in the way that they disaggregate human attributes, let alone the way they line them up in associated gendered patterns. But then ostensibly removing one whole half of the constructed picture takes the abstraction much further. We are left with a disembodied political public sphere, one which has humanity in any holistic sense emptied out of it and one that is partial in its construction of political economy, culture and society. This partiality is bound to be reflected in the form and scope of public sphere values and ethics, and their capacities to account for and make meaningful different factors. The abstractions and reductionism discussed here have practical implications for the very nature of the public sphere and its ethical potential and limitations, or the ways in which these might operate. It goes without saying that human experience is embodied as suicide bombing, war, torture, extraordinary rendition, detention without trial, all characteristic of the new age of terror, graphically demonstrate. Pain in multiple physical and psychological senses is a feature of all these manifestations of terror and counter terror, but where is its political meaning and force?

Disembodiment and the absence of pain as politically meaningful

I would argue that a disembodied political public sphere inevitably leads to one that ontologically and epistemologically cannot easily account for, and therefore, make meaningful the phenomenon of pain. Further, I would argue that the new age of terror has illustrated this problem on a grand scale and from multiple perspectives related to all sides of the terror, whether those who are perpetrating it, or those working to combat it. In the light of this, making pain politically meaningful could be argued as one of the most pressing challenges to arise out of the new age of terror, although for the reasons I have outlined above, it does not generally appear on mainstream agendas. The disembodied construction of public sphere politics ensures that this does not happen. The binary walls built around the public and the private make sure that human experience is abstracted within and across them. Human experience is thus in certain senses broken apart and disaggregated, so that its holistic fullness cannot easily be accessed in political terms.

The question of accessibility is particularly interesting in relation to the media saturation of the new age of terror (Hoskins and O'Loughlin 2010). Never have we been surrounded by so much news and commentary on pain, not only through traditional mass media outlets, but 24-hour news coverage and diverse (established and new) forms of online sources including interactive debates on social media and primary sources such as soldier blogs. The plethora of horizontal or bottom-up sources, that the new online informational environment facilitates, is an important aspect related to the political public sphere. We see an expansion of public sphere debate way beyond just the top-down few to many print and broadcast outlets, to include ever expanding horizontal forms where the experience of this new age of terror is shared. In addition, to the secondary media reporting that has historically dominated the political public sphere, we now have ever increasing primary material direct from actors of all kinds, including terrorists and their supporters, soldiers and their families, organisations for and against war, politicians and citizens in general (Karatzogianni 2009).

> The proliferation of new media technologies renders more of life matter to be recorded, disseminated and debated on near-instantaneous and deterritorialised scales. Hence, we now live in a 'new media ecology' in which people, events and news media have

become increasingly connected and interpenetrated through the technological compressions of time-space.

(Hoskins and O'Loughlin 2010: 18)

In this new interactive world of communication, perspectives on the pain
suffered because of terror and counter-terror activities have never been
more numerous or more accessible. Experiences and images of pain are
reported and commented on, shared and made available via traditional
media and new media forms and platforms, in multiple ways, which have
never previously been possible. It is relatively easy to access a whole range
of viewpoints and debates on the same incident, including across different
national settings. The amounts of primary and secondary data on pain in
the new age of terror are not only at record levels in historical context, but
also expanding all the time. This makes the questions addressed in this
chapter all the more pertinent and urgent, not least with the reams of
reporting on the 7/7 London bombings inquest prominent in the news at
the time of writing.

This reporting has not surprisingly had a distinctly embodied character
to it, with repeated graphic descriptions by those involved and the emergency personnel who assisted them of the terrible ordeals endured in dis-
covering and coping with major injuries and deaths. The power of the
memory of pain is completely fore-grounded in these reports and in
reading them one is drawn into the reliving of the past in the present, as
the individuals recount what happened from their different viewpoints
and experiences. As with all such recounting it is clear how much the past
does actually live in the present, not only through the lives of individuals
and their own specific narratives, but in major events such as a bombing
and the extent to which this is a shared experience with wide impact. The
public documenting of this, substantially contributed to by the media, is
intrinsic to the memory process, but as I asked at the beginning of this
chapter: what happens to this pain? It enters the political public sphere,
but almost seems to dissipate in political terms as soon as it arises. Why
does it not achieve some major political purchase?

I would argue that the disembodied character of mainstream politics, as
explained above, makes it very difficult for this to happen. The disembodied political public sphere, and its 'othering' of pain as something that sits
outside of it, configure political process and agency to mirror such exclu-
sions. Essentially, pain becomes a private, rather than a public matter, and
it is important to understand this in ontological and epistemological
terms. Such understanding allows us to see how memory is central over
time and space. Billions of bodies, dead, injured and tortured, civilian,
combatants and terrorists, litter the history of humanity, but the tendency
of mainstream politics is to reduce these to (rational) statistics rather than
to probe the real human toll, including in relation to the pain of it all. For
the kind of disembodied political public sphere I have described does not

ontologically or epistemologically account for, or accept, pain within its realm of (public) meaning. The generation of such meaning becomes either impossible or at the very least deeply challenging. Here, we need to concentrate too on the issue of process, because these problems cannot be understood in one-off event terms, but over time and across space. Too often, too little attention is paid to the binary process as dynamic and the concept of memory is potent in helping us to correct this. As I have highlighted, memories of pain have been and continue to be generated through history into the present. But the binary process ensures that as pain occurs, and is marked and remembered, it is othered in the political public sphere, and this is a process that continually repeats itself, as the mainstream disembodied character of this sphere is asserted again and again across time and space.

In the context of this process, political agency related to pain is hindered in ontological and epistemological terms and even, when it does arise, is likely to be treated as out of place and thus to struggle to have enduring impact. If we return here to the question of media saturation, there are two points that in particular are worth discussing with regard to agency. The first relates to the nature of the public sphere and the second to the new interactive horizontal dimensions of the online world. Traditional media play a major part in constructing the public sphere and for the most part will reflect the realities of mainstream politics. So, it might be argued all media saturation is likely to do predominantly is to embed those (disembodied) realities, rather than disrupt them, and this will be the case, whether that media saturation involves the coverage of embodied pain or not. No matter how much embodied pain is represented, it will always be othered in the political public sphere and the more that this othering occurs, the more it asserts the absence of embodied pain, as politically meaningful. Because this is a process that is repeated across time and space, the absence impacts on memory. Now it is clear, that the online interactive world of communication is stretching or disrupting the parameters of the public sphere, as perhaps the WikiLeaks phenomenon disseminating secret government documents related to the new age of terror and beyond demonstrates most starkly in recent times. It is worth thinking about whether the horizontality of new media over time, and the kinds of communication it facilitates, may increasingly enable political agency around areas such as pain, which are currently excluded. But the binary process I refer to can be expected to persist nevertheless, so such change may not be quick if it is possible at all. Furthermore, it draws our thinking to the question of how new media are increasingly becoming integrated into public sphere processes and will thus be a growing part of our thinking about the nature of the public sphere and the role of memory related to it (Garde-Hansen *et al.* 2009). Detailed discussion of this falls outside the scope of this particular chapter, but some relevant points are touched on in the next section that looks to the future.

Radical transformation: making pain count

A number of the areas I have already covered hint at the arguments I would present about the potential for radical transformation towards making pain count in political senses. Working towards a holistic political public sphere is fundamental. In terms of feminist politics this would involve much greater equality of diversity of all kinds in this sphere. But we do not have to wait for such equality to be achieved (bearing in mind the timeframes indicated earlier) to take on board the insights of feminist theory as I have set them out. The binary processes that constrain the nature of the political public sphere need to be overcome (Jónasdóttir and Jones 2009) so that the experience of pain is no longer othered and placed outside of its prime concerns, but is made central to them. This is arguably the only means by which pain can be made politically meaningful, in the ways that it is not now, and through this path contribute to politics that would be more actively and consistently directed towards reducing it in all forms, whether we are talking about domestic violence or war. This is a huge point, but as above, it is not the end point – important and optimistic as this is – that I want to concentrate on, but the process, because that is what counts in terms of there being possibilities to move towards such ends or not.

The constrained nature of the political public sphere I refer to in this chapter goes back through patriarchal theory and practice, through masculinist theory and politics, and the binary process across time and space has become embedded in long-term history across the different societies and cultures of the world in varied forms and with highly contrasting results. There are of course as many different political public spheres, as there are states and communities, and there are many distinctions across them, including in relation to some of the issues discussed here. However the broad-brush relevance of the major themes I have unpacked have sufficient general applicability to be worth taking seriously. This is the case in relation to the role of memory of the past as much as what is happening now and what may happen in the future because the connections across these are profound. As I have stressed, memory is not a static thing, it is constantly being remade whether we are thinking publicly or privately. Renewed framings of the political public sphere would not only have relevance to the present and future, but also to our capacities to learn in more potent ways from the past. Such moves would enable the reclaiming and revisiting of all kinds of histories related to pain, the generation of new analyses of them and political debates around them.

The new media environment has direct significance here, because of the extent to which, as already noted, its horizontal and interactive forms, can help to stretch and disrupt the familiar constraints of the public sphere. The multimedia power of the Internet is important when thinking about the possibilities of revisiting (and reclaiming) the past because the ability to combine the written and spoken word with diverse visual resources facilitates a richness of communication previously accessible in far less horizontal ways. The Internet is being used to make much more archive material available, including to the general public. But the implication of my arguments above is that it cannot be taken for granted, this will necessarily be productive politically, in terms of contributing to change. There are many ways in which the Internet is still primarily an informational sphere. In political terms, it is mostly adjacent to, and intersecting with, the mainstream public sphere, rather than wholly integrated with it. No one knows yet exactly how that integration might take place and it is bound to be highly variable across states as things stand.

I have used the term radical in the heading for this section of the article and want to say a little about that. The new age of terror, and the physical and psychological pain executed in its name, are yet further examples of the horrors of which humanity is capable and add to a long list of similar processes in current and historical affairs. It would be radical to transform the political public sphere into a realm, where the human and social costs of such processes could become meaningful, in ways that they are not now, to motivate political will and agency for change towards a less painful world. As I have argued, this would be both an ontological and epistemological transformation and its fundamental form is clear. The transformation would mean that memory of pain, instead of being continually effaced in political senses, would gain potency, not only in relation to the present and future, but also the past. The links across time and space are central here as are the connections between public and private. While the transformation and its effects relate to war and terror, they also relate to domestic violence. The transformation would involve preoccupations with all kinds of inflicted pain and how it could be countered, reduced and eradicated. This would undoubtedly be radical in comparison to the current situation, where it is othered and excluded from mainstream political process and motivations.

Conclusion

This chapter has focused on the new age of terror and the question of pain. Its prime orientation has been the engagement with pain from the standpoint of politics. It has addressed how to make pain meaningful in political terms. In adopting a feminist theoretical approach I have presented a series of arguments about how pain comes to be absent from the mainstream political public sphere. I have emphasised that this is a fundamental matter of how that sphere is constructed ontologically and epistemologically. In other words, how it is understood as a reality and how knowledge about it over time has been constructed. I have discussed the binary processes that have gendered this sphere along masculinist lines and the mutually reinforcing sets of binaries that operate to keep this reality in place. This needs to be understood as a process that continues to be reasserted over time and, just as pain is made absent as an effective political resource today, this has links to how this has happened previously.

This is matter of history and thus also of memory. It is also a matter of private and public, and the divide between them that is intrinsic to the construction of masculinist politics. I have argued that such politics are an abstraction. They are disembodied and deny political meaning to embodied experience of pain thanks to their binary constraints. The presence and persistence of pain therefore cannot be made to count politically, even in an age of media saturation, where we are immersed in reporting and images of pain more than ever before, and in 24-hour news cultures. The realities of pain are distorted by the realities of the mainstream political lens. This is one explanation for the limited political effect of increasing exposure to the collective experiences of pain. I have suggested that the new media environment, where many more horizontal and interactive forms of communication have been developing, cannot yet be considered fully integrated with the political public sphere. Rather, it is adjacent to and intersects with it, and thus has limited impact on it. However, its facilitation of expanded bottom-up communication and interaction has the potential to stretch the public sphere and disrupt its constraints to some extent. How this potential will develop in the future we cannot know, but the more integrated new media become in the mainstream public sphere the more possibilities open up.

Memory is part of the way we move through time and space both individually and collectively. It has not been a major concern of this chapter to talk about the many different kinds of memories and ways of understanding them. But the place of memory in relation to the pre-occupation here with pain and politics has been essential. On political fronts, memory is distorted by this binary process, and pain fails to inform and transform politics as it might, because it is made absent. Keeping memory to the fore helps to remind us that this is an ongoing process that stretches back and forward, and that it is not necessarily determined and can be changed. Radical transformation, not only creates possibilities for the future, but allows us to revisit and re-learn from the past. Memory is not static and politics can reclaim elements of it and give them new force. This would be part of the path towards making pain politically meaningful towards transformation to a more peaceful and less painful world.

Acknowledgement

This article developed out of the ESRC research seminar series 'Ethics and the war on terror: politics, multiculturalism and media' (RES-451-25-4188), 2006–09, led by the author with Prof. Simon Caney (University of Oxford) and Prof. Heather Widdows (University of Birmingham).

References

Elshtain, J. B. (1993) *Public Man, Private Woman: Women in Social and Political Thought,* 2nd ed. Princeton: Princeton University Press.

Garde-Hansen, J., Hoskins, A. and Reading, A. (eds) (2009) *Save As ... Digital Memories,* Basingstoke: Palgrave Macmillan.

Grosz, E. (ed.) (1999) *Becomings: Explorations in Time, Memory and Futures,* Ithaca, NY: Cornell University Press.

Hare, D. (2008) *The Reader* (screenplay), based on the book Der Vorleser by Bernhard Schlink. Film directed by Stephen Daldry and produced by The Weinstein Company.

Hoskins, A. and O'Loughlin, B. (2010) *War and Media: The Emergence of Diffused War,* Cambridge: Polity.

Jónasdóttir, A. and Jones, K. B. (2009) Out of Epistemology: Feminist Theory in the 1980s and Beyond. In Jónasdóttir, A. and Jones, K. B. (eds), *The Political Interests of Gender Revisited: Redoing Theory and Research with a Feminist Face.* Manchester: Manchester University Press, 17–57.

Karatzogianni, A. (ed.) (2009) *Cyber-conflict and global politics,* London: Routledge.

Misztal, B. (2003) *Theories of Social Remembering,* Maidenhead: Open University Press.

Radstone, S and Hodgkin, K. (eds) (2003) *Regimes of Memory,* London: Routledge.

Radstone, S. and Schwartz, B. (eds) (2010) *Memory: Histories, Theories, Debates,* New York: Fordham University Press.

Human Rights and Equalities Commission (2008) *Sex and Power.*

Neiger, M., Meyers, O. and Zandberg, E. (eds) (Forthcoming 2011) *On Media Memory: Collective Memory in a New Media Age,* Basingstoke: Palgrave Macmillan.

Pateman, C. (1988) *The Sexual Contract,* Stanford: Stanford University Press.

Pettman, J. (1996) *Worlding Women: Feminist International Politics,* London: Routledge.

Reading. A. (2002) *The Social Inheritance of the Holocaust: Gender, Culture and Memory,* London: Palgrave Macmillan.

Spike Peterson, V. (2003) *A Critical Rewriting of Global Political Economy: Integrating Reproductive, Productive and Virtual Economies,* London: Routledge

Walby, S. (1990) *Theorizing Patriarchy,* London: Wiley-Blackwell.

Walby, S. (2009) *Globalization and Inequalities: Complexity and Contested Modernities,* London: Sage.

Youngs, G. (ed.) (2000) *Political Economy, Power and the Body: Global Perspectives,* London: Palgrave Macmillan.

16 Corrective rapes

Rape narratives in South Africa

Bev Orton

Introduction

In this chapter I will be discussing rape narratives and rape myths using various studies and research on gender violence in South Africa. *Broken Dreams*, a play by Juliet Vuviseka Rozani, highlights some of the issues, perceptions and threats confronting lesbians in townships in South Africa. Using the literature and empirical data I promote support for the movement in South Africa by activists to petition the government to classify lesbian rape as a hate crime. It is through changing the law that perpetrators of lesbian rape would be subjected to harsher sentencing and that there would be an acknowledgement that 'corrective rape' is a violation of human rights.

South Africa has the worst figures for gender-based violence for a country which is not at war or involved in a civil conflict. Statistics reveal that a woman is raped every 83 seconds. According to a world report by the UNHRC, in 2010 South Africa has the highest rate of rapes reported to the police. One in 28 men had raped a woman and the conviction rate is very low – only 6 per cent. This low percentage of conviction contributes to the '...normalisation of rape and violence against women and girls in South Africa' (Human Rights Watch 20 January 2010). These statistics highlight the devastating information that rape and sexual assault against women in South Africa is increasing (Moffett 2006: 129; Vetten 1998). This is despite government legislation and a government ministry for women, girls and the disabled. South African history is one of violence and during the apartheid regime sexualised forms of violence were used by the apartheid government to control women. Rapists' narrative is that they rape because women ask for it.

Negative representations of lesbians in the media perpetuate homophobia. Young lesbian women aged between 16 and 25 are the most vulnerable. They are being evicted from their homes because of the stigma attached to being a lesbian. Lesbians have become the target of 'hate crimes' in the townships and report that they are being directly targeted for rape. 'Corrective rape' is a practice used by men to turn lesbians 'into a real African woman'. Men use rape to 'cure' lesbians – 'to make them go straight'.

Very often women are the silent victims of war (Merry 2009: 156). African women were the ones who suffered the loss of sons, husbands, brothers and fathers and who had to defend for themselves in the homelands or *bantustans*.[1] During periods of ethnic conflict rape, assault and killing women is a common feature. An overstretched criminal justice and health system in South Africa, which is unable to deal appropriately with rape and violence against women, suggests that there is an unacknowledged gender civil war in South Africa.

Justificatory narratives of rape

The overthrow of the oppressive apartheid government regime has left South Africa in a state of national fervour and political transformation. Parallel to urban and political regeneration, and constitutional and political restructuring, runs a seam of alarmingly high rates of gender violence (Vetten 1998).

Moffett argues sexual violence in South Africa post-1994 is motivated by justificatory narratives, which are rooted in apartheid discourses (Moffett 2006: 132). During the apartheid regime, the dominant white group used violence to regulate the lives of African people and to remind them of their subordinate status. This was not confined only to public and political spaces, but also penetrated private and domestic spaces. African men and women were subjected to conditions that perpetuated inequality, extreme disparities between the poor and the rich, violence in prisons and humiliating experiences of police harassment. Institutionalised racism led to feelings of inferiority and a lack of self worth, which contributed to acts to violence. With the main emphasis on protecting the white population, there was a lack of policing in the townships, which enabled criminal gangs and a criminal culture to prosper in a poor community subjected to particularly harsh living conditions (CSVR 2009: 6–8; Posel 2005: 30).

South African history is one of violence – colonialism was maintained by military force, which included rape and violence by the dominant group over the subordinate group. Sexualised forms of violence were used by the Apartheid government in order to control the political activities of women. This is highlighted explicitly in the speech by Thenjiwe Mthintso, Chairperson of the Gender Commission, who in her opening speech at the special women's hearings at the Truth and Reconciliation Commission in Guateng, South Africa, spoke of how men use women's bodies 'Because always, always in anger and frustration men use women's bodies as a terrain of struggle – as a battleground ... Behind every women's encounter with the Security Branch and the police lurked the possibility of sexual abuse and rape' (Krog 1999: 271–2). In August 1996, Zubeida Jaffer, at the Women's Hearing of the Truth and Reconciliation Commission in Cape Town, spoke of threats of rape and of pain to family members that women faced when threatened by the police force: 'The captain in charge of the interrogation turned to a policeman and told him to rape her' (Ross 2003: 66). When women were interrogated by the Security Branch they were called prostitutes, made to strip naked in front of policemen who made derogatory comments about their bodies, their fallopian tubes were filled with water and rats inserted into their vaginas. A man who did not break under torture gained the respect of the police, but a woman's refusal to break under torture angered the torturers because a 'a black meid,[2] a kaffermeid at that, had no right to have the strength to withstand them' (Krog 1999: 272).

Throughout the apartheid era, a veil of secrecy hid and silenced crimes of sexual violence. According to the South African Law Commission 1985, rape was not regarded as a social problem, and the supposedly high rates of rape was feminist propaganda (Posel 2005: 30). In fact, it has been argued that women are being regulated through sexual violence. Sexual violence is seen as a means of 'social stabilisation' (Moffett 2006: 132). Sexual violence is used by young men to force women to enter into relationships with them (Wood and Jewkes 2001 cited in Reid and Walker 2005: 65). Heather Reganass, whilst director of South Africa's National Institute for Crime Prevention and Rehabilitation of Offenders, expressed concern about the high level of rape crimes. She is of the opinion that rape and racial injustice during the apartheid years are linked. As she commented no white man has been executed in South Africa for raping a black woman, however the majority of men executed was for raping a white woman. The message being that raping a black woman was not as serious as raping a white woman. Gender violence and rape were perceived as being marginal issues to the struggle for liberation, and which could potentially be divisive, and divert attention from the national struggle for liberation and racism. What was happening, she found, was that 'rape, particularly of black women, was so prolific in South Africa that it was accepted by everybody' (Armstrong 1994: 36).

Prejudice and discrimination in rape cases

In 2007, South Africa amended legislation to broaden the definition of rape.[3] Having previously defined rape as vaginal penetration, the Criminal Law (Sexual Offences and Related) Matters Amendment Bill[4] broadened the definition of rape to include forced anal or oral sex. This is irrespective of the gender of the victim or perpetrator. The new legislation recognises male rape (formerly classified as indecent assault), the request by rape victims that offenders undergo HIV testing and for the provision of post-exposure state funded anti-Aids drugs (Le Roux 22 May 2007).

Cases of discrimination and prejudice against rape victims within South African law are reflected in three cases below. In 1987, a five year sentence for rape was set aside on appeal from two-and-a-half years because the judge, Justice Michael Corbett, regarded the woman as being sexually experienced and lacking a serious injury. Mr. Justice Botha acquitted a rapist, because he suspected a risk of false motive. Unfortunately, these attitudes have changed little over the years. In 1993 a policeman, convicted of four charges of sexual assault, was not fired from his job, because the magistrate, Peter Campbell, regarded the crimes as being not serious and that the women had over-reacted (1995: 103–5).

Reporting rape in the media sensationalises the sexual aspect and tends to neglect emphasising that rape is a form of violence (Armstrong 1994: 35). Vetten's report on the media coverage of the rape of Ms Gasa, wife of MP Raymond Suttner, on Robben Island in 1997 demonstrates the contradictory attitudes in reporting rape. In some newspapers, Ms Gasa was denounced as a liar and there were accusations that she was treated favourably, because she was a prominent person and had a high profile. Femina[5] magazine's approach, however, was to honour Ms Gasa as a woman of courage. This sensationalised reporting of rape tends to encourage women to refrain from reporting rape and this contributes to the silence that surrounds the act (Vetten 1998). Surveys, data collected and questionnaires by organisations such as Human Sciences Research Council, Medical Research Council, Statistics South Africa and the Centre for the Study of Violence and Reconciliation show that sexual violence is increasing. This combined with an overstretched criminal justice and health system unable to deal appropriately with the crisis suggests that there is an unacknowledged gender civil war. The high rate of rape is contributing to the spread of HIV/AIDS pandemic (Moffett 2006: 130).

Malamuth, Haber and Feshbach's investigation of the perception that 'rape is an extension of normal sexual patterns' in 1980 (in Larsen and Long 1985: 299) disturbingly revealed that 51 per cent of male subjects were of the opinion that more males would rape, if they felt that they could avoid punitive action. An article on a report by Baroness Stern into how rape complaints are dealt with in South Africa in *The Guardian* highlights the low level of reporting of and conviction for rape, as well as the high level of victims withdrawing before their case gets to court. The report found that there were problems with both the police and the prosecution system. The report found that only six per cent of reported rapes end in a conviction and that many offenders escaped prosecution (Williams 15 March 2010). According to USAID/South Africa the conviction rate for 50,000–54,000 rape cases reported is 7 per cent (USAID/South Africa 3 May 2010).

Rape myths

Ending women's oppression was high on the agenda of the democratically elected government in 1994. Women's groups lobbied to ensure that gender equity was a priority. The South African Constitution is one of the most progressive in the world and includes explicitly that the state may not discriminate directly, or indirectly, against anyone on grounds of race, gender or sex (Walker 2005: 227). It would seem that women's political and civil citizenship in post-apartheid South Africa is guaranteed by the South African Constitution. This is not so. According to Lewis *et al.* (1999: 38) an ethos of equal rights for women is undercut by sexism. Growing up with the ever-present threat of rape develops a society that is oriented towards 'male service' (Card 1996: 7). The act of rape communicates male domination. Patriarchal society reinforces the idea that men are entitled to sex and that female sexuality is something that men need to possess. Male dominated society perpetuates powerful myths about rape which sustains justification of male violence against women, ensuring that these violent acts are seldom punished whilst developing attitudes that blame and punish the victim. These rape myths are that all women want to be raped, that a woman cannot be raped unless she wants to be, that she asked for it, that she changed her mind after the act, a no actually means yes and that if a woman is going to be raped she may as well lay back and enjoy it. What underpins these rape myths are attitudes suggesting that the male could not control himself, that he was dominated by his biological needs and that he was seduced. In this scenario, the victim becomes the offender and vice versa thereby absolving the rapist, rationalising rape and protecting the patriarchal society (Sheffield 1997: 120–2). Heather Reganass found that there were myths being perpetuated in the black teenage community, such as not having sex was bad for a person's mental health, that a lack of sex would make one go crazy and that, therefore, if sex was not available legitimately, then sex should be sought illegitimately (Armstrong 1994: 37). A former rapist, Dumisani Rebombo, was 15 when he raped a young woman living in his village. He claims that he committed the rape, because he wanted to prove that he was a boy and that he wanted to be accepted. He believes that the problem is partly societal – that boys are brought up with a sense of entitlement and a belief that they are able to do whatever they would like to with women (Jecks 29 July 2009).

Niehaus's investigation into masculine sexuality as a political issue during the liberation struggle in Impalahoek, a multi-ethnic village in Northern Sotho in South Africa, provides insight into the rationale for 'sexuality (featuring) very prominently in masculine narratives about the liberation struggle' (Niehaus 2000: 390). Bantu Education in 1953 was repressive, oppressive and underpinned by a puritanical perspective of adolescent sexuality, which spread the ideology of Christian nationalism. Sex was regarded as being the worst transgression, as well as a form of subversion. Pupils were severely punished if they were suspected of writing love letters or having sexual intercourse. However, students felt that teachers were hypocritical about their attitude towards sex. One student revealed how a teacher at Impalahoek Primary School would leave his books in the classroom after class and then order a young girl to bring them to his office. The student felt that what happened to the young girl was rape. The girls were given money to keep quite about his activities. When the girls became pregnant the teacher would blame one of the boys (Niehaus 2000: 394).

After 1986, there was a reversal of power. At Mashile High School the Comrades, miltants who were opposed to apartheid, took over. Corrupt teachers were punished and some even feared they would be executed. What is revealing about the investigation is that while the Comrades condemned the exploitation of schoolgirls by teachers, they felt that they were able to exploit the most attractive schoolgirls. When a Comrade chose a schoolgirl, he felt he had the right to have sexual relations with her regardless of her opinions and those of family and friends. Comrade leaders enforced a strategy of *go yata* or operation production, a pro-natal strategy to replace Comrades who were killed in the Struggle. Girls were forbidden to use condoms, to have contraceptive injections and were forced to have unprotected sex with Comrades. This was regarded as rape by people opposed to the actions of Comrades (ibid.:399). Niehaus suggests that having suffered the punitive regime of the Bantu Education certain future leaders realised the '...intimate connections between political and sexual repression, as in the suppression of homosexuality and pornography' (ibid.: 406).

In a televised interview in South Africa, a taxi driver reveals how he and his friends cruise the streets at weekends all the while looking for a victim whom they can abduct and 'gang-bang'. The criteria for choosing the women were those regarded as being cheeky, those walking around as if they own the place and who looked them in the eye. The disturbing aspect of this interview was the negation of the taxi driver of rape and criminal behaviour. He seemed to be unaware that he had committed a crime and 'When the interviewer pointed out that his actions constituted rape, he was visibly astonished' (Moffett 2006: 138). His response was that women asked for it – that they forced the taxi driver and his friends to rape them. This interview illustrates how women in South Africa are punished for being independent or who demonstrate any form of autonomy. Sexual violence is used to punish, to control and to teach women a lesson.

According to Jecks (29 July 2009) gang rape amongst men in their twenties is regarded as a game. The marhasimani[6] meets a young woman in a club, buys her drinks and then takes her to a place to have sex with her. At this place his friends hide under the bed. When the first man has raped the woman and left the room, his friends than take turns to have sex with her. When the men were confronted with the possibility that they had raped the woman, they denied it, saying that the drinks were expensive, that they might have drugged the woman – but it did not happen all the time.

Homophobic violence

The Women's Charter for Effective Equality (1994)[7] Article Eight states that '...women have freedom of choice in establishing relationships' and

Article Ten states that '...here shall be legal protection for all women against sexual and racial harassment, all forms of abuse and assault' (Women's National Coalition February 1994). However, regardless of the Women's Charter, one of the most progressive Constitution's prohibiting discrimination based on sexual orientation and the Equality Act passed in 2000 which specifically outlaws hate crimes, gay and lesbian people are very vulnerable to violent attacks. The only cases that have been brought to court are those pertaining to race and gender (Martin *et al.* 2009: 5).

Zoliswa Nkonyana, 19, was the first case of homophobic violence to gain prominence. A mob of 20 youths clubbed, stoned and beat her to death on 4 February 2006 in Khayelitsha, a township in the Western Cape. It took at least two weeks for the media to report her murder. Nine men have been accused of her murder and to date none of them have been sentenced – the trial has been delayed 32 times (Middleton 7 March 2011).

Homophobic violence faced by Black lesbians is directly related to their poverty. Their vulnerability is exacerbated by inadequate and badly maintained means of transport,[8] problems with housing and their reputation as lesbians in the community, factors which results in their being subjected to ostracism and increases their vulnerability to violent attacks (Swarr and Nagar 2004: 506). In an article on how the law is failing lesbians on corrective rape, activist Ndumie Funda asserts that there is a lack of awareness in regards to hate crimes and corrective rape. She suggests a programme of action, intervention and a budget to research the problems that lesbian women face (Bucher 31 August 2010). The high rate of violence against Black lesbian women, particularly that of 'corrective rape', being reported has resulted in the South African Human Rights Commission recommending that the criminal justice system acts against these hate crimes (Human Rights Watch 20 January 2010).

Lesbians are ostracised and evicted by their families and subjected to sexual violence. Bucher states that young lesbians between the ages of 16 and 25 are the most vulnerable. They feel dislocated, depressed and have feelings of not belonging. Every day they are verbally attacked, insulted, told that they deserve to be raped and that if they are raped they will go straight (Martin *et al.* 2009: 7). As well being subjected to attacks and verbal abuse, they are victimised a second time, because the homophobic police officers are lax in their investigations (Bucher 31 August 2010). By legitimising brutal attacks on lesbians the message that is being sent to the community is that '...any deviation from the traditional constructions of masculinity and femininity aligned with African patriarchy is not acceptable' (Reddy 2001: 83).

Mufweba says that Zanele Muholi, a reporter for the lesbian and gay publication *Behind the Mask*, started a project called The Rose has Thorns. Since starting this project, she says, they have realised that corrective rape is happening everyday and everywhere. The perpetrators are friends, family and neighbours. Kekeletso Khena was raped three times before she

turned 19. She has now fled Soweto and condemns the practice called corrective rape, which is used by men to turn lesbians into real African
women. The first time she was raped was when she was 13 and afterwards
her mother walked into the room and remarked that that is what happens
to girls like her – meaning that she was regarded as being a 'butch child'
(Mufweba 7 November 2003).

Jody Kollapen, former chairman of the South African Human Rights
commission, says that the rationale for corrective rape is the belief that the
violent act of rape can change the sexual orientation of a person, thereby
altering their identity. The perception is that a woman who chooses to be a
lesbian is someone who has not been in a relationship with a man. Raping a
woman, subjecting her to violence and force, will convince her that her lifestyle is not appropriate. Kollapen feels that there are two factors which contribute to corrective rape – one is of prejudice that exists because of the
apartheid policy which forced people in separate categories and the other is
that South Africa is a violent society, within which, force has been traditionally used to settle problems (Schaap and Gim 10 May 2010).

A report by Action Aid published in the *Telegraph* (13 March 2009)
highlights the fact that crimes against lesbians are unrecognised by the
state and are unpunished by the legal system. Eudy Simelane, a former
member of the South African national football squad, Banyana Banyana,
was openly gay. She was viciously attacked, gang-raped, brutally beaten and
stabbed 25 times in her chest, legs and face. Her partially clothed body was
found in a creek in a park in Kwa Themba on the outskirts of Johannesburg. Her death provoked public outrage and disgust. Harrison, writing
for Reuters (13 March 2009), says that the murder of Eudy Simelane
'brought homophobic violence, especially towards women, to the fore'.
Her mother said that she feared for her daughter's life, but 'never imagined her life would be taken in such a way' (Kelly 12 March 2009). In February 2009, one man pleaded guilty to rape and murder. He was sentenced
to 32 years in jail. Three other men are pleading not guilty. The judge
made a statement saying that Eudy's sexual orientation played no significant part in her death, thereby reinforcing the government's evasion of
dealing with corrective rape (Martin *et al.* 2009: 6).

Carrie Shelver of People Opposing Women Abuse (Powa)[9] says that
lesbian women are being targeted, because of the macho culture that exists
in South Africa. This culture objectifies women as being merely sexual
beings, which need to be oppressed. A lesbian woman is vilified as an affront
to the macho culture – to their masculinity (Kelly 12 March 2009). Walker's
research (with the organisation Men For Change) with young men in Alex-
andra, a township in Johannesburg, revealed that men felt threatened and
anxious by 'women's improved status and their perception that woman have
attained equality' (Walker 2005: 168). Women were regarded as the enemy
– they are able to provide for themselves, they were more confident and
taking over roles previously viewed as being men's roles.

According to Hearn (1996), it is important that when trying to make sense of men's violence to women the problem is placed in an historical context. By doing so one can understand how a crime such as corrective rape has been accepted, condoned, ignored and normalised by some individuals and the state. Living in a society where there is an increasing macho culture and men's day-to-day domination of women is being endorsed by the state, regardless of the Equality Act, it is important to consider how men and women define violence. Women view violence as including emotional, sexual and physical aspects, which includes the threat of violence. Men seem to view violence in a narrower manner – as physical violence. Hearn states that most men do not define coercive and pressurised sex as violence. It is only when men are arrested and charged with rape that they define sexual violence as violence. Men resort to violence when their power and privilege is being challenged (Hearn 1996: Chapter 2).

In a case reported to ActionAid, Nomawabo revealed that she had been raped by her best friend. Under the pretext of inviting her to his house to study for an assignment, he fought with her and hit her so hard that she collapsed. Then he raped her saying that she needed to stop being a lesbian. This rape resulted in a pregnancy and a baby. The second time she was raped was when she and her soccer friends were kidnapped at gunpoint and held for three days where the men abused and raped them mercilessly. After reporting the incident to the police – nothing happened – the case did not come to court. To this day no one has been found guilty for the crime (ActionAid 12 March 2009).

Kaufman maintains that men's violence towards women 'is probably the clearest, most straightforward expression of relative male and female power' (Kaufman 1997: 40). Women are regarded as being the Other – an objectification of a person in a phallocentric society – onto whom men are able to vent their anger and frustration. Violence is used by men to reaffirm their masculinity, to cope with their feelings of powerlessness and negative self-image (Kaufman 1997: 41). Susan Brownmiller maintained that rape is the way men 'keep women in a state of fear' (Sanday 1997: 62). This state of fear is experienced by Phumla when she talks about the threat of violence. She describes this feeling as 'Every day you feel like it's a time bomb waiting to go off' (Kelly 12 March 2009). This threat of violence inhibits her movements, she feels restricted and she is always afraid. According to Triangle, a gay rights organisation, their research demonstrates that 86 per cent of black lesbians and 44 per cent of white lesbians are living in fear of being raped (*Telegraph* 13 March 2009). Vanessa Ludwig, the chief executive at Triangle, told Kelly from the *Guardian*, that lesbians who are raped are told repeatedly during the attack that 'being a lesbian was to blame for what was happening to them' (Kelly 12 March 2009).

By linking rape to the history of apartheid Moffett states that three pitfalls-discourses are generated that tend to sound like excuses, by merely dismissing the degradation of male pride as being the reason for rape results in a lack of critique of patriarchal society and the blame is focused on black men (Moffett 2006: 134). In cases of corrective rape in the townships, the perpetrator is a black man or men and rape is being used as a means of domination. In these cases of corrective rape, the rape narrative is about gender, not about race. Black lesbian women are demonised and seen as the Other. The Other is regarded as having the potential to be powerful and dangerous, and therefore needs to be kept in place (ibid.: 137). In a television broadcast for Channel 4 news, Samira Ahmed interviewed men about corrective rape – some of the responses were that 'if you are a man you are a man, if you are a woman then you are a woman' and 'that it is good (to show them what they are) because it is not good to be a lesbian' (Ahmed 12 March 2009). In a harrowing interview with Nonhlanhla Zwane she describes the rape of her twin 13-year-old daughters, one of whom committed suicide after being raped. The reason given by the rapists for raping these two young girls was to show them that they did not have to be like their mother – 'you are supposed to a woman – and women get fucked by other men'. Samira Ahmed felt challenged when she covered the story (ibid.).

Corrective rape is not being covered by editors in South Africa because the level of crime is so high that there is not much public interest in a lesbian who has been raped in the township (McCabe 2010). According to Ndumie Funda, who founded Lulekisiwze in memory of her fiancé Lulekisiwze, who was a victim of corrective rape in 2007, ten lesbians are raped or gang raped in Cape Town every week. Andile Ngcoza, raped, beat up and strangled Millicent Gaika for five hours with the intention to make her pregnant and to make her go straight. Andile Ngcoza raped Millicent Gaika because he hated lesbians. He was released on R60 bail, the equivalent of less than £6. Ndumie Funda, whose organisation provided support and advocacy for Millicent Gaika was forced to go into hiding as she feared for her life. Whilst in hiding, another victim of corrective rape, Bulelwa, committed suicide because of the lack of support and advocacy. There is movement by activists demanding that the government classify lesbian rape as a hate crime. Lulekisiwze has directly petitioned South African Justice Minister Jeffrey Thamsanqa Radebe. This petition was signed by 150,000 people. However, Justice Minister Jeffrey Thamsanqa Radebe responded by saying that motive crimes such as lesbian rape are irrelevant (Robertson 24 January 2011; News 2010 December 2010).

Broken dreams

Issues of lesbians being demonised and evil are highlighted in a play written by Juliet Vuyiseka Rozani, a writer, activist and performer in South Africa. Her play *Broken Dreams* is a play about the experiences of lesbian women in South Africa. In an interview with Rozani (Interview 10

December 2010) she said that after reading articles about the experiences of Lesbian women she decided to write a play. 'I wanted to make a change – to make a difference in society' (Interview 10 December 2010). She was disturbed by the documentaries she watched about lesbians where the men interviewed defended corrective saying that 'it was against our culture, they should marry a man – supposed to get raped to feel herself as a woman.' (Interview 10 December 2010).

In *Broken Dreams* the main character, Ayanda, is the daughter of a priest. She is a lesbian and during the play she is raped on the streets in the township. Her family is religious, her father is a priest. Ayanda attends a white private school and when she returns to her home in the township she feels different to her family and people in the township – she eats differently, speaks differently. When Ayanda tells her family that she is a lesbian they are devastated. Her family is very aware of and conscious of the opinions of their neighbours and congregation. Her father says that he has a reputation to uphold, that she has ruined his reputation and that she is a disgrace to the family. There are strong references in the play to religion and that being a lesbian is akin to being evil and a demon. Rozani mentioned that there is the perception that being lesbian is 'white stuff – being something that white people do' (Interview 10 December 2010). Ayanda's family tells her that she is not needed in the house, that she is not normal and that they do no want her anymore.

According to Rozani the guys who brutalise women 'are guys who do not have much to do. Just smoke … it is something to do. That's why they do it' (ibid.). While Rozani was doing the play a woman approached her and told her that she was being violated by some old man in the township and that she had reported this to police and nothing had happened. 'Society does not accept you for what you are, you are violated by your neighbours and you cannot walk freely in the township' (ibid.). Rozani described how a lesbian was stoned in front of her own house 'you have nowhere to hide, they do not respect you at all…. Old women are raped … old women with children, they rape the kids… we don't want you to be like your mother…' (ibid.). Rozani found the reaction to her play very touching. She worked on the play for six months and composed the music. For her watching the play is painful 'I cried every time the show was on … it made me emotional' (ibid.).

A report by McGreal (13 March 2008) revealed disturbing facts about South African schoolchildren, one being they are playing games called 'rape me, rape me' and the other that some schoolboys had committed corrective rape on lesbians which they justify using the pretext that sexual assault will make the victims heterosexual. The South African government is facing a very difficult dilemma of how to achieve gender equality in a country that has experienced years of oppression, discrimination and racism. During the years of the struggle for liberation the fight for gender equality was marginalised. Mandela acknowledged this in his speech when he opened the first democratically elected government in April 1994. He clearly stated that freedom can only be achieved once women have been freed from all oppression (Manjoo 2005: 2). Victims of corrective rape like Millicent Gaika[10] are only too aware of how far women in South Africa are from achieving Mandela's goal.

Notes

1 In 1951 the Nationalist government declared that each African – Xhosa, Zulu, Sotho and Venda-tribe should have its own homeland. About 13.7 per cent of land in South Africa was set aside to accommodate the African tribes.
2 Meid: derogatory term in Afrikaans for maid. Kaffermeid is African maid.
3 For information on The Principles of Legality in Constitutional Matters with reference to Mayisa v Director of Prosecutions and Others 2007 (5) SA 30 (CC) http://ajol.info/index.php/ldd/article/viewFile/55410/43878.
4 www.mrc.ac.za/public/facts18.htm.
5 A women's magazine in South Africa.
6 A marhasimani is the young man who leads the process by going to the club, meeting the woman and buying her drinks. He then leaves with her, to go and have sex.
7 The Women's Charter is officially recognised by National Parliament and nine regional parliaments and was accepted in 1994. There are 12 articles dealing with equality, law and administration, violence against women, health and media, custom, culture and religion, the economy, education and training, development infrastructure and the environment, social services, political and civic life, family life and partnerships.
8 For information on transport in the South African townships see www.socialistreview.org.uk/article.php?articlenumber=9682.
9 Powa is a non-governmental organisation offering support for women experiencing abuse.
10 Millicent Gaika was raped, beaten up and strangled for five hours by Andile Ngcosa. He wanted her to go straight. He was released on R60 (about £6) bail.

References

ActionAid (12 March 2009) 'Hate crimes: the rise of 'corrective' Rape in South Africa', at www.actionaid.org.uk/101756/hate_crimes_the_rise_of_corrective_rape_in_south_africa.html (accessed 12 October 10).

Ahmed, Samira (12 March 2009) 'Corrective rape' in South Africa, Channel 4 News, at www.channel4.com/news/articles/world/africa/corrective+rape+in+south+africa+/3027797.html (accessed 12 April 2011).

Armstong, S. (1994) 'Rape in South Africa: an invisible part of apartheid's legacy', *Focus on Gender*, Special issue: Population and Reproductive Rights (June 1994), 2(2): 35–9.

Bucher, N. (31 August 2010) 'Law failing lesbians on 'corrective rape', Inter Press Service News Agency, at http://ipsnews.net/africa/nota.asp?idnews=48279 (accessed 17 September 2010).

Card, C. (1996) 'Rape as a weapon of war', *Hypatia*, Special Issue: Women and Violence (Autumn 1996), 11(4): 5–18.

CSVR (2009) 'Why does South Africa have such high rates of violent crime? Supplement to the final report of the study on the violent nature of crime in South Africa'. Report commissioned by the Minister of Safety and Security, 7 April 2009, Braamfontein, South Africa: Centre for the Study of Violence and Reconciliation (CSVR). www.csvr.org.za/docs/study/7.unique_about_SA.pdf (accessed 12 April 2011).

Harrison, R. (13 March 2009) 'South African gangs use rape to 'cure' lesbians', Reuters at www.reuters.com/article/idUSTRE52C3MN20090313 (accessed 12 September 2010).

Hearn, J. (1996) 'Men's violence to known women: historical, everyday and theoretical constructions by men', in Fawcett, B., Featherstone, J., Hearn and Toft C. (1996) *Violence and Gender Relations*, London: Sage.

Human Rights Watch (1 November 1995) 'Violence against women in South Africa: state response to domestic violence and rape', at www.unhcr.org/refworld/docid/3ae6a8294.html (accessed 12 April 2011).

Human Rights Watch (20 January 2010) World Report 2010 – South Africa, 20 January 2010, at www.unhcr.org/refworld/docid/4b586ce132.html (accessed 12 September 2010).

Interview with Juliet Vuyiseka Rozani , 10 December 2010.

Jecks, N. (29 July 2009) 'Tackling South Africa's rape epidemic', BBC News, at http://news.bbc.co.uk/1/hi/world/africa/8171874.stm (accessed 2 September 2010).

Kaufman, M. (1997) 'The construction of men's masculinity and the triad of men's violence', in O'Toole, L. and Schiffman, R. (eds) (1997) *Gender Violence: Interdisciplinary Perspectives*, New York: New York University Press.

Kelly, A. (12 March 2009) 'Raped and killed for being a lesbian: South Africa ignores 'corrective' attacks', The Guardian, at www.guardian.co.uk/world/2009/mar/12/eudy-simelane-corrective-rape-south-africa (accessed 12/10/10).

Krog, A. (1999) *Country of My Skull*, London: Vintage.

Larsen, K. and Long, E. (1985) 'Attitudes towards rape', *Journal of Sex Research*, 24: 299–304.

Le Roux, Mariette (22 May 2007) 'South Africa broadens rape definition as it passes new law', at www.aegis.com/NEWS/AFP/2007/AF070516.html (accessed 12 September 2010).

Lewis, D., Kuzawayo, E. and Ramphele, M. (1999) 'Myths and citizenship in two autobiographies by South African women', *Agenda*, Special issue: Citizenship, 40: 38–44.

Manjoo, R, (2005) 'Case Study: the commission for gender equality, South Africa: promotion and protection of gender equality – are separate structures necessary?', *Griffith Law Review* 19; (2005) 14(2):268, at www.law.du.edu/latCrit/Publications/PublishedSymposium/SIGULR(2005)/14(2)_9_manjoo.pdf (accessed 10/12/10).

Martin, A., Kelly, A., Turquet, L. and Ross, S. (2009) 'Hate crimes: the rise of corrective rape in South Africa', Action Aid, London, at www.actionaid.org.uk/doc_lib/correctiveraperep_final.pdf (accessed 17 September 2010).

McCabe, J. (14 March 2010) 'Samira Ahmed, behind the scenes with C4 news', The f word blog, at www.thefword.org.uk/blog/2010/03/samira_ahmed_be (accessed 10 December 2010).

McGreal, C (13 March 2008) 'Traumatised South African children play "rape me" games', The *Guardian*, at www.guardian.co.uk/world/2008/mar/13/southafrica.internationalcrime (accessed 10 December 2010).

Merry, S. (2009) *Gender Violence: A Cultural Perspective*, Oxford: Wiley-Blackwell.

Middleton, L. (7 March 2011) 'Corrective rape': fighting a South African scourge, Time Magazine, at www.time.com/time/world/article/0,8599,2057744,00.html (accessed 10 March 2011).

Moffett, H. (2006) 'These women, they force us to rape them: rape as a narrative of social control in post-apartheid South Africa', *Journal of Southern African Studies, Special Issue: Women and the Politics of Gender in Southern Africa* (March, 2006), 32(1): 129–44.

Mufweba, Y. (7 November 2003) 'Corrective rape makes you an African woman,' IOL News – South Africa, at www.iol.co.za/news/south-africa/corrective-rape-makes-you-an-african-woman-1.116543 (accessed 12 September 2010).

Niehaus, I. (2000) 'Towards a dubious liberation: masculinity, sexuality and power in South African Lowveld schools, 1953–1999', *Journal of Southern African Studies* (September, 2003), 26(3): 387–407.

Posel, D. (2005) 'Baby rape: unmaking secrets of sexual violence in post-apartheid South Africa', in Reid, G. and. Walker, L. (eds) (2005) *Men Behaving Differently: South African men since 1994*, Wetton: Double-Story Books.

Queerlife (December 2010) 'Tackling corrective rape in South Africa', at www.queerlife.co.za/test/news/december-2010/5993-tackling-corrective-rape.html (accessed 10 March 2011).

Reddy, V. (2001) 'Homophobia, human rights, and gay and lesbian equality in Africa', *Agenda* (African Feminism 1 Special Issue), 50: 3–86.

Reid, G. and. Walker, L. (eds) (2005) *Men Behaving Differently: South African men since 1994*, Wetton: Double-Story Books.

Robertson, D. (24 January 2011) 'South African Lesbians Targeted for Rape and Violence', Voice of America News, at www.voanews.com/english/news/africa/South-African-Lesbians-Targeted-for-Rape-and-Violence-114495619.html (accessed 09 March 2011).

Ross, F. (2003) *Bearing Witness*, London: Pluto Press.

Sanday, P. (1997) 'The socio-cultural context of rape: a cross-cultural study', in O'Toole, L. and Schiffman, R. (eds) *Gender Violence: Interdisciplinary Perspectives*, New York: New York University Press.

Schaap, J. and Gim, B. (10 May 2010) 'Female athletes often targets for rape', ESPN Sports, at http://sports.espn.go.com/espn/e60/news/story?id=5177704 (accessed 12 September 2010).

Sheffield, C. (1997) 'Sexual terrorism', in. O'Toole L and Schiffman, R. (eds) *Gender Violence: Interdisciplinary Perspectives*, New York: New York University Press.

Swarr, A. and Nagar, R. (2004) 'Dismantling assumptions: interrogating "lesbian" struggles for identity and survival in India and South Africa', *Signs*, 29: 491–516.

Sweetman, C. (ed.) (1998) *Violence against Women*, Oxford: Oxfam GB.

Telegraph (13 March 2009) 'Lesbians subjected to 'corrective rape' in South Africa', at www.telegraph.co.uk/news/worldnews/africaandindianocean/southafrica/4982520/Lesbians-subjected-to-corrective-rape-in-South-Africa.html (accessed 12 September 2010).

USAID/South Africa (3 May 2010) Democracy Program Description, at http://sa.usaid.gov/south_africa/node/54 (accessed 10 December 2010).

Vetten, L. (1998) 'Reporting on rape in South Africa', CSVR, Braamfontein, South Africa: Centre for the Study of Violence and Reconciliation (CSVR). Previously published by Women's Media Watch. www.csvr.org.za/wits/articles/artrape3.htm (accessed 17 September 2010).

Walker, L. (2005) 'Men behaving differently: South African Men since 1994', *Culture, Health and Sexualities* (African Sexualities, May 2005), 7(3): 225–38.

Walker, L. (2005) 'Negotiating the boundaries of masculinity in post-apartheid South Africa', in Reid, G. and. Walker, L. (eds) (2005) *Men behaving differently: South African men since 1994*, Wetton: Double-Story Books.

Williams, R. (15 March 2010) 'Rape conviction rate still important, says solicitor general', The Guardian, at www.guardian.co.uk/society/2010/mar/15/rape-conviction-rates-solicitor-general (accessed 10 December 2010).

Women's National Coalition (February 1994) The Women's Charter for Effective Equality, at www.kznhealth.gov.za/womenscharter.pdf (accessed 10 December 2010).

Wood, K. and Jewkes, R. (2001) *Dangerous Love: Reflections on violence among Xhosa township youth*, Morrell, 317–36.

Index

3/11 *see* Madrid bombings
7/7 *see* London bombings, 2005
9/11 *see* September 11
120 rue de la Gare 31, 33–7, 41–2

Abkhazia 223, 230
accumulated experience 14
active resistance 216, 218
activism 216–18
Admoni, Nahum 173
advertising culture and BDSM 95–6, 100
affairs of men and media 67–8
airplanes, nose art 47
Al-Qaeda 119
A11MAT 120, 125, 127
American frontier 78, 80, 81, 83, 84
American guilt 79–80, 85, 88
American history and the Western 78–80
American identity 78–80, 81, 83, 88
Anti-terrorism Crime and Security Act 2001, UK 155
anti-war movement, 2003–09: UK 131–2, 133, 136, 138; US 131–2, 133, 140
Antigone 133, 134
Apartheid and sexual violence 261–2, 268–9
Army Times 58–9
Arnold, Brigadier General Chaplain William 47, 48, 49, 52, 55–6, 57–8
articles of war 21
artificial invisibilities 206–7
artificial vision 206, 208, 210
Asociación de Víctimas del Terrorismo (AVT) 119, 127
Asociación 11M Afectados del Terrorismo *see* A11MAT
asylums, French Occupation 36–40, 41
Autonomous Community of Madrid 125

Bantu Education 264–5
Barak, Ehud 180

Battle of the Little Big Horn 82, 83, 84, 87, 88
Battle of Washita 85
BDSM: and advertising culture 95–6, 100; associations with perversion and violence 97; and boundaries of normal and abnormal 96–100, 106–7; definition of BDSM community 100, 101; imagery in popular culture 97; and litigation 104; mainstreaming of sex 93–6; motivation for crimes 101; and pornography 104; as psychiatric disorder 100–2; representations in media 92, 105–6, 107; and stigma 103–4; and torture 99–100; and trust 102, 103
BDSM chic 93–6
Blair, Tony 136, 149, 156, 158
Blears, Hazel 156, 157, 160
bodies of war dead 131–45
Bohemian Revolt 13
Bondage Domination Sadism and Masochism *see* BDSM
book licensing and copyright law 15–16
Bosnian war 194–8
botnets 225, 226, 227
Boulevard des Branques 31, 33–7
British Muslims: and Britishness 161–2, 163; as critical audience 152–4, 164; in Manchester 152, 153, 157, 160, 162, 163; and media 148–66, 150–1, 157; post-7/7 154; in Stoke-on-Trent 152, 153, 157, 159, 162; victim identity 164; web forums 154, 160, 161, 163–4; women 157–8
Broken Dreams 269–71
Bronze Soldier of Tallinn 223
Bush, George W. 99, 131, 135, 141, 149, 156, 192; Gulf War 194; retaliation for 9/11 131, 135; war on terror frame 99, 192; 'war on two fronts' 149, 156;

Bush, George W. *continued*
  weapons of mass destruction frame 193
bystanders 65, 66, 75, 76, 116

Cambodia, US invasion of 80
camp newspapers 50, 51, 59
capitalism 210
Carrel, Alexis 38, 39–40
cartoons 51
censorship: film 215; of images of
  returning US coffins 141; self-censorship
  16–17, 72, 208; Thirty Years War 16; in
  World War II 34, 49–50, 55, 56
chaplains *see* United States Army
  chaplains
Chaplains Corps 46, 52
China and cyber crime 226, 229, 232
cinema: and the Internet 215–16; and
  myth 210–11; and September 11
  212–13; and war 212–13; *see also* film
citizen journalists 72
citizenship 163–4
Civil Contingencies Bill 2004, UK 155
civil war, Bosnia 196
civilian accounts of war, Thirty Years War
  20, 22–4
Civilian Conservation Corps (CCC) camps
  46, 47, 48–9
civilian resistance 216–17
Climate Research Unit (CRU) 224
Climategate hack 224, 232–4
Clinton, Bill 195–8
CNN effect 189
College Humor 54–5
combat simulators 214
communications: early modern
  communications revolution 14, 15–18,
  25; and framing 150; integration 15, 16;
  interactive world of 254, 255, 258; near-
  instant 210, 214
community cohesion 158–9
community of mourning 133
compassion for victims of suffering 70
computer security 225
Concurrent Return, US 140
conflict: generic representation of 74;
  hidden 71–4; internecine 115; media
  actors in 188–99; and visibility 67–8,
  69–70, 74, 188–9; *see also* cyber conflict
consent in BDSM culture 92, 103, 104
'Contest 2' report 161, 165
Cooperative Cyber Defence Centre of
  Excellence 231
Coroner's inquest, UK war dead 143
corrective rape 260–71
counter-terrorism 156, 159, 160, 161, 165
credibility gaps 72

crime fiction and wartime violence 31, 32,
  42
crimeware networks 226
Criminal Justice Act 2003, UK 155
crisis, risk of 210
Croatia 195
cultural lens 5–6
cultural war 160
culture: BDSM imagery in 97; of
  commemoration 131; and hardcore
  pornography 94; pornification of 94;
  sexual representation in 96–100;
  sexualisation of 93, 97
Custer, General George Armstrong 82,
  83, 84, 85, 87–8
cyber conflict: background 223–4; and
  cyber crime 227, 231; and Russia
  hackers 224–6; theory 228
cyber crime, Russia: gangs 224, 225; as
  'patriotic' hacking 226–9; and the state
  227, 231; superhackers 224–6
cyber espionage 226, 229
cyber security 229–30
cyber warfare 232
CYBERCOM 232

Dannatt, General Sir Richard 137
dark times 71, 73
Dayton Accord 195, 196
de-realisation of war 205, 208
Defenestration of Prague 13, 17
demonisation 150–1, 164–5
denial 73
deterrence 211, 217
deviance, and BDSM 93, 101, 106
disaster capitalism 208
discrediting 73
discussion forums 164
disembodied politics 251–6
distributed denial-of-service attacks
  (DDoS) 226–7, 228, 231
documentary photography 75
dominant frames 155–6, 164, 197–8
dual nationality and Britishness 161, 163
duty vs sacrifice 138, 145

early modern communications revolution
  14, 15–18, 25
embodied politics 249–58
enemy within 156, 161–3
Esquire 58
Estonia cyber attacks 223, 227–9
ETA victims 119, 120
eugenics 37–41
European attitudes to violence 14
European Day of Victims of Terrorism
  119

Execution of Emperor Maximilian, The 65–6, 73–4
eyewitness accounts 18, 20, 209

Facebook 153, 154, 158
Factiva database 115, 116
fashion industry and pornography 94–5, 99–100
Federal Republic of Yugoslavia (FRY) 195
feminist politics 251, 256
feminist theory 251–2
fetishism 95, 99, 100
film: and BDSM 96; censorship 215; and the Internet 215–16; and military perception 205; and war 212–13
flagbody 141
flashmobs 214, 228
forums for discussion 164
framing: in Bosnian war 196–8; and communications 150; in decision making 190; and post-7/7 narratives 148, 150–2; in war on terror 150–2, 190
France, occupation of (1940–1944) 30–42
Frontier, mythology of 81, 85, 86

gains and losses 190
gaming 214–15
gang rape 265
Gavison, Ruth 173, 177
gender inequalities 251
gender studies lens 8–9
gender violence 260, 261–2
generic representation of conflict 74
genocide, Bosnia 196
Georgian cyber attacks 223, 227, 229, 230–1
girlie magazines *see* pulp magazines
global vs local 150, 206, 216
globalisation 68, 165
Ground Zero 118
Gulf War 1991 193–4

Habsburg dynasty 13
hackers, Russian 221–35
hacktivism 228, 231
Haeberle, Ronald 85, 86
Halutz, Dan 172, 175, 176, 178–9
hardcore pornography and mainstream culture 94
hate crimes 260, 266
Help for Heroes 138–9
'Heroes of 2001' commemorative US postage stamp 117–18
Hersh, Seymour 85
Hezbollah terrorist organisation 171, 183
hidden conflict 71–4
historical lens 3–5

Holy Roman Empire 13, 15–16, 17
homecoming parades, UK 136, 137–8
homophobic violence 266–9
human rights abuses 73, 151, 160, 260
humanitarian disasters 70, 189

images, unreality of 207–8
imaginary 66, 68
indecent publications, for GIs 46, 47–52
information war 206–7
inquisitorial perception 209
intelligence 159
internecine conflicts and victims 115
Internet: and archive material 257; and British Muslims 152–3, 154, 160; and Virilio's theory of vision 213–16
invisibility in war 206–7
Iraq war 131–45, 148, 149
Islamophobia 151, 156, 157, 163
Israel–Hezbollah War 171–84
Israeli Defense Forces (IDF) 171, 175, 176, 178

Jews and French Occupation 34–5, 41
Jordan (Katie Price) 94
journalists 72, 190, 191, 209, 215–16
journalists and the state 215–16
just wars 21
justification 73

Kaspersky, Evgeny 224
Kent State shootings 81

Lebanon 171–2, 174, 182, 183
lesbian rape 260, 266–7, 269–70
lesbians and media 260, 269
Liberation of Paris (1944) 30
Life 85–6, 87
literature, indecent for GIs 46, 47–52
Little Big Man 79–80, 82–5, 86–9
logistical perception 206, 213, 214, 215
logistical power 216–18
London bombings, 2005 148–66, 254; and Iraq war 156–7
loss aversion phenomenon 190, 192–3, 198

Madonna 95
Madrid bombings, 2004: and charitable donations 127; commemoration of 118–20, 127; compensation of 124–5, 127; and ETA victims 119, 120, 127; psychological trauma 125; victims, definition of 116–17
magazines *see* pulp magazines
Magdeburg, sack of 20
mail coach services 16

mainstreaming of sex 93–6
male rape 262
Malet, Léo 31, 32–3, 34–5, 41–2
malicious software 224, 225
mamlakhtiim 177
Mandela, Nelson 271
Manet, Edouard 65–7, 73–4
massacre 13
Maximilian I 65–6
media: activism, coverage of 217; and
    affairs of men 67–8; and Bosnian war
    195, 197–8; and British Muslims
    148–66, 150–1, 157; and foreign-policy
    making 188–9; and frames 148–9, 164,
    190–2; and grief 132; institutions 68–9,
    71, 72; invisible impact of 192–3; and
    Iraq War 2003 192; lesbians,
    representations of 260; and London
    bombings 148–66; and loss aversion
    192; and new age of terror 253; and
    pain 253–4; and political leaders
    190–4; portrayal of Russian hackers
    224–6, 227, 229, 232–4; rape,
    reporting of 263; representation of
    Mylai atrocities 86; representations of
    BDSM culture 92, 105–6, 107;
    saturation 253, 255, 258; and state
    actors 72; and terrorist attacks 149–50;
    as traders of information 191; and UK
    remilitarisation 137; in war and
    conflict 188–99; and war dead 142, 144
mediapolis 68–9
mediation 66, 71–2
medico-moral and legal discourses 92, 97
Meisel, Steven 95, 99
memory and pain 250, 255, 256, 258
mental hospitals, French Occupation
    36–40, 41
militarised frames 148, 149
militarising frames 155, 156, 164, 165
military covenant 137
military perception and film 205
military publications 51–2
mobilisation via Internet 214, 228
momentary experience 14
morale, World War II 51
morality play narratives 74
mourning, work of 134, 135, 136, 145
Muslim extremism 158
Muslim media 151
Muslim victims of terrorism 117
Muslims, UK *see* British Muslims
Mylai massacre 85–6
MySpace 153
myth 210–11
Myth of Conquest 81, 85, 86, 87
Myth of the Frontier 81, 85, 86

Napoleon III 66
Nasrallah, Sheikh Hassan 171
National Armed Forces Memorial 136
National Organization for Decent
    Literature (NODL) 56–7
National Police Gazette 57
Native Americans 81, 82, 84–5, 87, 88
NATO 228, 229–30, 232
Netanyahu, Benjamin 179, 180, 181, 184
new age of terror 249, 251–6
new Cold War rhetoric 229–32
New Hollywood 79
new media: and British Muslims 154–64;
    and pain 256–7, 258; and Virilio's
    theory of vision 213–16
news framing contests 190–3, 194, 197
newspapers: and cyber crime 226; and
    post service 16; and reporting of Thirty
    Years War 17; US armed services 46, 49,
    51, 59
Nixon, President Richard 80–1, 88
normalisation: of BDSM 98, 101, 106; of
    the perverse 95
nose art, airplanes 47
'not in my/our name' 133, 135, 136
nude photographs 48, 93

Oklahoma City attacks 113–14
Olmert, Prime Minister Ehud 171, 172,
    173, 175, 178, 179–82, 183–4

pain 249–58; and disembodiment 253–5;
    and portrayal by media 253–4, 258;
    radical transformation 256–7
patriotic hacking 226–9, 231
Peace of Westphalia 13
Pécherot, Patrick 30–42; *120 rue de la Gare*
    31, 33–7, 41–2; and eugenics 37–41;
    and Malet, Léo 32–3, 41–2
perception, automation of 206
Peretz, Amir 172, 175, 176, 179
perverse sexual imagery 95
photographs: BDSM 95; caskets of war
    dead 141, 142; documentary 75;
    fashion 92, 96, 99; girlie 58–9; Iraq War
    72, 100, 141, 142; Mylai massacre 85,
    86; nude 48, 93; *Sex* 95, 99; 'State of
    Emergency' 92, 99; torture 72, 100
photography and visibility 75–6
pin-ups 47, 48
pocket-sized novels 49–50
Police Gazette 57
police investigation 209
political hacking 226, 231
political leaders and media 190–4
political lens 7–8
political public sphere and pain 251–8

politics of grief 131, 135
politics of mourning 131, 134, 136, 145
politics of vision 204–7, 212
popular culture *see* culture
popular defence 211, 213, 216–18
pornification of contemporary culture 94
pornography 92, 93–4; and BDSM 104;
    and fashion industry 94–5, 99–100;
    hardcore and mainstream culture 94;
    porn chic 94; violent 92, 104
postal system, Europe 15
poverty 70
power-pleasure spiral 101, 106
power struggle 216–18
Preventing Extremism Together groups
    158, 159
propaganda 24, 139
prospect theory 189–90, 192, 193, 194
protests against Vietnam War 81
public grief 144
public obituaries 132
public realm and visibility 68, 70–1
publications, indecent for GIs 46, 47–52
publicity and visibility 67
pulp magazines 52–9

radical transformation and pain 256–7
rape: and HIV/AIDS 262, 263;
    justificatory narratives of 261–2; as
    means of control 260, 261, 265, 267,
    268; media reporting of 263, 269; myths
    263–4; prejudice and discrimination
    262–3
reactive resistance 216, 218
remilitarisation, UK 136–40
remoralisation, US 140–2
renormalisation of military, UK 137, 138
repatriation of war dead 131; UK 143–4;
    US 140–1
Resistance, France 30
resistance of civilians 216–17
revisionist Westerns 80, 81, 82, 85
role performance, military 138
Rozani, Juliet Vuyiseka Rozani 269–70
Russian Business Network (RBN) 224, 225
Russian hackers 221–35; and Climategate
    hack 224, 232–4; portrayal by media
    224–6, 227, 229, 232–4

sacrifice, of war dead 140, 141, 142, 145
sadomasochism *see* BDSM
science fiction and war 212
second-class mailing privileges 52–5, 57
Secretary 96, 97, 98–9
security 211–12
segregation effect 194
self-censorship 16–17, 72, 208

sensory deprivations 208
September 11 113–14; and charity
    donations 121, 122–3, 126; and cinema
    212–13; commemoration of 117–18,
    126; compensation of 120–4, 126;
    emotional distress, recognition of 122;
    hero status of victims 117–18, 123, 126;
    and media 114, 116, 118, 121, 122,
    123–4; occupational status of victims
    118, 126; survivors of 118, 122, 123–4,
    126; victims, definition of 116
Serbia 196
service personnel, aftercare 137
Sex 95, 99
sex, mainstreaming of 93–6
sexual citizenship 97
sexual imagery 92, 95
sexual representation in popular culture
    96–100
sexual violence, South Africa 261–2,
    265–8
sexualisation of Western culture 93
Shahak, Amnon Lipkin 172
Shariah TV 154
sightless vision 206
Slovenia 195
SM *see* BDSM
social networks 153, 163
social question 70
society and image bombardment 207–8
sociological lens 6–7
soldiers' accounts, Thirty Years War 21,
    22
South Africa and rape 260–71
South Ossetia 223, 230
special forces 19–20
Stars and Stripes 46, 51, 52
state: as arbiter of knowledge and rights
    156, 159–61; and artificial vision 210;
    and cyber crime, Russia 227, 231;
    deterrence 211; and grief 132, 133; and
    journalists 215–16; and security 211–12
'State of Emergency' 92, 99–100
stealth equipment 206
Stirrup, Sir Jock 137
stop-and-search of Muslims 156, 157
stratification of loss 121, 123
Straw, Jack 157–8
superhackers, Russia 224–5, 226
surveillance society 15

technologies of vision 205, 206
telepresence 209–10, 214, 218
television: detective and police dramas
    209; imprisoning people 207; role in
    diplomacy and foreign policy 188;
    Shariah TV 154

terrorism: counter-terrorism 156, 159,
160, 161, 165; Muslim victims of 117; as
publicity stunt 217–18; transnational
113–14, 125–7; victims of 113–27
Thirty Years War 13–26; civilian accounts
of war 20, 22–4; compared to World
Wars I and II 13–14; and early modern
communications revolution 17–18, 25;
'little war' 19; major warfare 19; nature
and level of violence 18–21;
perceptions of violence 21–6; soldiers'
accounts of 21, 22
Thurn und Taxis post 15
torture porn/chic 100
transnational terrorism 113–14, 125–7
trust and BDSM 102, 103
Twin Towers attack *see* September 11

United Service Organization (USO) 46,
50
United States Army chaplains 46–60; and
censorship 49–50, 55, 56; role of,
upholding morality 46–7, 59–60
United States Post Office and indecent
publications 52–5
University of East Anglia 224, 233–4
UNPROFOR 195, 196
US: and Bosnian war 195–8; guilt 79–80,
85, 88; history and the Western 78–80;
identity 78–80, 81, 83, 88; invasion of
Cambodia 80; relationship with Israel
182–3
US Cyber Command (CYBERCOM) 232

veil, Muslim 157–8
Vichy regime 30, 40, 41
Victim Compensation Fund, US 121
victim hierarchies 115, 117, 120, 121,
125–7
victim identity 164
victims of terrorism: ambiguity between
victims and perpetrator 114–15;
commemoration of 117–20;
compensation of 120–5, 126, 127;
definition of 113, 116–17; media
worthiness 113–14; worth and
legitimacy 117–25
video-games 214–15
Vietnam War 80–2, 85–6, 88

violence: and BDSM 92, 97, 99, 100,
102–3, 104; early modern definitions of
20–1; European attitudes to 14;
perceptions of 21–6; perceptions of in
early modern communications
revolution 13–26; and pornography 92,
104; Thirty Years War 18–21; visibility of
188–9
Virilio, Paul 204–18
virtual communities 213
visibility *see* visible world
visible world 66, 67–71
vision, politics of 204–7, 212
vision machine 206
Vogue 92, 99–100

war: and cinema/film 212–13;
de-realisation of 205; at home 155,
156–9; media actors in 188–99
war dead 131–45; contending the
meaning of 135–6; mourning and grief
132–5; numbers, US and UK 141–2;
remilitarisation of civic life, UK 136–40;
remoralisation, US 140–3; repatriation
of 131, 140–1, 143–4; virtual 229
war-machines 205, 206, 212, 213, 214
war on terror 99, 145, 148, 149, 150, 164,
192; *see also* new age of terror
wargaming 214–15
Washita massacre 86–8
web forums and British Muslims 154, 160,
161, 163–4
Western Frontier 78
Westerns 78–89, 209
Winograd, Dr. Eliyahu 173, 174, 177
Winograd Committee: background 172–3;
criticisms of 173–4, 177; final report
177–9, 180, 181, 182; Interim Report
174–6, 179; mandate 173; member 173,
177; scope of operation 173–4
women: influence of 251–2; Muslim
157–8; objectifying of 97, 267, 268; rape
and violence, South Africa 260–71
Wootton Bassett 143
work of mourning 134, 135, 136, 145
World War II: censorship in 34, 49–50, 55,
56; compared to Thirty Years War
13–14; morale 51